These spiritually based prayers for your children will give you a deep, settled confidence before the throne of grace. Knowing that God has heard your prayers will keep your heart in great hope.

FERN NICHOLS
Founder, Moms in Prayer International

There is one thing you can pretty much count on: a godly parent's desire to parent well. Yet at the end of the day we find ourselves woefully inadequate. We can't change the hearts of our children. We can't bring them to faith. No matter how consistently we teach them, their hearts are not in our hands. And that is why this wonderful gem of a book is so important. In it, you'll not only be encouraged to read through the Bible every year for the sake of your own faith, you'll also be encouraged to do the most important thing when it comes to your parenting: You'll be encouraged to pray. My friend Nancy has given you a priceless gift—a book of devotions and prayers so you can read and pray through the year for your little (or big) darlings. The Lord, in whose hands are their hearts, is able to do wonderful things.

ELYSE FITZPATRICK
Author of *Good News for Weary Women* and coauthor of *Give Them Grace*

Regardless of the other areas of life in which I have convinced myself I am making straight As, parenting shows me my need for my heavenly Parent with complete clarity. Nothing has brought me to my knees quite like being a mom. What Nancy gives us in this book is better than a how-to on prayer or on parenting. It doesn't guarantee us a safe child or a successful child or an obedient child if we follow its words. But it does point us toward words of life. Nancy helps us invoke the pattern of Scripture in our daily battle for holiness as parents as we make our requests known to God with humility and hope. Where our own words fall short, His Word supplies our need.

JEN WILKIN
Author, Bible teacher, and mom of four

I love how Nancy Guthrie has taken the method of praying the Bible and applied it specifically to parents praying the Word of God with and for their children. Each devotional is simple and easy to use, including a brief Bible passage, a paragraph or so of devotional thought, and a prayer Nancy composed in connection with the Scripture selection. She has even included blanks so you can insert the name(s) of your child(ren) as you pray for them. I wish Caffy and I had had this book when our daughter was growing up. I'll certainly be giving a copy to her and her husband to use with our grandchildren.

DONALD S. WHITNEY

Professor of biblical spirituality at the Southern Baptist Theological Seminary; author of *Praying the Bible*

The One Year®
Praying through the Bible
for Your Kids

THE ONE YEAR®

PRAYING
through the
BIBLE
for your
KIDS

Nancy Guthrie

FOREWORD BY SINCLAIR B. FERGUSON

TYNDALE
MOMENTUM®

The Tyndale nonfiction imprint

Visit Tyndale online at www.tyndale.com.

Visit Tyndale Momentum online at www.tyndalemomentum.com.

Tyndale, Tyndale's quill logo, *Tyndale Momentum,* the Tyndale Momentum logo, and *The One Year* are registered trademarks of Tyndale House Ministries. *One Year* and The One Year logo are trademarks of Tyndale House Ministries. Tyndale Momentum is the nonfiction imprint of Tyndale House Publishers, Carol Stream, Illinois.

The One Year Praying through the Bible for Your Kids

Designed by Beth Sparkman

For information about special discounts for bulk purchases, please contact Tyndale House Publishers at csresponse@tyndale.com, or call 1-800-323-9400.

ISBN 978-1-4964-3376-3 (HC)

ISBN 978-1-4964-1336-9 (SC)

Printed in the United States of America

27   26   25   24   23   22
14   13   12   11   10   9

Foreword

I REMEMBER AS A YOUNG STUDENT being startled by a paragraph in the journal of the nineteenth century Danish writer Søren Aabye Kierkegaard (1813–1855). He wrote that the "greatest danger" a child could experience is not to have a "free-thinker" as a parent but to have an orthodox father from whose life the child subliminally draws the conclusion that God is not infinite love. Kierkegaard was an unusual man (he wanted the words *The Individual* on his gravestone!). But unusual men often have unusual insights, and this one has lingered with me from those early years until now.

It is all too easy to be drawn into a performance-based mind-set when we think about being Christian parents—to say and do all the right Christian things, and in the process produce the kind of atmosphere in the home that Kierkegaard described. But the truth is that children breathe in the spiritual air their parents have breathed in and out—the sense of who God is as Father, of the love of Jesus as Savior, of the help of the Holy Spirit—*or otherwise*. And if I am to be wholly honest, I would say that it is this element that is often absent from the counsel and the how-to-be-a-Christian-parent manuals offered to us by parenting gurus. We can try to program our lives and our homes to do the "right thing," but parenting is much more about *being*, about *who we are* as Christians, and about our communion with God. It is about our trust in him as our Father, our love for Jesus Christ as our Savior and Lord, and our walking in the wisdom the Spirit gives to us in the pages of Scripture.

Our children are not simply atoms and molecules to be manipulated by the use of the right techniques. In fact, breathtakingly, if we are their birth parents, we have participated in bringing into being eternal creatures who bear the image of God. If we are adoptive parents, we still welcome into our homes and hearts little people who are destined to last for all eternity. And it is our first, our highest, and our most demanding role in life to prepare them to live eternally. Yes, parenting is *that important*. And the key to it is our own walk with God.

Since you have picked up and begun to leaf through the pages of *The One Year Praying through the Bible for Your Kids*, this is where Nancy Guthrie enters the picture. If you have not already done so, I urge you to get a copy for yourself! For this book is a labor of immense love (not only Nancy's, but shared by her husband, David). It is *not* a "how to do" manual. No, it is a "how to be" guidebook. It is about who we are, what we become, and how well we know God in our joys and trials, our burdens and our prayers as parents. It does not take the low road of offering us a series of things we must do to be successful Christian parents. Instead it takes the high road of patiently, daily, guiding us through the message of the whole Bible so that we may reflect on it and pray through it, all in a way that is related to the nitty-gritty, day-in and day-out experience of being a mom or a dad.

In these pages Nancy illustrates the wise adage that "it takes a whole Bible to make a whole Christian" and applies it to being a parent. She has a fine grasp of the plotline of the Old Testament and a real appreciation of the importance of the Psalms in our praying and the book of Proverbs in our parenting. She has woven this into a book that will encourage and challenge you to read through the entire Bible (and keep you going, perhaps for the first time). The counsel is simple: Breathe in (the Word of God) and breathe out (the love of God). Richard of Chichester (1197–1253) was right to reduce his requests to the basics: "For these three things I pray: To see thee more clearly, to love thee more dearly, to follow thee more nearly." In its expositions of biblical teaching and in Nancy's openhearted and honest guides to prayer, *Praying through the Bible for Your Kids* helps us all to do just that.

One final word. Nancy Guthrie is well-known as someone who speaks to large gatherings of women and has a deep love for and joy in the treasures she has found in God's Word. It is possible for the rest of us therefore to assume she belongs to the superior rank of the superwoman. But those who are familiar with the Guthries know of their ministry to hurting parents and of the pilgrimage they continue to make as they bear the burdens of life. In this devotional, Nancy simply points us to the fountain from which she herself has drunk. To mirror Paul's words to the Corinthians, she is sharing with us the comfort with which God has comforted her, the challenges through which God has brought her, the joys God has given her, and the Word God has spoken to us all. She knows that the mother of the very best child experienced a sword piercing her soul (Luke 2:35); and she knows, too, how to be an Anna who carried her own sorrows with grace "coming up at that very hour . . . to speak of him to all who were waiting for the redemption of Jerusalem" (Luke 2:38, ESV).

So now, let your yearlong journey begin. You are in safe hands with your guide, because she carries with her the best of guidebooks in God's Word. Pause daily at the side of the road to read it, and pray through it for your children. If you do, I believe you will be grateful for this immense labor of love on Nancy Guthrie's part—and even more so for the wisdom and grace of God.

Sinclair B. Ferguson
Pastor, Author, Professor, Father, and Grandfather

A Word from Nancy before You Begin

PARENTING BRINGS INCREDIBLE, indescribable joys. But because our children matter so much to us, parenting can also bring incredible challenges and even devastating heartbreak. For such an important task, we need to have our thoughts and attitudes and our dreams and desires shaped by Scripture. So I've written this devotional as a way to allow God to speak into this all-important task on a daily basis.

In putting together *The One Year Praying through the Bible for Your Kids*, I set out to write the book that I have really needed myself. While many of my desires and expectations for my child might be godly, I recognize that they are easily corrupted by things like the culture around me, a twisted sense of competition with other parents, an inadequate understanding of what a parent should be and do, as well as my own idolatries and blind spots. So I need the Scriptures to go to work in me to reshape my deepest longings for my child. I also need a daily dose of perspective, a daily infusion of hope, and a daily reminder of grace in regard to my parenting.

I need the Word to convict me of my own sin because I easily become overly focused on my child's shortcomings. I need the Word to challenge me to change because I can be tempted to think it is only my child who needs to change. I need the Word to remind me of the gospel—that my sins have been paid for in Christ's death and my future hope is anchored in his resurrection—because I sometimes think that my child is more in need of the gospel than I am.

Maybe you do too. If so, *Praying through the Bible for Your Kids* is for you.

Another reason I set out to write this book and wrote it in the way I have is that I know I need to pray for my child more than worry about my child. I need to pray for God to do what he has promised to do rather than presume upon him to do it. I need to talk to God about what only he can do in my child's life more than I talk to others about my anxieties about my child's life. But over the years, my prayers have tended to be more self-directed than Scripture-saturated, which means that I pray the same things over and over. My prayers have often been shaped more by my stunted and sometimes selfish desires for my child than by God's grand purposes for all of his children. So I need the Scriptures to inform and direct my prayers and to encourage me to persevere in prayer. I need the Word of God to provide me with fresh words and renewed passion to pray for my child day by day.

Maybe you do too. If so, *Praying through the Bible for Your Kids* is for you.

What I don't need is another list of things I've got to be or do if I want my child to turn out "right." I don't need a how-to guide to getting my child to have self-confidence, avoid drugs, say no to premarital sex, and keep the faith. It's not that I don't want these things or that I'm not open to fresh ideas or expert advice about how to approach this difficult job of parenting.* It's that I've seen too many great and godly parents bring up children who struggle significantly or walk away from faith, and too many less-than-great—dare I say ungodly—parents raise terrific kids. As a result, I know there are no simplistic formulas for parenting.

I need much more than good advice. I need the commands and expectations of Scripture to keep me from complacency in parenting, and the grace and mercy presented in Scripture to save me from guilt in parenting. I need Scripture to puncture the pride that rises up in me when my child is doing well and I'm tempted to take the credit. And I need Scripture to save me from the despair that threatens to sink me when my child is floundering and I'm tempted to take all the blame.

---

*In fact, I consulted a wide variety of sources while writing this book—from Christian parenting classics to Bible commentaries to recorded sermons—as I explored what Scripture has to teach us about rearing our children. I've listed many of the reference materials in the "Notes" section, which begins on page 367. The sources for direct quotations within the daily readings are listed there as well.

I need the constant reminder that while I have influence and responsibility, I don't have control over my child or everything about his or her world. While I can teach my child the Scriptures, I can't be the Holy Spirit in my child's life. While I can confront sinful patterns that need to change, I can't generate spiritual life in my child that will lead to lasting change. Only the Holy Spirit can do that. What I can do is pray for my child and parent my child the best I know how, which will always be imperfectly. I can seek to trust God and keep trusting God to do what I cannot.

At this point in parenting I recognize that the things I want most for my child are things only God can do. And I want to be faithful and persistent in asking him to do them.

Maybe you do too. If so, *Praying through the Bible for Your Kids* is for you.

Hearing from God and Responding in Prayer

As parents, we want to hear everything God has to say to us. So we want to grow in our consistency of opening up his Word day by day to listen. In writing *Praying through the Bible for Your Kids*, I haven't searched out passages specifically about parenting. The truth is, there aren't that many. Instead, this book works its way through the whole of the Bible over the course of a year, mining every day's Scripture reading for insight for parents. *Praying through the Bible for Your Kids* provides and follows the One Year Bible Reading Plan. I strongly encourage you to read through the listed passages each day, knowing that God promises that his Word "always produces fruit. It will accomplish all I want it to, and it will prosper everywhere I send it" (Isaiah 55:11). But if you miss a day or more, don't give up! You don't even have to try to catch up. Just pick up the daily readings whenever you can.

Each day's devotion drills down into one part of that day's Scripture reading to find a nugget of truth and hope for parents to take hold of. Each day offers fresh words to begin your prayers for your child based on the text for that day.

By coming to the Word this way, we receive the whole counsel of God rather than simply going to the parts that interest us. We let God set the agenda and provide the emphasis for our conversation with him.

And after we listen to what he has to say, as we do in any good relationship, we respond. In the prayer starter for most days, you'll find a blank in which you can insert your child's name or your children's names. In this way you will deepen your ability and develop the habit of praying through the Bible in a specific way for your child or children.

Making Adjustments as You Read

Because I've sought to write this book so that it will be applicable to a wide range of readers, you may need to make some adjustments as you read. Out of my desire to be as inclusive as possible, to keep sentences as uncomplicated and unencumbered as possible, and to make reading and praying with this book as personal as possible, I've used a variety of pronouns and plurals throughout. You'll find that I go back and forth between referring to your child as a him or a her. Sometimes the reference is to a singular child and sometimes to children. When I use "him" and your child is a "her," I hope you'll make the needed adjustment in your mind as you read. When I speak in the singular and you have multiple children, I hope you'll make the needed modification.

I use "we" most often in the prayers as I'm hopeful couples will read these devotions together as they get ready in the morning, over the phone during the day, after the kids go to bed, or before they drift off to sleep at night. But I also recognize many moms and dads will be reading alone—either because their spouse is not reading with them, or because they are single parents. If you're working through this book on your own, when I use "we" in prayers, I hope that you'll make the adjustment to "I" and that this "we" wording will never be off-putting to you.

Another challenge to applying the Scriptures broadly is that all of our families and our children are in such different places spiritually. In fact, we often have a hard time knowing where our children are. None of us, no matter how tuned in we are as parents, can clearly see into the interior of our child's spiritual state. The continual focus throughout this book is on asking

God to save and sanctify us and our children. To pray for God to draw your child to himself does not imply that he or she has not already been drawn to Christ for salvation. To pray this way recognizes that Scripture speaks of salvation as something God has accomplished in the past, is doing now, and will do in the future. He *has saved* us by putting our sin upon Christ and crediting Christ's righteousness to us. He *is saving* us by sanctifying us through his Word and Spirit. And he *will save* us by glorifying us and bringing us into our forever home with him at the Resurrection.

Some who read this book will be confident that their children have been savingly connected to Christ by faith. Others will be hopeful but honestly unsure if this has happened. Still others will be quite sure that their children have not yet taken hold of Christ. My desire has been to write the prayers so that parents in every category will find fitting words to pray for their children. We all share the desire for our children to be drawn to Christ and, once brought into his family, to grow in godliness and be increasingly conformed to the image of Christ. And because we know that this is the will of God, we can be sure that this is a prayer he delights to answer.

Praying through the Bible for Your Kids is not written for parents of children of a particular age range. From the day our children are born until the day they watch as we are put into our graves, we will be always in need of godly wisdom for guiding and encouraging them. Likewise, they will always need the Spirit of God to do work in their lives as only he can do. So no matter how old our children are, the Scriptures help us to pray that God will continue to draw them to himself, transform them into his image, keep them, and one day take them to himself.

My Prayer for You as You Begin

As I've written *Praying through the Bible for Your Kids*, I've not only been taking in these truths for my own parenting and praying these prayers for my own child, but I've been praying for you and all the other parents who will pick up this book. I've prayed for all of the unique joys and satisfactions you are finding along this path of parenting, as well as the challenges you face and the fears you fight against. I'm praying that the year ahead will be one in which you will discover new insights in regard to parenting and that you'll also experience a fresh sense of the grace that covers you.

But it seems only right that my prayers for you are shaped by Scripture. So this is my prayer for you, my friend, adapted from Ephesians 1:

I'm praying for you as you work your way through this book, asking God, the glorious Father of our Lord Jesus Christ, to give you spiritual wisdom and insight as parents so that you might grow in your knowledge of God. I pray that your hearts will be flooded with light so that you can understand the confident hope he has given to those he called—his holy people who are his rich and glorious inheritance.

I also pray that you will understand the incredible greatness of God's power for us who believe him. I pray that you will sense this power at work in your parenting and see it at work in your kids. This is the same mighty power that raised Christ from the dead and seated him in the place of honor at God's right hand in the heavenly realms. May this resurrection power bring new life to you and to your family over this coming year.

Nancy Guthrie

Formless, Empty, Dark

In the beginning God created the heavens and the earth. The earth was formless and empty, and darkness covered the deep waters. And the Spirit of God was hovering over the surface of the waters. GENESIS 1:1-2

IN THE BEGINNING, when God spoke the Creation into being from nothing, the earth was a mass of raw material, a dark and barren wilderness with no shape to it. But it was brimming with possibility because the Spirit of God was hovering over it in anticipatory power, waiting for the Word to go out. Then God said, "Let there be light," and there was light. The power of God's spoken word penetrated and eradicated the darkness. As he continued to speak, the formlessness of creation gave way to the order of earth and sky, land and sea. The emptiness was filled with plant, animal, and human life.

And still God's Word goes out with shaping, filling, illumining power. Still the Spirit hovers over homes and families where there is chaos and emptiness and darkness with the power to bring something out of nothing. Still the Spirit works through the Word so that what emerges is truly good.

❊ ❊ ❊

Creator, we need you to do a creative work in our home that only you can do. We need your Spirit to hover as we open up your Word day by day this coming year. Let there be light in our home. May it penetrate the dark corners and expose what is hidden. Bring order to our disordered ways of relating to each other and to you. Fill up the empty places with your beauty and life.

As parents, we don't have the power to create spiritual life in _____. Only you can do that. So won't you do your creative work in _____? Shape his life into something beautiful for your glory. Enlighten his eyes to see you. Fill his life with your good gifts.

JANUARY 2

Unashamed

She took some of the fruit and ate it. Then she gave some to her husband, who was with her, and he ate it, too. At that moment their eyes were opened, and they suddenly felt shame at their nakedness. So they sewed fig leaves together to cover themselves.
GENESIS 3:6-7

WHEN GOD'S FIRST CHILDREN, Adam and Eve, rebelled against him by eating what they were told was forbidden, they went from being naked and feeling no shame to being keenly aware of their nakedness and full of shame. They went from intimate relationship with God to alienation from God. They went from living in a world of blessing to living in a world under a curse.

It could have been the end of the story; instead, it was the beginning of a new story of grace. There in the Garden of Eden, God covered the nakedness of his disobedient children with the skins of an animal, a preview of the greater sacrifice of one who would provide a covering once and for all. And God gave them a promise. God assured them that one day a descendant of Eve would be born. He, too, would be tempted, but he would obey instead of rebel. He would take the curse upon himself and put an end to the evil that now infiltrated all creation.

In the midst of the curse, the Lord offered a word of grace, a word of hope. Today he offers that same favor to you—no matter how deep or prolonged your family's struggles are.

❋ ❋ ❋

Father, it helps me to know that you understand how it feels to have a child disobey your clear instruction. You have felt the disappointment and heartbreak of having a son and daughter assume that you are keeping them from something good rather than protecting them from something evil.

Father, you are the only one who can provide an adequate covering for _____'s shame through the righteousness of your obedient Son. Help _____ to accept and embrace that all of her shame was placed upon Christ on the cross so that she can stand before you forgiven and blameless, with no need to hide.

Favor

The LORD observed the extent of human wickedness on the earth, and he saw that everything they thought or imagined was consistently and totally evil. So the LORD was sorry he had ever made them and put them on the earth. It broke his heart. And the LORD said, "I will wipe this human race I have created from the face of the earth. . . ." But Noah found favor with the LORD. GENESIS 6:5-8

HUMANITY had become thoroughly and pervasively evil. There was no goodness, no kindness, no joy—just never-ending selfishness and never-enough indulgence. This is the world Noah was born into and the nature he was born with. Noah was born a sinner like everyone around him. The same selfishness came naturally to him, and the same debauchery tempted him. But Noah was not like everyone around him. Noah's life was not guided by his environment and inherited tendencies. How do we know? Noah found favor, or grace, with the Lord. Or perhaps it would be better to say that grace found Noah.

It's not that God looked over humanity and found the one person who sought to please him, thereby granting Noah favor and providing him salvation in the ark. The grace came before the goodness. Noah did not earn this favor from God. It was a gift, pure and simple and undeserved. In fact, God's favor is never something that can be earned or purchased. It is always a gift. The grace that found Noah changed Noah. In fact, it shaped everything about his life and identity. Though he was surrounded by evil and perversion, the grace at work in Noah's life implanted within him the desire to keep himself pure and uncontaminated.

※ ※ ※

Lord, may _____ find favor with you. Would you grant him your grace that cannot be earned through good behavior and therefore cannot be lost by bad behavior? And may the grace that finds _____ change him so that he might, like Noah, be a blameless person in his generation, one who walks in fellowship with you.

Wisdom Shouts

Wisdom shouts in the streets.
She cries out in the public square. . . .
Come and listen to my counsel.
I'll share my heart with you
and make you wise. PROVERBS 1:20, 23

ALL OF US, if left to ourselves, are naturally foolish. But God is too good to leave us floundering in our foolishness. He comes to us offering wisdom. Yet he is even more active than that. God does not quietly make the offer of wisdom known; he shouts it in the streets. It's as if he is standing on the back of a flatbed truck waving his hands, trying to get us to stop barreling down the highway of life and choosing our own way so that he can point us in another direction. He wants to save us from ending up where that dead-end road will take us. He wants us to find our way home—to him.

In the pages of the Bible, and especially in the book of Proverbs, God calls out from the highest heights to us, and to our children, insisting that there are really only two paths in this life—one that leads to death and misery, and one that leads to life and joy. He offers exactly what we need to navigate life while enjoying his presence along the way and finding him fully at our final destination.

※ ※ ※

God of all wisdom, we hear you shouting in the street, offering to share your heart with us and to make us wise. As much as we love our children, we want to love them the way you love them. So please share your heart with us. And as much as we want to lead and guide our children, we know that we can't do it without the wisdom that comes from you. So please make us wise.

Lord, please keep shouting in the streets to _____. Keep crying out to her to come to you and listen to your counsel. Give _____ the will to open up your Word day by day to hear from you. Don't let _____ be a fool who hates knowledge. Make _____ wise.

Blessing from God

The LORD had said to Abram, "Leave your native country, your relatives, and your father's family, and go to the land that I will show you. I will make you into a great nation. I will bless you and make you famous, and you will be a blessing to others. I will bless those who bless you and curse those who treat you with contempt. All the families on earth will be blessed through you." GENESIS 12:1-3

IN GENESIS 11 we read about the people in Babel who, wanting to make a name for themselves, built a tower into the heavens intending to make their way to God. Then in Genesis 12, we discover something radically different. God came down to a man who wasn't even looking for him and made incredible promises to him. God told Abram that he would make his name great and that he would bless him. God promised to be Abram's security and to give his life significance. God's promise of blessing was a sheer gift of grace.

Surely we want this name, blessing, and significance for ourselves and for our children too. We don't want the name we can make for ourselves. We don't want the security we can assemble for ourselves or the wealth we can amass for ourselves. We want the blessing of God that is a work of God.

❊ ❊ ❊

Lord, as I think about the life that lies ahead for _____, I find myself wanting him to make something of himself. I want him to be somebody. I want him to do what he needs to do to create financial and relational security. But I'm also realizing that I don't want _____ to have a life that is all about what he can accomplish. Rather, I'm asking you to bless him in the way only you can. Shower him with the blessings that are ours in Christ. Make his life all about what you have done, what you will do, what you will give. Make his life all about your grace and goodness to him.

Counted Righteous

The LORD took Abram outside and said to him, "Look up into the sky and count the stars if you can. That's how many descendants you will have!" And Abram believed the LORD, and the LORD counted him as righteous because of his faith. GENESIS 15:5-6

ABRAM COULD HAVE taken stock of the promises made to him by God and discounted them. He could have simply deemed them too good to be true and disregarded them. Instead, he went against intuition and logic, against what he saw and felt, and believed God. Abram trusted God's promise, not only that he would have many descendants, but that one of them would bless the world and be its Savior.

Because Abram believed God, a miraculous and mysterious transaction took place. Abram was "counted" as righteous. A deposit was made to Abram's spiritual account in the sight of God, a deposit of righteousness. It wasn't wages that he earned, and neither was it something that magically appeared out of nowhere. This was real righteousness. But it was not Abram's righteousness. Abram believed God, and his faith became the channel through which he received the perfect righteousness of another. When Christ came, living a life of sinless obedience and loving devotion to God, the true and perfect source of the righteousness credited to Abram was revealed.

❊ ❊ ❊

Oh, God, would you give _____ this saving faith? Would you give _____ the faith to take stock of your promises and grab hold of them? Please deposit to her account the same righteousness that was deposited to Abram's account—the righteousness of Christ.

Pray like This

Our Father in heaven,
  may your name be kept holy.
May your Kingdom come soon.
May your will be done on earth,
  as it is in heaven.
Give us today the food we need,
and forgive us our sins,
  as we have forgiven those who sin against us.
And don't let us yield to temptation,
  but rescue us from the evil one. MATTHEW 6:9-13

IT SEEMS SIMPLE ENOUGH: Prayer is talking to God. And yet we struggle with it. Often when we pray as a family, such as before a meal, our prayers sound like we're just going through the motions with no real desire to connect with our Father in praise, thanksgiving, confession, or petition. Just the same old "bless this food."

But we want so much more for ourselves and our children. We want them to know how to truly commune with God in prayer. Just like Jesus' disciples, we need to learn to pray. We want to learn to begin not with our requests, but with his honor. We want to welcome his Kingdom to come and his will to be done in our home and in our hearts. We want our children to know that God is our ultimate provider who delights in being depended upon. We want to be a family who is real about our sin and our need for forgiveness as well as our need to forgive. So as parents, we humble ourselves to name our sin and ask forgiveness. We humble ourselves to name the temptation from which we need to be rescued.

❊ ❊ ❊

Father, may we keep your name holy. May our home be an outpost of your Kingdom, and may all who live here gladly conform to your will and your ways. You are the source of everything we need, and we ask you to provide as you see fit. You are the only one who can grant us forgiveness and the grace to forgive each other. You are our only source of power to say no to sinful desires, and our only source of rescue from the evil one who wants to claim us and our children as his own for eternity.

JANUARY 8

Hidden Dangers

When Lot still hesitated, the angels seized his hand and the hands of his wife and two daughters and rushed them to safety outside the city, for the LORD was merciful.
GENESIS 19:16

BACK IN GENESIS 13, we read that Lot surveyed the fertile plains of the Jordan Valley and chose to settle there. When he took that long look, did he not see what Moses later wrote about that place? "The people of this area were extremely wicked and constantly sinned against the LORD" (Genesis 13:13). Yes, it was fertile, but it was also perilous. Lot seemed so enamored by the obvious comforts that he ignored the hidden dangers.

As Lot and his family made their home in Sodom, they evidently became desensitized to the pervasive sin and evil. Even when the wickedness in the city threatened his daughters, and even though he was warned of the coming destruction, Lot "hesitated" to leave. Clearly he and his family were in need of a rescuer who would overcome their attraction to the city. If Lot and his family were dependent upon their own wisdom, their own response, their own choices, they would have been destroyed with the rest of Sodom. But at the center of this horrific, even sickening, story, we find hope. Though Lot and his wife and daughters had been seduced by the allures of Sodom and lulled into ignoring the danger, and though they were far too slow in turning away from the evil of the city, the Lord was gracious. In mercy, he saved those who had closed their eyes to danger as they made themselves at home in the world.

※ ※ ※

Lord, give us eyes to see the hidden dangers in what may look good on the surface as our children move out of our home and into the world. Give _____ discernment beyond her years to wisely assess opportunities that are presented to her. Even as _____ seeks to be salt and light in the world, keep her from losing her saltiness and being pressed into the world's mold. Don't let _____ become desensitized to sin and evil. And as you write our family's story, would you make it a story of your mercy? May your mercy overcome our compromise and outweigh the influence of our surroundings.

Too Hard?

The LORD kept his word and did for Sarah exactly what he had promised. She became pregnant, and she gave birth to a son for Abraham in his old age. This happened at just the time God had said it would. GENESIS 21:1-2

WHEN WE MEET SARAH in the Scriptures, she seems to be defined by her emptiness. "But Sarai was unable to become pregnant and had no children" (Genesis 11:30). Her situation appears even more poignant when we read that God had promised to give her husband descendants as numerous as the stars of heaven (Genesis 15:5), descendants who would come from a son born to her. This promise seemed to be an impossibility.

Sarah knew her own body—that it was worn out and dried up. The idea of becoming pregnant was laughable. And so she was amused when she heard God say that life would emerge from her lifeless womb. Hearing Sarah's laughter of unbelief, God asked her, "Is anything too hard for the LORD?" (Genesis 18:14). Sarah had been focused on whether it was too hard for her and Abraham, and there was no question it was. But the Lord turned to her with the more important question, which was, "Can I do it?" And of course he could.

Isaac was born so that, by a miraculous work of God, "a whole nation came from this one man who was as good as dead—a nation with so many people that, like the stars in the sky and the sand on the seashore, there is no way to count them" (Hebrews 11:12). In fact, God still accomplishes the impossible, creating life out of death apart from human effort. "God . . . when we were dead in our trespasses, made us alive together with Christ. . . . And this is not your own doing; it is the gift of God" (Ephesians 2:4-5, 8, ESV).

※ ※ ※

Lord, sometimes the growth and change we want to see in _____ seem impossible, even laughable. We need faith to keep believing that what is impossible in human terms is not too hard for you. Indeed, our hopes for ourselves and for _____ are grounded in the reality that you still accomplish the impossible. You create life out of death, which is not dependent upon human effort. Nothing is too hard for you!

JANUARY 10

You Can Heal Me

Suddenly, a man with leprosy approached him and knelt before him. "Lord," the man said, "if you are willing, you can heal me and make me clean." Jesus reached out and touched him. "I am willing," he said. "Be healed!" And instantly the leprosy disappeared. MATTHEW 8:2-3

HIS DISEASE probably started with just a few painful spots. Then the spots went numb. Slowly his body became a mass of ulcerated growths. To be a leper in Jesus' day was to have no future and no hope, to know only ongoing deterioration, disfigurement, and despair.

The effects of leprosy on a person's body provide a vivid picture of the effects of sin on a person's soul. Just as it takes only one spot to indicate that a person's body is permeated with leprosy, one spot of sin in our lives reveals that we have the spiritual disease that has permeated our whole selves. Our thoughts, our emotions, and our wills have all become infected with sin. Like leprosy, it infects the whole person, and it is ugly, loathsome, corruptive, contaminating, and alienating. Ultimately our transgressions lead to death.

So in reaching out to heal leprosy, Jesus showed that his touch can heal us of the most destructive, deadly disease in our lives—the disease of sin. When he touches us, we become joined to him so that his very own life and health flow into us. And as much as we pray for our children to be physically healthy and whole, we realize that this is the health and wholeness that matters most of all.

❄ ❄ ❄

Lord, we come to you knowing that you are the only one who can deal with the deadly disease of sin. And we are desperate for your healing touch. Won't you please touch _____ and bring healing to the wounded places where sin has left its ugly mark? Won't you please cleanse _____ of the sin that only leads to death? Give to _____ your very own life and health. We know that this healing will be a lifetime process, but we beg you, do not delay or withhold your healing touch even as we look forward to the day when we will be completely healed and whole.

Godless like Esau

"Look, I'm dying of starvation!" said Esau. "What good is my birthright to me now?"
But Jacob said, "First you must swear that your birthright is mine." So Esau swore an
oath, thereby selling all his rights as the firstborn to his brother, Jacob. Then Jacob gave
Esau some bread and lentil stew. Esau ate the meal, then got up and left. He showed
contempt for his rights as the firstborn. GENESIS 25:32-34

AS THE ELDEST SON, Esau was entitled to a double share of the family fortune when Isaac
died. But this birthright was about more than money or cattle or land. It was about covenant promise. God had made incredible promises to bless Esau's grandfather, Abraham,
and those promises had been passed down to his son, Isaac. But evidently, receiving
those promises and being a part of what God was doing to bless the whole world simply
weren't of any value to Esau. God's promises were intangible and unreal to him.

By contrast, his brother, Jacob, believed the promise and wanted in on it. His problem was that he didn't think the promise could be his apart from his own sinful manipulation. But interestingly, when we get to the New Testament, it's not Jacob's deception
that is condemned, but rather Esau's godlessness. The writer of Hebrews warned the
people of his day, "Make sure that no one is immoral or godless like Esau, who traded
his birthright as the firstborn son for a single meal" (Hebrews 12:16).

As fellow heirs with him, all who are in Christ have been given an invaluable birthright. We have an eternal inheritance that is being kept in heaven for us. What we long
for, as parents, is for our children to have eyes of faith to see the incredible worth of this
inheritance and to refuse to trade it away to satisfy a momentary craving.

※ ※ ※

God, all that you have promised and are preparing for those who love you is of such
monumental worth. But it takes eyes of faith to see it and a willingness to wait for it
when so much in this world promises immediate gratification. _____ has been raised
in a home where your great promises are known and loved, but, Lord, we know that
_____ must value and take hold of them for himself. Lord, don't let _____ be
immoral or godless like Esau. Don't let him trade all of the blessings of Christ to satisfy
a momentary craving.

JANUARY 12

Which Is Easier?

"Is it easier to say 'Your sins are forgiven,' or 'Stand up and walk'? So I will prove to you that the Son of Man has the authority on earth to forgive sins." Then Jesus turned to the paralyzed man and said, "Stand up, pick up your mat, and go home!" And the man jumped up and went home! MATTHEW 9:5-7

WHEN THE FRIENDS of the paralytic brought him to Jesus, they came in faith that he could and would deal with what they saw as the man's most significant problem—his inability to walk. When Jesus' first words to their friend were, "Be encouraged, my child! Your sins are forgiven," they must have looked at one another in confusion, thinking that Jesus had not truly grasped the situation. But in reality Jesus could see through the physical paralysis to a much more fundamental problem—a paralysis of the soul caused by sin. Jesus knew that while restoring this man's health might save him from *years* of suffering, restoring his soul would save him from an *eternity* of suffering.

When we look at the lives of our children, we tend to focus our concern and effort on what we see as the most significant problem. We see the learning disability, the lack of or the wrong sort of friends, the ongoing health issue, the rebellious attitude, or the relentless perfectionism. Perhaps we don't see and don't often feel desperate for Jesus to address the most profound need our children have, the most profound need we all have—our need for forgiveness of sin.

✳ ✳ ✳

Lord, forgive us for taking your forgiveness for granted. Your grace toward us addresses our most critical need, even though it might not always be so obvious to us. As we bring the many other needs our family has before you, give us proper perspective—that it is your healing work being accomplished in the soul of _____ that matters most now and into eternity.

More Workers

When he saw the crowds, he had compassion on them because they were confused and helpless, like sheep without a shepherd. He said to his disciples, "The harvest is great, but the workers are few. So pray to the Lord who is in charge of the harvest; ask him to send more workers into his fields." MATTHEW 9:36-38

THERE WAS JESUS, surrounded by confused and helpless crowds of people—people who were crippled by the effects of sin and confused about how to please God. Jesus hurt for them and with them. But there was so much more need than what could be met by the twelve disciples who surrounded him. So Jesus told these twelve to pray to the one who is in charge of the harvest of souls and to ask him to send more workers into his fields. By the end of the book of Acts, it becomes clear that their prayers were being answered. Workers had spread out throughout the known world, proclaiming the Good News. More and more sheep were hearing the voice of their Shepherd and coming into the safety of the fold.

Still today there are multitudes of confused and helpless people. And still compassion drives workers to leave the comforts of home to learn new cultures and languages. Still the Lord of the harvest sends workers who are willing to be persecuted and misunderstood and willing to give their lives away in order to announce the good news about the Kingdom. And still we are to pray for the Lord of the harvest to send more workers into his fields. Perhaps that's because when we do so, our hearts are drawn away from our own causes, and we become more invested in his cause. Surely if we give ourselves to pray for more workers to be sent into his fields, it opens us up to pray that we might be those workers and that our children might leave the safety of our homes and the closeness of our communities to work in his fields.

❋ ❋ ❋

Lord, you are in charge of the harvest of the souls of men and women. Only your Spirit can call and convict and convert. But your Spirit uses the proclamation of your Word to bring this about. So I'm praying that you will send more workers, more proclaimers to bring in a harvest of souls. But I can't pray for more workers without also praying that you would show us what it means for our family to be workers in your fields. And I can't pray for _____ without offering her up to be a worker in your fields, even if that proves uncomfortable or costly.

I Must Have It

When Rachel saw that she wasn't having any children for Jacob, she became jealous of her sister. She pleaded with Jacob, "Give me children, or I'll die!" GENESIS 30:1

WE THINK WE KNOW what we must have to be happy. Jacob was convinced he had to have Rachel to be happy, so much so that he was willing to work another seven years to get to marry her after Laban tricked him into marrying her older sister, Leah. Leah was convinced she had to have her husband's love to be happy, so she kept giving him more sons, hoping they would turn his heart toward her. But Rachel was the one who came right out with it. She was convinced that if she did not have the family she desired, she would die.

As much joy as family can bring into our lives, if our contentment is dependent on having the family we think we must have to be happy, we'll never be happy. Our idolatry will warp our expectations and interactions. Family simply can't bear the weight of being the primary source of our happiness. The truth is, anything about which we say "I must have this to be happy" is an idol. And idols never deliver what we hope they will. They enslave rather than provide. They disappoint rather than deliver.

❈ ❈ ❈

Lord, protect us from staking our happiness on our children. You are the center and source of our happiness. You are the only thing we must have or else we will die. So we will not insist that we have a certain number of children or that the children we have must be healthy or smart or successful. Our happiness will not be dependent on our children's saintliness or sinfulness, on the lifestyle they choose or their willingness to change. Our meaning in life and significance in this world don't come from the family we create or anything else. You provide the only meaning and significance that last.

More than Me

If you love your father or mother more than you love me, you are not worthy of being mine; or if you love your son or daughter more than me, you are not worthy of being mine. If you refuse to take up your cross and follow me, you are not worthy of being mine. If you cling to your life, you will lose it; but if you give up your life for me, you will find it. MATTHEW 10:37-39

EVEN AS JESUS SPENT time with his disciples, he began preparing them for when he would no longer be with them. Jesus knew the costs the disciples would be required to pay for being identified with him after his departure. Halfhearted love and halfway commitment would not be enough to kindle the kind of courage they would need to endure the persecution and rejection that was ahead for all who were called by his name.

Jesus didn't want his followers to be surprised when they experienced tremendous pressure to forget about following him and return to Judaism. In the early church, Jews who embraced Christ were no longer welcome at the synagogue, which would be where their families had found their home and place of belonging for centuries. Many had to make very painful choices between pleasing their parents and following Christ.

Even today, as our children emerge into adulthood, Jesus' call for them is to love him more than us. He still calls them to refuse to cling to the plans they may have had for their lives and the plans we may have had for where they would live, how they would live, and what they would live for.

❈ ❈ ❈

Lord, it seems a bit strange to pray that _____ would love you even more than he loves us, but we know that's what you've called him to. More than that, we know that as his love for you makes him more determined to obey you than to obey us, more determined to give up his plans and dreams for you than he is for us, he will be living the blessed life. And that's what we want for him. So we give _____ to you, Lord, asking you to fill him with that kind of love and level of commitment to you, so that nothing and nobody—not even his parents—will deter him from a life devoted to the cause of your Kingdom.

JANUARY 16

Genesis 32:13–34:31
Matthew 11:7-30
Psalm 14:1-7
Proverbs 3:19-20

Unless You Bless Me

This left Jacob all alone in the camp, and a man came and wrestled with him until the dawn began to break. When the man saw that he would not win the match, he touched Jacob's hip and wrenched it out of its socket. Then the man said, "Let me go, for the dawn is breaking!" But Jacob said, "I will not let you go unless you bless me."
GENESIS 32:24-26

JACOB HAD BEEN WRESTLING all his life. He had wrestled the birthright from his brother, words of affirmation from his father, and a wife from his father-in-law. But something had clearly shifted in Jacob that made the wrestling match on this dark night different. Jacob had come to the place where God's blessing meant more to him than life itself. He wanted to do whatever it took to experience the singular blessing that comes from knowing and being known by God himself. Less concerned about getting all he wanted from God, Jacob wanted God to have all of him.

Jacob would forever bear on his body the marks of this painful yet grace-filled encounter with God in which to survive and cling was to triumph. For the rest of his life, Jacob would walk with a limp. And yet we also read that God "blessed Jacob there" (verse 29). To be truly blessed by God is not to emerge from the struggles of life unscathed, but to emerge from them having been pressed more deeply into him. To be truly blessed is to become more desperate for him. It is to be convinced that having our identity flow from his victory in our lives is worth more than walking away from the struggle with our health, position, and lifestyle perfectly intact.

None of us relish the idea of our kids having to struggle either. And we certainly don't want them to be marked for life from the struggle. Yet we've lived long enough to know that when the hard and dark places of life force us to become desperate for God, we're changed by it and marked by it in the best of ways.

❋ ❋ ❋

Lord, I don't want ________ to have to go through this life with a limp, but I do want ________ to know you in the intimate way that only comes through intense desire, determination, struggle, and sometimes suffering. So, Lord, please do what you must do to bring ________ to the end of herself so that she can see that having your blessing in her life is worth everything it may cost her. And in the process, give ________ a new sense of identity that is defined by her life-altering encounter with you.

My People

These are the names of the twelve sons of Jacob: The sons of Leah were Reuben (Jacob's oldest son), Simeon, Levi, Judah, Issachar, and Zebulun. The sons of Rachel were Joseph and Benjamin. The sons of Bilhah, Rachel's servant, were Dan and Naphtali. The sons of Zilpah, Leah's servant, were Gad and Asher. GENESIS 35:22-26

YOU AND I DIDN'T get to choose where we were born, when we were born, or into what family we were born. And neither did our children. But God did. God called Abraham away from his own family to establish a new one—a family that God would uniquely call "my people." One day God would enfold himself into the womb of a virgin, a woman who was a descendant of this family.

So since God got to choose the family he was born into, what kind of family did he select? When we read their story in Genesis, we think we might have chosen better for him. No effort is made by the biblical writer to sanitize the portrait of this family. They were a polygamous group marked by manipulation, incest, prostitution, jealousy, murder, rape, sibling rivalry, idolatry, deceit, and estrangement. These are not exactly the kind of people who inspire confidence for putting God's name on display in the world. They do not seem to be worthy of the honor of being God's people. So what do we do with this?

We find hope in it and pass along that hope to our children. The story of these twelve sons—who became fathers of the twelve tribes who became the people of God into which we are adopted—illustrates that God is not looking for perfect people with spotless records to be a part of his family. There is only one Son born into this family who had a perfect record. Only one Son who is worthy of being called God's child. But this Son is our brother. He makes all who are joined to him by faith worthy of being part of God's family.

⁂ ⁂ ⁂

Lord, when we take stock of the family that you chose to be born into, it sets our hearts at rest. We realize that you are not looking for perfect people to become a part of your own family. Instead, you are populating your family, your church, with imperfect but repentant people, flagrant but forgiven sinners. When our children sin in outrageous ways, when they act in ways that dishonor you, help us to remember that you still choose to dwell among your people, though we are unworthy of you. Thank you for making us worthy by joining us to Christ.

JANUARY 18

Loved Him More

Jacob loved Joseph more than any of his other children because Joseph had been born to him in his old age. So one day Jacob had a special gift made for Joseph—a beautiful robe. But his brothers hated Joseph because their father loved him more than the rest of them. They couldn't say a kind word to him. GENESIS 37:3-4

JACOB SHOULD HAVE REMEMBERED the pain inflicted upon him by the failings of his father, Isaac, who obviously favored his brother, Esau. But evidently he didn't. He should have been determined not to inflict the pain of parental favoritism on his own sons. But evidently he wasn't.

Favoritism. It's one of the many ways we sin in parenting our children—one of many ways we may make adverse, lasting impressions on our children. So what do we do with our inner agony over the way our sin has impacted our children? Joseph helps us with that.

It was Jacob's sin of favoritism that filled Joseph's brothers with murderous hate toward him and led them to sell him into slavery. And yet when his brothers came to Egypt years later, he said to them, "Don't be upset, and don't be angry with yourselves for selling me to this place. It was God who sent me here ahead of you to preserve your lives" (Genesis 45:5). Joseph was able to see how God used even the great sin against him to accomplish his good purposes in his own life and that of his people.

Joseph's God is our God. We can trust that he is able to use our sins and failures as parents—our inconsistencies and our hypocrisies and even our cruelties—to accomplish his good purposes in the lives of our children.

❋ ❋ ❋

Lord, I see again and again in the Scriptures that you redeem the worst situations and the most stubborn people. But sometimes I find it hard to trust that you can redeem the things I've done and failed to do in the lives of my children. Will you show me how my attitudes and actions impact _____ in ways that pain him and shape who he will be as a parent someday? And will you give me the faith to trust in your providential plan for _____ as well as your grace toward me?

A Wicked Thing

*"Come and sleep with me," she demanded. But Joseph refused. "Look," he told her,
"my master trusts me with everything in his entire household. No one here has more
authority than I do. He has held back nothing from me except you, because you are
his wife. How could I do such a wicked thing? It would be a great sin against God."*
GENESIS 39:7-9

JOSEPH WAS YOUNG and good-looking. He was far away from the support and accountability of home. And he was being relentlessly pursued by the wife of his master. Yet
when this woman insisted that he sleep with her, Joseph refused. Where did this resolve
come from? As parents we'd like for it to be bottled and sold in bulk so we could force-
feed it to our children.

First, Joseph knew he was not a free agent, but rather a trusted servant. The goodness
of his master instilled in him a sense of loyalty that he did not want to violate. Second,
he was clear about the true nature of what he was being asked to do. It wasn't just a bit
of harmless fun or a love story that was meant to be. Joseph called it "a wicked thing."
Third, Joseph saw that it would be a great sin against the God he loved. He simply loved
God too much and feared him too greatly to take a casual approach to sin. Joseph was
able to see through what presented itself as pleasure to recognize its true ugliness. He
saw past the pleasure to the pain it would bring to his master and the offense it would
be to his God. And so he refused.

Our sons and daughters are deluged with the message from our culture that being
sexually active, regardless of marital status, is normal and even necessary to live a full
life. They face ongoing temptation to look at and indulge in what is wicked. Oh, that
they would have the clarity to recognize wickedness when it pursues them!

✷ ✷ ✷

*Lord, I can't protect _____ from every temptation, and I can't instill in _____
a resolve not to sin when temptation comes after her. Only you can protect her from the
enemy that seeks to rob, kill, and destroy. Only you can instill in _____ a desire to
please you that is greater than her desire to please herself. Would you give _____
clarity about the wickedness of sexual sin? Would you give _____ resolve to live a
pure life? And would you fill _____ with a growing love for you that would make
it more and more unthinkable to sin against you?*

JANUARY 20

Great Value

The Kingdom of Heaven is like a treasure that a man discovered hidden in a field. In his excitement, he hid it again and sold everything he owned to get enough money to buy the field. Again, the Kingdom of Heaven is like a merchant on the lookout for choice pearls. When he discovered a pearl of great value, he sold everything he owned and bought it! MATTHEW 13:44-46

ALL OF US—including our children—are constantly making trades. We trade an allotment of time spent on a project for the satisfaction of the job completed. We trade the effort of exercise or athletic practice for achievement of physical goals or victory in competition. We trade money for food, clothing, services, and such. Sometimes we make really good trades so that we end up ahead. Other times, we make foolish trades so that what we gain is worth nowhere near as much as what we traded away to get it.

But Jesus promises us that we will never be disappointed by anything we let go of to get more of him. He promises that having him as our King now and into eternity will be worth our submission to his authority and our embrace of his economy. The good news of his gospel is that we can lose everything this world tells us has value—reputation, opportunity, wealth, power, attractiveness—and still have everything that will make us happy forever if we have him. When the apostle Paul compared the value of things of this world to the person of Christ, he was able to say, "Yes, everything else is worthless when compared with the infinite value of knowing Christ Jesus my Lord. For his sake I have discarded everything else, counting it all as garbage, so that I could gain Christ" (Philippians 3:8). Oh, that our children will have eyes to see what is—namely *who* is—of infinite and eternal worth so that they will discover the happy trade-off of losing everything on earth to gain Christ.

※ ※ ※

Lord, I not only want _____ to see the great value of knowing and being ruled by you, but I need to see it and believe it too. Because I hate to see _____ lose out on anything in this life, I find that I want him to have everything the world offers as well as everything to be found in Christ. And that simply doesn't make sense. Lord, if it costs _____ everything to have you, he will not be losing out. Just don't let him gain the whole world but lose his soul.

He Reached Down

He reached down from heaven and rescued me;
  he drew me out of deep waters.
He rescued me from my powerful enemies,
  from those who hated me and were too strong for me.
They attacked me at a moment when I was in distress,
  but the LORD supported me.
He led me to a place of safety;
  he rescued me because he delights in me. PSALM 18:16-19

WHEN OUR CHILDREN ARE SMALL, we keep their tiny hands away from hot stoves, train them to look both ways before they cross the street, and warn them about talking to strangers. We've been their protector, their rescuer. But as our children grow, the threats are multiplied as well as diversified. And we simply don't have the power to keep them safe from every potential threat or unexpected attack. Our children need a better rescuer, a stronger savior. And that is exactly what they have.

Psalm 18 begins with an inscription that says David "sang this song to the LORD on the day the LORD rescued him from all his enemies and from Saul." In the psalm, David is celebrating the God who has had his back over a lifetime of difficulties. After God plucked him out of the fields and placed him on the royal throne, David endured the insurrections of his own subjects and the attacks of foreign enemies, as well as an overthrow attempt by his own son. David knew that he had not emerged from the abyss of his troubles by his own skill. He recognized that he had repeatedly been drawn out of deep waters and distress by the hand of God.

When our kids get in a tough spot, we tend to kick into high gear to accomplish a rescue or at least strategize a solution. But what our kids need most is to experience what David experienced—divine rescue, divine support. They need to be the object of divine delight as the Lord rescues them.

❈ ❈ ❈

Lord, I mistakenly put my confidence in coming up with a human solution or in manipulating a situation. But I know that's not what _____ needs most. What we all need is to experience the kind of rescue that has to come from you. Lord, help me to know when to hold back my help and keep my suggestions to myself, so that _____ can experience your support and safety.

I Will Bear the Blame

I cannot go back to my father without the boy. Our father's life is bound up in the boy's life. If he sees that the boy is not with us, our father will die. We, your servants, will indeed be responsible for sending that grieving, white-haired man to his grave. My lord, I guaranteed to my father that I would take care of the boy. I told him, "If I don't bring him back to you, I will bear the blame forever." So please, my lord, let me stay here as a slave instead of the boy, and let the boy return with his brothers. For how can I return to my father if the boy is not with me? I couldn't bear to see the anguish this would cause my father! GENESIS 44:30-34*

IF WE'VE BEEN TRACING Judah throughout the story of his brother Joseph, we recognize in this scene that something in Judah had shifted. Judah had been the one who'd come up with the idea to sell Joseph to the slave traders years earlier. It was Judah who slept with his daughter-in-law, Tamar, thinking she was a prostitute, and then wanted to have her burned to death when she became pregnant. Along with his brothers, Judah kept silent all those years while Jacob mourned over Joseph.

Something had clearly changed. Judah was no longer resentful over the intensity of Jacob's love for another brother, Benjamin. He was no longer anxious to get rid of his father's favorite. He couldn't bear the idea that his father would have to experience the anguish of losing a second son. So Judah offered himself in place of another out of love for his father. He was willing to bear the blame. How very Christlike.

But sadly, there is something that hadn't changed about Jacob. His life was still "bound up" in the life of a favored son. His other sons saw it. They knew that if this son died, life would not be worth living to their father.

❊ ❊ ❊

Lord, as much as I love my children, don't let me put them in the place that should be reserved for you alone. Protect me from allowing my identity or my happiness to be "bound up" in them. Instead, as I grow older, keep changing me. Make me more compassionate, more self-denying. Likewise, help me to trust that you intend to work in _____'s life over the course of a lifetime to make _____ more like Christ.

Words You Speak

You hypocrites! Isaiah was right when he prophesied about you, for he wrote, "These people honor me with their lips, but their hearts are far from me.". . . The words you speak come from the heart—that's what defiles you. For from the heart come evil thoughts, murder, adultery, all sexual immorality, theft, lying, and slander.
MATTHEW 15:7-8, 18-19

JESUS WAS SPEAKING to a group of people who were rigid in their religious observance. They were frustrated that Jesus was not following their rules. Jesus was more concerned, however, with the way they had managed to develop a system of manageable dos and don'ts that they thought would make them acceptable to God while ignoring the hardness of their hearts toward him and one another. There was a significant disconnect between the religious commitment they claimed and the true condition of their hearts, which was evident by their words.

And it is that disconnect—that hypocrisy, as Jesus names it—that we eschew in ourselves and in our children. We can sometimes be so concerned that our kids act right and go through the motions of church life that we miss the real issue—their need for hearts that are being made new by the power of the Holy Spirit. Only then will evil thoughts progressively be transformed into holy thoughts and desires.

We don't want to have a home in which outer conformity covers up inner rebellion that goes unrecognized or unchallenged. We long for sincere faith and a humble awareness of our need for God, by his Spirit and through his Word, to give us and our children new hearts, pure hearts, sincere hearts.

✳ ✳ ✳

Lord, I'm thinking about the words my children hear me speak each day and how they reveal the true condition of my heart—specifically, the sins that have made themselves at home there. Save me from the hypocrisy of church activity without genuine repentance. Save me from the hypocrisy of praying over meals without praying about what matters. Save me from the hypocrisy of reciting your commands without living under your authority. And Lord, don't let me confuse rule-keeping in _____ with regeneration and repentance. You are the one who can replace a heart of stone with a heart of flesh, so I ask you to do that in _____ today.

JANUARY 24

Whole-Body Focus

Guard your heart above all else,
*   for it determines the course of your life.*
Avoid all perverse talk;
*   stay away from corrupt speech.*
Look straight ahead,
*   and fix your eyes on what lies before you.*
Mark out a straight path for your feet;
*   stay on the safe path.*
Don't get sidetracked;
*   keep your feet from following evil.* PROVERBS 4:23-27

"DON'T TEXT WHILE DRIVING." It's the kind of instruction we give to our kids so they won't end up in the ditch or worse. We want their full attention and focus to be on navigating the road ahead of them. Similarly, the father speaking in Proverbs 4 calls his son to pay attention to the path ahead so he won't get lost along the way of life. If the son wants to have the full life that is available in God, he must orient his whole self in God's direction.

The father works his way through numerous body parts that must be dedicated and disciplined in this direction: the heart must be guarded from worldly affections, the mouth can't spew perverse talk, the eyes must be fixed on the prize of the upward call of God, and the feet must take him places where he will experience more of God instead of more of what the world offers. If we and our children are going to go after Christ, we can't simply invite him along on the life we have charted out for ourselves. Christ must be our constant companion as well as our destination.

We are all vulnerable to having hearts that grow cold toward the things of God—mouths that talk in ways that diminish Christ, eyes that flit from thing to thing rather than focus on his Word, and feet that don't follow in the footsteps of Christ. But the Bible calls us to deploy the entirety of our bodies in pursuing Christ by offering them as living sacrifices.

❈ ❈ ❈

Lord, you have set out a course of life for _____. Keep him watchful for what would make his heart grow cold toward you. Fill his mouth with words of grace, and rid it of corruption. Fix his eyes on all you have promised, and keep him headed in your direction.

Give Up Your Life

Then Jesus said to his disciples, "If any of you wants to be my follower, you must give up your own way, take up your cross, and follow me. If you try to hang on to your life, you will lose it. But if you give up your life for my sake, you will save it. And what do you benefit if you gain the whole world but lose your own soul?" MATTHEW 16:24-26

PETER HAD JUST RUNG the bell with his solid confession about who Jesus is: "You are the Messiah, the Son of the living God" (verse 16). Jesus responded by saying that Peter was blessed because he didn't come up with this himself, but in fact the Father in heaven had revealed it to him. But then Jesus said that he was headed to Jerusalem, where he would be killed at the hands of the religious leaders. Peter blew it this time. His response? "Heaven forbid, Lord," he said. "This will never happen to you!" This time Jesus didn't say he was blessed. Instead he said, "Get away from me, Satan! You are a dangerous trap to me. You are seeing things merely from a human point of view, not from God's" (verses 22-23). And then he told the disciples that if they were going to follow him, they would have to give up their lives too. But in losing their lives for his sake, they would actually save them.

Next Jesus asked the question that reverberates from his day to our day, from the disciples who surrounded Jesus to the disciples sitting around the table in our homes: "What do you benefit if you gain the whole world but lose your own soul?" That's the potential tragedy that keeps us setting the treasures of Christ before our children day after day, even as we point out the vacuousness of what the world tells them will make them happy. And that is the promise for all who are willing to suffer for and follow after Christ: We can face losing everything because we know we stand to gain everything.

❋ ❋ ❋

Lord, if I'm honest, I don't like the possibility that _____ might have to lose in this life to follow after you. When my heart is broken over what she may not obtain in this life, give me eyes to see all she stands to inherit, all she will never lose but in fact all she will gain in you. Show me how to help her see the temporal value of this world and the eternal value of having you.

Exodus 2:11–3:22
Matthew 17:10-27
Psalm 22:1-18
Proverbs 5:7-14

Rescued for Worship

*The LORD told him, "I have certainly seen the oppression of my people in Egypt.
I have heard their cries of distress because of their harsh slave drivers. Yes, I am aware
of their suffering. So I have come down to rescue them from the power of the Egyptians
and lead them out of Egypt into their own fertile and spacious land. . . . When you
have brought the people out of Egypt, you will worship God at this very mountain."*
EXODUS 3:7-8, 12

ANY OBSERVER WATCHING the Hebrew people working day after day in the hot sun for
Pharaoh would not have expected that a generation later these people would be settling
into a land of milk and honey, a place where they could live at rest. No observer would
have believed that these people, immersed in the culture of Egyptian gods, would put
their trust in the promises Yahweh made to their ancestor Abraham. And certainly, apart
from divine intervention, it would have been impossible.

Perhaps as an observer of your family, you can't see how you or your children will
ever break free of deeply ingrained patterns that have made you slaves to consumerism,
slaves to body image, slaves to spending time and money in ways that do not honor
God. You can't imagine that you and your children could ever be transformed into a
family of glad worshipers, a family who finds your greatest happiness in praising and
pleasing God.

But when we open the Scriptures, from Genesis to Revelation, we discover a God
who intervenes to help his people. He comes down. He came down to dwell among
his people in the Tabernacle. He came down to deliver his people in the person of Jesus
Christ. And he still condescends by his Spirit to rescue and redeem. He still moves in
the lives of people who are slaves to sin and leads them into freedom, transforming them
into glad worshipers.

❋ ❋ ❋

*Lord, when things aren't changing as quickly as we'd like and in the way we'd like, we
wonder if you have really seen the need in our family. We wonder if you've heard our cries.
But we know that you see and you hear and you rescue. Please rescue us from the things
that enslave us to what is evil. Transform us into a family of glad worshipers.*

As Humble as a Child

About that time the disciples came to Jesus and asked, "Who is greatest in the Kingdom of Heaven?" Jesus called a little child to him and put the child among them. Then he said, "I tell you the truth, unless you turn from your sins and become like little children, you will never get into the Kingdom of Heaven. So anyone who becomes as humble as this little child is the greatest in the Kingdom of Heaven." MATTHEW 18:1-4

JESUS' DISCIPLES wanted to be great. But they had a profound misunderstanding of greatness, seeing it in terms of human endeavor, accomplishment, and status. So Jesus provided both a visual and verbal rebuke, answering their question about who would be greatest in the Kingdom by demonstrating what is required just to get into the Kingdom. The requirement: childlike trust. Proud adults must approach God in unself-conscious dependence.

We, too, long for greatness. We want the day to come when our children tell us we were great parents. We want people around us to think we are great parents. We want to look in the mirror and be able to say to ourselves that we're doing great at this daunting endeavor called parenting.

But what will make us truly great? How can we best point our children toward the Kingdom of God, which must certainly be at the heart of good parenting? Evidently it is not by always doing the right thing and never letting our children see us sweat. Evidently it is not about our greatness at all, but instead about recognition of our neediness. It is about living out before our children an ongoing childlike dependence upon our heavenly Father.

❋ ❋ ❋

Lord, I recognize that even though I am a parent, I will never outgrow my need of coming to you as a child. I'm also seeing that what _____ needs most from me is not a parent who has everything figured out and does everything right. What _____ needs most is to see my childlike trust, my vulnerability, and my inability to make progress apart from your help, direction, and resources. Lord, I don't want my self-reliance to cause any of your little ones to fall away into the sin of self-sufficiency. Please give me the grace to humble myself so that _____ will see that I live in childlike trust and dependence on you.

My Shepherd, My Host

The LORD is my shepherd;
I have all that I need. PSALM 23:1

DAVID WAS A SHEPHERD. But he also knew he was a sheep in the care of the Great Shepherd. His prayer expressing recognition of the joys of being in the care of such a good shepherd inspires us to pray the same way.

❀ ❀ ❀

Lord, you are not just my shepherd. You are _____'s shepherd. And you are a good shepherd, not a careless, unkind, or incompetent one. Because _____ has you as his shepherd, he has everything he needs.

As a shepherd, you are leading him into your abundance and beauty and rest. You are renewing his strength when it is gone by feeding him with your Word. You are guiding him toward a life of right living so you will be glorified in his life.

Because you are _____'s shepherd, I can be sure that even when _____ is in very dark places, even when he faces great danger, he does not need to be afraid and neither do I. You are right there beside him, so he is never alone. I can't always be with him, but you are always with him.

As a good shepherd, you use your rod to discipline and protect him and your staff to take hold of _____ and draw him to yourself.

Not only are you a good shepherd; you are a good host. You have not only taken _____ into the safety of your fold; you have welcomed him into the abundance of your home. You are feeding him with the broken body and blood of Christ, a salvation feast, even as he is surrounded by enemies who make false promises of satisfaction. You are filling his being with your Spirit and flooding his life with undeserved favor and blessing.

While there are many things I can't be sure of as I look into the future, one thing I can be sure of is that your grace and goodness will be chasing after _____ all the days of his life. Even after my days on this earth come to an end, _____ has a shepherd to guide and provide for him, and a host who has made a home for him where he can live forever.

Rich, Religious Ruler

Someone came to Jesus with this question: "Teacher, what good deed must I do to have eternal life?" . . . Jesus told him, "If you want to be perfect, go and sell all your possessions and give the money to the poor, and you will have treasure in heaven. Then come, follow me." But when the young man heard this, he went away sad, for he had many possessions. MATTHEW 19:16, 21-22

THE YOUNG MAN who came to Jesus with a question appeared to have everything our culture says we should want for our children. He was rich, he was religious, and he was a ruler. He had plenty of resources to finance a comfortable lifestyle, he had plenty of morality and religiosity to engender the respect of others, and he had plenty of authority to use to exert his will over others. Not only that, he asked good questions.

He wanted to know what he needed to do to get eternal life. Everything else in his life seemed to have been so manageable, so attainable. And it can seem that way to our kids, who are constantly told by our culture that they can be anything they want to be and accomplish anything if they believe in themselves and go after their dreams.

Jesus offered this young man the opportunity of a lifetime when he told him to let go of the worldly wealth and powerful position that had such a grip on his heart so that he could follow after Jesus. But the man went away sad, unwilling to surrender it all. Imagine all the amazing experiences this wealthy young ruler missed out on by holding on to his possessions—the joy of being with Jesus, being taught by Jesus, being used by Jesus. What a tragedy to be large and in charge but to miss out on rich relationship with Christ and life lived under the authority of Christ.

✖ ✖ ✖

Lord, save me from settling for the American dream for _____. I don't want _____ to follow after a dream of financial security or privilege. I want _____ to be rich—rich in a reward that he can never lose, rich in relationship with you. I want _____ to rule—not over men and millions in this world, but as a coheir and co-ruler with you in the new heavens and new earth. I want _____ to be religious—to have a pure and genuine religion in your sight, caring for orphans and widows in their distress and refusing to let the world corrupt him.

What's Your Ambition?

The mother of James and John, the sons of Zebedee, came to Jesus with her sons. She knelt respectfully to ask a favor. "What is your request?" he asked. She replied, "In your Kingdom, please let my two sons sit in places of honor next to you, one on your right and the other on your left." MATTHEW 20:20-21

SURELY THE MOTHER of James and John had some ambition for her sons. But when she approached Jesus with her bold request, you can almost see her sons pushing her toward him, thinking, perhaps, that Jesus would be more inclined to say yes to the nice lady. When Jesus replied to her question, he talked around her and spoke directly to them. "You don't know what you are asking! Are you able to drink from the bitter cup of suffering I am about to drink?"

Their ambition had not only twisted their understanding of the Kingdom; it had inflated their sense of themselves. "'Oh yes,' they replied, 'we are able!'" (Matthew 20:22).

We all have ambition for our children. We want them to make the team, be admitted into the desirable school, and get the part in the play, knowing that others will not. It's not that having ambition for our children is necessarily bad. The issue is this: Have our ambitions for our children been shaped by the kingdom of the world or by the Kingdom of God? Jesus says that while people in the world look to lord over others, that's not how it works in his Kingdom. "Whoever wants to be a leader among you must be your servant, and whoever wants to be first among you must become your slave. For even the Son of Man came not to be served but to serve others and to give his life as a ransom for many" (Matthew 20:26-28).

Though our culture constantly pushes our children to focus on excelling and climbing the ladder to success academically, athletically, and socially, Jesus calls them to come down from that ladder to serve the needs of others.

❈ ❈ ❈

Lord, I can't help but have hopes and dreams for _____. But like everything else that flows out of my heart, I need my ambitions for _____ to be purified by you. Give me the grace to lead the way in having an ambition to serve others out of love for you. And give _____ a true sense of the good life—a life of taking up a cross, confident of the crown that is to come.

When He Sees the Blood

Moses called all the elders of Israel together and said to them, "Go, pick out a lamb or young goat for each of your families, and slaughter the Passover animal. Drain the blood into a basin. Then take a bundle of hyssop branches and dip it into the blood. Brush the hyssop across the top and sides of the doorframes of your houses. And no one may go out through the door until morning. For the LORD will pass through the land to strike down the Egyptians. But when he sees the blood on the top and sides of the doorframe, the LORD will pass over your home. He will not permit his death angel to enter your house and strike you down." EXODUS 12:21-23

IMAGINE what it was like in Hebrew homes on this night. God's instructions were that they had to take a lamb into their home. Then, four days later, as the sun was beginning to set, Dad had to take the innocent lamb that everyone had become so fond of and slit its throat. Perhaps many firstborn sons asked him, "Dad, do we really have to kill the lamb? He has done nothing to deserve this." To which the father replied, "Son, either the lamb dies, or you die."

The Israelites' killing of lambs and sprinkling of the blood was an act of faith. The blood on the lintel and two doorposts was proof that they were taking God at his word about the judgment to come and the protection he would provide through the death of the lamb. And it is the same for us. If we take God at his word that judgment is coming, the proof is that the blood of the Lamb has become our covering, our hiding place, our source of protection. Our lives are marked by that blood.

Many people think a Christian is someone who believes in God and tries to be good, or someone who lives by the Ten Commandments or the Sermon on the Mount (as if anyone could!). But what we and our children must understand is that a Christian is a person who recognizes that he or she is a sinner deserving nothing less than the terrifying judgment of God and who takes refuge only in the blood of the Lamb of God, Jesus Christ.

❊ ❊ ❊

Lord, how I wish I could do something tangible and physical to ensure the safety of my children from judgment. Instead I must trust you and thank you for providing the Lamb of God who takes away sin. I ask you to give _____ a deep sense of need for her life to be marked by his blood.

FEBRUARY 1

What the Lord Hates

There are six things the LORD hates—
no, seven things he detests:
haughty eyes,
a lying tongue,
hands that kill the innocent,
a heart that plots evil,
feet that race to do wrong,
a false witness who pours out lies,
a person who sows discord in a family. PROVERBS 6:16-19

As WE READ through the list of things the Lord hates, as it zeros in on every body part that has been engaged in hateful and hurtful attitudes and actions toward others, we wonder if someone has been spying on what goes on behind closed doors at our house. After all, we've seen these offenses, both in ourselves and in our children.

We've seen haughty eyes rolled at us and our rules. We've caught our children in outrageous lies. We've had children who bit other kids in the nursery, bullied other kids on the playground, and ruined the reputations of other kids on the Internet. We've figured out their plans to deceive us about where they will be and seen them race out the door to go where we told them not to go. Our children have twisted the truth in their tattling and persisted in conflict with siblings.

When we read through this list, we hope it really is true that God hates the sin but loves the sinner. And indeed there is hope for those infected with things the Lord hates. There is grace for sinners—the kind of grace that changes haughty eyes into eyes filled with tears of repentance, grace that transforms a lying tongue into a tongue that tells the truth, grace that cleanses away the blood of the innocent, grace that melts a cold heart into one that desires to please God, grace that changes the course of feet quick to do wrong so that they follow after Christ, grace that transforms troublemakers into peacemakers.

❋ ❋ ❋

Oh, Lord, our family needs your transforming grace if we're ever going to experience the kind of deep heart change that will transform how we relate to one another. We need your Spirit to convict us when we selfishly hurt each other. Would you do a work by your Spirit in us so that we increasingly love what you love and hate what you hate?

Grumbling and Grace

The LORD said to Moses, "I have heard the Israelites' complaints. Now tell them, 'In the evening you will have meat to eat, and in the morning you will have all the bread you want. Then you will know that I am the LORD your God.'" EXODUS 16:11-12

GOD HAD HEARD the cries of his people and sent a deliverer to bring them out of slavery in Egypt. He had held back a wall of water so they could cross through the Red Sea on dry ground and then released it to drown their enemies. Most recently he had brought them to an Eden-like oasis and sweetened the bitter water there to slake their thirst. They should have been overflowing with gratitude. But instead, God's people grumbled, accusing him of bringing them out into the wilderness to die of hunger.

God would have been just to let them starve right there in the desert. But God's grace is greater than his people's grumbling. His gracious response to their grumbling was to supernaturally provide for them. Every day as they gathered just enough manna to meet the day's needs and went to bed expecting it to rain down again the next morning, they were learning what it meant to live by faith in God's promised provision.

We long for our children to learn what it means to live by faith. We sometimes think it is all about knowing the right things and acting the right way. But isn't it really more about sensing a great need for what only God can provide and waking up each day to that provision? Though we are quick to notice when our kids gripe and grumble, how often do they hear us complain—about their messy room, an annoying neighbor, or about our own parents? What we all need is for gratitude to crowd out our impulse to complain.

❈ ❈ ❈

Lord, forgive us for our grumbling against you when you are providing everything we need, including what we need most—the Living Bread that came down from heaven, Jesus himself. Lord, give _____ a desperate hunger for you. Help _____ to see that only your provision nourishes and satisfies the human soul. As he takes and eats your provision, the body and blood of Christ, make him truly know that you are the Lord his God.

What You Want Most

One of them, an expert in religious law, tried to trap him with this question: "Teacher,
which is the most important commandment in the law of Moses?" Jesus replied, "'You
must love the LORD your God with all your heart, all your soul, and all your mind.'
This is the first and greatest commandment. A second is equally important: 'Love your
neighbor as yourself.'" MATTHEW 22:35-39

IF SOMEONE WERE to ask your children what you want most for them or from them
based on what they hear you say or see you get worked up about, how would they
respond? Would your children sense that what is most important to you is that they
have a clean room, good grades, and that they live up to their potential?

Or would your children sense that your greatest desire for their lives is grounded in
the greatest commandment? Do your actions, words, and attitudes communicate that
what will please you most is what will please God most—that your children love God
most of all?

Our children probably know that we want them to obey the Ten Commandments—
to honor their mom and dad, to be sexually chaste now in anticipation of being faithful
one day to a spouse, to tell the truth, and to be content with what they have rather than
covetous over what they don't. But perhaps we haven't been as clear with them about
this all-important affection. Perhaps we haven't been clear that the reason we take them
to church and read the Bible is because we want them to know God in such a way that
his beauty and perfection will stir up in them an all-encompassing affection for him.

❊ ❊ ❊

Lord, I know that my children see what I'm drawn to, what I get excited about, what
I think and talk about, what I put effort toward. What I want _____ to see in me
is that I love you with all of my heart and that I am not coldhearted or simply going
through the motions, but that I have a genuine loving relationship with you. I want
_____ to see that I love you with all of my soul, that the deepest part of who I am has
a bent toward you. I want _____ to see that I love you with all of my mind—that
I think about you more than my favorite team, activity, or meal. Lord, let my love for
you in our home be contagious so that _____ might love you with all of her heart,
soul, and mind.

Nothing to Fear

When the people heard the thunder and the loud blast of the ram's horn, and when they saw the flashes of lightning and the smoke billowing from the mountain, they stood at a distance, trembling with fear. . . . "Don't be afraid," Moses answered them, "for God has come in this way to test you, and so that your fear of him will keep you from sinning!" EXODUS 20:18, 20

GOD HAD JUST COME DOWN on Mount Sinai to give his law to his people, and the earth shook with the force. The Israelites who gathered at the foot of the mountain would soon see in the inscribed tablets that God demanded their total allegiance. They could also see in the fire and smoke the judgment that awaited lawbreakers. If they came near the mountain, they would die, so they were understandably afraid.

God wanted them to know that he had rescued them. But he also wanted them to know that he is not a domesticated deity. He is a good God, and he is also a dangerous God. As his mediator, Moses told them that the Lord had given them this law not to destroy them, but so they could develop a life of glad obedience to him. This law that revealed the goodness of God was being given so that they might share in his goodness.

God has told us what to do. But there's a problem. We can't do it! If we were able to keep the law, we could be saved by it. But since we cannot keep it, we can only be condemned by it. Fortunately, we have a better mediator than Moses and have received a better covenant than the old covenant. "The law of Moses was unable to save us because of the weakness of our sinful nature. So God did what the law could not do. He sent his own Son in a body like the bodies we sinners have. And in that body God declared an end to sin's control over us by giving his Son as a sacrifice for our sins" (Romans 8:3).

In the book of Hebrews, we learn that we who live under the new covenant don't approach God at Mount Sinai like his people did in Moses' day. We go to a different mountain—Mount Zion. Zion is where Jesus reigns now at the right hand of the Father, who is still ablaze in holiness and abundant in mercy. Because of Christ's finished work, we can approach God with nothing to fear and everything to gain.

※ ※ ※

God, you are a consuming fire. You are pure and holy, and you demand perfection. The day will come when _____ will stand before you. Oh, how my heart yearns for him to be ready for that day by taking hold of Christ as his mediator, by standing before you covered in Christ's perfect record of obedience.

Exodus 21:22–23:13
Matthew 24:1-28
Psalm 29:1-11
Proverbs 7:6-23

Seduced

So she seduced him with her pretty speech
and enticed him with her flattery.
He followed her at once,
like an ox going to the slaughter.
He was like a stag caught in a trap,
awaiting the arrow that would pierce its heart.
He was like a bird flying into a snare,
little knowing it would cost him his life. PROVERBS 7:21-23

IN THIS PROVERB, the father tells his son how he looked out his window one day and saw a naive young man doing something stupid. The young man had gone out of his way to stroll by the house of an immoral woman. He was curious and foolishly unaware of his own vulnerability. The imagery seems to fit exactly the situation we as parents face today. We may take a look at the Internet history on the computer and discover our child has gone on a search for pornographic images. What is a wise parent to do?

The wise father in this proverb remains engaged in order to safeguard the sexual purity of his son. He is a realist about the aggressive tactics of peddlers of sex and about his son's susceptibility. So he spells out how his son will be approached, preparing him to be alert and ready for it. He provides a preview of what he will be promised, how his ego will be stroked, and how beautiful and pleasurable it will appear. But he is also clear about the high cost if his son follows the enticement by pursuing what is offered. Sexual sin, though pleasurable in the moment, will have a deadening impact. It will rob him of life rather than add to it.

Our savvy sons and daughters think of themselves as smart and in control, but we recognize their susceptibility to seduction. So we are wise to set up practical safeguards and install accountability software—for ourselves and for them—even as we point out where the path of sexual sin leads.

❊ ❊ ❊

Father, I need wisdom from you to know how to guide _____ toward purity in a world of available sexual images, aggressive sex peddlers, and acceptance of sexual perversion. Give me wisdom to confess my own need for your power to overcome sexual temptation and words to express the availability of forgiveness and cleansing for sexual sinners.

Good Intentions

Moses went down to the people and repeated all the instructions and regulations the LORD had given him. All the people answered with one voice, "We will do everything the LORD has commanded." EXODUS 24:3

GOOD INTENTIONS. That's what the people of Israel had after they heard God's law through Moses. They genuinely desired to live in the way God prescribed for them as a holy nation and his treasured possession. But less than forty days after the Israelites promised to have no other gods and to make no idols (God's first and second commandments), they stood around a fire pitching their gold jewelry into the smelting pot to become part of a golden calf.

We, too, have good intentions. Yet we are people who bow before other gods, such as our investment portfolios and other people's opinions. We call ourselves Christians and then act completely un-Christlike when we don't get the service we think we ought to at a restaurant. We inundate ourselves with entertainment that normalizes sex outside the covenant of marriage. We shade the truth to make ourselves look good at someone else's expense. We covet the better cars in the carpool line, the better figures and physiques in magazines. We are lawbreakers.

Fortunately, Jesus can do for us what the law could not. The grace of God at work in us gives us the power to obey "the perfect law that sets [us] free" (James 1:25). We can worship God wholeheartedly and take his name upon ourselves with integrity because Christ liberates us from our slavery to other gods. Our security in Christ frees us to enjoy his Sabbath rest. He fills our hearts with the same love he has for his Father so that we can honor our parents. He fills us with his very own faithfulness so that we can live in sexual purity. He enables us to treat our children as precious gifts rather than as evidence of our great parenting skills. He convinces us of all that is ours in him forever so that we can stop coveting things that will not last beyond this life.

✳ ✳ ✳

Lord, we need so much more in our home than a code of good behavior and a load of good intentions. We need your Spirit to write your law on our hearts so that we will want to obey you. We need your holy law to work its way through the hidden places in our hearts and the habits in our home so that we can be set free from idolatry and infidelity, disrespect and dishonesty. We long to be a holy people who together enjoy the freedom not to sin, which is made possible by the work of your grace in our lives.

37

Entrusted

The Kingdom of Heaven can be illustrated by the story of a man going on a long trip. He called together his servants and entrusted his money to them while he was gone. He gave five bags of silver to one, two bags of silver to another, and one bag of silver to the last—dividing it in proportion to their abilities. He then left on his trip.
MATTHEW 25:14-15

JESUS TOLD HIS DISCIPLES this parable as he was preparing to leave on a "trip." Ahead of him, in the next few days, would be crucifixion, followed by resurrection and then ascension. He was teaching his disciples how to live as his servants in his absence, between his resurrection and his return, which is exactly where we find ourselves. Our master, Jesus, has entrusted each of us with resources to invest in the growth of his Kingdom until he returns. We've all been given many things to steward: abilities, opportunities, experiences, health, strength, intellect, and advantages. The question is: How are we investing what has been entrusted to us by our Master to earn a return for his Kingdom, not ours?

In our Western world of entitlement and independence, we need—and our children need—the Spirit to work in us so that we begin to see ourselves as stewards rather than as owners of our money, time, abilities, and opportunities. We need the Spirit to redirect our heart's desire away from using what we've been given to build our own earthly kingdoms and toward stewarding what we've been entrusted with to expand the Kingdom of God. We need the Spirit to work the truths of this parable into our hearts so that we desire to hear our Master say, "Well done, my good and faithful servant."

❋ ❋ ❋

Lord, you have blessed me with so many things, including my children. I want to be a good steward of this family so that we might be a part of expanding your Kingdom. I can see that you have entrusted _____ with experience, abilities, and opportunities as well. Would you help _____ to see that all this does not belong to her but has been entrusted to her so it can be invested for a return for your Kingdom, rather than used to build her own kingdom? Would you implant in _____ a longing to one day hear you say, "Well done, my good and faithful servant"?

In Your Hands

I am trusting you, O LORD,
*   saying, "You are my God!"*
My future is in your hands. PSALM 31:14-15

FROM THE TIME they are newborns, we are concerned about how our children are progressing. In the early days we follow their weight and growth on percentile charts. We are proud when our children seem to be ahead of the game in terms of reading or verbal or physical coordination skills. We want to know what we can do—what we can feed them, teach them, how we can train them—to keep them moving toward a bright future. During the school years, our parental fear or confidence rises and falls on how well our children are progressing in school and sports, as well as socially and physically. As they emerge into young adulthood, we can't help but set timelines for them to finish their education, find a mate, and establish a career. And all along the way, we often think and act and feel as if it is up to us and our children to chart out a path for their lives and make it happen.

But King David knew otherwise. When he looked at his past, he remembered how he had been plucked out of the shepherd's field and anointed king of Israel. As he took stock of his present situation, which was full of distress and uncertainty, he determined to trust the God who had made him his own. And as he looked toward the future, he recognized that he was not ultimately in control. Neither did he want to be. "My future is in your hands," David said to his God.

Sometimes we want to take the Lord's place in our children's lives and are foolish enough to think we actually could. But their future is not in our hands. It's not under our control, nor is it our responsibility. And ultimately our children's future is not in their hands either, but in God's.

※ ※ ※

I would like to say that I am trusting you, Lord, with _____'s future. But the truth is, I find myself obsessing over many aspects of who _____ will be, what _____ will do, and where _____ will be. If I'm honest, I have my own expectations and timeline for how _____'s life should progress. But I know that _____'s future is not in my hands. And deep down I don't want it to be. I know that the safest place to be, the place of favor and blessing, is in your hands. So I am trusting you, O Lord, saying, "You are _____'s God. _____'s future is in your hands."

Your Will, Not Mine

He went on a little farther and bowed with his face to the ground, praying,
"My Father! If it is possible, let this cup of suffering be taken away from me.
Yet I want your will to be done, not mine." MATTHEW 26:39

WE TEND TO THINK that if we are really good and really godly, then God will be inclined to say yes to our prayers. We think the secret to getting the answer we want from God is to try our best to be in close fellowship with him. But in the prayer of Jesus to his Father in the garden of Gethsemane, we discover the fallacy of that assumption. Was there ever anyone as good or godly as Jesus? Was there ever anyone who was in closer fellowship with God the Father? Yet here is Jesus, asking his Father to accomplish the salvation of sinners in some other way, and God, through his silence, says no.

It is good that we get to overhear this conversation between Jesus and his Father. It helps to know that Jesus wrestled with God's plan for his life—and his death—even as he submitted to it. We, too, have wrestled with God's plan for our lives even as we have sought to submit to it.

Perhaps you have wondered: *God, could it possibly be your plan for us to never be sure if we'll have enough money to pay the bills? Could it possibly be your plan for us to spend years in a less-than-perfect marriage? Could it possibly be your plan for our children to struggle instead of sail through life?* How can you come to a place of acceptance when God says no to your reasonable, repeated requests?

Let's listen closely to how Jesus did it. Even though Jesus was struggling as he told God what he wanted, he was resolute about what he wanted most of all: "I want your will to be done, not mine" (Matthew 26:39). Jesus was able to submit what he wanted to what he wanted more. He had a greater longing that trumped and trampled his desire to avoid enduring the judgment of God on our behalf. And that was to fulfill the purpose and plan of God.

✳ ✳ ✳

Father, I need to grow in my confidence in your perfect plan and purposes so that I can put my desires into proper perspective. I need my faith in your goodness and justice to loom so large that I can entrust myself and our family to you without fear or resentment. Help me to truly believe that the joy of surrendering to your will—whatever it may be—will be worth whatever it may cost.

The Grace of Conviction

Oh, what joy for those
  whose disobedience is forgiven,
  whose sin is put out of sight! . . .
When I refused to confess my sin,
  my body wasted away,
  and I groaned all day long.
Day and night your hand of discipline was heavy on me.
  My strength evaporated like water in the summer heat. PSALM 32:1, 3-4

TO COME UNDER CONVICTION of sin and to gain a sense of clarity about the offensive nature of our selfish actions and rebellious attitudes is not necessarily pleasant. We would much rather close our eyes to the ugliness of our sin. To name it for what it is and to admit that we've been foolish, selfish, and rebellious is also unpleasant. It's humbling and uncomfortable.

Perhaps part of the pain of conviction and confession is the recognition that we're being called to forsake that sin. And the truth is, we like our sin. We don't want to say no to it forever. It seems like it's adding to our life. At least for a while. Until we figure out what David expressed in Psalm 32, which was that the sin that seems pleasant in the moment ultimately brings pain. What we thought would add to our life proves to rob us of life.

But to come under conviction is evidence of the Spirit at work. To experience the heaviness of our reluctance to confess is a gift of God. We want our children to experience this same heavy and uncomfortable grace of conviction. We want the Spirit to hound them to forsake whatever creates a barrier between them and God.

❋ ❋ ❋

Lord, how I long for _____ to know firsthand the joy of your forgiveness and the clean conscience made possible by your work of putting sin out of sight. And I know this is a unique joy that comes only after confession. So, Lord, send your Spirit to do his convicting work in _____'s life. Let him feel the weight of his sin, as well as the confidence that if he will confess his sin, you will surely forgive.

FEBRUARY 11

Life without God

The LORD said to Moses, ". . . Go up to this land that flows with milk and honey. But I will not travel among you, for you are a stubborn and rebellious people. If I did, I would surely destroy you along the way." EXODUS 33:1, 3

WHILE MOSES WAS up on the mountain getting plans from God for the sanctuary in which he would come down and dwell among his people, something evil was happening below. The Israelites were throwing all of their gold into a fire to melt it and shape it into a calf to worship. Their outrageous idolatry put them at risk of losing the one thing that defined them as a people, the one thing that gave them hope for the future—the presence of God in their midst.

When the Lord came down to deal with their sin, they learned that God still intended to give them the land he had promised to them. He was going to drive their enemies out of the land so they could take possession of it and enjoy the good life there. But there was a problem. God wasn't going with them. An angel would lead them there. Essentially what this meant was that they would get the best of everything this world had to offer . . . minus relationship with God.

The Israelites were facing life without God. Word must have spread quickly around the camp. "God is not going to go with us!" And when we read about it, we realize it presents a test for us and for our children. Do we just want the good stuff God gives to us, or do we genuinely want him? The reality is that many people want his provision and perhaps his protection, but they have no interest in his presence. And as parents that should make us consider: Is it evident in the way we talk about God and about his blessings, and in the way we pray to God and for his blessings, that we truly believe that his presence in our lives in the person of the Holy Spirit—speaking to us through his Word, binding us to Christ, comforting, teaching, and convicting us—is the blessing we cherish most?

❊ ❊ ❊

Lord, help us to love you more than we love your blessings. Give _____ an unquench-able desire for your presence in her life so that when she faces the choice of having what the world offers apart from you, she will see that it will ultimately leave her empty. Lord, we love your blessings, but it is your presence with us by your Spirit that we cherish most of all.

Sins of the Parents

Yahweh! The LORD!
  The God of compassion and mercy!
I am slow to anger
  and filled with unfailing love and faithfulness.
I lavish unfailing love to a thousand generations.
  I forgive iniquity, rebellion, and sin.
But I do not excuse the guilty.
  I lay the sins of the parents upon their children and grandchildren;
the entire family is affected—
  even children in the third and fourth generations. EXODUS 34:6-7

MOSES HAD ASKED TO SEE THE GLORY OF GOD. And while Moses couldn't see the fullness of God's glory and live, God did allow Moses to catch a glimpse of him as he passed by. And as he moved past, he called out to Moses these words that revealed the essential essence of his character. He is the God of compassion, meaning he feels for us at the center of his being. He is a God of mercy, meaning he doesn't give us the punishment we deserve. He lavishes love and forgives rebellion. But we're not sure what to do with what comes next. What does God mean when he says that he lays the sins of parents upon their children and grandchildren? Does it mean that God punishes sinless children for the sins of their parents?

God does not take out the punishment you deserve on your children. If you have been joined to Christ, you can be sure that God exhausted the punishment you deserve on him. It was dealt with at the Cross. All of it.

But God does let the effects of parents' sin take their natural course, infecting and corrupting the hearts of their children. Sadly, some of the consequences of our sinful actions and attitudes fall on our children. Surely this is one of the most sobering texts of the Bible for parents who love their children. All the more reason to forsake sin. All the more reason to follow Christ.

❊ ❊ ❊

Lord, please show me the patterns of sin in my life that are finding their way into the lives of my children, and give me a heart of genuine repentance. Give me the grace to trust you with the regrets that haunt me over my sins and their effects on my children.

Freed from Fears

I prayed to the LORD, and he answered me.
  He freed me from all my fears.
Those who look to him for help will be radiant with joy;
  no shadow of shame will darken their faces. PSALM 34:4-5

WE STARTED INTO THIS LIFE of faith in Christ by putting our confidence in him. We told him we wanted to trust him with our lives in this world and in the next. But as we walk down this road of parenting, we continue to come upon new obstacles that prevent us from truly depending on God for everything. Somehow telling him that we trusted him with our eternal future seemed so much easier than trusting him with the struggles we are facing with our child.

As we see harmful patterns taking shape, and when change is slow in coming, fear begins to set in. It starts to alter our perspective, rule our emotions, and twist our responses. We don't want to be naive about what could happen, but neither do we want to be gripped by fear. So what do we do? What comes naturally to us is to worry, to strategize solutions, to manipulate, to catastrophize. What we must do instead is to take all of our fears and turn them into prayers. We must look to God for help, not just with our child's situation, but with our own fears that rob us of joy, peace, and rest.

"Let all who are helpless take heart," says the psalmist in verse 2. Are you feeling helpless? "Oh, the joys of those who take refuge in him!" says the psalmist in verse 8. Are you finding joy as you rely on the unparalleled strength and unending purposes of your God, or are you swallowing daily doses of misery as you indulge in imagining the worst for the future? "Those who trust in the LORD will lack no good thing," the psalmist assures us in verse 10. The place of rest and safety, hope, and blessing is found not in indulging all of our fears, but in nurturing our trust in the Lord by meditating on his Word.

❀ ❀ ❀

Lord, I'm praying to you, asking you to free me from all of my fears about _____'s health and safety, friendships and future. I'm looking to you for help, asking you to transform my countenance from its expression of anxiety to one that radiates joy and confidence in you.

FEBRUARY 14

Make Disciples

Jesus came and told his disciples, "I have been given all authority in heaven and on earth. Therefore, go and make disciples of all the nations, baptizing them in the name of the Father and the Son and the Holy Spirit. Teach these new disciples to obey all the commands I have given you. And be sure of this: I am with you always, even to the end of the age." MATTHEW 28:18-20

IN JESUS' COMMISSION to his disciples before ascending to the right hand of the Father, we also find a commission for ourselves as a family. Our chief responsibility as parents is to make disciples of our children, to lead them toward having their identity flow from their connectedness to Christ and his body, and to teach them to live in obedience to Christ. We want his Kingdom authority to reign supreme in the hearts of all who live in our home.

This commission is meant to become the core calling of our family as well. Of course, different families will live out this calling in different ways that reflect their unique circumstances, location, season of life, gifting, and passions. Christ's charge should impact how we spend our money, what we do with our vacation and recreational time, and what motivates our academic pursuits and career goals. What this means is that instead of raising up our children to pursue the American dream of a good job, a few kids, a nice house, and a comfortable life, we should orient the culture of our family toward making disciples of those who do not know Christ and teaching new disciples what it means to live in obedience to him.

Fortunately, just as the disciples weren't given an impossible task to complete on their own but instead were assured that Christ was empowering and directing them, so we can be sure that we are not left on our own to live out this calling as parents and families. What Jesus calls us to do, he equips us to do.

⌘ ⌘ ⌘

Lord, I recognize that so many dreams and desires get in the way of our family keeping the mission of making disciples at the core of who we are and what we do. We need your help to readjust our misplaced priorities, ignite our cold hearts for the lost, and eradicate the fears that prevent us from following you. Lord, we know we communicate our dreams and desires for ________'s life to ________ in so many ways. Won't you work in us so that our true desires will conform to your commands?

Our Priest

The craftsmen made beautiful sacred garments of blue, purple, and scarlet cloth—clothing for Aaron to wear while ministering in the Holy Place, just as the LORD had commanded Moses. . . . The ephod consisted of two pieces, front and back, joined at the shoulders with two shoulder-pieces. . . . They mounted the two onyx stones in settings of gold filigree. The stones were engraved with the names of the tribes of Israel, just as a seal is engraved. He fastened these stones on the shoulder-pieces of the ephod as a reminder that the priest represents the people of Israel. EXODUS 39:1, 4, 6-7

EACH PRIEST who served in the Tabernacle and later in the Temple wore an ephod, which was likely a long, sleeveless apron or vest with two straps that went over his shoulders. Two semiprecious stones mounted on the shoulder straps were inscribed with twelve names—the names of the tribes of Israel. Attached to the front of the ephod was a chestpiece with twelve precious stones mounted on it, one for each tribe of Israel, signifying that these people were precious to God. So in a sense, when the priest entered into the presence of God in the Tabernacle's Most Holy Place, he carried God's people on his shoulders and close to his heart. If you were an Israelite in those days, when you saw the name of your tribe on the high priest's breastplate, you could be sure that he carried out his work before God on your behalf.

As believers under the new covenant, we have an even better priest who shoulders our burdens and keeps our concerns close to God's heart. He has entered into an even better sanctuary, the heavenly sanctuary. And this is good news for us as parents. We do not bear the full load of the needs of our children. We simply can't. And it is not just *our* hearts that are touched by our children's needs and concerns. In Christ, our children have a Great High Priest who bears their burdens and keeps their interests close to his heart.

※ ※ ※

Father, we need Jesus. We need Jesus as our Great High Priest to intercede for us in your holy presence. We need Jesus to intervene in what would otherwise be a hopeless situation. We need an advocate who asks you to treat us and our children not as we deserve, but as he deserves.

Two Ways

The woman named Folly is brash.
  She is ignorant and doesn't know it.
She sits in her doorway
  on the heights overlooking the city.
She calls out to men going by
  who are minding their own business.
"Come in with me," she urges the simple.
  To those who lack good judgment, she says,
"Stolen water is refreshing;
  food eaten in secret tastes the best!"
But little do they know that the dead are there.
  Her guests are in the depths of the grave. PROVERBS 9:13-18

THROUGHOUT THE BOOK OF PROVERBS, the father points out to the son that there are two "ways" or "paths" open to him and that he will have to choose one or the other. One path is the way of wisdom, which leads to life in its fullest sense. God is calling out to walk this way and is with those who take this path. "He is a shield to those who walk in integrity, guarding the paths of justice and watching over the way of his saints" (2:7-8, ESV). Those who follow this path find it straight and secure and are led to a blessed life.

The other path is the way of folly. Folly, too, calls out to all. This path is called "dark" (2:13) and "crooked" (2:15). Its dangers include evil people who take pleasure in doing wrong and hidden snares that may appear good but ultimately bring harm. Most significant, however, is this path's destination—death and destruction. "There is a way that seems right to a man, but its end is the way to death" (14:12, ESV).

When our children are small, we take hold of their hands to cross the street. As they grow, we teach them the skills to reach an agreed-upon destination. But as they mature, they begin making choices for themselves about the way they will take. And, oh, how we want them to choose the right path.

※ ※ ※

Lord, how I sometimes wish I could keep making choices for my child. I want _____ to walk in your way. I want _____ to recognize the voice of Folly with its false promises of pleasure that bring only pain. Help me to trust the power of your voice to call _____ to walk in your ways.

An Offering for Sin

When you become aware of your guilt in any of these ways, you must confess your sin. Then you must bring to the LORD as the penalty for your sin a female from the flock, either a sheep or a goat. This is a sin offering with which the priest will purify you from your sin, making you right with the LORD. LEVITICUS 5:5-6

IMAGINE THE EXPENSE of taking the best animal in your herd down to the Temple in Jerusalem just to be sacrificed and burned up. That was the animal that would have produced the best offspring, and it wouldn't have been easy to give up. Imagine the time burden, especially if you didn't live in Jerusalem. You would have had to travel and find a place to stay. Imagine the emotional and spiritual burden as you made this trek, knowing you would have to identify and confess your sin to the priest in offering your sacrifice. Yet when you slit that animal's throat and watched it burn, and when the priest declared your sin forgiven, you would think, *It should have been me. I am the one who deserves to die. But this innocent animal has become my substitute. This animal has died so I can live.*

The visceral and immediate nature of offering an animal sacrifice would leave a lasting impression on you and your children. It would speak of the seriousness and the cost of sin. Year after year, animal after animal, it would repeat the message that sin brings death and that forgiveness of sin requires the shedding of blood.

Of course, none of the animals offered in these sacrifices could, in themselves, take away a person's guilt or truly pay the debt for sin. But by offering these sacrifices, the people of the Old Testament demonstrated their faith in the superior, once-for-all sacrifice who was to come. Jesus was God's provision of a sacrifice sufficient to put an end to the need for the sacrifices prescribed in Leviticus. "He has appeared once for all at the end of the ages to put away sin by the sacrifice of himself" (Hebrews 9:26, ESV).

❋ ❋ ❋

Lord, as we live and breathe in an atmosphere of such grace, made possible by the sacrifice of your Son, we don't want to take our sin lightly. We need your help, as parents, to rightly emphasize the gravity of sin and the costliness of forgiveness to our children, while also relishing the freedom from punishment provided for in the once-for-all sacrifice of Christ.

Heart's Desires

Trust in the LORD and do good.
Then you will live safely in the land and prosper.
Take delight in the LORD,
and he will give you your heart's desires. PSALM 37:3-4

WE'RE TEMPTED to use Psalm 37:4 as a formula, or even as a tool of manipulation, offering God our interest and dutiful obedience in order to get what we want in return. It's a verse often quoted to communicate something like: *Get really serious about God, throw yourself into working for him, read your Bible and pray a lot, and then God will finally be able (or be obligated) to give you what you want most—whether it's a spouse, a new job, or a compliant and happy child!*

But delighting in God is not a means to get what we want from him. That is manipulation. Genuine affection for God is an end in itself, not the means to some further ends. Genuine delight has no ulterior motives, no additional demands. Delight says thank you to God for his many blessings, such as good food to eat, a house to live in, people who love you, and a job to go to, but it also says, *I will not worship these things by demanding them from you.*

As we delight ourselves in the Lord—enjoying his holiness and purity, experiencing the pleasure of his ways—we begin to see the desires of our hearts in a different way. Our delight in the Lord loosens our grip on the things we've longed for. We are able to see what is standing in the way of true delight. We discover that the Holy Spirit is working in us to change what we desire most so that increasingly what we want most is more of Christ.

❈ ❈ ❈

Lord, I know that you are not after simply an external change in our behavior; you want an internal change in our affections. You want to transform and redirect our most personal and passionate longings and then to satisfy them fully. So, Lord, help me to keep my focus for _____ on an internal change in affections rather than merely an external change in behavior. Transform _____ into a total pleasure seeker who recognizes that you are the greatest pleasure to be found.

True Family

Jesus' mother and brothers came to see him. They stood outside and sent word for him to come out and talk with them. There was a crowd sitting around Jesus, and someone said, "Your mother and your brothers are outside asking for you." Jesus replied, "Who is my mother? Who are my brothers?" Then he looked at those around him and said, "Look, these are my mother and brothers. Anyone who does God's will is my brother and sister and mother." MARK 3:31-35

WHEN MARK WRITES that Mary, Jesus' mother, and his brothers were "outside," he is talking about more than where they were physically. They were outsiders spiritually. And why had they come now? They were on a mission to save Jesus from his saving mission, which they found embarrassing. And it was not the last time they'd try. In John's Gospel, we read about a later time when Jesus' brothers tried to convince him to leave Galilee. Perhaps they knew about the plot stirring among the Pharisees to destroy him. Perhaps they simply wanted to shut him up. John interpreted their actions this way: "Even his brothers didn't believe in him" (John 7:5).

But there is something here for those of us who have family members who are "outside" when it comes to Jesus. There is hope. So often when we despair of our children ever coming to Christ, we don't realize that we've not yet reached the end of the story.

The Gospel accounts are not the last time that we see Jesus' family in Scripture. After the Resurrection and on the Day of Pentecost, when the Holy Spirit came down in power on those gathered inside the upper room, we read, "They all met together and were constantly united in prayer, along with Mary the mother of Jesus, several other women, and the brothers of Jesus" (Acts 1:14). Outsiders had become insiders. Through faith they had become part of the true family of God. Jesus' brother James went on to become head of the church in Jerusalem and to write the epistle that bears his name. That letter begins with this self-identification: "James, a slave of God and of the Lord Jesus Christ" (James 1:1).

※ ※ ※

Lord, I'm taking hold of the hope that is to be found in the transformation of Jesus' family. They went from ridiculing Jesus to embracing him, from being cynical about Jesus to describing themselves as slaves and followers of him. I believe the same power that replaced their cold hearts toward Jesus with hearts on fire for the gospel can warm the hearts of those in my family who are cold toward you.

A Heartbroken Parent

Aaron's sons Nadab and Abihu put coals of fire in their incense burners and sprinkled incense over them. In this way, they disobeyed the LORD by burning before him the wrong kind of fire, different than he had commanded. So fire blazed forth from the LORD's presence and burned them up, and they died there before the LORD. LEVITICUS 10:1-2

As SONS OF AARON, the first high priest of Israel, Nadab and Abihu had participated in a fellowship meal with the seventy elders of Israel in the presence of God on the mountain. They had gotten a glimpse of the glory of God and lived to tell about it. One would think they would not easily forget this experience or take it for granted.

But evidently they did. With presumptuous arrogance, Nadab and Abihu decided for themselves how they wanted to offer worship in the Tabernacle instead of following the specific instructions God had given to Moses on the mountain. Just as "fire came out from the presence of the LORD and consumed the burnt offering and the fat portions on the altar" (Leviticus 9:24, NIV), the judgment of God in the form of fire consumed Nadab and Abihu. This time, it burned up the sinners themselves instead of a substitute. It was a vivid demonstration of God's justice.

How it must have broken Aaron's heart. And yet Aaron was commanded not to go through the motions of mourning before the people so that, as high priest, he would demonstrate his confidence in and acceptance of God's justice before them. Did Aaron question his parenting, wondering if his own imperfect example steered his sons astray? (There was that golden calf incident.) Did Aaron wonder if he had failed to communicate the holiness of God and the importance of obeying God's instruction? Perhaps. We're not told in the text.

But it does make sense to us, because that's the first place we go when our children are casual or dismissive of worship. It's the first place we go when our children brazenly sin against God's clear command. We think, *It must be my fault.*

❋ ❋ ❋

Lord, forgive us for our arrogance in thinking our good parenting accounts for the best of what we see in the lives of our children. And give us the grace we need to reject the lie that tells us our poor parenting is the sole reason for the things in our children's lives that break our hearts and yours. Free us, Father, and forgive us.

Make Us Clean

By these instructions you will know what is unclean and clean, and which animals may be eaten and which may not be eaten. LEVITICUS 11:47

WHEN WE LOOK at everything designated as unclean in Leviticus 11–15, we see that each reflects the effects of the curse of sin on this world. Animals fed on other animals only after the curse. Childbirth became painful only after the curse, and sexual relations between men and women became infected with sinful passions only after the curse. Bodies bled and developed disease only after the curse. Children were born with birth defects only after the curse. Mold and mildew, the visible evidence of decay, came into being only after the curse. Everything designated unclean in Leviticus demonstrated that things are not the way they once were in the Garden—the way God originally intended them to be.

As we read in Leviticus about the provision God made for what was unclean to become clean, and for what was clean to become holy, we realize that God was vividly demonstrating his promise that he would not abandon our world to being unclean forever. He would make it clean through the blood of an all-sufficient sacrifice, his own Son.

Jesus, who is completely clean and pure, continually touched unclean things. In Mark 5 we read about Jesus touching unclean person after unclean person—a man with an unclean spirit who cut himself and lived among the dead near a herd of pigs, a woman who had a discharge of blood for twelve years, the dead daughter of the ruler of the synagogue. Each shows us a picture of the way Jesus makes sinners clean.

Even today he reaches out to touch us, taking upon himself our sin sickness and uncleanness, and then imparting to us his health, wholeness, and acceptance. We are cleansed because the Holy One of God became unclean for us.

❋ ❋ ❋

Holy One of God, we are unclean. And we are desperate for your touch. We are as desperate for deliverance as the demon-possessed man, as desperate for life to stop draining out of us as the hemorrhaging woman, and as desperate as the synagogue ruler for you to bring us and our loved ones from death to life. Won't you touch each of us and make us clean? We look forward to the day when you touch us again and make our dead bodies not just clean, but holy, so that we can dwell in your righteous presence forever.

A Bold Reproof

People who wink at wrong cause trouble,
  but a bold reproof promotes peace. PROVERBS 10:10

WHEN WE READ THE WORDS "a bold reproof promotes peace," we think, *Well, evidently the writer of this proverb hasn't spent any time at my house.* When we refuse to wink at wrong and instead confront it, it sometimes results in yelling and tears, hard conversations and hurt feelings, costly consequences and slammed doors.

Sometimes we get weary of the battle, and the possibility of winking at wrong or simply closing our eyes to it starts to sound pretty good. Following through and going against the flow require so much consistent energy. Parenting would be a lot easier if we didn't care so much, if we didn't love so fiercely, if we were willing to let some issues go that really need to be addressed, if we just didn't make a fuss about modesty or purity or kindness.

But we know that there is wisdom in this proverb pushing us toward bold reproof of wrong—disrespect and disregard of others, unkept promises and unfinished assignments, chasing after the world and caring nothing about holiness. We know that keeping the peace now may likely leave the door open for trouble later. And we know that a bold reproof now may result in a lifetime of peace for our children—peace with us; peace with other people, including a future spouse; and, most important, peace with God.

❊ ❊ ❊

Lord, when I am weary of the battle and just want to retreat, give me the energy to engage. Give me the wisdom to know what I really should let go of and what I should address and keep addressing for _____'s good and for your glory. Protect me from wanting to be the cool parent in ways that make me hesitant to reprove. Give me the long view in parenting _____ so that I will have the will to take the hard steps now that will save _____ from heartache later.

In Serious Trouble

Late that night, the disciples were in their boat in the middle of the lake, and Jesus was alone on land. He saw that they were in serious trouble, rowing hard and struggling against the wind and waves. About three o'clock in the morning Jesus came toward them, walking on the water. He intended to go past them, but when they saw him walking on the water, they cried out in terror, thinking he was a ghost. They were all terrified when they saw him. But Jesus spoke to them at once. "Don't be afraid," he said. "Take courage! I am here!" Then he climbed into the boat, and the wind stopped.
MARK 6:47-51

SOMETIMES WE THINK that if we are obeying God then we will be spared from hardship, and that if we run into difficulty we must be disobeying him in some way. We think if we're parenting right then we should have smooth sailing with our kids. But here we see that the disciples were crossing the lake just as Jesus had told them to do and yet they were in grave danger. Likewise we can parent in just the way Scripture tells us to yet end up in serious trouble with one or more of our children.

When we're facing serious problems, we tend to do what the disciples did. We row harder. We try to come up with strategies and plans to still the storm in our child's life. We worry. We talk to our friends and to counselors. We struggle against what sometimes seems like gale-force winds pushing back against our wise counsel.

It is precisely when we or one of our kids is in deep trouble that we are in the place to see and experience Christ as never before. In the storm, we come to the end of ourselves. Jesus comes to us in a way that no mere human could, unlimited by human power or strategies. He comes as the only one who has the power to either still the storm or preserve us through it. He climbs into the boat with us and tells us that we don't have to be afraid because he is here.

※ ※ ※

Lord, we often find ourselves in serious trouble, with no ability to make any progress on our own. We need you to come to us in the way that only you can. Make your presence known to us in the midst of the storm. Calm our fears. Take us from little faith to firm faith, confident in your power to save and preserve us and our family.

Defiled

It's not what goes into your body that defiles you; you are defiled by what comes from your heart. MARK 7:15

WHEN WE READ laws in the Old Testament about what made a person clean and unclean, we hardly know what to do with them. (Rules for dealing with various bodily discharges? Detailed guidelines on how each sacrifice must be performed?) They seem foreign, strange, and extreme. God's intention was to reveal to his people how sin had corrupted creation since Adam rebelled in the Garden, as well as how this corruption of sin can and will be dealt with—through the blood of an atoning sacrifice.

When we come to the New Testament, we discover that the keeping of these laws had become an empty ritual devoid of any true sensitivity to sin. Speaking to those who washed their hands for show while tolerating the sins in their hearts, Jesus quoted the prophet Isaiah, who said, "These people honor me with their lips, but their hearts are far from me" (Mark 7:6).

Jesus made it clear what defiles a person: "It is what comes from inside that defiles you. For from within, out of a person's heart, come evil thoughts, sexual immorality, theft, murder, adultery, greed, wickedness, deceit, lustful desires, envy, slander, pride, and foolishness" (Mark 7:20-22).

As parents, we strive to help our kids understand that their attitudes and outlook—which are often betrayed not just by their actions but by their facial expressions and courtesies extended to others (or not)—have great significance. That's because these matters of the heart indicate how close they are, both to us and to God.

※ ※ ※

Lord, in this list of things that defile, we see the sins of our children. And, yes, Lord, we see our own sins too. We are all in desperate need of the cleansing that only the blood of Christ can provide.

I pray for _____ today, asking you to cleanse him of evil thoughts and fill him with thoughts of the beauty of Christ. Help _____ to see the ways he has broken your commands, and lead him into repentance. Rid him of deceit, envy, and greed, and make him a man of integrity. Transform any lustful desires into eagerness for your transforming work. Humble him in whatever way you have to. Transform his foolishness into the wisdom that comes by being joined to Christ.

FEBRUARY 25

Desperate

A woman who had heard about him came and fell at his feet. Her little girl was possessed by an evil spirit, and she begged him to cast out the demon from her daughter. MARK 7:25-26

A DESPERATE MOTHER—desperate for Jesus to do something about the evil that had taken hold in her daughter's life—must have felt a flicker of hope when she first heard about him. Surely she listened eagerly as people described how he'd fed the hungry, cleansed the leper, given sight to the blind, and raised a paralytic to walk. Clearly this Jesus was a person of compassion. More important, he was a man of power. And this mother was tired of being so helpless, so alone, so afraid.

So she came to where Jesus was and fell down before him. She begged him to release her child from the demon's control. She put herself at the feet of the only one who had the power to overcome the evil in her child's life. A bundle of hurt and need begging for a crumb of grace.

As a Gentile, this woman had no sense of entitlement to the deliverance she knew Jesus could provide. Yet she seemed to understand that God had always intended for his grace and goodness to spread beyond the boundaries of those who appeared to have the inside track based on religiosity or race. Jesus affirmed her recognition that he was the only hope for her daughter so trapped in the cords of evil. He healed the little girl from afar, making this bold and persistent mother the recipient of his undeserved favor.

❊ ❊ ❊

Lord, I come to you so aware of the evil that has so much power in this world and in my child's life. I know there are unseen forces at work that want to destroy her life and dishonor you. Like this woman in Tyre, I'm well aware of your power and ability to relieve suffering and overcome evil. So I'm putting myself at your feet. I'm begging you to save _____ from the enemy of her soul. I'm asking for a taste, a crumb, of all that awaits us in the new creation—when evil will be gone for good—to be given to us in the here and now. Let our family taste the joy of freedom from this evil power. I come not demanding or with any sense of entitlement, but confident in your power, your grace, and your goodness.

True Life

Calling the crowd to join his disciples, he said, "If any of you wants to be my follower, you must give up your own way, take up your cross, and follow me. If you try to hang on to your life, you will lose it. But if you give up your life for my sake and for the sake of the Good News, you will save it." MARK 8:34-35

To be a true follower of Jesus is not easy. There is a cost. It requires a relinquishment of the selfish ambition that makes this life all about what we can accomplish and acquire. It requires that rather than charting out a course for a life that we think will provide happiness and fulfillment, we must entrust the course of our lives to Christ. It requires that we fix our gaze firmly on him as we anticipate his benefits and presence in the life to come, even as we accept the losses and disappointments that are part of this life.

As parents we want to protect our children from pain and difficulty. Too often we want a life for them that does not include a cross. We have ambitions for our children that, if we're honest, are often less about living the crucified life than they are about creating a comfortable life. We want them to soar, not stumble. We want them to be admired, not marginalized.

We need faith to believe that what Jesus said to his disciples is really true for us and for our children—that the only way to find true life is by putting self-determination and self-centeredness to death.

❋ ❋ ❋

Lord, I want to follow after you and find true life. And, Lord, I want this true life for _____. I want him to be willing to give up his life for your sake and for the sake of the gospel. I don't want him to gain the whole world but lose his soul. When Jesus returns in glory, I long to see _____ there with him, sharing his glory. Would you give _____ a passion for your Kingdom that will squeeze out selfish ambition? Would you give him eyes to see what Jesus is worth, shoulders that are willing to bear your cross, and perseverance in following after you?

Help My Unbelief!

"How long has this been happening?" Jesus asked the boy's father. He replied, "Since he was a little boy. The spirit often throws him into the fire or into water, trying to kill him. Have mercy on us and help us, if you can." MARK 9:21-22

FAITHLESS PEOPLE. We don't want to think we fall into that category. We say that we've trusted Christ with our lives and deaths. But we find it so very hard to trust him with our children. We find it hard to trust his methods, his timing, and certainly his good purposes in what only looks bad to us.

It is difficult to imagine the sadness, the fear, and the weariness of the father of a son who couldn't speak, a son who foamed at the mouth and ground his teeth. Ever since his son was small, an evil spirit would seize the boy and make him fall into a fire, seeking to burn him to death, or make him plunge into water, trying to drown him. This heartbroken father longed for a miraculous healing, but Jesus wanted him to want much more than that. Jesus wanted this distraught dad to put his full confidence in who he was and what he had come to do in the world. And he had come to "destroy the works of the devil" (1 John 3:8).

"I do believe, but help me overcome my unbelief!" the father replied when Jesus told him to put his complete trust in him. We're glad these words are there for us, spoken by a father wearied by his long-term love for a child in the grip of forces over which he had no power. It was a simple prayer prayed out of spiritual weakness—a prayer that God always answers with a glad yes.

❋ ❋ ❋

Lord, I easily become so focused on problems that I don't see the bigger issue: my lack of faith in you. But your Word is helping me see that you are the source, not only for the intervention I long for, but for the faith I need to trust you for it. I do believe, but help me overcome my unbelief. Show me the ways I simply want to use you without deeply and fully trusting you. As I feed on your Word, increase my confidence in your promised help and in your preordained plan for _____ and for our family. Like the father in this story, I come to you asking you to have mercy on us and to help us.

Rest

You have six days each week for your ordinary work, but the seventh day is a Sabbath day of complete rest, an official day for holy assembly. It is the LORD's Sabbath day, and it must be observed wherever you live. LEVITICUS 23:3

FROM THE BEGINNING, God established an ongoing pattern of work and worship. God rested on the seventh day and invited Adam and Eve to do the same. Every seventh day would be a day to rest in who he is and what he accomplished in his creation, a time set aside to enjoy with him the goodness of all he had made. Then when God called his people out of slavery in Egypt, where they likely worked seven days a week, he instructed them to stop their work on the seventh day so they might assemble for worship.

The Sabbath was never meant to be a burden but rather a gift of God to his people. When we set aside work for worship, we demonstrate to ourselves, our families, and the world around us that God is worthy of our glad worship and that we find our home among God's people. But more than that, we live out our very real trust in God's provision for our needs with six days of work, not seven.

※ ※ ※

Lord, I confess that our family has not always accepted the gift of your Sabbath in its glorious fullness. We've put other activities before gathering with your people. We've been more concerned about what we will have for lunch than our need for the feast set before us at your table.

Give us the grace and resolve we need to change our deeply ingrained ways of spending this day that belongs to you. Give us wisdom on how to make adjustments out of love for you without capitulation to legalism. Develop in _____ a delight in the Sabbath as a demonstration of trust in your provision and delight in your Word and ways.

MARCH 1

Genuine Love

"Teacher," the man replied, "I've obeyed all these commandments since I was young."
Looking at the man, Jesus felt genuine love for him. "There is still one thing you haven't
done," he told him. "Go and sell all your possessions and give the money to the poor, and
you will have treasure in heaven. Then come, follow me." MARK 10:20-21

WE WANT SO MUCH more than for our children to simply follow the rules or to appear successful to the world around us. We want Christ to be their supreme joy and treasure. Because we love them, we want them to love God above everything else.

To love our children in this way is to love as Jesus loved. When a man who had great wealth came to Jesus and asked what he needed to do to get the life Jesus was offering, we read that "Jesus felt genuine love for this man as he looked at him" (Mark 10:21, TLB). Jesus could see that as good as the man had been at obeying the Ten Commandments—at least on the surface—he had actually failed at the very first command, which is "You must not have any other god but me" (Exodus 20:3).

Jesus could see that another god had taken the place reserved for God alone—the god of wealth and possessions and the comfortable, privileged life they brought. When an idol threatens the eternal joy of the person you love, the compassionate thing to do is to point out the idol and call that person to forsake it, kill it, dethrone it, repent of it, and turn toward Christ, recognizing that he is the true source of everything the idol falsely promises.

❈ ❈ ❈

Lord, help me see beneath _____'s behaviors—good and bad—into the passions that drive them. Give me insight into the idols that need to be torn down, the desires that have morphed into demands, the gifts you've given that she has come to love more than the Giver. But more than that, shine your light in me to help me see the idols that I have tolerated in my own heart. Lead me to genuine and pervasive repentance so that I might love _____ well by leading the way in putting such idols to death.

Blind Eyes

Bartimaeus threw aside his coat, jumped up, and came to Jesus. "What do you want me to do for you?" Jesus asked. "My Rabbi," the blind man said, "I want to see!"
MARK 10:50-51

BARTIMAEUS had a sense of who Jesus was, and he was clear on what he wanted Jesus to do for him. Even though he was physically blind, somehow Bartimaeus could see that Jesus was the King his people had waited for since God promised King David that one of his sons would sit on his throne in a Kingdom that would never end. He could see that Jesus was the Servant the prophet Isaiah wrote about who would make the lame walk, the deaf hear, and the blind see. Surely Bartimaeus had sung the psalm, "The LORD opens the eyes of the blind" (Psalm 146:8). And so he told Jesus that he wanted to see.

Oh, that our children would call out to Jesus and ask him to give them spiritual sight like this man asked for physical sight! King Jesus is able to give sight to the blind. He shines the light of his truth into a person's life and eradicates the darkness. He brings clarity where there is confusion. When our children can't see how beautiful Jesus is and how ugly their sin is, when they can't see how valuable Jesus is and how worthless the treasures of the world are, when they can't see how loving Jesus is and how much they are hated by the enemy of their soul, Jesus can open their blind eyes to see.

※ ※ ※

Lord, I don't want _____ to go through this life spiritually blind, unable to see how sin only takes and destroys while you give and bless. Don't allow him to sit on the sidelines as you pass by. Son of David, have mercy on him. Do for him what only you can do. Give _____ eyes to see your goodness, faith to trust you, and the will to follow you.

MARCH 3

Belongs to the Lord

One-tenth of the produce of the land, whether grain from the fields or fruit from the trees, belongs to the LORD and must be set apart to him as holy. LEVITICUS 27:30

BEGINNING WITH THE FIRST TIME we give our child an allowance, we have the opportunity to speak into how our child will deal with money as we encourage him to spend some, save some, and give some to God. In this way we have the opportunity to shape our child's understanding of himself as a steward—someone entrusted with God's money, which is to be used in ways that please and honor God. We can also begin to help our child build a hedge against covetousness. Every time an amount is set aside for God, he will have to deal with his desire to spend it on something for himself. To give to God is to not spend on ourselves. And to face this crisis with every allowance and later every paycheck he receives will test him again and again.

But like everything else we set out to teach our children, they learn more from our example than from our instructions. As our children grow, they begin to grasp more about money—not only about how much we make and how we spend it, but also about our attitudes toward it and God's claims on our money. They see whether we are cheerful or reluctant givers. And every time they see us live out our confidence that we can live on 90 percent or less of our income, it's as if we say to them, "This same God who takes care of me will supply all your needs from his glorious riches, which have been given to us in Christ Jesus" (Philippians 4:19).

✻ ✻ ✻

Lord, we want to be cheerful givers, and we want to raise cheerful givers. But we also find that there are so many other things we want, so many things that promise to make us happier than giving back what already belongs to you. Help us to reject the lie that what we need is more to spend on ourselves and instead choose to believe that you will supply all of our needs.

A Lasting Foundation

When the storms of life come, the wicked are whirled away,
but the godly have a lasting foundation. PROVERBS 10:25

WE CAN'T HELP but wonder if Jesus had this proverb in mind when he told the story of the wise builder and the foolish builder. In the Sermon on the Mount, Jesus said: "Anyone who listens to my teaching and follows it is wise, like a person who builds a house on solid rock. Though the rain comes in torrents and the floodwaters rise and the winds beat against that house, it won't collapse because it is built on bedrock. But anyone who hears my teaching and doesn't obey it is foolish, like a person who builds a house on sand. When the rains and floods come and the winds beat against that house, it will collapse with a mighty crash" (Matthew 7:24-27).

The wise builder and the foolish builder have at least two things in common. First, they both hear the teaching of Jesus. (We could think of them as two people who both hear the same sermon at church on Sunday.) The second thing they have in common is the storm, which descends on both of them with the same destructive power.

But there's also something they don't have in common. When the wise builder hears God's Word, he follows it. Another translation says he "work[s] these words into [his] life" (MSG). And that makes all the difference when the storm comes. The person who has not just heard God's Word but has put it into practice and made it a part of who he is does not need to fear the storms of life. It's not that he won't be affected by the storms but that he won't be destroyed by them. His life will have been built on something solid that won't give way under the pressure of the storm—the sure and certain Word of God.

✖ ✖ ✖

Lord, how I long for _____'s life to be built on something solid and secure—the truth of your Word. Show me, day by day, how I can help _____ not just to hear your Word, but to work your Word into her life. May your Word become part of the fabric and foundation of her life so that when the storms come, _____ will not be destroyed by them.

MARCH 5

Loving Others Well

One of the teachers of religious law was standing there listening to the debate. He realized that Jesus had answered well, so he asked, "Of all the commandments, which is the most important?" Jesus replied, "The most important commandment is this: 'Listen, O Israel! The LORD our God is the one and only LORD. And you must love the LORD your God with all your heart, all your soul, all your mind, and all your strength.' The second is equally important: 'Love your neighbor as yourself.' No other commandment is greater than these." MARK 12:28-31

ANY PARENT of a toddler knows that self-love does not need to be commanded or taught. It comes so very naturally to us. We all have a powerful instinct to take care of ourselves—to diminish our own pain and increase our own happiness. And this instinct is not necessarily evil. There's nothing bad about wanting to be safe or healthy or respected or to have our needs met. There is nothing wrong with our kids wanting to do well in sports or school or to enjoy nice clothes and fun activities. But this natural tendency can become evil, and Jesus' command in Mark 12 reveals whether our self-love has become evil.

The heart of this command to love our neighbor as we love ourselves means that we are to be as committed to the comfort and safety of our neighbor as we are to our own. Jesus calls our kids to desire good friends for others as much as they want good friends for themselves, to be as committed to others getting recognition for achievement as they are to receiving acknowledgment themselves.

When we truly understand the weight of this command, we realize that we and our children need supernatural help to love the Lord in this way and to love others to the degree that we love ourselves.

❊ ❊ ❊

Lord, as we consider this important command, we are undone by it. Our innate love for ourselves keeps us from loving you in the all-encompassing way you require and keeps us far more committed to taking care of ourselves than we are to meeting the needs of others. We know that only one person loved you and loved his neighbor in this perfect, self-giving way. Our desire is that as we abide in Christ, this kind of love will increasingly become our way of life.

The Lord Bless You

Then the LORD said to Moses, "Tell Aaron and his sons to bless the people of Israel with this special blessing: 'May the LORD bless you and protect you. May the LORD smile on you and be gracious to you. May the LORD show you his favor and give you his peace.'" NUMBERS 6:22-26

WHEN GOD INSTRUCTED Moses to have the priests speak these words over the people of Israel, the blessing was given not as a request for the Lord to grant them his favor, but rather as an announcement of God's intention to shower his grace upon them. God wants his people to enjoy the assurance of his plan to bless them. Isn't it good to know that the Lord's settled disposition toward you and your family is to bless you?

But what does it mean to be blessed? When we pray and ask God to bless our plans, we are essentially inviting his presence right into the center of our lives. Experiencing God's blessing is not merely getting good things *from* God. The essence of blessing is getting more *of* God.

To be blessed is to be deeply content in God, to find our home so securely in him that adverse circumstances cannot shake us. To be blessed means that we are pervasively happy in God alone. It means we can lift our eyes and see God's smile on our lives and on our family. His face is radiant because he sees us not for who we are on our own, but for who we are in Christ. He is not focused on what we've done, good or bad, but on what Christ has done on our behalf. To be blessed is to live each day in peace because we know our God is not stingy with grace. His settled intention is to show us his favor, or grace, when we turn to him.

※ ※ ※

Lord, what a good God you are to bless us, protect us, smile on us, extend grace to us, show us your favor, and give us your peace. We know that we stand under the stream of your abundant blessing only because Jesus plunged himself under the stream of your curse in our place. He endured the full weight of your wrath so that we could enjoy the vast wonders of your favor. We know that you will protect our souls for eternity only because there was no protection for your own Son. You can turn your face toward us only because you turned your face away from him. We rejoice in your unfailing love and mercy, and we ask that you increase our love for you.

Our Guide

On the day the Tabernacle was set up, the cloud covered it. But from evening until morning the cloud over the Tabernacle looked like a pillar of fire. This was the regular pattern—at night the cloud that covered the Tabernacle had the appearance of fire. Whenever the cloud lifted from over the sacred tent, the people of Israel would break camp and follow it. And wherever the cloud settled, the people of Israel would set up camp. NUMBERS 9:15-17

ISRAEL was on the verge of a new start. They were about to set out from Mount Sinai, where they had been camping for almost a year, to make their way through the wilderness to the Promised Land. So much about the journey and the destination ahead was unknown, but this much they knew: They wouldn't be going into the wilderness alone. God was going with them. He had come down to dwell in their midst in the Tabernacle on the first day it was set up. His radiant glory descended in a pillar of fire on this tent in the middle of their camp and stayed there.

The day would come when, once again, the people of God would set out into the unknown—on the Day of Pentecost. The risen Jesus had ascended into heaven and told them to wait together. And similar to the pillar of fire descending on the Tabernacle in Moses' day, tongues of fire descended on God's people on the Day of Pentecost. It was an outward sign that the Holy Spirit had descended to dwell in all believers.

As we face the unknowns of each new stage of parenting our children through life in the wilderness of this world, we sometimes wish for a pillar of fire to lead us and show us where to go. But we have something even better. We have the Holy Spirit indwelling us, guiding us, and empowering us for every unknown.

❊ ❊ ❊

Lord, some days I wish your presence was as visible and your leading as recognizable as a pillar of fire. As we make our way through the wilderness in this world, we do not take your presence for granted. We want to move forward when you move and stay where we are when you stop. Thank you for your Holy Spirit, who lives in us and illumines your Word, helping us to know and understand your will. Thank you for the way you are renewing our minds so we will know the good and pleasing and perfect will of God for our lives.

Cravings

Then the foreign rabble who were traveling with the Israelites began to crave the good things of Egypt. And the people of Israel also began to complain. "Oh, for some meat!" they exclaimed. "We remember the fish we used to eat for free in Egypt. And we had all the cucumbers, melons, leeks, onions, and garlic we wanted. But now our appetites are gone. All we ever see is this manna!" NUMBERS 11:4-6

EVIDENTLY THE GRUMBLING started with those who lived on the fringes of the camp— the people of various nationalities who came out of Egypt with God's people—and worked its way inward, spreading its infectious discontent throughout the camp. What were the Israelites complaining about? The same thing we complain about when the signs for restaurants at upcoming exits on the interstate don't display the familiar logo we're looking for, or when the food set in front of us doesn't quite suit our tastes. It's not that they had nothing to eat. It's that they wanted something to eat besides the manna God graciously rained down on them every day.

God had spectacularly delivered them from slavery without asking them to fight a battle. He had supernaturally fed them in the desert without asking them to work. He had given them the most humble and faithful leader imaginable. But they couldn't see any of it because they were consumed by their craving. They became one-dimensional people who thought about life only through the knothole of their craving. Their desire for more variety in their diet became a demand that blinded them to anything and everything else.

We see this in our children—cravings for toys and technology, clothing and cars. But we see it in ourselves, too. Many of us have a craving that blinds us so that we can't see all that God has done for us and given to us. Yes, we appreciate salvation and all that, but what we really crave is to be thin, to have a nicer house in a better neighborhood, to have a job with more authority and opportunity, to have children who make us look good and friends who make us feel important.

For the Israelites, everything was about food. What is everything about for you? How is it causing you to lose sight of God's goodness?

❊ ❊ ❊

Lord, we don't want our family to be ruled by our cravings. We want to learn the secret Paul learned when he said he had learned to be content while living with nothing or with everything, with a full stomach or an empty one. Lord, we need that same strength to be content.

67

Grand Intentions

Peter said to him, "Even if everyone else deserts you, I never will." Jesus replied, "I tell you the truth, Peter—this very night, before the rooster crows twice, you will deny three times that you even know me." "No!" Peter declared emphatically. "Even if I have to die with you, I will never deny you!" And all the others vowed the same. MARK 14:29-31

WHEN PETER SAID IT, he meant it. He was all in when it came to Jesus and his mission—at least what he understood to be Jesus' mission. But he was unaware of his own weakness and his misunderstanding of what the Kingdom of God really is and what it requires. So he arrogantly proclaimed his own fidelity to Christ as superior to everyone else's. He confidently put himself forward as an exception to what Jesus told him would happen. Mark tells us that all of the other disciples then made the same vow. Their grand intentions only seem to add to the tragedy when we read a few verses later, "Then all his disciples deserted him and ran away" (verse 50).

We are more like Peter and the rest of the disciples than we would care to admit. We convince ourselves that we are wiser, stronger, and more righteous than we really are, and because of our overconfidence, we step into danger. We are certain we can peek at pornography and not become enslaved by it. Our children are certain they can go to the party and not be persuaded to drink alcohol. We want to think that we will be strong enough in our faith to put everything on the line when we're pressed to compromise, but we cave.

It was the discovery of his weakness that made Peter strong. His self-confidence vanished, and a sense of utter dependence upon the Lord grew in its place. Perhaps that's why Peter encourages the readers of his letters to "prepare [their] minds for action" (1 Peter 1:13), "stay alert" (1 Peter 5:8), and "be on guard" (2 Peter 3:17). Peter knew firsthand that good intentions are not enough to protect a person from the darts of the evil one.

✳ ✳ ✳

Lord, as much as _____ may want to be strong in the face of opposition and temptation, and as good as his intentions may be to be true to you, _____ is weak and so in need of your Spirit. _____'s spirit is willing, but his flesh is weak. Keep calling him to watch and pray so that he will not give in to temptation.

Not a Single One

God looks down from heaven
*   on the entire human race;*
he looks to see if anyone is truly wise,
*   if anyone seeks God.*
But no, all have turned away;
*   all have become corrupt.*
No one does good,
*   not a single one!* PSALM 53:2-3

"NOBODY'S PERFECT," people like to say. But of course the situation is far more grim than that. David describes the reality of humanity clearly in Psalm 53. He pictures God stooping to observe the conduct of his creatures, scanning the crowd to find a single person who is seeking him. And he can't find even one.

It is not that there is no human goodness in the world, but rather that humans do not do good naturally. This shouldn't surprise anyone who is a parent. No one has to teach a young child to be selfish, but often the lesson of sharing has to be taught. And as our children grow into teenagers, we know that they often are more likely to be influenced to do bad than to do good. Even when they do what is right, their good deeds are often tinged with self-serving motives.

The scene from heaven's vantage point appears hopeless. David longs for God to intervene in this desperate situation, asking, "Who will come from Mount Zion to rescue Israel?" Salvation for Israel will have to come out of Zion, that is, out of God's dwelling place. David places all his hopes in the day "when God restores his people," for only then "Israel will rejoice" (Psalm 53:6). That glad day arrived with the coming of Jesus Christ.

David's hope for sinful humanity is the same hope we have for our sinful children—that God will rescue them. Our hope is in the Savior who seeks after those who are not seeking after him.

※ ※ ※

Lord, I lament with David over the corruption in my heart and the hearts of my children. But my heart also hopes with David's heart—that you will rescue and restore us.

MARCH 11

Never Abandoned

At noon, darkness fell across the whole land until three o'clock. Then at three o'clock Jesus called out with a loud voice, "Eloi, Eloi, lema sabachthani?" which means "My God, my God, why have you abandoned me?" MARK 15:33-34

JESUS MUST HAVE BEEN meditating on Psalm 22, written a thousand years before he was born, as he hung on the cross. In it he found the words that expressed his own agony of soul. Up to this point Jesus had been beaten and whipped, and he'd had thorns pressed into his temples and nails pounded into his hands and feet. Yet he had said nothing. And then suddenly from the cross, he cried out these words from Psalm 22. He was experiencing something infinitely more painful than even his physical agony—he felt the spiritual agony of having the familiar presence of God withdrawn.

At the cross Jesus became sin for us. And because God cannot look upon sin, the Father had to turn away. Out of hatred for sin and love for sinners, the Father cast aside his beloved Son. Yet Jesus was not abandoned for all time. Once the wrath of God had burned itself out in the very heart of Jesus, Jesus spoke again from the cross, shouting the words of Psalm 31:5: "Father, into your hands I commit my spirit!" (Luke 23:46, ESV). The price for sin was paid and the relationship restored.

Though it pains and perhaps confuses us to think of God turning away from his own Son, we must see that this abandonment was purposeful and profitable. Because God turned aside from his Son on that day, you and I need never fear that God will abandon us or our children. Jesus experienced the separation that we deserve to experience forever so that we will never have to experience it. While we may sometimes feel abandoned by God, we have never been and never will be. Because Jesus was alienated from God as our substitute, we can draw near to him. Because God turned his face away from Jesus, we can be confident that he will never turn away from us.

※ ※ ※

Lord, I am the one who deserves to experience this agonizing abandonment by God. I'm the one who has sinned. Yet you bore not only my sin and my children's sin, but also the abandonment of your Father that we might experience his presence forever. Thank you for your extravagant love for _____ and for me, which cost you everything and gives us all our hearts truly long for!

A Warning to Grumblers

The LORD said to Moses: "Place Aaron's staff permanently before the Ark of the Covenant to serve as a warning to rebels. This should put an end to their complaints against me and prevent any further deaths." So Moses did as the LORD commanded him. Then the people of Israel said to Moses, "Look, we are doomed! We are dead! We are ruined! Everyone who even comes close to the Tabernacle of the LORD dies. Are we all doomed to die?" NUMBERS 17:10-13

THROUGHOUT THE STORY of the wilderness wandering, we read that the congregation of Israel grumbled. They complained about the food that showed up outside every morning, the lack of water, and the route they were taking, and in Numbers 16, we see they grumbled about the leaders God gave them in Moses and Aaron. God had had enough of their grumbling. He instructed the leaders of all twelve tribes to submit their staffs to Moses. They were placed before the Lord in the Tabernacle and left there overnight. During the night, one staff not only sprouted; it budded, blossomed, and produced almonds! In this way the Lord definitively demonstrated his choice of Aaron to serve him and stand in his presence, and he put an end to the people's grumbling.

So how are we to deal with the grumbling in our own hearts and homes? How should we respond when our kids complain about their schools, curfews, or chores? We can't exactly bring a dead stick in from the yard and make it bud and produce almonds overnight to show who's boss. We can, however, remember that we are all—parents and kids—like those old dead sticks, fit only for the fire and unfit to stand in the presence of a holy God. Grumbling and rebellion can be overcome only as we contemplate another tree—the cross. There Jesus took upon himself the curse deserved by all rebels for our grumbling. God has made us alive and is making our lives fruitful! Because he took our rebellion and grumbling upon himself and gave us his perfect record of obedience and gratitude, we are able to do what Old Testament believers could not do: draw near to God's presence with boldness and confidence.

※ ※ ※

Lord, in the Cross we see Jesus absorbing the punishment we deserve for our rebellion and grumbling. And in his resurrection, we see the almond branch blossom, the firstfruits of the harvest of eternal life. When _____ complains, grant us the patience and wisdom to extend the same grace you give to grumblers.

The Hearts of the Fathers

Don't be afraid, Zechariah! God has heard your prayer. Your wife, Elizabeth, will give you a son, and you are to name him John. You will have great joy and gladness, and many will rejoice at his birth, for he will be great in the eyes of the Lord. He must never touch wine or other alcoholic drinks. He will be filled with the Holy Spirit, even before his birth. And he will turn many Israelites to the Lord their God. He will be a man with the spirit and power of Elijah. He will prepare the people for the coming of the Lord. He will turn the hearts of the fathers to their children, and he will cause those who are rebellious to accept the wisdom of the godly. LUKE 1:13-17

JOHN THE BAPTIST had a unique role in the history of redemption. He came in the spirit and power of the prophet Elijah to call the people of God in his day to turn, to repent, and to change. John's ministry would so affect the hearts of his people that it would revolutionize the way they lived in their homes. Parents would awaken with fresh love and commitment to their children. Rebellious children would accept the wisdom of their godly parents.

What a picture of the grace of God at work in the hearts of every member of the family! What a lesson in how the gospel transforms the way parents and children relate to and respect one another. Parents whose passions have been invested more in work or sports or activities begin to invest their best energies in meeting the needs of their children. Parents who have been abusive in the way they speak to each other and to their children begin to speak with kindness and gentleness and affection. Parents who have withdrawn from their children because of repeated disappointment or apparent ingratitude begin to engage and forgive.

While we sometimes experience that a soft answer turns away wrath, no parent or child holds all the power to turn the heart of the other. Sometimes our best efforts fail to soften or turn the hearts of our children. But because our Father has turned his heart toward us in Christ, our hearts can be turned toward our children, and we can keep asking him to turn our children's hearts toward us.

❋ ❋ ❋

Father, the more we experience your grace and mercy, the better able we are to turn toward our children with that same grace and mercy. We are not able to turn _____'s heart toward us or toward you. But you can. Please turn all of our rebellious hearts toward you and toward one another.

Look and Live!

The LORD sent poisonous snakes among the people, and many were bitten and died. Then the people came to Moses and cried out, "We have sinned by speaking against the LORD and against you. Pray that the LORD will take away the snakes." So Moses prayed for the people. Then the LORD told him, "Make a replica of a poisonous snake and attach it to a pole. All who are bitten will live if they simply look at it!" So Moses made a snake out of bronze and attached it to a pole. Then anyone who was bitten by a snake could look at the bronze snake and be healed! NUMBERS 21:6-9

THE PEOPLE WERE complaining about being brought up out of Egypt, longingly remembering the good food they ate there but apparently forgetting their bitter slavery. And so the Lord sent snakes. Why snakes? The symbol of Egyptian power—featured on the Pharaoh's crown—was a serpent. So these serpents said with every hiss: "Is this really what you want? Do you want to be afflicted with suffering by the mighty serpent of Egypt again?" The serpents were also a reminder of the ancient serpent who slithered into the Garden of Eden and tempted Adam and Eve, causing them to be ejected into the wilderness.

God instructed Moses to mount the symbol of Israel's mortal enemies—Egypt and Satan—lifeless and defeated on a pole. It was a picture of how the power of sin would one day be defeated for good when the seed of the woman would crush the head of the serpent (Genesis 3:15). The Israelites received life and healing when they fixed their gaze on the bronze snake on the pole, a picture of the future defeat of the ancient serpent when Jesus would be lifted up on the pole of the cross.

❊ ❊ ❊

Just as Moses lifted up the bronze snake on a pole in the wilderness, so Jesus was lifted up on the cross so that everyone who believes in him will have eternal life. You love _____ so much that you gave your one and only Son, so that if _____ believes in you, she will have eternal life. You sent your Son into the world not to judge _____ but to save her through him. Please call _____ to yourself so that she might fix her gaze on the cross, where her salvation is found.

Keeps Quiet

It is foolish to belittle one's neighbor;
*   a sensible person keeps quiet.*
A gossip goes around telling secrets,
*   but those who are trustworthy can keep a confidence.* PROVERBS 11:12-13

FOR MOST PARENTS, the day comes when we discover that our children are more likely to do what we do rather than do what we say. They're watching our actions, and it shapes what they do for good and for bad. Likewise, when we think our children aren't listening, they are—even when we're not talking to them. In fact, our children absorb a great deal from what we say to each other—to people in the halls after church, to our best friends over the phone, to and about the policeman who stops our vehicle, to the referee who goes against us, to the neighbor who annoys us.

What are your children overhearing in your conversations with other adults? Do they hear you constantly belittling others—coworkers about the quality of their work, other parents about the way they parent, your own parents about the choices they're making? A sensible parent keeps quiet.

Do your children overhear you gossiping—about the secret habits, the secret faults, the secret failures, the secret heartbreaks of those you pretend to care about? Those who are trustworthy can keep a confidence.

How much better would it be if our children were to overhear us praising the Christlike qualities of others, celebrating their accomplishments and affirming their gifts? How much would our children learn from us if they observed us squelching gossip rather than joining in? How would their willingness to trust us with their secrets grow if they observed us keeping the confidences of others?

❊ ❊ ❊

Lord, I have foolishly belittled others, gossiped, and shared things that were not mine to tell in private and in the presence of my children. Today I am naming these things as sin and asking you for divine help to forsake this sin. Won't you empower me, instead, to choose to bless rather than belittle, to keep quiet rather than to share secrets?

Thoughts Revealed

Jesus' parents were amazed at what was being said about him. Then Simeon blessed them, and he said to Mary, the baby's mother, "This child is destined to cause many in Israel to fall, and many others to rise. He has been sent as a sign from God, but many will oppose him. As a result, the deepest thoughts of many hearts will be revealed. And a sword will pierce your very soul." LUKE 2:33-35

NEVER HAS A CHILD RECEIVED a more celebratory welcome than the one the baby Jesus received when Mary and Joseph took him to the Temple and placed him in the arms of the aging Simeon. The Lord had revealed to Simeon that he would not die until he had seen the Messiah with his own eyes. And this was that day. The baby he was holding was the Savior. But just as God revealed to Simeon that this child would bring salvation to people from every nation, God also revealed to him that this child would be opposed and rejected by many in Israel. Because of this, one day Mary would feel the blunt force of that hatred in her own soul. Surely Mary thought of Simeon's words when she wept at the foot of the cross. Surely she thought the sword that pierced her soul then was cutting her heart into pieces.

Simeon was right. Many opposed Jesus. "He came into the very world he created, but the world didn't recognize him. He came to his own people, and even they rejected him. But to all who believed him and accepted him, he gave the right to become children of God. They are reborn—not with a physical birth resulting from human passion or plan, but a birth that comes from God" (John 1:10-13).

This sword cuts through our own lives, and perhaps even through our families, separating those to whom Jesus is a joy from those who ignore, reject, and oppose him. This sword that will one day separate the sheep from the goats pierces our very souls too.

❊ ❊ ❊

Sovereign Lord, I know that my future and _____'s future are bound up in our response to the Savior you sent into the world, Jesus Christ. Your Word is a two-edged sword that goes deep into every one of us, revealing our deepest thoughts and motives. I ask, Lord, that the sword of your Word, wielded by your Spirit, would work to cut away anything and everything that would keep _____ from recognizing you as the true and only Savior.

Jesus Grew

Jesus grew in wisdom and in stature and in favor with God and all the people.
LUKE 2:52

WHAT MUST IT have been like to be the parents of Jesus? Imagine parenting a sinless child. Sounds good, doesn't it? Of course the fact that Jesus was sinless doesn't mean that he was born fully formed with no need for his human parents. Parenting Jesus meant parenting a child going through the process of growing up. And though this verse doesn't tell us everything we'd like to know about what that was like, it is clear that Jesus grew in all of the ways we want our own children to grow. Over the years of his childhood, adolescence, and young adulthood, Jesus grew. He changed. He developed. While the Holy Spirit was clearly at work through the Scriptures in the development of Jesus, his parents were certainly a key part of the process.

Likewise, as parents we have a significant role in the process of how our children develop and who they will become. But it is not all up to us. We need the Holy Spirit to work through his Word in the lives of our children.

We want our children to grow in wisdom. This is less about good grades than it is about godly living. We want to see steady growth, not just in their knowledge of the Scriptures, but also in their ability to apply God's truth to their relationships, priorities, and pursuits. We want our children to grow in stature. Long after the pediatrician is assigning our child a number on the growth chart, we want to see that our children are healthy in body and mind, healthy in habits, and healthy in terms of body image as well as eating and drinking to the glory of God. We want our children to develop a life under God's favor. We want them to experience what it means for God to smile on them because of their connection to Jesus. And finally, we want them to have good relationships with the people around them.

✼ ✼ ✼

Lord, I am desperate for wisdom from you to know how best to guide _____ toward growth in wisdom, how to encourage _____ to embrace favor with you through Christ, and how to model to _____ the way to love others well in this world. Give me the patient perseverance I need for the long-haul task of parenting.

Numbers 26:52–28:15
Luke 3:1-22
Psalm 61:1-8
Proverbs 11:16-17

Daughters of Genuine Faith

One day a petition was presented by the daughters of Zelophehad—Mahlah, Noah,
Hoglah, Milcah, and Tirzah. Their father, Zelophehad, was a descendant of Hepher
son of Gilead, son of Makir, son of Manasseh, son of Joseph. These women stood
before Moses, Eleazar the priest, the tribal leaders, and the entire community at the
entrance of the Tabernacle. "Our father died in the wilderness," they said. "He was
not among Korah's followers, who rebelled against the LORD; he died because of his
own sin. But he had no sons. Why should the name of our father disappear from his
clan just because he had no sons? Give us property along with the rest of our relatives."
NUMBERS 27:1-4

ZELOPHEHAD HAD DIED during the forty years the Israelites had wandered in the wilderness—and he had died without any sons to carry on his name and inherit his stake in the
land allotted to his family in Canaan. Having a name that endured through your descendants was a vital part of being a partaker in the promises of God. As it was, Zelophehad's
name would be forgotten, and his land would be absorbed by another clan. But Zelophehad
had five daughters—women who were convinced that the promises of God were valuable
enough to fight for. So they went to Moses and appealed their case. In spite of their father's
sin, by God's grace and mercy, these daughters were given a stake in the land.

What these daughters wanted was an inheritance that was promised by God but not
yet possessed. Unlike the men in the family's previous generation, who had lacked the faith
to enter into the land God had promised them, these daughters declared by their actions,
"We believe what God has promised, and we want all that he has promised to give!"

If there's anything we want in our children, it is bold faith like these daughters of
Zelophehad—children who, despite the sins of their parents and the doubts their parents might have had about the goodness of God, want everything he has to give and are
willing to do whatever is required to take hold of it.

※ ※ ※

Lord, won't you fill _____ with the same passionate desire for what you provide, the
same rugged confidence in your goodness, the same bold intention to take hold of all you
have to give? Help me to rest in the truth that my failures to trust and obey you do not
determine the future inheritance of my children in your Promised Land.

MARCH 19

Dearly Loved Son

One day when the crowds were being baptized, Jesus himself was baptized. As he was praying, the heavens opened, and the Holy Spirit, in bodily form, descended on him like a dove. And a voice from heaven said, "You are my dearly loved Son, and you bring me great joy." Jesus was about thirty years old when he began his public ministry. Jesus was known as the son of Joseph. Joseph was the son of Heli. . . . Seth was the son of Adam. Adam was the son of God. LUKE 3:21-23, 38

ADAM WAS GOD'S FIRST SON (LUKE 3:38). Adam had the potential to bring his Father great joy, but instead he brought his Father tremendous grief. Adam's disobedience required his exile from the Garden of Eden and from the presence of God. Then God had another son, the nation of Israel. "I called my son out of Egypt," Hosea wrote about Israel (11:1). The Lord intended this son, his treasured possession, to live in his holy land in obedience to his law, which was given at Mount Sinai. But the Israelites were disobedient too. And so, just as Adam was exiled from the Garden, Israel was exiled from the Promised Land.

But God was not content for his people to live in alienation from him. So he sent his dearly loved Son, Jesus, who brought him great joy, into the world. And this Son obeyed! But he, too, was exiled—not because of his own disobedience, but because of ours. By taking our sin upon himself, Jesus has made it possible for God to say to us and to our sons and daughters, "You are my [child], whom I love; with you I am well pleased" (Mark 1:11, NIV).

We love our children, and our children bring us both joy and sorrow. What matters most is not that our children please us, but that they please their heavenly Father, which happens only as they are joined to Jesus by faith and receive his perfect record of obedience as a gift. We are all born spiritually dead because of the sin of our ancestor Adam. But when we are joined to Jesus by faith, the Father showers on us the same love and approval he showers on his Son, Jesus.

❊ ❊ ❊

Father, I admit that I am very concerned about _____ living a life that will bring me great joy, a life I can affirm and approve of. But I realize what is most important is that _____ is joined to your dearly loved Son by faith so that _____ is under your smile, granted your welcome, and made acceptable by him.

Bound with an Oath

Moses summoned the leaders of the tribes of Israel and told them, "This is what the LORD has commanded: A man who makes a vow to the LORD or makes a pledge under oath must never break it. He must do exactly what he said he would do."
NUMBERS 30:1-2

AS GOD'S PEOPLE PREPARED to start a new life in the land he had promised them, the place where they were to live as God's treasured possession and be a light to the Gentiles, the Lord told them something very important. They were to put the character of God on display to the world around them by being truth tellers and faithfully following through on what they promised.

Even today, God's people are to be people of their word, even when it is costly. Specifically, when we make a vow, we are to fulfill our promise and keep the commitment we made. When we fail to keep our vows to our children, or to other people in full view of our children, we undermine their confidence, not only in our reliability to keep our word but also in the faithfulness of the God whose name we bear. That is why it is so crucial that our yes be yes and our no be no, as Jesus told us in Matthew 5:37.

But as much as we want to be people who live up to our promises, we are promise breakers in big and small ways. Fortunately there is one who has kept his vows perfectly in our place. What's more, this one we are united to by faith has borne the punishment for all of our broken promises. Joined to Christ by faith, we have become part of God's family, heirs in Christ to all the promises of God. Our inheritance—and our children's confidence—rests on his faithfulness, not ours. Our salvation is secure precisely because it does not rest on our ability to keep our vows to God but on his ability to make good on all of his covenant promises to us.

❀ ❀ ❀

God, you have bound yourself to your people with an oath, so that those who received the promise could be perfectly sure that you would never change your mind. You have given both your promise and your oath. These two things are unchangeable because it is impossible for you to lie. Therefore, we who have fled to you for refuge can have great confidence as we hold to the hope that lies before us. This hope is a strong and trustworthy anchor for our souls.

Progress in the Wilderness

This is the route the Israelites followed as they marched out of Egypt under the leadership of Moses and Aaron. At the LORD's direction, Moses kept a written record of their progress. These are the stages of their march, identified by the different places where they stopped along the way. NUMBERS 33:1-2

NUMBERS 33 is one of those lists in the Bible that we think has little for us in the tedium of the detail. But if we put our feet into the sandals of those who stood on the edge of the wilderness, preparing to enter into the Promised Land, we realize that this list of every place they camped along the way would have evoked many memories. We might also see that this inventory was meant to shape Israel's perspective on forty years in the wilderness. Likewise, it has something to say to us about our years spent traversing the wilderness of this world as we make our way to God's holy land.

Three different kinds of places are included in this list. There are places that would have reminded the Israelites of the Lord's faithfulness in meeting their needs—like when they found an oasis in the desert at Elim. Then there are places that would have called to mind their own failure and rebellion against the Lord—like when they complained against Moses at Rephidim when there was no water to drink. Interestingly, this divinely inspired list doesn't mention the great sins of the people in these places. It is as if God had forgiven and forgotten and had no desire to throw it back in their faces. Then there are places where nothing of significance happened. These were ordinary days when God faithfully fed, led, and preserved them.

If you were to write down a record of your family's journey through the wilderness of this world, wouldn't it consist of the same three kinds of places—places and times in which God worked in significant ways to meet your needs, markers of great failures and sins in your family that threatened your progress, and then many ordinary days when God fed, led, and preserved you?

※ ※ ※

Lord, as we think back through the days and months and years of our lives, we thank you for the many points when you worked in unmistakable ways on our behalf. We are grateful for your divine forgetfulness of our sins—that you remove them as far as the east is from the west. And we thank you for all of the ordinary, unremarkable days when you fed us, led us, and preserved us as a family.

He Saw a Tax Collector

Later, as Jesus left the town, he saw a tax collector named Levi sitting at his tax collector's booth. "Follow me and be my disciple," Jesus said to him. So Levi got up, left everything, and followed him. LUKE 5:27-28

EARLIER THAT DAY, most of the people in town had crowded into a house to hear Jesus speak and to see a man who had been paralyzed jump up, pick up his mat, and go home praising God. But not Levi, the local tax collector. Money was his god. Now Jesus was passing by with a large crowd following him, and still Levi sat. But then Jesus saw Levi. Jesus saw his greed and corruption. He saw his loneliness and need. Jesus moved toward the man who was not moving toward him. When Jesus looked at Levi, this person who was hated for his robbery, Jesus saw who Levi would become. Jesus could see he would become Matthew, which means "gift of God"—Gospel writer, gift to the church.

In this unpredictable call to Levi and his unexpected, instantaneous, all-out response, we see that Christ's call to followership is completely sovereign and irresistible. To the leper Jesus says, "Be healed!" and he is healed. To the paralyzed man he says, "Stand up," and he stands up and walks. And to Levi Jesus says, "Follow me," and he immediately follows. But the authority of Jesus does not discount Levi's genuine response. When Levi "got up, left everything, and followed him," we see his genuine human response of faith. His response of faith was lived out by following Jesus.

As parents, when we see our children sitting instead of following after the Lord, we can't see them as Jesus sees them. We can't see all that he has planned for them and all of the ways he intends to transform them. But we can pray for Jesus to see our children and to call our children to himself. And we can trust that his call is irresistible.

✳ ✳ ✳

Lord, sometimes when I look at _____, all I can see is who he is now, the choices he's making, and his need for significant change. I just know that you are sovereign and that if you see him and call him to follow you, your call cannot be resisted. So come. Call _____ to yourself as your disciple. How I long for it to be said about _____ that he "got up, left everything, and followed" you.

Those Who Think They Are Righteous

Jesus answered them, "Healthy people don't need a doctor—sick people do. I have come to call not those who think they are righteous, but those who know they are sinners and need to repent." LUKE 5:31-32

OUT OF A DESIRE for our children's holiness, we sometimes set them up to be hypocrites. Rather than recognizing that our children are sick with the disease of sin and in need of the healing touch of Christ, we bandage them up with church activity and dress them up in good behavior so that they learn to look healthy and good when that may not at all be the reality in their souls.

"Before sin is a matter of behavior, it is always a matter of the heart." Sin, quite simply, is part of our nature. The frustrating thing for us as parents is that we don't have the power to change our children's hearts. So in our zealousness to see them doing what is right, we "ask the law to do in the lives of [our] children what only grace can accomplish." We put our hope in creating the "right set of rules, the right threat of punishment, and consistent enforcement." We fool ourselves into thinking that if we can regulate our children's behavior, we will have done our job well.

But if the right set of rules (the Ten Commandments), the right threat of punishment (exile from the land of promise), and consistent enforcement (the perfect justice of God) had the power to create lasting change in the lives of people, there would have been no need for a Savior. But Jesus has come, and he still comes into the homes of people who are sick with sin. He never calls us as parents to do what only he can do, but instead "he lifts the burden of change" in our children off us and onto himself.

❋ ❋ ❋

Lord, we want to teach _____ your law, which we know is right and good. And we want to faithfully exercise authority and loving discipline in _____'s life. We want to be tools in your hands to create the heart change that is needed in _____'s life. Please show us where we're substituting rule-keeping for genuine love for you. Keep reminding us that you come to call not those who think they are righteous, but those who are sick with sin and in need of your grace of repentance.

Supernatural Love

To you who are willing to listen, I say, love your enemies! Do good to those who hate you. Bless those who curse you. Pray for those who hurt you. If someone slaps you on one cheek, offer the other cheek also. If someone demands your coat, offer your shirt also. Give to anyone who asks; and when things are taken away from you, don't try to get them back. Do to others as you would like them to do to you. LUKE 6:27-31

IT IS PERFECTLY NATURAL to love people who love us. And it comes quite naturally to hate those who are against us, those who hurt or humiliate us. So it is also natural for us to want to water down this command of Christ to love and do good to our enemies to something more manageable, more reasonable. As parents, we can't stand the idea of our children being taken advantage of, so we're more likely to teach them how to protect themselves and stand up for themselves than we are to teach them how to pray for those who have hurt them. But what if we did? And before you answer, understand this will mean that you will have to demonstrably love *your* enemies and audibly bless those who curse *you*.

What attitudes do your children see and hear from you in regard to neighbors who park on your lawn, bosses who abuse their power, referees who officiate poorly, or church leaders who make undesirable changes? What if you and your kids invited the annoying neighbors over for dinner? What if your kids heard you blessing your boss, thanking the referee, and praying for your church leaders rather than complaining? Is this even possible?

The gospel, with its staggering promises of great reward, offers the resources we need for this Spirit-driven behavior. As we love our enemies, we model God's own character, which was manifested fully in Jesus. We love as we have been loved. This command to love our enemies is a call to unnatural deeds of kindness, unnatural words of blessing, and unnatural prayers for pardon. It is a command for supernatural love.

※ ※ ※

Lord, I cannot rely on what comes naturally when it comes to dealing with people who are against me and those who have hurt me or my family. I need supernatural power to love as I have been loved. You are a God who demonstrated love toward us even when we were your enemies. Won't you fill me with that kind of love and fill _____ with that kind of love so we can love like you do?

MARCH 25

Deuteronomy 4:1–49
Luke 6:39–7:10
Psalm 68:1–18
Proverbs 11:28

The Speck in My Child's Eye

How can you think of saying, "Friend, let me help you get rid of that speck in your eye," when you can't see past the log in your own eye? Hypocrite! First get rid of the log in your own eye; then you will see well enough to deal with the speck in your friend's eye. LUKE 6:42

AS PARENTS, we're always peering into the lives and character and habits of our children, taking note of areas of growth and progress as well as areas that still require maturation and sanctification. We are quick to correct our children when they speak harshly and complain. We set limits on their screen time and sweet consumption. We are quick to name their jealousy and pride.

Certainly our children's sins need to be lovingly confronted. But before we speak, before we point, we would be wise to take a look in the mirror with eyes willing to see our own vanity, our own idolatrous obsessions, our own selfishness. Our children struggle with the same sins we do; we've just become better at justifying and ignoring them. We need to examine ourselves to see if we're disciplining our children for sins that we allow ourselves to get away with. Ultimately parents who are grieved and humbled over their own sins are best prepared to deal with the "speck" in their child's eye. If we deal as firmly with our own sins as we do with our children's, demonstrating a commitment to obedience as well as an expectation of grace and mercy, we'll be living out authentic faith before them, the kind of faith they'll likely want to live out themselves.

❊ ❊ ❊

Lord, I don't want to be a hypocrite in my own home. But it is so very hard for me to be humble before my children and to confess my own sins. It is so hard to let them see how much I need your Spirit to empower me for ever-increasing holiness. But I do! I need your power to choose humility and eradicate hypocrisy. Help me to be as rigorous in calling out and forsaking my own sin as I am in calling out and correcting the sins of my children.

Repeat Them Again

You must love the LORD your God with all your heart, all your soul, and all your strength. And you must commit yourselves wholeheartedly to these commands that I am giving you today. Repeat them again and again to your children. Talk about them when you are at home and when you are on the road, when you are going to bed and when you are getting up. Tie them to your hands and wear them on your forehead as reminders. Write them on the doorposts of your house and on your gates.
DEUTERONOMY 6:5-9

MOSES WAS STANDING at the edge of the Promised Land with God's people. He wouldn't be entering with them, so he was telling them everything they needed to know to live well in the land God was giving them. He reiterated the Ten Commandments that God had written on stone tablets forty years before, when most of those standing with him were children or hadn't yet been born.

The weight and wisdom of Moses' instructions echo through the centuries to us today. Moses was calling on parents to talk to their children about how God had saved them from slavery in Egypt and had given them his loving law to live by when they sat around the table, when they traveled, at bedtime, and in the morning. In other words, the grace of God as well as the law of God were to be authentic parts of their conversation throughout the day, in every place and situation. Since they were people whose souls had been shaped by the deliverance of God and whose lifestyle was being shaped by the law of God, it would be only natural that these truths would shape their conversations with their children.

But it's not always natural for us, is it? We fear letting our kids see our weaknesses, our neediness, our failures. Yet this great parenting passage is not telling us how good we must be at parenting or anything else. Instead, it reminds us how real we must be about our need for Jesus.

❋ ❋ ❋

Lord, this passage seems to condemn me from the start because I do not love you with all my heart, soul, and strength. But I want to. I haven't been wholeheartedly committed to your commands or made them a consistent part of my daily conversation with _____. Lord, loosen my tongue with _____ to speak about my need for your grace and forgiveness, as well as my confidence that you supply both to me.

MARCH 27

The Lord Loves You

The LORD did not set his heart on you and choose you because you were more numerous than other nations, for you were the smallest of all nations! Rather, it was simply that the LORD loves you, and he was keeping the oath he had sworn to your ancestors. That is why the LORD rescued you with such a strong hand from your slavery and from the oppressive hand of Pharaoh, king of Egypt. DEUTERONOMY 7:7-8

THE OLD TESTAMENT tells the story of the people God chose from all the nations of the earth to showcase his redeeming work. But the reasoning and purpose behind his choice is not obvious in human terms. God didn't set his affections on Israel because they had done anything to deserve it or because they were strong or numerous or impressive. He loved them because he chose to love them. He promised Abraham and Isaac and Jacob that he would love them when he said, "This is the everlasting covenant: I will always be your God and the God of your descendants after you" (Genesis 17:7). His choosing was not random, and neither was it without meaning. "I created Judah and Israel to cling to me, says the LORD. They were to be my people, my pride, my glory—an honor to my name" (Jeremiah 13:11).

Perhaps the only way we can begin to understand this kind of love is to explore the nature and source of our love for our own children. We don't love them because of anything they've accomplished or because they are necessarily lovable. In fact, the radical and inexplicable nature of our love for our children is best demonstrated when our children are at their worst, when on the surface of things, they are demonstrably unlovable. We love them because . . . we love them. We love them because they are ours.

❋ ❋ ❋

Gracious God, even before you made the world, you loved us and chose us in Christ to be holy and without fault in your eyes. You decided in advance to adopt us into your own family by bringing us to yourself through Jesus Christ. This is what you wanted to do, and it gave you great pleasure. Lord, it is only your irresistible grace that can bring _____ to the place of choosing you. Please work in _____ so that _____ will cling to you, so that _____ will be your pride and your glory, bringing honor to your name.

Patience for the Harvest

The seeds that fell on the good soil represent honest, good-hearted people who hear God's word, cling to it, and patiently produce a huge harvest. LUKE 8:15

JESUS TOLD THE PARABLE of the sower and the soils at a time when few were following him. To the disciples it didn't make sense. Here was the Messiah the Israelites had been waiting and longing for, here was the King who was promised, yet the people were rejecting him instead of embracing him, picking up stones to kill him rather than bowing the knee to him.

The parable doesn't explain *why* people respond the way they do, but it does identify the source of the problem—human hardness, shallowness, and self-indulgence.

As we spread the seed of the Good News of Jesus in our own home, how we pray it will fall on good soil in the hearts of our children! We don't want it to fall on shallow or rocky soil. We want them to "cling to it" as if their lives depend on it—because they do. We don't want them to easily let go of it when they walk out the door of our home. We want the seeds we are spreading to produce a huge harvest in their lives over the seasons ahead. But we have to be patient. We can't expect an instant, enormous harvest.

Not every Christian produces the same amount of fruit. There are different conditions in the soil that cause different levels of fruitfulness in the crop. If the seed of the gospel has taken root in the lives of our children, it will bear some fruit. It may be just a little fruit. Perhaps it will only be the fruit of a convicted conscience that—at least for now—does not develop into fully flowering repentance. What we're looking for is even the smallest sign of fruitfulness. And what we need is the patience to wait for the seed we have planted to produce a huge harvest over a lifetime as our children grow in fruitful discipleship to Jesus.

✳ ✳ ✳

Father, you are the Master Gardener. You know the soil of my heart and that of _____'s. My prayer today is that you would plow up the soil in all of our hearts by your Spirit so that we are ready to receive your Word, so that it will be implanted deep into our lives. Give us the will to cling to it. Help us to wait patiently for its flowering.

Authority

The disciples were terrified and amazed. "Who is this man?" they asked each other. "When he gives a command, even the wind and waves obey him!" LUKE 8:25

IT MIGHT SEEM that the four scenes Luke records in chapter 8 of his Gospel are merely a chronicle of happenings in the ministry of Jesus. But Luke has put his record together with divinely inspired intention. In this series of scenarios, we're meant to see something significant about Jesus, namely about his power and authority. First, a storm came up on the Sea of Galilee. The disciples were terrified, certain that their boat was about to sink. But with a word, Jesus rebuked the wind, and there was instant calm. Next we read about a naked man who had been driven mad by the inhabitation of demons. Jesus commanded the unclean spirit to come out, and after all the commotion, the townspeople came out to see the former madman clothed and in his right mind. Later, a woman who had been hemorrhaging for twelve years dared to press in to Jesus. With just a touch, the flow of blood ceased. Finally, a synagogue leader's daughter had died, but Jesus told her to arise, and she got up and ate.

Luke wanted the readers of his Gospel to grasp the pervasive nature of the power and authority of Jesus. And because the Word of God is living and active, when we read this chapter, we can be sure that God wants us to grasp the pervasive nature of the power and authority of Jesus too. Sometimes as parents we feel completely out of control, like we are about to sink in a storm of raging forces beyond our control. But these circumstances are not out of Christ's control. Sometimes we fear that the enemy has taken over and threatens to rob us and our children of sanity and dignity. But his power is firmly subservient to Christ's power. We are tempted to give up hope that long-term issues will be resolved or that new life can invade the dead places in our lives. That's why we need the hope found in Luke 8, or more specifically the Hope Giver of Luke 8.

❆ ❆ ❆

Jesus, you know the storm that rages in our family and the fear we feel that this will take us down for good. Speak your peace into our chaos. Jesus, you know the evil that threatens the sanity and purity in our home. Protect us from the evil one. Jesus, you know the long-term issues that never seem to find resolution. Touch us with your healing power. Jesus, you know the dead places in our hearts and in our relationships. Infuse us with your life.

Bond-servant

Suppose your servant says, "I will not leave you," because he loves you and your family, and he has done well with you. In that case, take an awl and push it through his earlobe into the door. After that, he will be your servant for life. And do the same for your female servants. DEUTERONOMY 15:16-17

WHEN WE INTRODUCE ourselves to someone we're meeting for the first time, we usually weigh carefully what we'll say about who we are and what we do. We want our words to give us some credibility and status in that person's estimation. This insight into ourselves adds meaning to the way Paul, James, Peter, and John refer to themselves at the beginning of their letters in the New Testament. They introduce themselves using a status described in the Old Testament book of Deuteronomy. In Romans 1:1, James 1:1, 2 Peter 1:1, and Revelation 1:1, each of these writers introduces himself the same way—as a "bond-servant" or "bond-slave" of Jesus Christ. It's as if they were saying, "The most important thing about me is that I've made Jesus Christ my master. Obeying him is the focus of my life. He is so precious to me that I've willingly bonded myself to him as his servant for life."

A bond-servant is not just a slave, but a slave who has willingly committed himself to serve a master he loves and respects even after he has been given the freedom to go. This kind of slavery is chosen, not imposed; it's the result of freedom, not compulsion.

❋ ❋ ❋

My Lord and Master, I realize that you are not forcing me into slavery. Becoming your bond-servant is my choice. And my choice is made. I want to relinquish my independence, surrender my will, and declare my loyalty to you.

And as I parent _____, so concerned about what he will accomplish and who he will become, help me to keep this central identity as a bond-slave to Jesus Christ at the heart of my dreams and desires for him. May _____ sense from me during our conversations and obligations today that my greatest desire for him is that he would be defined by his yieldedness to Jesus Christ.

Take Up Your Cross

"The Son of Man must suffer many terrible things," he said. "He will be rejected by the elders, the leading priests, and the teachers of religious law. He will be killed, but on the third day he will be raised from the dead." Then he said to the crowd, "If any of you wants to be my follower, you must give up your own way, take up your cross daily, and follow me." LUKE 9:22-23

As PARENTS, we want to smooth out the way in front of our children. We want them to be included and appreciated, not mistreated or alienated. We want them to experience the smile and embrace of the world around them, not rejection or ridicule. And yet deep down we know that it is not comfort that forms character. It is not applause and approval that develop humility. It is not ease that tests integrity. These grow by God's grace in the fertile ground of difficulty and adversity.

Our greatest hope as Christian parents is not that our children have comfortable or successful lives on this world's terms. Our greatest hope is that we will raise children who will willingly lay down their lives for Christ. So rather than protect them from hardship, we pray for them in hardship, asking God to use each painful experience to make their satisfaction less dependent on the things of this world and to convince them that the way of Jesus—the way of dying to oneself and pursuing his Kingdom—is the only way to live a truly fulfilling life.

❀ ❀ ❀

Lord, I know that _____ will not wear the crown of glory unless she bears your cross. May the crushing blows that come _____'s way serve to conform her more fully to your likeness and affirm to her more deeply the lasting joys of sharing in your suffering, confident that she will also share in your glory.

Finally Understood

I tried to understand why the wicked prosper.
But what a difficult task it is!
Then I went into your sanctuary, O God,
and I finally understood the destiny of the wicked. PSALM 73:16-17

IN PSALM 73, Asaph tells his own story of being immersed in the ministry of leading the Temple choir and then almost walking away from God. It's a picture of a person questioning the value of life with God and beginning to slip away.

When we read Asaph's account of his flirtation with the world's ways of satisfaction and his frustration with God's ways, it can strike fear into our hearts as parents—especially if we've seen signs of this kind of questioning in the lives of our own kids. It can send us into an immediate strategy session to figure out what we're going to do or say to convince them to keep a firm grip on faith in Christ.

So it is important for us to take note of what brought a turn of direction for Asaph. In verse 17, he says, "I went into your sanctuary, O God, and I finally understood the destiny of the wicked." God drew him into his presence and gave him a more vivid grasp of the judgment that awaits those who chase after the world rather than following after God. Asaph realized that though his heart had become bitter, he still belonged to God. The Lord had taken hold of him and would not let go. Asaph's perspective changed so that when he looked into the future he saw God guiding him to a glorious destiny and could say to the Lord, "I desire you more than anything on earth" (verse 25).

There is hope for our sons and daughters who think life outside of Christ is where the fun and satisfaction are and that serving Christ brings nothing but trouble. Our hope as parents is not in our power of persuasion. Neither is it in our children's ability to keep hold of Christ. Our hope is that God will give them a fuller understanding of the ruin that awaits those who reject God and the glory that awaits those who desire him.

✳ ✳ ✳

Sovereign Lord, you are my shelter; you are my hope. And I'm grateful to know that you are a more patient parent than I am. You sometimes allow your own to almost lose their way. You sometimes allow your own to question your ways. But you also protect your own. You draw them to yourself. You strengthen them to listen to you and love you. Won't you do what only you can do in _____'s life so that _____ will be able to say that he desires you more than anything on earth?

Refuses to Obey

Suppose a man has a stubborn and rebellious son who will not obey his father or mother, even though they discipline him. In such a case, the father and mother must take the son to the elders as they hold court at the town gate. The parents must say to the elders, "This son of ours is stubborn and rebellious and refuses to obey. He is a glutton and a drunkard." Then all the men of his town must stone him to death. In this way, you will purge this evil from among you, and all Israel will hear about it and be afraid. DEUTERONOMY 21:18-21

THIS PASSAGE IS DIFFICULT for any loving parent to read without a shudder. So how are we to understand it?

As the Israelites prepared to move into Canaan, Moses instructed them on how to live there as God's holy people. He also explained how they were to deal with issues that might threaten their security. He included the case of a family in which the firstborn son was proving unworthy of his inheritance and future family leadership. This was not a naughty young child or a rebellious teen, but an adult who lacked any character and persisted in vile behavior. If this was how he behaved now, what would he do with the family's resources when he became head of the family?

When God gave his people the law, he promised a reward for honoring one's parents: "Then you will live a long, full life in the land the LORD your God is giving you" (Exodus 20:12). A foolish, wicked son would not be honoring his parents. So rather than experiencing the blessing of a long, full life, he would experience the curse of an early death—but only if both of his parents and the town elders agreed on this penalty.

While there is no record of anyone being executed under this law, this instruction still alarms and perhaps even embarrasses us because it doesn't seem very godlike. But there is actually great hope in this dark scene. Centuries later, a firstborn Son who obeyed his Father perfectly would be put to death—not for his own stubborn rebellion, but for ours. He would experience the curse that all rebellious sons deserve so that we can experience the blessing of the long, full life that he deserved. He experienced the ultimate curse so that we can enjoy unending blessing.

※ ※ ※

Lord, we hardly know how to thank you for putting the punishment we deserve for our stubborn, rebellious ways on your own innocent Son so that we can experience a long life of blessing. Will you help us know how to encourage _____ toward this life of blessing, especially when _____ is stubborn, rebellious, and refuses to obey?

Registered in Heaven

Don't rejoice because evil spirits obey you; rejoice because your names are registered in heaven. . . . No one truly knows the Son except the Father, and no one truly knows the Father except the Son and those to whom the Son chooses to reveal him. LUKE 10:20, 22

JESUS HAD SENT THE SEVENTY-TWO disciples out for ministry, and they returned amazed by the supernatural power they experienced. They commanded demons to depart, and the demons obeyed! Jesus assured them that this was just the beginning of the defeat of the devil that they would get to be a part of. But then he gave them a sense of perspective regarding the thrill they felt from what God had done through them. There was something that should provide them with an even greater sense of joy—the security of having their names written on the register in heaven that lists all of those who will live in God's presence forever.

Jesus looked up and expressed joy and thankfulness to his Father for revealing the mystery of his Kingdom and Satan's ultimate defeat to the disciples with their childlike faith. And then he turned to the disciples and told them that they were blessed because they were being given eyes to see the person of Jesus and ears to hear the call of Jesus. Although the Old Testament prophets wrote about the coming Messiah and his Kingdom, they only saw it in shadows. Jesus was celebrating that his disciples were beginning to see him for who he was and embrace his Kingdom for all it would be.

And this is what we so desperately want for our children. We long to peer into that registry in heaven and be assured that our children's names are there. We want them to have eyes that are open to seeing Jesus. And we realize that "no one truly knows the Father except the Son and those to whom the Son chooses to reveal him." So we want to pray that Jesus will reveal himself to our children!

✵ ✵ ✵

Lord, I'm well aware that no one deserves to have his or her name registered in your holy presence. But you are gracious. Lord, would you extend your grace to _____ by revealing yourself to her? Would you give _____ the joy of seeing your goodness, hearing your Word, and being used by you in this dark world to restrain the forces of evil? I thank you, Father, that you have hidden these things from the wise and understanding and revealed them to little children.

How Much More

You fathers—if your children ask for a fish, do you give them a snake instead? Or if they ask for an egg, do you give them a scorpion? Of course not! So if you sinful people know how to give good gifts to your children, how much more will your heavenly Father give the Holy Spirit to those who ask him. LUKE 11:11-13

JESUS WANTED to encourage his disciples to pray to God as a father. To help them understand the Father's heart toward those who are persistent in prayer, he appealed to their understanding of a parent's heart. Most parents genuinely want to respond positively to the requests of their children and provide for their needs. Most parents would never intentionally do anything that would hurt or harm them. Their orientation is toward the good of their children.

Jesus says that when parents understand their own hearts and inclinations toward their children, they have a glimpse of insight into his Father's heart and his inclinations toward his sons and daughters. If parents whose hearts are infected with sin respond to their children with kindness and good intentions, how much more will the Father whose heart is pure and holy respond to his children this way? We parent from hearts that are sometimes stingy, sometimes hard, sometimes deceived, and sometimes filled with pride. We simply aren't smart enough to always know what is best for our child. That means we sometimes give our kids what makes us feel better instead of what is best for them.

So we rest in the reality that our children have a heavenly parent who is exceedingly wiser, more generous, and more consistent than the earthly parents they were given. His orientation is to respond to their prayers by giving them what is good. And only he is able to give them the very best—the Holy Spirit.

※ ※ ※

Heavenly Father, thank you for this glad welcome to come to you and ask for what we need! Parenting often brings us to the end of ourselves, and that brings us to you. So we intend to keep on asking for your help, keep on seeking your wisdom, and keep on knocking on your door, asking that you will give us and give _____ the good gift of the Holy Spirit.

Blessed

You will experience all these blessings if you obey the LORD *your God:*

Your towns and your fields
will be blessed.
Your children and your crops
will be blessed. . . .
Wherever you go and whatever you do,
you will be blessed. DEUTERONOMY 28:2-4, 6

THE BLESSING OF GOD—that's what we really want for ourselves, our families, children, businesses, and endeavors. And from the beginning of the Bible, where we read about the Creator blessing all that he had made, we understand that the orientation of God is to bless his people. When God's people came out of slavery in Egypt, God met them at Sinai and gave them his loving law. Every command came with a blessing that would be theirs if they obeyed that command. And at the end of Deuteronomy, as Moses spoke to the next generation preparing to enter into the land of Canaan, he called on them to obey God's law, reminding them of God's promise that if they would obey, they would be blessed. Their children, too, would be blessed. Everything would go well for them as families and as a nation.

But later in this same chapter, Moses warned of what would happen if they didn't obey God's law. And it was horrifying. If they refused to obey, they would be cursed, defeated, afflicted, enslaved, exiled.

This passage sends disobedient parents running into the arms of the gospel. We are brought to our knees in gratitude that we live under the new covenant instead of the old covenant. God's blessing in our lives is not dependent upon our perfect obedience to God's law, but on Christ's perfect obedience. We do not live in fear of being cursed for our disobedience, because he bore the curse for us. We receive the blessing of God, not through our obedience, but through faith. We use the freedom we've been given to pursue glad obedience, not out of fear of the curse, but out of gratitude for the blessings provided to us in Christ.

✻ ✻ ✻

Lord, we want every blessing you have to give! Bless our family and make our family a blessing to those around us. Bless us in spite of our failures to fully obey because of the complete obedience of Christ.

God Will Change Your Heart

When you experience all these blessings and curses I have listed for you, and when you are living among the nations to which the LORD your God has exiled you, take to heart all these instructions. If at that time you and your children return to the LORD your God, and if you obey with all your heart and all your soul all the commands I have given you today, then the LORD your God will restore your fortunes. He will have mercy on you and gather you back from all the nations where he has scattered you. . . . The LORD your God will change your heart and the hearts of all your descendants, so that you will love him with all your heart and soul and so you may live! DEUTERONOMY 30:1-3, 6

MOSES TOLD the people of God that after they entered Canaan, they would disobey God and be exiled and scattered from the land. But the day would also come when they would be regathered there. At that time, God would change their hearts. We learn more about this change from the words God spoke through Ezekiel: "I will give you a new heart, and a new spirit I will put within you. . . . I will put my Spirit within you, and cause you to walk in my statutes and be careful to obey my rules" (Ezekiel 36:26-27, ESV).

This happened on the Day of Pentecost, when the Holy Spirit came down to indwell those who embraced Christ by faith. This is the change we and our children still desperately need. Until the Spirit of God does this supernatural work, our children will have no heart to love the Lord, no power to obey him.

As parents, we can't make this happen, but we can create an atmosphere that opens them to the Holy Spirit's work. We can read, discuss, and revere God's Word in our homes. We can pray that God, by his Spirit, will do what only he can do, which is to call and then unite our children to Christ. We can challenge our children to choose the God who chose them in Christ before the foundations of the world. And we can live in such a way that they see the beauty of having a heart that is being changed by the Spirit of God.

❄ ❄ ❄

Lord, just as I am powerless to generate genuine spiritual life in myself apart from the work of your Spirit, so I am powerless to generate spiritual life in _____. So I am taking hold of your Word and your promise that the change of heart you accomplish in your people is also for our children and our children's children. Transform us into people who obey you out of an intrinsic desire rather than an imposed demand.

What's the Use of Worry?

Can all your worries add a single moment to your life? And if worry can't accomplish a little thing like that, what's the use of worrying over bigger things? LUKE 12:25-26

JESUS WAS SPEAKING to disciples who were filled with anxiety about having enough—enough food to eat, enough clothes to wear. We, too, are disciples who are filled with anxiety about whether or not we will have enough—enough insight into our child's issues, enough energy for meeting our child's needs, enough income for our child's education, enough influence to open up doors for our child. We worry about whether our sons and daughters have enough friends, enough talent, enough intelligence, enough common sense, enough ambition, and enough opportunity. So we need to consider the question Jesus poses and the instruction he gives to his disciples.

Jesus tells them to look at the birds that are fed by God and the lilies of the field that are made beautiful by God. He tells us that we have something unbelievers don't have that should make all the difference when we are tempted to worry about not having enough—we have a Father who knows our needs and will give us everything we need.

Jesus asks his disciples if our worries have the creative power to actually add to our lives. And as soon as we hear the question, we know the answer. We know that all of the energy we give to worry is really only robbing us of peace. None of us have enough control over our lives or our children's lives to add a single hour to them through worry or manipulation. Our children have nothing to gain by our ongoing anxiety, which becomes evident in our interactions and surely does not escape their notice. Do we really want to breathe out our fears about the future into the lives of our children, or do we want to radiate restful confidence in God?

❊ ❊ ❊

Father, I don't want to be afraid. I don't want to lie awake at night working my way through all of my worries. I don't want my conversations with friends or my words to my children to be saturated with the sin of worry. I'm taking you at your Word that it gives you great happiness to give us the Kingdom. And if we have that, we have everything we need.

Empty Words

When Moses had finished reciting all these words to the people of Israel, he added: "Take to heart all the words of warning I have given you today. Pass them on as a command to your children so they will obey every word of these instructions. These instructions are not empty words—they are your life! By obeying them you will enjoy a long life in the land you will occupy when you cross the Jordan River." Deuteronomy 32:45-47

Moses had come to the end of his before-I-say-good-bye message to the Israelites as they prepared to take possession of the Promised Land. He wanted God's people to take his words to heart. He was also concerned that the parents pass along God's promises of blessing and warnings of curses to their children. They couldn't expect that their children would absorb these truths simply by living in their homes. These parents needed to be purposeful in passing them on. Of all of the words spoken between family members each day, it was these words—God's promises and warnings—that simply had to be uttered. These words were not about empty, fleeting things. These words had the power to impart life.

It makes us wonder what a recording device in our homes might reveal. Just think of all the words traded between parents and siblings, all of the words that penetrate the environment of our homes from the airwaves and Internet, all of the words muttered under our breath—words of instruction, warning, criticism, encouragement, cynicism, and even hope. So many words.

But many of them don't give life. So we need to hear Moses' instruction to parents to pass on God's Word—with its promises to bless and its warnings of curses—to our children. Our aim should be that they will not simply hear but will obey. Our children need so much more than to be taught the Bible at church. They need to hear us, as parents, discussing Scripture. They need to hear how the Word of God intersects with our thinking. They need to hear how God's Word informs the way we spend our money and our vacation time, how we deal with a difficult situation at work and a difficult relationship in the extended family. These are words that bring genuine life to our children over the long haul.

❀ ❀ ❀

Lord, only you can take my many words and make them life-giving. As I seek to infuse my words with your true, unavoidable, unimpeachable words today, may they bring life to _____.

It Grows

Jesus said, "What is the Kingdom of God like? How can I illustrate it? It is like a tiny mustard seed that a man planted in a garden; it grows and becomes a tree, and the birds make nests in its branches." He also asked, "What else is the Kingdom of God like? It is like the yeast a woman used in making bread. Even though she put only a little yeast in three measures of flour, it permeated every part of the dough." LUKE 13:18-21

JUST AS THE JEWS of Jesus' day wanted the Kingdom of God to come triumphantly and comprehensively in one swift show of power and transformation, so we tend to want the reign of Christ to come into our children's lives triumphantly and comprehensively in one swift show of power and transformation. But this isn't how his Kingdom comes into the world, and it's not how his rule and reign comes to our lives or the lives of our children. It starts small, like a tiny seed that requires nourishment and light to grow. It begins almost invisibly, doing its work from within, like yeast. The Holy Spirit works through the Word to make a dead heart come alive, and over time, that radical inner change works its way through the whole person. This means we, as parents, have to be patient. It means we should not be surprised that our children are not now everything we long for them to be.

And it should also fill us with hopeful anticipation of all King Jesus will do over the course of our child's lifetime. Just as the impact of yeast on dough will be comprehensive over time, we can be sure that what began as something small and almost imperceptible in the life of our child will grow and will one day be complete. The grace of God will have its full effect in the lives of our children, changing them from the inside out. "The Lord—who is the Spirit—makes us more and more like him as we are changed into his glorious image" (2 Corinthians 3:18).

※ ※ ※

Lord, how we long for your Kingdom to come in our home and in our lives! We want to see and experience more of your justice, more of your mercy, more of your wisdom, more of your ways. And it is coming, though often not as quickly or comprehensively as we might like. Would you give us patience with ourselves and with our children, the kind of patience a farmer must have after the seeds have been planted and the kind of patience a baker must have after the dough has been kneaded? Thank you for the grand privilege of watching your Kingdom grow in _____'s life.

As a Hen Protects Her Chicks

O Jerusalem, Jerusalem, the city that kills the prophets and stones God's messengers! How often I have wanted to gather your children together as a hen protects her chicks beneath her wings, but you wouldn't let me. LUKE 13:34

MERRIAM-WEBSTER'S DICTIONARY defines a *mother hen* as "a person who worries about, cares for, or watches over other people in a way that is annoying or unwanted." Certainly this is not how we as parents want to care for our children. Instead, we want to be mother hens in the way that God describes himself. Throughout the Bible, God uses the familiar imagery of a hen that gathers her chicks under her wings to provide protection from danger. It's a picture of shielding the chicks with her own body to preserve their lives.

Oh, how deep is our instinct to draw our children to ourselves to try to protect them from every threat. And, oh, how typical the tendency is for our children to assume they need no protection. They want to take their chances out in the world on their own, apart from our careful watch and covering.

We should probably take away two things from this picture. When we long for our children to come in close so that we can protect them, we're parenting them the way God parents us. This impulse is God-given and God-like. Chicks are meant to look to their parents for protection. But we must also recognize that there is a far greater security that can only be provided to our children by God himself. Christ is like that hen we see gathering her chicks under her wings. Only he can shield us from the wrath of God. Christ has provided the protection needed for all who will come under the shelter of his wings. He absorbed the wrath of God so that we, and our children, might be protected.

❀ ❀ ❀

Lord, as _____ hears you calling out to come to you, won't you break through every strain of resistance and independence? Give _____ a healthy and right fear of you so that he will see his need for protection. Give _____ a longing for you so that there is nowhere he would rather be than under the shelter of your wings.

What Do These Stones Mean?

Joshua said to the Israelites, "In the future your children will ask, 'What do these stones mean?' Then you can tell them, 'This is where the Israelites crossed the Jordan on dry ground.' For the LORD your God dried up the river right before your eyes, and he kept it dry until you were all across, just as he did at the Red Sea when he dried it up until we had all crossed over. He did this so all the nations of the earth might know that the LORD's hand is powerful, and so you might fear the LORD your God forever." JOSHUA 4:21-24

AS SOON AS THE FEET of the priests carrying the Ark of the Covenant touched the Jordan, the river instantly stopped flowing south toward the Dead Sea. Instead, the water piled up in a heap upriver so that the people passed through on dry ground. As they crossed through the Jordan, they remembered how the previous generation had crossed through the Red Sea forty years before. But Joshua did not want the remembering to end with that generation. He wanted future generations to know what happened there—to know that Yahweh's hand is powerful enough to make a way for his people to enter into all that he intends to provide for them.

So Joshua gave instructions for building a memorial. The men were to take twelve stones from the dry riverbed to the camp in Canaan. The memorial would be a sign to ensure that the people of God would never forget how the Lord, on this remarkable day, worked to lead his people into promised rest.

In our sinfulness and weakness, we tend to forget the good things that God has done for us in the past. So God has also given us a sign—a memorial to remind us of what the Lord's powerful hand has done to make it possible for us to look forward to life in his Promised Land. Instead of a stone memorial, we partake of a memorial meal in the bread and the cup. So when our children ask, "What does this meal mean?" we want to be prepared to tell them that God has given this meal "so all the nations of the earth might know that the LORD's hand is powerful, and so you might fear the LORD your God forever."

❀ ❀ ❀

Lord, thank you for the memorial sign you have given to your people and to our family, so that we will remember your saving work on the cross. We look forward to life in your land, enjoying your rest. Give us the words we need to teach our children the meaning of this meal, and give us the rest that is promised to us in it.

Lost

His father said to him, "Look, dear son, you have always stayed by me, and everything I have is yours. We had to celebrate this happy day. For your brother was dead and has come back to life! He was lost, but now he is found!" LUKE 15:31-32

IN LUKE 15 we read about a series of lost treasures—a lost sheep sought after and brought home, a lost coin searched for and rejoiced over, and a lost son waited for and welcomed. But really there are two lost sons in the third story.

One son is in "a distant country" seeking pleasure, evading responsibility, and self-medicating his madness. He is lost in the delusion that the world will fill him up, but in reality it is chewing him up and leaving him desperately empty. The other son remains in his father's home and yet is so very far away from sharing his father's heart. He is lost in such a haze of angry resentment, self-righteous protest, and arrogant entitlement that he doesn't realize that he has never lost what matters most—the presence of his father. All of his life he has shared in all that belongs to the father.

As parents we tend to get so worked up over sons and daughters who stray from us, living lifestyles that are nothing like the one they grew up in. And rightly so. Any lost child grieves us. But we must also be on watch for sons and daughters who may be going through the motions of being "the good kid" while having hearts that are so very far away from the Father.

✳ ✳ ✳

Father, just as you have all kinds of prodigals in your family, so do we. So we appeal to you to seek and save the lost. Do what you must to bring to their senses those who are far away from you, seeking satisfaction in anything and everything apart from you. If severe mercy is the only thing that will bring them to saving grace, then be as severe as the wonders of your love require. If things have to get much worse in their lives, then give us the patience, trust, and assurance that you are at work. And should we be tempted to rescue them before your work is done, grant us grace and power to resist doing so.

And for our prodigals who haven't gone anywhere but have confused proximity to you and work for you with love for you, show them how much they need the grace of the gospel.

The Valley of Trouble

Joshua said to Achan, "Why have you brought trouble on us? The LORD will now bring trouble on you." And all the Israelites stoned Achan and his family and burned their bodies. They piled a great heap of stones over Achan, which remains to this day. That is why the place has been called the Valley of Trouble ever since. So the LORD was no longer angry. JOSHUA 7:25-26

JUST BEFORE GOD brought the walls of Jericho tumbling down, Joshua commanded the people not to loot the city. But evidently Achan just couldn't resist. He coveted and gave in to temptation. He brought home a beautiful cloak, two hundred shekels of silver, and a bar of gold that he had lifted from the city. Achan mixed these spoils in with his own things and hid it all under his tent. His sin was his secret—or so he thought.

Then came the next battle. And this time, instead of fighting for his people, the Lord seemed to abandon them to their enemies. When Joshua fell before God asking why they faced such a bitter defeat, the Lord told him it was because Israel had taken things from Jericho. Joshua got up early the next morning and brought all the people before him tribe by tribe, then clan by clan, then family by family, and finally man by man. Eventually Achan was the only one left. He confessed, so "Joshua and all the Israelites took Achan, the silver, the robe, the bar of gold, his sons, daughters, cattle, donkeys, sheep, goats, tent, and everything he had" (Joshua 7:24) to the valley of Achor, where they stoned Achan and his family. They piled a great heap of stones and called it the Valley of Trouble—a monument to sin, defeat, and death.

But then one day God spoke through his prophet Hosea promising that he would "transform the Valley of Trouble into a gateway of hope" (Hosea 2:15). How would he do this? Through Christ. A heap of stones as a monument to sin becomes, in Christ's power, an empty tomb from which the stone has been rolled away. Families once covered with sin and shame become displays of his grace.

❈ ❈ ❈

Lord, sometimes as I look at the landscape of our family, I see piles of stones that seem to serve as monuments to hidden habits, ongoing deceptions, and forbidden lusts. Without you, that is all there would ever be. Our family would forever be lost in the Valley of Trouble. Will you, through the power of Christ's sinless obedience, come down to this valley and transform it into a gateway of hope? Will you infuse us with resurrection life so that each of us can look toward the future with the confidence that our past failures will not define us forever?

In Need of a Miracle

"If another believer sins, rebuke that person; then if there is repentance, forgive.
Even if that person wrongs you seven times a day and each time turns again and asks
forgiveness, you must forgive." The apostles said to the Lord, "Show us how to increase
our faith." The Lord answered, "If you had faith even as small as a mustard seed, you
could say to this mulberry tree, 'May you be uprooted and be planted in the sea,' and
it would obey you!" LUKE 17:3-6

"WRONGS YOU SEVEN TIMES A DAY." It can sound like the repeated refrain we hear from the backseat of the car or from the playroom or around the dinner table. We tell our children to say they're sorry, and we tell the offended party to forgive. But we know that to be truly repentant and to truly forgive real wrongs require so much more than words. These acts take a miracle in the heart, which seems to be what Jesus promises in these verses.

Recognizing that they didn't have in themselves the needed resource for this radical kind of forgiving, the apostles told Jesus they needed more faith. But Jesus said it wasn't *more* faith they needed; they already had enough. Jesus was saying that if his gospel had any place at all in their hearts—even the size of a mustard seed—they had what they needed to forgive. The same is true for us and for our children: If we have enough faith to believe that God has forgiven us our enormous debt of sin, we have what we need to forgive the debts of others.

Just a mustard seed's worth of comprehension of God's forgiveness is enough to break our hearts over the enormity of our own sin and the greatness of his mercy. We, in turn, can extend mercy to someone who has hurt or offended us. Jesus wants to help us become as forgiving as he is, but he knows that we don't have what it takes to do that on our own—but then, if we are in him, we are not on our own.

❊ ❊ ❊

Lord, you have given us the faith we need to entrust our lives to you, but sometimes the
faith to entrust the deep hurts and ongoing offenses we've experienced from both inside
and outside our family seems harder to come by. Would you help us to grasp the enormity
of our sin and the generosity of your forgiveness so we might extend that kind of forgive-
ness to each other? We don't want to just demand that our children forgive; we want them
to see it in the lives of their parents.

Homesick

How lovely is your dwelling place,
*   O LORD of Heaven's Armies.*
I long, yes, I faint with longing
*   to enter the courts of the LORD.*
With my whole being, body and soul,
*   I will shout joyfully to the living God.* PSALM 84:1-2

PSALM 84 is an expression of longing written by an eager and homesick man, one of the Korahite Temple singers. Pilgrims making their way to the Temple in Jerusalem sang this psalm to cultivate their delight in the Lord and to open their eyes and hearts to the staggering privilege of being a welcome guest in God's own house. Singing this psalm was a way of impressing upon their own souls the conviction that nothing the world offers remotely compares to the joy and pleasure of God's house.

What they longed for was not simply an attachment to a place. The living God was the true object of this yearning. This is the homesickness we want our children to have—the desire we pray will take hold of them. We want this longing to keep drawing them to find their home among God's people. We want this anticipation of God's blessing to enable them to expect that the most difficult places in their lives will become places where God will rain down his blessings. We want this enthrallment with God's presence to keep them pursuing greater intimacy with him. And we want this confidence in God's grace and glory to keep them convinced of his goodness.

※ ※ ※

Lord, I need this homesickness for you to become a reality in my soul. I simply can't pray for _____ to have this kind of passionate desire for you when I don't have it myself. Will you give me eyes to see your loveliness and the joy that comes from your goodness? Will you set my mind on a pilgrimage to the New Jerusalem?

And when _____ walks through the Valley of Weeping, will you make it a place of refreshing springs? Rain down your blessings. As _____ makes this lifelong pilgrim journey, may she continue to grow stronger until the day she appears before you in the New Jerusalem.

I Am a Sinner

The tax collector stood at a distance and dared not even lift his eyes to heaven as he prayed. Instead, he beat his chest in sorrow, saying, "O God, be merciful to me, for I am a sinner." I tell you, this sinner, not the Pharisee, returned home justified before God. For those who exalt themselves will be humbled, and those who humble themselves will be exalted. LUKE 18:13-14

JESUS' STORY about the Pharisee and tax collector begins, "Jesus told this story to some who had great confidence in their own righteousness and scorned everyone else" (verse 9). Evidently Jesus could see past the Pharisees' strict observance of the law and recitation of the Torah and look deep into their hearts. And what he saw was a tremendous amount of self-righteousness that generated arrogant scorn for others.

We don't want to think of ourselves as self-righteous. Yet without realizing it, we often exude aloofness and superiority. Our conversations in the car and across the dinner table reveal that we don't like others' morals, their music, or their preferred news channel. It comes out with our kids as we talk with them about other people. We can easily sound as if we think that if everyone else were like us, the world would be a much better place.

God wants to change the conversation from what's wrong with everyone else to what's wrong with us. He wants to lead us to a place of repentance and dependence on his mercy. A hard heart never admits anything. But when the people of God melt and confess their sins, that's when the presence of Jesus is felt among us. It's our repentance, not our perfection, that makes the beauty of Christ shine through our lives and through our families.

❀ ❀ ❀

Lord, we're much more comfortable talking about the faults and the sins of others than we are confessing our own. And we're realizing this is an area where we must take the lead—to become the chief repenters in our home. Lord, forgive us for exalting ourselves as those who don't struggle against temptation and who never fail when tempted. Give us the courage and grace to humbly name our sin in the presence of our family so that we become more than simply parents and children but also brothers and sisters in Christ.

Impossible

When Jesus saw this, he said, "How hard it is for the rich to enter the Kingdom of God! In fact, it is easier for a camel to go through the eye of a needle than for a rich person to enter the Kingdom of God!" Those who heard this said, "Then who in the world can be saved?" He replied, "What is impossible for people is possible with God."
LUKE 18:24-27

WHEN THE RICH MAN turned away from Jesus, it was because he was in love with the world. And this scares us a bit, because we see how much our children love the world. They love its thrills and its technology. They love its promises of becoming somebody and its paths to getting ahead. They love its entertainment and its enticements. We think that it's going to be really hard to figure out how to wean them away from all that the world offers and instill in them a desire for what the Kingdom of God offers. But the truth is more dire. It is *impossible* for parents to do what is necessary to keep their children from loving the world more than Christ and his benefits. So where does that leave us?

It leaves us wholly dependent on God to do what is impossible for us to do. When we're discouraged about the hold that worldly things and worldly ways of thinking have on our children, we remember that what is impossible for people is possible with God. When it seems foolish to hope or expect that there will be change deep in their hearts, we recall the Lord's limitless mercy and grace. While it may be impossible for us to convince our children to change, impossible for us to generate their interest in the things of God, impossible for us to penetrate the defenses that have been built to keep out the truth, it is not impossible for God. Our children's future and destiny are not determined by what we can make happen. Change is possible because God does what is impossible for us to do.

❀ ❀ ❀

Lord, I hear you telling me that I should put to rest all my planning and manipulating, and bring to mind your power and your purposes. While I have influence as _____'s parent, I simply don't have the power to create life from death, intensity from apathy, new affections for Christ from deeply ingrained attachments to the world. But you do. Will you do what is impossible for me to do in _____'s heart and life?

APRIL 18

A True Son of Abraham

Jesus responded, "Salvation has come to this home today, for this man has shown himself to be a true son of Abraham. For the Son of Man came to seek and save those who are lost." LUKE 19:9-10

ON THAT DAY when Jesus came through town, Zacchaeus wanted to see who Jesus was. But up on his sycamore perch, he was surprised to discover that Jesus already knew who *he* was. Jesus was in hot pursuit of this one who was lost in the delusion of riches, this one whose greed brought financial ruin to those around him. Jesus told Zacchaeus that he simply had to be a guest in his home that day.

In Jesus' time, eating with someone—going to his home and sharing a meal—was a sign of intimate fellowship. It communicated acceptance. So Jesus didn't tell Zacchaeus that if he would clean up his life, he would accept him. Jesus reversed that. He offered Zacchaeus acceptance, and that acceptance worked its way through this tax collector in such a way that it changed him. The grace of Jesus shown around the table generated deep change in Zacchaeus's heart. Zacchaeus knew that the law of Moses required someone who'd stolen from another to confess his sin and offer full restitution plus 20 percent to the wronged party. But Zacchaeus was not interested in merely living up to the rules. The grace of Jesus had done such a work in his heart that he vowed to return far more than was required.

The Pharisees, who took great pride in being the physical descendants of Abraham, thoroughly disapproved of Jesus' choice of dinner companion. But while they grumbled at grace, Zacchaeus was made generous by grace. His desire and determination to live out a costly repentance demonstrated that the same righteousness that was credited to Abraham was becoming a reality in him. As a true son of Abraham, Zacchaeus transferred his confidence from his own financial stockpiles to Christ's salvation riches.

❊ ❊ ❊

Lord, we want to show ourselves to be true sons of Abraham by the way your gospel of grace is changing us from people who are consumed with taking care of ourselves into a family that joyfully and sacrificially gives. We don't want to live as if we presume that our church membership and religious activity alone make us a part of your family. We want the salvation that has come to our home to change every person living here.

Full of Troubles

O LORD, God of my salvation,
  I cry out to you by day.
  I come to you at night.
Now hear my prayer;
  listen to my cry.
For my life is full of troubles,
  and death draws near.
I am as good as dead,
  like a strong man with no strength left. PSALM 88:1-4

SOMETIMES we have sharp but short-term troubles with our kids. Other times we have deeper, ongoing, seemingly intractable issues—a chronic condition, an ongoing addiction, an unresolved conflict. And we get worn down. We can't see any light ahead. We can find no reason for hope.

The writer of Psalm 88 seems to understand such weariness. "My life is full of troubles," he says. No strength left. Seemingly forgotten by God. Alone. Trapped. Tearful. In the dark. Most laments in the Psalms let in a ray of sunshine, closing on a confident note of determination to trust God. But not this psalm. There seems to be no resolution. But that does not mean there is no genuine hope.

This psalm gives words to those who need to keep crying out to the Lord day and night—not to a powerless or uncaring God, but to the "God of my salvation." Faith can be real even when it can't be tied up into a tidy conclusion, even when it cannot articulate strong hope, even when it's barely holding on, even when everything seems very dark.

Parents who take up this divinely inspired song are led to keep coming to the Lord, even when it feels as if he does not hear and is refusing to act. And though the light of redemption is faint in this psalm, it helps us recognize that the God of our salvation is the only one with the ability to pierce through the darkness of our difficult circumstances.

※ ※ ※

God of my salvation, save me from despair over what seems unbearable. Save me from my inclination to run away from you with all of this very real pain rather than to cry out to you. Save me from the voice inside my head that is telling me that you have forgotten, that you are angry, that you have turned your face from me. Enter into my darkness and illumine me.

All the Good Promises Fulfilled

The LORD gave to Israel all the land he had sworn to give their ancestors, and they took possession of it and settled there. And the LORD gave them rest on every side, just as he had solemnly promised their ancestors. None of their enemies could stand against them, for the LORD helped them conquer all their enemies. Not a single one of all the good promises the LORD had given to the family of Israel was left unfulfilled; everything he had spoken came true. JOSHUA 21:43-45

GOD HAD MADE ABRAHAM, the Israelites' forefather, an incredible promise. His descendants would be held captive for four hundred years, but then God would bring them out and bring them into the land he intended to give them. And so God came to Joshua, their leader, and told him, "Be strong and courageous, for you are the one who will lead these people to possess all the land I swore to their ancestors I would give them" (Joshua 1:6). God promised he would go before them in battle and eliminate the evil that had made its home in God's Holy Land so that his people could live there securely, at rest, with God dwelling in their midst. When we come to the end of the book of Joshua, we discover that not a single promise the Lord had given to Abraham and his descendants was left unfulfilled. God's people were at rest in his land.

And this should deeply encourage us as we realize that the promises made and fulfilled to Abraham and his descendants are a foreshadowing of far greater promises God has made to all who have become sons of Abraham by faith. God has promised to bless us. Even now he is at work reclaiming more and more territory in our lives from evil impulses and patterns. He is at work making our very lives holy land. The day will come when our greater Joshua—Jesus Christ—will lead us into the true land of milk and honey. Heaven will be the land we've always longed for, the land that Canaan was always pointing toward, the land where we will finally be at home.

❋ ❋ ❋

Lord, our hearts become so enamored with the here and now. Will you lift our eyes to our promised inheritance? Will you fill our hearts with anticipation of all we stand to inherit when we enter into your Holy Land? And, Lord, we long to be there together as a family, every one of us, enjoying your rest. Bring us all home to you.

A Snare and a Trap

If you turn away from him and cling to the customs of the survivors of these nations remaining among you, and if you intermarry with them, then know for certain that the LORD your God will no longer drive them out of your land. Instead, they will be a snare and a trap to you, a whip for your backs and thorny brambles in your eyes, and you will vanish from this good land the LORD your God has given you. JOSHUA 23:12-13

WE WANT SO MANY THINGS for our children. But surely at or near the top of the list is that if they marry, they marry someone who loves Christ, someone who will share this life-encompassing, identity-defining commitment. But oftentimes even some believing children toy with relationships that grow deeper than they expect, sometimes ending in marriages in which either the Christian relegates Christ to the margins of life, or the unbelieving partner is marginalized, leaving both parties feeling lonely and unhappy.

When our children's hearts become entwined with those who do not share faith in Christ, they resist the reality that pursuing a relationship with another person who has little to no interest in building a life around Christ will make them miserable over the long haul. They're convinced that somehow *their* case will be the exception. They insist that the unbelieving spouse will be supportive of their Christian faith. They are convinced that the two of them are soul mates. Blithely optimistic, they're sure that their passion and commitment will overcome all obstacles.

So we need the ancient word—this ancient warning—to do a work in our thoroughly modern children, convincing them that a romantic entanglement with an unbeliever has the potential of becoming a snare and a trap, something that may seem so very right in the moment but will bring great sorrow and loneliness over their lifetime.

※ ※ ※

Lord, I want _____ to enjoy every blessing you have to give your children, including the blessing of being joined heart to heart, soul to soul with a spouse as one flesh. Use your Word and your warnings to keep _____ from assuming that somehow she is an exception to the reality of the misery of being unequally yoked. Give her wisdom and discipline in matters of the heart. And give her such a passion for you that it will rule over all other passions.

As for Me and My Family

Fear the LORD and serve him wholeheartedly. Put away forever the idols your ancestors worshiped when they lived beyond the Euphrates River and in Egypt. Serve the LORD alone. But if you refuse to serve the LORD, then choose today whom you will serve. Would you prefer the gods your ancestors served beyond the Euphrates? Or will it be the gods of the Amorites in whose land you now live? But as for me and my family, we will serve the LORD. JOSHUA 24:14-15

ABRAM'S ANCESTORS LIVED in Ur of the Chaldees where they worshiped the moon god. Later, his descendants lived in Egypt, where the sun, the Nile, and many other false gods were worshiped. When his descendants prepared to enter Canaan, where the Canaanites worshiped many pagan gods, Joshua called on the people to get rid of all their household idols. Some of these families must have had images and statues associated with pagan deities that they had brought with them from Egypt.

Joshua called them to renounce all false gods and to serve the Lord exclusively. And their glad answer was yes! Even when Joshua warned them that they wouldn't be able to live up to their grand commitment, they said, "No, we will serve the LORD!" (Joshua 24:21).

Clearly the spirit was willing on this day, but the flesh proved to be weak over the days and years to come. And so is ours. We don't want our families to bow down to materialism, but those catalogs keep coming in the mail. We don't want to serve the gods of sexual perversion, but we find it hard to censor the television shows or movies we watch. We don't want to worship the god of image and success, but we find ourselves wanting to put out the impression of the perfect family like we see every day on social media and read about in Christmas letters.

So what should we do? We refuse to give up. We decide that our family will serve the Lord *today*. And we make the same choice tomorrow. We ask for his power to keep choosing to serve him in all the days to come.

✳ ✳ ✳

Lord, as much as we would like to close our eyes to the false idols that have made themselves at home in our lives, we know we can't. We've got to choose this day. So make us relentless in identifying our false idols. Give us the will to cast them far away so that they don't work their way back into our home.

Let Our Children See Your Glory

Lord, through all the generations
you have been our home! . . .
Satisfy us each morning with your unfailing love,
so we may sing for joy to the end of our lives.
Give us gladness in proportion to our former misery!
Replace the evil years with good.
Let us, your servants, see you work again;
let our children see your glory. PSALM 90:1, 14-16

MOSES WAS A MAN without a country, having left Egypt and knowing he would not cross over into Canaan. God's people were also without a country when this psalm was written. So we might expect Moses to describe the land of Canaan, the Promised Land, as Israel's dwelling place. But Moses began his psalm, "Lord, through all the generations *you* have been our home!" (emphasis added). Moses understood that our truest home is not a place but a Person. In God alone we find the security, safety, and peace that our hearts long for as we wander our own wildernesses in this world. Moses recognized that this is how it has been for all generations—that every generation before his and every generation after his lives in a world marked by mortality and sin, and we are all in great need of finding our true home in God.

So Moses gives us—one of the many "generations"—a song that provides us with words to petition God for what we need most as we seek to make our home in him. We need perspective about the brevity of life so we don't view our time on earth as all there is. We need the satisfaction that comes from knowing we are recipients of God's unfailing love. We need hope that our lives will not be forever defined by the evil and suffering of this life but instead will be made radiant with the glory of God. We long to experience his redeeming, resurrecting power in our lives and in the lives of our children. And so we sing to the Lord who, through all generations, has been our home.

❋ ❋ ❋

Lord, teach us to realize the brevity of life so that we may grow in wisdom. Satisfy us each morning with your unfailing love so we may sing for joy to the end of our lives. Give us gladness in proportion to our former misery! Replace the evil years with good. Let us, your servants, see you work again; let our children see your glory.

Another Generation Grew Up

After that generation died, another generation grew up who did not acknowledge the
LORD or remember the mighty things he had done for Israel. The Israelites did evil
in the LORD's sight and served the images of Baal. They abandoned the LORD, the
God of their ancestors, who had brought them out of Egypt. They went after other
gods, worshiping the gods of the people around them. And they angered the LORD.
JUDGES 2:10-12

THE GENERATION THAT had been small children when the Israelites walked away from
Egypt and through the Red Sea had died. Gone, too, was the next generation who marched
around Jericho for seven days and saw its walls fall down. Something terrible had happened
as that generation died off: Those who'd first entered the Promised Land had failed to
pass along a living faith to their children. This new generation had *heard* the stories about
Yahweh and his powerful deliverance, guidance, and provision, but they hadn't *experienced*
them. This generation was much like our own—born into prosperity and fascinated with
the search for spiritual meaning among the many options presented in the colliding cultures
around them. They saw God's Word as terribly old-fashioned and irrelevant.

As parents, we want the secret formula for passing along a living faith to our children, and we are frustrated that there is none. But surely our kids need more than to
hear about how we have experienced God in the past or even the present. Surely our
children need to be *involved* in ongoing experiences of putting faith to the test. Yet
most of us do everything we can to avoid situations in which our families are forced to
depend on God as our only hope, our only supplier, our only security. But if the next
generation is going to know the Lord, they have to know more than Bible stories or
even correct doctrine. They have to *experience* what it means to trust God to deliver on
his promised help. Maybe we shouldn't always be so quick to be our children's savior.
Maybe we should be willing to allow our children to experience the need for God to
come to their rescue and discover how he does that.

❈ ❈ ❈

Lord, we don't want the story of the next generation of Israelites to be the story of the
next generation in our family. We long for _____ to experience your saving power
in her life, not just read about it or hear about it. Keep us from trying to be _____'s
savior. Keep us from trying to protect _____ from every trouble and every need that
would require her to look to you.

Let Your Glorious Justice Shine Forth!

They crush your people, LORD,
hurting those you claim as your own.
They kill widows and foreigners
and murder orphans.
"The LORD isn't looking," they say,
"and besides, the God of Israel doesn't care."
Think again, you fools! PSALM 94:5-8

THERE'S NOTHING QUITE LIKE seeing our children being mistreated or abused to make our blood boil with a determination to protect them and punish the people who have hurt them. It begins with the kids who bite in the nursery, includes the unfair coaches or teachers, and extends to the girlfriends or boyfriends who break their hearts. Of course, sometimes a far greater evil is done to the child we cherish, a far more injurious hurt.

So what are we to do with our raging desire for vengeance? What are we to do when it seems that the evildoers in our children's lives will never experience true justice?

Psalm 94 gives us words to pray, words to plead to the God of vengeance that his glorious justice—far more pure and powerful than our own—would shine forth into the darkness of our situation. It reminds us in mocking tones that the Lord is not deaf to what is being said. He is not blind to what has been done. He is not ignorant about the private thoughts and motives of the perpetrators. Psalm 94 invites us to entrust to God our demands that the wrongdoers pay—to trust the Lord's timing, his way, and his perfect justice. And until that day comes, the Lord is our fortress. Our confidence in him enables us to wait without being consumed by frustration and anger.

❊ ❊ ❊

Lord, when doubts fill my mind about whether those who have hurt my child will get what they deserve, your comfort gives me renewed hope and cheer. Help me to trust that your perfect justice will be perfectly satisfied either in the punishment they receive or in the punishment borne for them on the cross. You are my fortress where I find safety from cynicism and despair. You are the mighty Rock where I hide to experience your comfort.

I Will Be with You

The LORD turned to him and said, "Go with the strength you have, and rescue Israel from the Midianites. I am sending you!" "But Lord," Gideon replied, "how can I rescue Israel? My clan is the weakest in the whole tribe of Manasseh, and I am the least in my entire family!" The LORD said to him, "I will be with you. And you will destroy the Midianites as if you were fighting against one man." JUDGES 6:14-16

IT WAS A DESPERATE SITUATION. For seven years terrorists from Midian had been regularly attacking the Israelites, taking all of their livestock and destroying all of their crops, leaving them to starve. The Israelites had left their cities in fear and hidden in caves with their families. Finally, they cried out to the Lord for help. And the Lord appointed a rescuer—a reluctant rescuer.

Gideon was well aware of his own inadequacy. But interestingly, when he told the Lord that he wasn't up to the job, the angel didn't try to assure Gideon that he was, in fact, adequate. He didn't assure Gideon of his untapped potential or encourage him to find the strength inside himself. Instead of pumping up Gideon's self-confidence, he infused Gideon's dangerous reality with confidence from God. "I will be with you," the Lord promised him.

We've heard Yahweh say this before to unwilling or hesitant servants. To Moses when he didn't want to face Pharaoh, God said, "I will be with you" (Exodus 3:12). To Joshua as he faced all of the cities inhabited by Canaanites, God said, "I will be with you as I was with Moses" (Joshua 1:5).

Perhaps we've discounted it. But the truth is, we can face really hard circumstances with this promise. Our children can face a new school, an overwhelming challenge, and untold temptations with this promise. God doesn't answer all of our questions about the details, but he provides what is essential: the assurance that he will be with us.

❊ ❊ ❊

Lord, we are sending _____ out into this world where he will have to fight, not against flesh-and-blood enemies, but against evil rulers and authorities of the unseen world, against mighty powers in this dark world, and against evil spirits in the heavenly places. We pray that _____ will know that you are with him and that his victory over these enemies does not lie in his own adequacy or abilities, but in your sufficiency and your power put on display in his weakness.

Remember Me

One of the criminals hanging beside him scoffed, "So you're the Messiah, are you?
Prove it by saving yourself—and us, too, while you're at it!" But the other criminal
protested, "Don't you fear God even when you have been sentenced to die? We deserve
to die for our crimes, but this man hasn't done anything wrong." Then he said, "Jesus,
remember me when you come into your Kingdom." And Jesus replied, "I assure you,
today you will be with me in paradise." LUKE 23:39-43

IT CAN BE HARD to hold on to hope when a family member continues to show no interest in Christ or even scoffs at him. Our hearts break at the possibility that this person
might not be with us when we enter eternity in the presence of Christ. And we can
barely think about what his or her future will be like apart from God.

So this criminal, hanging beside the Lord at the bitter end of his life, gives us hope.
Finally he can see the holiness of Jesus, the worthiness of Jesus, the kingship of Jesus. If
he could come down from the cross, he would bow his knee before this one who hangs
under the mocking sign that says "King of the Jews." At last, in these final moments
of life, this criminal can see his own guilt. He knows he deserves the punishment he's
receiving. He knows he has no basis for his bold request, and yet he asks. He has no
moral résumé to put forward to gain acceptance but simply open acknowledgment of
his sin and his desperation for Jesus.

The story of the criminal putting his faith in Christ encourages us to pray up to the
very end for those we love who have so far seen no need for Christ. We pray that they
will see their real guilt but that what will loom much larger will be a strong Savior. He
is a merciful King who responds to our desires to be with him by assuring us that we
will live with him forever.

❈ ❈ ❈

King Jesus, I pray now for the one I love who is living far away from you, far away from
your grace and mercy. Melt her hardened heart, open her blind eyes, and drain her of
the cynicism that keeps her scoffing at you. Bring her to her knees before you so that your
Kingdom becomes beautiful and desirable, so that the paradise that is defined by your
very presence is what she longs for most.

Our Ruler

The Israelites said to Gideon, "Be our ruler! You and your son and your grandson will be our rulers, for you have rescued us from Midian." But Gideon replied, "I will not rule over you, nor will my son. The LORD will rule over you! However, I do have one request—that each of you give me an earring from the plunder you collected from your fallen enemies." JUDGES 8:22-24

IF WE'VE SPENT MUCH TIME reading and teaching the Bible to our children, we've often been befuddled about how to explain the failings of those who seemed to live in obedience to God and yet messed up along the way. Noah courageously stood alone among the people of his day and built the ark, yet later fell into drunkenness and indiscretion. Abraham left Ur at God's command but then lied and told the Egyptians that Sarah was his sister. Moses faced down Pharaoh but then put on a show of self-righteousness by pounding the rock when the people cried out in thirst. And now we come to Gideon. He led a small band of men to defeat the Midianites. He seemed to recognize that he was not the one to be king over Israel—that God himself was their King—yet he just couldn't resist being treated like a king and assuming some of the privileges of royalty.

And it is not just in the pages of the Bible that we and our children are forced to figure out how to respond to seemingly godly people who disappoint us. Over the course of the years that they grow up in the church, our children will likely witness leaders who have affairs, abuse their power, or even walk away from faith. A shadow of inconsistency hangs over God's servants. So we keep pointing our children toward our true ruler, our righteous King.

⌘ ⌘ ⌘

Lord, we've been so blessed to be a part of God's people and for our children to see good shepherds who watch over the sheep in their care. We thank you for the integrity, faithfulness, and authentic faith our children have witnessed in the body of Christ. But we also know that at some point they will be disappointed by Christians who fail to be all you intend for them to be. So we ask you to guard _____'s heart from cynicism about the church. Save _____ from disillusionment with your people. Clarify to _____ that you are the true ruler of your church and that you will never fail or disappoint.

This Message Proclaimed

And [Jesus] said, "Yes, it was written long ago that the Messiah would suffer and die and rise from the dead on the third day. It was also written that this message would be proclaimed in the authority of his name to all the nations, beginning in Jerusalem: 'There is forgiveness of sins for all who repent.'" LUKE 24:46-47

AFTER HIS RESURRECTION, Jesus proclaimed that his disciples should take the message that there is "forgiveness of sins for all who repent" to all nations. As disciples today, we should ask: Is this the message we are proclaiming in our own homes? Or do our children hear us proclaiming a message about good morals, good behavior, and good citizenship?

What is the gospel according to your family? Is it that if you work hard and treat people well, God will bless you? Is it that if you respect authority and go to church every Sunday, you'll have a good life? While these activities have some value, they aren't the gospel of Jesus Christ. And we want to be gospel proclaimers in our own homes!

Parents who verbalize the need to forgive, who find joy in being forgiven, and who lead the family in walking out genuine repentance are true gospel proclaimers. Children who hear Mom and Dad name their own specific sins that need to be forsaken will be less likely to hide their sins that need to be forsaken—from God and from their parents. Children who see genuine change in their parents will more easily believe that God's power really can provide what is needed for them to change. Proclaiming the gospel in this way is more than simply challenging our children to accept Christ. It is living with the recognition that we are accepted *by* Christ and not on the basis of our good behavior, but because our bad behavior has been forgiven.

✳ ✳ ✳

Lord, would you help me to humble myself so that I might be able to admit my own constant need of a Savior to _____. I don't want to be busy giving lip service to a gospel that isn't real and life-changing within the walls of our own home. I want our family to be a part of proclaiming your gospel to a dying world. Help us to begin by proclaiming to one another that there really is forgiveness of sins for all who repent.

APRIL 30

A Birth That Comes from God

He came into the very world he created, but the world didn't recognize him. He came to his own people, and even they rejected him. But to all who believed him and accepted him, he gave the right to become children of God. They are reborn—not with a physical birth resulting from human passion or plan, but a birth that comes from God. JOHN 1:10-13

THE DAY OF OUR CHILD'S BIRTH is unforgettable as the pain of childbirth gives way to indescribable joy. But as significant as our child's birth is to both the child and to us, we know that another birth is needed—"not a physical birth resulting from human passion or plan, but a birth that comes from God." Why? Because our children are born spiritually dead.

This idea that our children are born spiritually dead can be hard to accept. As they grow, we might be willing to agree that they have some deficiencies and areas where improvement is needed. But the reality of their spiritual condition is far more serious. The Bible tells us that we are all spiritually dead apart from a miracle of life that God births in us. Apart from this grace, our children may look good on the outside but continue to have no real spiritual life on the inside.

But none of us can decide to be born spiritually any more than we decided to be born physically. Something has to happen *to* us—a work of the Spirit. So how does this happen? We are infused with new life when we no longer try to make our lives work through our own power or effort and say to Jesus: *I need you. Apart from you, I have no life, no hope. I want the life that is available only by coming alive to you. I need you to take hold of me in a way that will change me at the very core of my being.*

❋ ❋ ❋

Lord, give _____ the ability to recognize you. Don't let _____ reject you. Give _____ the faith to believe, the will to accept, and the right to become a child of God. We long for so much more for _____ than going through this life physically alive but spiritually dead. Call _____ to life so that _____ will never die.

The Lord Was at Work

His father and mother objected. "Isn't there even one woman in our tribe or among all the Israelites you could marry?" they asked. "Why must you go to the pagan Philistines to find a wife?" But Samson told his father, "Get her for me! She looks good to me." His father and mother didn't realize the LORD was at work in this, creating an opportunity to work against the Philistines, who ruled over Israel at that time. JUDGES 14:3-4

AFTER YEARS OF INFERTILITY, Manoah and his wife lived in anticipation of all that their son, Samson, would be and do. They taught him God's law and watched the Spirit of the Lord stir in him as he grew up. But then one day a Philistine girl from Timnah caught Samson's eye, and he just had to have her. All their years of teaching, training, praying, and sacrificing seemed to have little power to restrain him. Samson's parents must have been devastated. But the writer of Judges reveals to us a gap in their knowledge that could have made all the difference about their sense of the situation. "His father and mother didn't realize the LORD was at work in this" (verse 4). How could the Lord be at work through Samson's desire to do exactly what the law of God forbade—for an Israelite to marry someone who worshiped other gods?

Certainly they weren't wrong to object to Samson's demands. And certainly Samson's desires were not virtuous. But Yahweh is not bound by a parent's ability to grasp the big picture or limited by a child's foolishness. The Lord is able to use even our sinfulness and stupidity to bring about his purposes. This should offer hope to us as parents when our children make unwise decisions and when we can't see God at work in the midst of their sinful choices. Just because we can't understand these choices doesn't mean the Lord is not creating an opportunity to work in our child's life.

※ ※ ※

Lord, when we consider our own sinful inadequacies, even as we have sought to faithfully teach, pray for, discipline, and love _____, we find comfort in the reminder that we cannot always expect to see the full picture of what you're doing. We praise you for being sovereign over our lives and over _____'s life—so sovereign that you can cause even _____'s foolish choices to work together for her good. Today we choose to trust that you are working in a way we can't yet see.

He Knows How Weak We Are

The LORD is like a father to his children,
tender and compassionate to those who fear him.
For he knows how weak we are;
he remembers we are only dust. PSALM 103:13-14

AS PARENTS we tend to be pretty hard on ourselves. We're well aware of our deficiencies and our hypocrisies. We're so determined not to parent our own children in some of the ways we were parented, yet we find ourselves instinctually repeating similar patterns. We want to listen, but we're distracted. We want to play, but we have so much work to do. We want to engage helpfully, but we recognize that so much of what we throw out there just doesn't seem to stick. Even our most brilliant efforts at parenting don't always work well.

So here in Psalm 103 we find good news for parents who have failed their child, for parents who have been angry, impatient, or cold. We have a Father who is tender and compassionate toward us. He's not pointing fingers or putting us on trial. He is mindful of our limitations and frustrations. He is more aware than we are of how the way we were parented imperfectly impacts the way we parent. He knows how weak we are in faith, in discipline, in consistency, in wisdom, and in relational skills. He remembers that we are dust and that we are doing the best we can in a world we don't control to parent children we don't ultimately control.

The good news for imperfect parents is that we have a perfect parent. He is strong and faithful enough to use even our failures to glorify him. He works in and through our weaknesses to show his power and strength.

※ ※ ※

Father, we need you to be a Father to us as we seek to parent _____. We need your wisdom and guidance. We need your tenderness to release us from our regrets, and we need your compassion to assure us of your long-term commitment to see us through all of the seasons and struggles of parenting over the years to come. Help us to parent as those who fear you, as people made of dust who have been infused with the breath of life that comes only from you.

Humans Can Reproduce Only Human Life

Jesus replied, "I assure you, no one can enter the Kingdom of God without being born of water and the Spirit. Humans can reproduce only human life, but the Holy Spirit gives birth to spiritual life. So don't be surprised when I say, 'You must be born again.' The wind blows wherever it wants. Just as you can hear the wind but can't tell where it comes from or where it is going, so you can't explain how people are born of the Spirit." JOHN 3:5-8

NICODEMUS, a respected religious leader, came to Jesus hoping to have a theological conversation. Specifically, he came to investigate Jesus' miracles. But Jesus ignored the question implied in Nicodemus's initial comment to turn the conversation toward a far more urgent issue—Nicodemus's need to be born a second time. Jesus told him that if *he* did not experience a supernatural transformation, his religiosity would ultimately prove empty and useless. Nicodemus's present condition was hopelessly unresponsive—like a corpse on the gurney that has no life or ability to breathe life into itself. There was no way Nicodemus could improve himself or study his way into God's good graces. He did not need "five steps to becoming a godly person." He needed a miracle.

This is the transformation we want for our children. But clearly it is not something we can make happen. Only the Holy Spirit gives birth to spiritual life. And there is no standard-issue, one-size-fits-all experience by which to assess ourselves or our children. Some people can point to a specific date when they knew that they were born a second time—changed by God from a spiritually dead person into a spiritually alive person. Others, who grow gradually in their understanding of the gospel, may have a hard time nailing down a particular moment when they were reborn. But even if we can't identify exactly when this transformation occurred, that instantaneous event has to happen—when God the Holy Spirit, in an unseen, invisible way, calls a person to new spiritual life.

❊ ❊ ❊

Lord, we need this miracle of new life. We simply can't make this second birth happen on our own. Only your Spirit can make what is dead come alive to you. We long for your Spirit to blow through our home and through the lives of our children, bringing us all from death to life.

MAY 4

He Must Become Greater

He must become greater and greater, and I must become less and less. JOHN 3:30

WE'RE PARENTING in the age of the selfie, an age in which we're constantly grooming our online image to make ourselves appear more beautiful, more interesting, and more connected than we really are. Through social media we say daily to the world around us, "Look at my face! I'm here! I'm important! I matter!" We're constantly seeking a place for ourselves in the spotlight—wanting as much recognition as we can get for who we are, who we know, and what we've accomplished.

John the Baptist knew what it was to be in the limelight. Lines of people waited to be baptized by him; his disciples hung on his every word. But when Jesus stepped onto the scene and John recognized him as the fulfillment of all that the Old Testament had been promising, John settled happily into the background. That "voice crying in the wilderness" began to proclaim that Jesus had to be put forward and followed, while John had to fade further into the background—into Jesus' shadow.

Surely we go against the tide when we resist constantly reshaping our image and searching for recognition and when we help our children recognize their desires for applause and adulation. Yes, we want our kids to have a sense of their worth because they're made in the image of God. Yes, we want them to experience the joy of accomplishment, and we want to encourage them with our affirmation. But we want something much more for them than simply chasing after the world's ever-elusive adulation and attention. We want them to be so mesmerized by Jesus that the genuine desire of their lives becomes to use every opportunity available to make much of him, and thereby less of themselves.

※ ※ ※

Lord, help us to love your glory more than our own. Give us the wisdom we need as parents to know when to affirm and celebrate _____ and when to point out pride and self-centeredness. Increasingly, as people look in our direction, may they see that Jesus is all-important, all-sufficient, altogether worthy of worship.

They Settled There

In the days when the judges ruled in Israel, a severe famine came upon the land. So a man from Bethlehem in Judah left his home and went to live in the country of Moab, taking his wife and two sons with him. The man's name was Elimelech, and his wife was Naomi. Their two sons were Mahlon and Kilion. They were Ephrathites from Bethlehem in the land of Judah. And when they reached Moab, they settled there.
RUTH 1:1-2

THE BOOK OF RUTH tells the story of one ordinary Israelite family living in the town of Bethlehem during the period of the judges—a time when there was no king in Israel and all the people did what was right in their own eyes. We discover in the book's first verse that there was no bread in this little town, whose name means "house of bread." This was supposed to be the land flowing with milk and honey. God had promised his people that they would never hunger if they obeyed him. The report of famine reveals that God's people had not obeyed, so God sent the famine to lead them to cry out to him.

That's what Elimelech should have done. But instead of repenting and waiting for God to meet his family's needs, Elimelech decided he himself would save his family. He took them away from the one place on earth where God had promised to bless his people to a pagan land, Moab. Perhaps Elimelech left thinking it would be only temporary, but the writer says they "settled there." And then tragedy struck. The family's pursuit of satisfaction and security apart from God's place of blessing was a failure that would be inscribed on gravestones in Moab.

Peter warns us "as 'temporary residents and foreigners' to keep away from worldly desires that wage war against [our] very souls" (1 Peter 2:11). His warning encourages us, as parents, to ask if our family is living in this world with the mind-set of being temporary residents, or if we have "settled" here, adopting this world as our home, putting down roots, and storing up our treasure here.

✳ ✳ ✳

Lord, this world is all we have known. It is all we can see with our eyes and experience with our senses. So we need eyes of faith to set our sights on the home that you are preparing for us. Protect us from putting our roots down too deep in this alien land. Show us what it will mean to lead our family in a pilgrim lifestyle during our days on this earth.

Better than Seven Sons

The women of the town said to Naomi, "Praise the LORD, who has now provided a redeemer for your family! May this child be famous in Israel. May he restore your youth and care for you in your old age. For he is the son of your daughter-in-law who loves you and has been better to you than seven sons!" RUTH 4:14-15

SO MUCH HAD CHANGED since Naomi returned to Bethlehem without her husband and sons. She told those friends who barely recognized her, "Don't call me Naomi. . . . Instead, call me Mara, for the Almighty has made life very bitter for me. I went away full, but the LORD has brought me home empty" (Ruth 1:20-21). Nothing about Naomi's family had worked out the way she wanted it to, and she found it impossible to believe that God could actually be working out a plan for her life that was better than her own.

Now Naomi's friends gathered around her to celebrate the birth of a baby to Ruth and Boaz, a child who would perpetuate the name of her late husband, Elimelech, in the land. As they celebrated, they deemed having Ruth as a daughter-in-law better for Naomi than having seven sons. "Seven sons" was another way of saying "the perfect family." They were telling Naomi that God's plan for her family and her life was better than any plan she might have had. God gave the women around Naomi the eyes to see that he was doing something much bigger than just the redemption of her own little family. Through this baby would come a greater Redeemer who would make this blessing available to all the families of the earth.

Whenever we're tempted to become bitter and see ourselves as cheated by God because our family is not living up to what we had hoped and dreamed, the story of Ruth reminds us that God is at work behind the scenes of our disappointments, working out his good plans.

※ ※ ※

Praise you, Lord, for providing a Redeemer for your people, which includes our little family. Throughout Scripture, I can see that you are committed to accomplishing your work in the world through less-than-perfect families. You work in and through situations filled with heartache and need, disappointments and difficulties. Help us to believe that we don't have to have the perfect family to enjoy your perfect peace.

You Honor Your Sons above Me

The sons of Eli were worthless men. They did not know the LORD. The custom of the priests with the people was that when any man offered sacrifice, the priest's servant would come, while the meat was boiling, with a three-pronged fork in his hand, and he would thrust it into the pan or kettle or cauldron or pot. All that the fork brought up the priest would take for himself. . . . Now Eli was very old, and he kept hearing all that his sons were doing to all Israel, and how they lay with the women who were serving at the entrance to the tent of meeting. 1 SAMUEL 2:12-14, 22, ESV

IT WAS A TRAGIC SCENE. Eli was the high priest serving in the Tabernacle. This was the tent in which God had come down to dwell among his people, the place where God's people went to have their sin dealt with. Eli had two sons serving with him. They lived at the one place on earth where it would seem impossible to avoid a life-altering encounter with the living God. And yet we read that they "did not know the LORD." Their appetites for rich food and illicit sex—rather than an appetite for God—dominated their lives.

It's not just the sinful passions and patterns of these two sons we see in this scene. We also see a brokenhearted, confused, perhaps even embarrassed, but ultimately complacent father. Eli knew what they were doing—taking the best portions of the sacrificed meat for themselves and seducing women. He knew their actions were an offense to God and a disservice to the people of God, but he didn't act. He didn't immediately plead with them to repent. Finally, the Lord sent a man to Eli who spoke for God, asking, "Why then do you scorn my sacrifices and my offerings that I commanded for my dwelling, and *honor your sons above me* by fattening yourselves on the choicest parts of every offering of my people Israel?" (verse 29, ESV, emphasis added). This reveals how the Lord saw Eli's complacency. Eli honored his sons above God. Sadly, he feared the wrath or rejection of his own sons more than he feared God.

⌘ ⌘ ⌘

Lord, please save ________ from growing up in the church without truly knowing you. Help ________ to value your sacrifice for sin and to fear abusing it. And give me the courage to not merely complain about sinful behavior, but to confront it, rebuke it, and do what is right to restrain it. I never want to honor my children above you! May you be honored in our home and in our hearts. May we truly know you so that we will long to please you.

Did Not Yet Know the Lord

Now in those days messages from the LORD were very rare, and visions were quite uncommon. One night Eli, who was almost blind by now, had gone to bed. The lamp of God had not yet gone out, and Samuel was sleeping in the Tabernacle near the Ark of God. Suddenly the LORD called out, "Samuel!" . . . Samuel did not yet know the LORD because he had never had a message from the LORD before. 1 SAMUEL 3:1-4, 7

WE WANT OUR CHILDREN TO KNOW THE LORD. We want them to recognize his voice speaking to them. We don't want them to be like Eli's sons, who lived according to their own pleasures and did not know the Lord. Instead, we want them to be like Samuel— listening to hear God speak and willing to obey God's Word when it is heard.

But what does it mean today to hear the voice of God speaking? How does this happen?

It is clear that on this occasion the word of the Lord came to Samuel in an audible voice. He did not merely have a subjective sense that God was speaking to him, which is the way many people describe receiving what they are quite sure is a divine message. What we must understand, and help our children to understand, is that "Long ago, at many times and in many ways, God spoke to our fathers by the prophets, but in these last days he has spoken to us by his Son" (Hebrews 1:1-2, ESV).

Direct guidance of individuals by dreams, visions, and prophetic words decreased as the repository of God's revealed will grew. Today we have the whole of the Old and New Testament Scriptures. God leads his people today by his Word. He continues to speak to us and to our children powerfully and personally as we open up the Bible and it becomes living and active in our lives. So we should prepare our children to hear the Lord speak, and we should impress upon them the expectation that God will speak to them personally and powerfully through his Word.

※ ※ ※

Speak, Lord, your servant is listening. When we open up your Word together as a family, you are speaking to us just as powerfully and personally as Samuel heard you speaking to him. We don't want _____ to be like Eli's sons, who could have heard you but through defiance and disobedience forfeited that privilege and therefore never knew you. Instead, Lord, open _____'s ears to hear you speaking through your Word today, tomorrow, and every day of his life.

Getting Rid of God

*After the Philistines captured the Ark of God, they took it from the battleground
at Ebenezer to the town of Ashdod. They carried the Ark of God into the temple of
Dagon and placed it beside an idol of Dagon. But when the citizens of Ashdod went
to see it the next morning, Dagon had fallen with his face to the ground in front of the
Ark of the LORD! So they took Dagon and put him in his place again.* 1 SAMUEL 5:1-3

THE PHILISTINE SOLDIERS assumed they had prevailed over Israelite forces because their
god Dagon had proven superior to Yahweh. So they placed the Ark of the Covenant,
which represented Yahweh himself, next to the statue of Dagon as one of his worshipers.
But the next morning when they came to Dagon's temple, the idol was facedown before
the Ark, apparently bowing before it. So what did the Philistines do? They propped
Dagon back up. But that didn't work either. The next morning Dagon was facedown
again. But this time his head and hands had broken off.

The Philistines had the presence of God in their midst exposing the impotence of
their false god. So did they get rid of their false god to worship the one true God? "The
rulers discussed it and replied, 'Move it to the town of Gath'" (1 Samuel 5:8). They went
to great lengths to keep their sin and get rid of God.

It is a grace from God when he exposes the powerlessness of our idols. It doesn't feel
like grace; it feels like conviction or even loss. We find ourselves grasping and desperate. But then we have a choice. We can turn away from whatever we're looking to for
significance and security and turn instead toward God to meet our needs. Or we can
keep trying to prop up our idol, giving it another chance to satisfy us. We can do everything in our power to rid God from our lives—or at least some parts of them—or we
can invite God to have his way in the whole of our lives.

❊ ❊ ❊

*Lord, we sometimes fool ourselves into thinking that you can comfortably coexist among
our idols, that your supreme holiness can be compartmentalized, that your powerful hands
can be tied so as not to interfere with the things we've decided we must have to be happy.*

*As we pray for you to show yourself strong in _____'s life, we know that will
mean knocking down the idols in her life, and that they will not be struck down without
a struggle. Show us what it means to encourage her as you deal with her idols one by one.*

Those the Father Has Given Me

Jesus replied, "I am the bread of life. Whoever comes to me will never be hungry again. Whoever believes in me will never be thirsty. But you haven't believed in me even though you have seen me. However, those the Father has given me will come to me, and I will never reject them." JOHN 6:35-37

"THOSE THE FATHER has given me will come to me." As parents we can't help but read this statement and wonder if our children fall into this blessed group. We want to know what we can do to make this happen. But we're not really in this picture. We discover in this passage what God the Father has done, what our child must do, and what Jesus has promised to do. The Father has given, the sinner comes, and the Son receives.

Only God the Father can give our child to Jesus. He is sovereign over the work of our child's salvation, and he will not let his ultimate purposes for anyone fail. He does not wait for his chosen ones to come to Jesus. If he did, they never would. He chooses them for his own, and he secures their coming. He draws them with his irresistible grace.

But our children must come. We simply can't do it for them. They must take the Bread of Life offered to them in the person and work of Christ and eat. They must take the cup, believing that Jesus will satisfy the deepest part of them, and drink.

And what does Jesus do? He knows whom the Father has given to him, and he is watching with his arms outstretched for the first movement in the heart. And when they come to him, he keeps them. "I will never reject them," he says. But really what he's saying is stronger than that. It's more like "I will never ever reject them"—not when he sees how weak our child's faith is, not when our child is slow to change or grow, not when our child fails in some big way. When our child has been given by the Father and is being kept by the Son, he or she can never fall or be driven away.

❇ ❇ ❇

Lord, your words shake us out of our self-reliant, self-determining, self-exalting, self-absorbed presumptions about what our reason, our wills, and our persuasion can do. We simply cannot provide the decisive impulse for _____ to come to Christ. Only you can give that. So we ask you to give it. Draw _____ to yourself in an unmistakable way. And help us to trust the path you take _____ on. Help us to trust your timing. Help us to trust your keeping power.

Anyone Who Feeds on Me

Jesus said again, "I tell you the truth, unless you eat the flesh of the Son of Man and drink his blood, you cannot have eternal life within you. But anyone who eats my flesh and drinks my blood has eternal life, and I will raise that person at the last day. For my flesh is true food, and my blood is true drink. Anyone who eats my flesh and drinks my blood remains in me, and I in him. I live because of the living Father who sent me; in the same way, anyone who feeds on me will live because of me." JOHN 6:53-57

"THIS BREAD, which I will offer so the world may live, is my flesh" (verse 51). Jesus' words made no sense to those surrounding him. They were just hoping for another miracle like the one they'd experienced the day before when Jesus fed five thousand people by multiplying five barley loaves and two fish. Jesus was pushing them to think more deeply about what this miracle really meant. And he's pushing us, too.

We don't eat this bread simply by listening to his teaching on the hillside or by observing his miracles among the masses. To eat the Bread of Life means that we must savor his sacrificial death as our life. Jesus offers himself to us and invites us to nourish our souls with the benefits of his atoning death. But sometimes we respond to this offer like the people of his day did. This is not what we were hoping to get from Jesus. We had a different miracle in mind, a miracle that would take care of what we see as our most pressing problem today: the lack of work or money in our bank account, the struggle going on at school, the health issue that just isn't getting any better. As we see Jesus offering himself to us as the Bread of Life, perhaps we grumble on the inside. So often we want to use God to get from him what we think we need, when *he* is what we need. And he offers himself freely.

What we want for ourselves and for our children is far more than simply believing that certain events that happened long ago are true. What we need and want is true communion with Jesus so that we feed on him, share fellowship with him, and draw strength from him.

※ ※ ※

Here you are, Jesus, offering yourself to us as the true bread that will save and sustain. All we need to do is take and eat. Forgive us for refusing to believe that you are what will satisfy and sustain us over the long haul.

MAY 12

Even His Brothers Didn't Believe in Him

Jesus traveled around Galilee. He wanted to stay out of Judea, where the Jewish leaders were plotting his death. But soon it was time for the Jewish Festival of Shelters, and Jesus' brothers said to him, "Leave here and go to Judea, where your followers can see your miracles! You can't become famous if you hide like this! If you can do such wonderful things, show yourself to the world!" For even his brothers didn't believe in him. JOHN 7:1-5

JESUS HAD FAMILY MEMBERS who didn't believe in him. They had lived with him for thirty years yet stubbornly refused to recognize him for who he really was. In fact, they were embarrassed by his actions and his words. They just wanted to get rid of him.

Perhaps sibling rivalry got in the way. It must have been very hard to have Jesus for a brother. He always did the right thing. He always obeyed his parents. He always acted out of humility, putting others first. It must have made his siblings increasingly self-conscious of their own sinful motives and actions. Perhaps Mary and Joseph treated Jesus differently from his siblings. When family stories were being swapped, it would have been hard to compete with a star appearing at your brother's birth.

Those of us who wonder if our family members would put their faith in Christ if only we were a better witness, if only we had the words to convince them, if only we were all-around better Christians, can find consolation as we look into the unbelief in Jesus' own family. Evidently having a perfect witness in the household doesn't guarantee that our loved ones will see and embrace Christ.

But we can also find hope as we consider the rest of the story. While it must have seemed unlikely that Jesus' brothers would ever become his disciples, after his resurrection, they did! In Jesus' own family we find hope for our own as we see that long-term resistance to Christ can give way to a glad embrace of him as Savior.

❊ ❊ ❊

Lord, we sometimes grow weary in our prayers for those in our family who remain far away from you. We sometimes think it is going to take a bigger miracle on your part to save our unbelieving family members than it took to save us—that somehow we were more inclined toward you, an easier project on the sliding scale of salvation challenges. We repent of our arrogance and prayerlessness and hopelessness. We ask you to do for our family members what you did for the members of your own family—open their eyes to see and believe in you.

Appearing Spiritual

The men of Israel were pressed to exhaustion that day, because Saul had placed them under an oath, saying, "Let a curse fall on anyone who eats before evening—before I have full revenge on my enemies." . . . But Jonathan had not heard his father's command, and he dipped the end of his stick into a piece of honeycomb and ate the honey. 1 SAMUEL 14:24, 27

SAUL SHOULD HAVE BEEN leading his people into battle against the Philistines, confident that the Lord would give his people victory. Instead he was hiding back at the camp, gripped with indecision and grasping at vain gestures of spirituality as a means to secure a military victory. Saul imposed a fast on his soldiers, seeking to appear as a man wholly dedicated to the Lord. He thought their fasting plus the presence of a priest in his priestly garments would impress God. Saul is a tragic example of a person who tried to appear religious but who lacked a living faith in God and a heart to honor him.

Saul's son was quite different. Jonathan was confident in the Lord's strength. Though he was young and had an even younger armor bearer with him, together they launched an assault on the Philistine camp, saying, "Perhaps the LORD will help us, for nothing can hinder the LORD. He can win a battle whether he has many warriors or only a few!" (verse 6). Later, when Jonathan learned about his father's foolish oath to put to death anyone who had eaten that day, which left his army faint with hunger and unable to fight, Jonathan said, "My father has made trouble for us all. . . . A command like that only hurts us" (verse 29).

This father and son stand in stark contrast to each other: a father who wanted to appear to honor the Lord but had no real passion for God or confidence in him, and a son whose heart had been emboldened by God's promises and who fully expected God to be true to his word.

We may be older than our children, but sometimes we discover they actually have deeper faith, greater confidence in God, and keen perception about our own attempts to appear more spiritual than we really are.

❋ ❋ ❋

Lord, may ________ never be forced into saying, "My father [or mother] has made trouble for us all!" Instead, make me wise so I will not make foolish promises. Give me genuine faith so I will not settle for vain gestures of spirituality. Strengthen my confidence in you as the enemy of my soul wages war against me and my family.

The Lord Looks at the Heart

The LORD said to Samuel, "Don't judge by his appearance or height, for I have rejected him. The LORD doesn't see things the way you see them. People judge by outward appearance, but the LORD looks at the heart." 1 SAMUEL 16:7

GOD HAD REJECTED SAUL and was preparing to give his people a king after his own heart: the kind of leader through whom he wanted to reign over his people. When Samuel got to Bethlehem and saw Jesse and his sons, Samuel was sure he saw Saul's replacement. David's oldest brother, Eliab, was tall and handsome and looked positively kingly. But the Lord told Samuel that Eliab was not what he was looking for.

It is the way of human beings to make external and superficial judgments. Certainly our children pick up on it when we make these types of judgments about people based on the way they appear physically, financially, or socially. This is not the way of the Lord. The living God looks at a person's heart to see what his or her true character is, what his or her real life is all about.

Some of us look so put together on the outside that no one would guess what is going on inside our hearts. People around us can't always see the stubborn disobedience, the steady stream of defeats in our battles against ongoing sin, the stifling darkness that permeates our inner lives. But God does. Likewise, other people can't always see the secret sacrifices, the costly surrenders, and all the little deaths to self that shape those hearts that have been invaded and ruled by King Jesus. But you can be sure that God does.

※ ※ ※

Lord, I know that the heart is deceitfully wicked and that I fool myself when I think I completely know my own heart. But I am grateful that you do and that you show mercy to those whose hearts are not pure. As I seek to walk in your ways, would you close the gap between the image I try to portray and the reality of my heart's condition before you? And as _____ considers the truth that you see the heart, may that realization bring comfort rather than condemnation. Give _____ a heart of integrity before you.

Threatened with Lifelong Slavery

Goliath, a Philistine champion from Gath, came out of the Philistine ranks to face the forces of Israel. He was over nine feet tall! He wore a bronze helmet, and his bronze coat of mail weighed 125 pounds. . . . Goliath stood and shouted a taunt across to the Israelites. "Why are you all coming out to fight?" he called. "I am the Philistine champion, but you are only the servants of Saul. Choose one man to come down here and fight me! If he kills me, then we will be your slaves. But if I kill him, you will be our slaves!" 1 SAMUEL 17:4-5, 8-9

GOLIATH WAS UNDILUTED EVIL. He came out day after day mocking the people of God. He was covered head to toe with bronze armor that looked like the scales of a snake. He was like a nine-foot-tall serpent.

But with one smooth stone hurled at Goliath, David crushed the head of the serpent. The victory won single-handedly by the Lord's anointed became the shared victory of God's people. They didn't go out to battle, yet they could claim victory vicariously through the one who faced the enemy as their representative.

Our families face an enemy—an army of enemies, in fact—that is as real, as powerful, and as terrifying as Goliath. "For we are not fighting against flesh-and-blood enemies, but against evil rulers and authorities of the unseen world, against mighty powers in this dark world, and against evil spirits in the heavenly places" (Ephesians 6:12). Our enemy is not covered in bronze and hurling heavy spears; he is armed with darkness and deception. He hurls condemnation and lies at us and tempts us to indulge in pleasures that only bring pain. He threatens to enslave us to destructive addictions and defeating patterns and incapacitating fears.

And we would turn and run, certain that we were doomed, certain that we were going to be slaves forever to binging and purging, to pornographic lust, to selfish ambition, to self-righteous snobbery, to materialism and greed . . . except that we have a champion. Just when we are tempted to give way to despair, we hear the voice of the greater son of David saying, "Let no man's heart fail because of him. Your servant will go and fight" (verse 32, ESV).

❉ ❉ ❉

Jesus, whenever I am tempted to despair, thinking we will never be free of the sins that enslave members of this family, I will look to you, our champion. You have defeated the enemy that threatened us with lifelong slavery to sin and death. Our victory and security come from being united by faith to you.

MAY 16

1 Samuel 18:5–19:24
John 8:31-59
Psalm 112:1-10
Proverbs 15:12-14

They Do Not Fear Bad News

Praise the LORD!
How joyful are those who fear the LORD
and delight in obeying his commands. . . .
They do not fear bad news;
they confidently trust the LORD to care for them. PSALM 112:1, 7

PARENTS WHO HAVE REPEATEDLY RECEIVED bad news—from the doctor, from the school, from the counselor, from the police—find themselves always bracing for more bad news. Anticipating the next blow can become a way of life. But this is not the life being held out to us in Psalm 112.

This psalm presents an idyllic picture of the life of those who put their hope in the gospel and thereby receive the righteousness of Christ by faith. As is typical in the Old Testament, the prosperity promised is described largely in material terms. Yet it does not ignore how the person who fears the Lord is made prosperous in spiritual and emotional ways. Such a person, according to this psalm, does not fear bad news.

And surely the blessedness of not living in fear of bad news is something we want and need as parents. We want the blessedness of confident trust that the Lord is committed to caring for us and for our children. We want the blessedness of not always living on edge, but instead living at peace, confident that our children are in God's hands. The answer to our ongoing anxieties is not a hoped-for turn of events, but rather a God-centered stance of trust.

Surely what our children need most is a joyful, hopeful, peaceful parent who trusts and rests in God. But how will this happen? "Faith comes from hearing, that is, hearing the Good News about Christ" (Romans 10:17). We need to drink from a steady stream of God's Word, which assures us that he is always bringing life out of death, healing out of brokenness, and hope out of despair. He is a God who loves to bless his people. And when we know this deep in our souls, instead of living in fear of bad news, we live in the confident expectation that he is at work.

❋ ❋ ❋

Lord, increase my fear of you, my sense of awe at your power, and my glad obedience to your Word. I know that as my fear of you increases, my anxieties about the problems we're facing today and my fears about the future will give way to confident trust that you are at work and that you care for us.

That the Power of God Could Be Seen

*As Jesus was walking along, he saw a man who had been blind from birth. "Rabbi,"
his disciples asked him, "why was this man born blind? Was it because of his own sins
or his parents' sins?" "It was not because of his sins or his parents' sins," Jesus answered.
"This happened so the power of God could be seen in him."* JOHN 9:1-3

THE DISCIPLES THOUGHT like we think—that suffering has to be somebody's fault. They
thought this blind man was being punished for sin—they just didn't know whose. In
fact, this assumption must be deeply ingrained in how we think as humans because it
is exactly what Job's friends thought—that Job's suffering was Job's fault, that he was
being punished. And we get it, too, don't we?

Did you think your miscarriage or your child's disability was God punishing you for
sin in your past? Have you lived in fear that something bad is going to happen in your
family because you think that's what you deserve? Is that how things work with God?
Does God punish us for our sin with suffering in this life?

If you are united to Christ by faith, you should never think that God is punishing you
for your sin. How can you be sure? Because someone has already been punished for your
sin. The punishment for your bad choices—your utter apathy toward God; your outright
rebellion; the ugliest, most shameful things you've said or done—has all been laid on Jesus.
He was punished for your sin so you don't have to be. Your loving Father will discipline
you to make you more holy, but he will not punish you simply to make you pay.

In asking who was to blame for the man's disability, the disciples were focused on
finding the cause. But Jesus wanted to focus on the purpose for his suffering, which
was to put the power of God on display. The larger miracle than restoring this man's
physical sight was opening his spiritual eyes to see who Jesus was. He was given faith to
believe. This man went from wanting to get something *from* Jesus to meet what he saw
as his greatest need, to worshiping Jesus for *being* everything he truly needed. Can you
see that this is the miracle Jesus wants to accomplish in your family and in your heart?

❊ ❊ ❊

*Lord, we long for your power to be put on display in our lives. Give sight where we are
blind. Give life where there is deadness. Put your power on display in _____'s life
today by generating in her the fruit of your Holy Spirit.*

They Know His Voice

The one who enters through the gate is the shepherd of the sheep. The gatekeeper opens the gate for him, and the sheep recognize his voice and come to him. He calls his own sheep by name and leads them out. After he has gathered his own flock, he walks ahead of them, and they follow him because they know his voice. JOHN 10:2-4

THERE WERE PLENTY of shepherds in Judea, a rocky plateau that wasn't very good for growing crops but provided grazing land for sheep. Shepherds had to be relentlessly vigilant to protect their sheep from precipices and crevices into which they could fall. They also had to keep watch for predators or thieves. Every village around the Judean hills had a sheepfold where various shepherds brought their herds each night to keep them safe. In the morning, the shepherds would call their particular sheep out from among the animals of various herds kept in the fold overnight. Because the sheep recognized their shepherd's voice, they would come to him, and he would lead them out.

This is the beautiful picture Jesus paints to illustrate his intimate knowing of those who belong to him. Jesus wants us to know that he is not just our King ruling over us. He's not just our Redeemer paying the ransom for us. He's not just our Mediator making peace for us. He's our Shepherd, taking care of us, calling out to us, feeding us, caring for our wounds, and protecting us from falling and from predators.

As good as we seek to be as parents, our children need something more. They need a Shepherd. And they have one. The Good Shepherd will care for them in ways that we can't and at times when we can't. He will protect them from pitfalls we don't see and wolves we don't recognize. Best of all, we can be sure that when he gathers his flock, he will call his sheep by name and lead them.

✸ ✸ ✸

Great Shepherd of the sheep, I find such peace in knowing that it is not all up to me to care for and protect _____. You are the Good Shepherd. You know your sheep, and your sheep know your voice. Good Shepherd, call out to _____ to come into the safety of your fold. Feed _____. Care for _____'s wounds. Protect _____ from harm. Lead _____ into the abundant life that is found only as a sheep of your fold.

No One Can Snatch Them

My sheep listen to my voice; I know them, and they follow me. I give them eternal life, and they will never perish. No one can snatch them away from me, for my Father has given them to me, and he is more powerful than anyone else. No one can snatch them from the Father's hand. The Father and I are one. JOHN 10:27-30

IT IS A BEAUTIFUL THING to be held in the Father's hand. In fact, the Father and the Son provide a two-handed grip that gives ultimate security to our children. If they are sheep in the flock of God, we don't have to be afraid that something or someone will come along and sever that saving relationship. Though physical death will one day come, our children will never ultimately perish. There are no exceptions to this assurance and no end to it either. "Never" is a very long time, but it is not longer than preserving grace will last. Likewise "no one" is a very broad category, broader than the list of potential predators:

- Illegal drugs or alcohol cannot snatch our children from the Father's hand.
- An atheist or agnostic philosophy cannot snatch our children from the Father's hand.
- An unbelieving boyfriend, girlfriend, or spouse cannot snatch our children from the Father's hand.
- Sexual experimentation cannot snatch our children from the Father's hand.
- A drunk driver or deadly disease cannot snatch our children from the Father's hand.

Even our children's own sins and failures do not have the power to snatch them from the saving grip of God. A double-handed force keeps our children safe against all danger. Nothing and no one will ever snatch them out of the hand of Jesus or the hand of his Father. "Who shall separate us from the love of Christ?" (Romans 8:35, NIV). No one!

❀ ❀ ❀

Father, into your hands I commit my spirit. Into your hands I entrust _____. Your sheep listen to your voice. Give _____ ears that are tuned to the sound of your voice. Your sheep follow you. Train _____'s heart to follow after you. I cannot force _____ into your fold or into your hand. But I'm trusting you, as a good shepherd, to take hold of _____.

MAY 20

The Resurrection and the Life

Martha said to Jesus, "Lord, if only you had been here, my brother would not have died. But even now I know that God will give you whatever you ask." Jesus told her, "Your brother will rise again." "Yes," Martha said, "he will rise when everyone else rises, at the last day." Jesus told her, "I am the resurrection and the life. Anyone who believes in me will live, even after dying. Everyone who lives in me and believes in me will never ever die. Do you believe this, Martha?" JOHN 11:21-26

MARTHA BELIEVED there would be a grand resurrection on a day far in the future. But she couldn't seem to find any comfort in it—at least not enough to balance out the pain she felt in the present. Her response exposed her belief that resurrection was a completely future event, offering no comfort in the here and now of deep grief. Martha simply couldn't find solace in the future tense.

But when Jesus says he is the Resurrection and the Life, he is speaking not only about something he will do in the future. He is telling us not just who he will be, but who he is now and forever. He is life after death and life right now. Jesus is life to our bodies and our souls. He is the source from which all life springs: "In him we live and move and exist" (Acts 17:28). Once we are made alive in Christ, our lives can never be extinguished. Jesus is not just the giver of victory over death in an obscure future. He provides victory over death in the actual present.

Resurrection can seem so religious, so unreal, so far removed when we stand by a grave with our family. It's possible to have a theological understanding of resurrection life but to find no joy or comfort in it, to have no ability to rest in it, or simply to not believe it. And Jesus knows our belief in him as the Resurrection and the Life is pivotal—foundational—to how we face grief and sorrow. So he asks us along with Martha, "Do you believe this?"

❊ ❊ ❊

Lord, we do believe. Help our unbelief. Help us respond to death in our family in a way that reflects a genuine belief in resurrection life. Give us the grace we need to grieve with hope and not as those who have no hope.

Finding Strength

David was now in great danger because all his men were very bitter about losing their
sons and daughters, and they began to talk of stoning him. But David found strength
in the LORD his God. Then he said to Abiathar the priest, "Bring me the ephod!" So
Abiathar brought it. Then David asked the LORD, "Should I chase after this band
of raiders? Will I catch them?" And the LORD told him, "Yes, go after them. You will
surely recover everything that was taken from you!" 1 SAMUEL 30:6-8

IN 1 SAMUEL 28, we learn that Saul was in difficult circumstances and desperate to
know what to do. Samuel had spoken for God to Saul, but now Samuel was dead. Saul
had slaughtered all but one of the priests in a murderous rage, so there was no priest to
go before God to inquire on his behalf. So what did Saul do? He sought help from a
medium, a woman who called on the dead.

At the same time, David was also in difficult circumstances and desperate to know
what to do. The Amalekites had raided his camp and carried off the women and children. In their grief, David's men were looking for someone to blame and began to talk
about stoning David. But rather than seek help from a medium, "David found strength
in the LORD his God." David called the only living priest and sought out God's voice
by means of the priestly ephod. We don't know exactly how the process worked, but we
know he received God's answer.

When we're desperate to know what to do with and for our kids, we can consult
counselors, read books by parenting experts, and talk to our friends. But while we might
get some ideas or strategies from them, none of these resources can provide us with the
insight or power most necessary. We need the wisdom that comes from God's Word,
the divine power that comes to rest on us when we are joined to Christ by faith, and
the peace that is found only in resting in the promises of God.

❈ ❈ ❈

Lord, I'm so grateful for the wise counselors you've given us—the caring friends, the
excellent models, and the many other resources that give us direction on this parenting
journey. But we don't want to depend primarily or solely on these things. We are wholly
dependent on you for the strength we need to parent _____ over the long haul. It's
your wisdom we seek.

Dying Young

Jesus replied, "Now the time has come for the Son of Man to enter into his glory. I tell you the truth, unless a kernel of wheat is planted in the soil and dies, it remains alone. But its death will produce many new kernels—a plentiful harvest of new lives. Those who love their life in this world will lose it. Those who care nothing for their life in this world will keep it for eternity." JOHN 12:23-25

WHEN THE WORLD talks about dying young, it is cast as a tragedy, a promising life cut short. But when Jesus calls our sons and daughters to die, even in their youth, it is not a tragedy. Instead it is an invitation to a life lived with no regrets, a life of adventure and intensity, a life that will matter into eternity.

To die young is to determine at a young age that this life is not about pleasing ourselves, comforting ourselves, or enjoying ourselves. It is about beginning to die now to self-interest, self-love, and self-importance. It is to determine that life will be about much more than a good education, a nice house, some winning seasons for a favorite sports team, and saving for a comfortable retirement. Instead it will be about giving one's life away in ways that will bear fruit for the gospel of Christ.

The call of Jesus to our children to care nothing for their lives in this world so they can anticipate everything in the life to come goes against the grain of all our society says about raising our children to be "successful." So when our children embrace this call to die to themselves early, we find that we are being called to die too. We may be called to die to our dream of having our grown children nearby as they chart a course to take the gospel to people on the other side of the world. We may be called to die to our desires for our children's financial security as they follow Christ into work that forces them to live radically by faith. But as we die to ourselves, we will discover that we're living the abundant life.

✳ ✳ ✳

Lord, I pray for _____ that he would "die young." I'm asking you to begin a lifetime of sanctifying work right now. Let the years of _____'s youth not be wasted or bring only regret. Instead, make them fruitful years that generate a plentiful harvest in your Kingdom.

And, Lord, I know that I'm not too old to die young. Give me the supernatural power I need to put to death anything that keeps me from being fruitful for your Kingdom.

He Began to Wash

Jesus knew that the Father had given him authority over everything and that he had come from God and would return to God. So he got up from the table, took off his robe, wrapped a towel around his waist, and poured water into a basin. Then he began to wash the disciples' feet, drying them with the towel he had around him. JOHN 13:3-5

WASHING THE DIRT off guests' feet was a task reserved for only the lowest-ranking Gentile servants. Jewish slaves were usually exempted from this demeaning duty. But there were no slaves in the borrowed room where Jesus and his disciples had gathered to share the Passover meal. So there was no slave to wash the feet of the disciples—no slave except the one who, though he was God, did not think of equality with God as something to cling to, but instead gave up his divine privileges and took the humble position of a slave.

Even as Jesus adopted the dress of a slave and took the position of a slave to wash everyone's dirty feet, he was preparing to die the kind of death that was usually reserved for slaves—crucifixion. "He humbled himself in obedience to God and died a criminal's death on a cross" (Philippians 2:8).

Probably all of the disciples felt uncomfortable as Jesus took hold of their dirty, smelly feet. But Peter was the one who resisted, saying that Jesus would never wash his. Clearly Peter didn't recognize that Jesus was doing far more than washing feet. He was giving his disciples a picture of the way he would, in his shameful death on the cross, provide the cleansing they needed most of all—a washing away of their dirt and shame that couldn't be seen with the human eye, a cleansing of the soul.

Sometimes we give our children the idea that the Christian life is all about what they must do for God. But at the heart of what it means to be a Christian is the willingness to accept the cleansing touch of Jesus so he can do for us what we cannot do for ourselves. "The Son of Man came not to be served but to serve others and to give his life as a ransom for many" (Mark 10:45).

※ ※ ※

Lord, I want _____ to serve you. But more importantly, I want _____ to be served by you, to experience the cleansing that only you can provide. Help me to get the gospel right as I talk about it day by day with _____. It's not primarily about what _____ must do for you, but about what you have done for _____, and what _____ must receive from you.

143

They Anointed Him King

Then all the tribes of Israel went to David at Hebron and told him, "We are your own flesh and blood. In the past, when Saul was our king, you were the one who really led the forces of Israel. And the LORD told you, 'You will be the shepherd of my people Israel. You will be Israel's leader.'" So there at Hebron, King David made a covenant before the LORD with all the elders of Israel. And they anointed him king of Israel. 2 SAMUEL 5:1-3

DAVID WAS A TEENAGER when the prophet Samuel anointed him to be king over Israel. But many years later, he still was not ruling on the throne. After Saul's death, David was finally made king of Judah in the south, but Ishbosheth, one of Saul's sons, was made king of Israel over the ten tribes in the north. "That was the beginning of a long war between those who were loyal to Saul and those loyal to David" (2 Samuel 3:1). When Ishbosheth was eventually killed, the people of the northern tribes had to decide if they would accept the king God had chosen and anointed and submit to his rule for their lives.

It's the same decision we, and each of our children, have to make. Will we submit to the rule of God's chosen king—King Jesus? Or will we continue to reject his rule? Anyone who has ever parented a child—from toddler to teenager—knows that we are all born with a determination to rule ourselves. Our children are naturally self-sovereigns until the day they come under the rule of Jesus. We are all in need of grace to put an end to our dangerous hope for autonomy.

Every day, as our children learn to accept our authority as their parents, they're learning what it means to submit to an authority greater than their own. And as we use our influence for their good, we're teaching them something about the goodness of life under the supremacy of King Jesus.

※ ※ ※

Lord, even as I begin to pray for _____ to grow in glad submission to King Jesus, I realize that I, too, have a heart and a will more inclined to autonomy than authority. Forgive me for believing the lie that your rule in my life will somehow diminish my life and my freedom rather than give me life and freedom. May my life of glad submission to you provide a picture to _____ of the joy of having you as King over all.

Secure Forever

For when you die and are buried with your ancestors, I will raise up one of your descendants, your own offspring, and I will make his kingdom strong. . . . Your house and your kingdom will continue before me for all time, and your throne will be secure forever. 2 SAMUEL 7:12, 16

GOD PROMISED DAVID that he would make his name great and give his people a place of security. He did that in David's day. God promised that he would establish a dynasty from David, that his son would sit on his throne and would build a house for him. God did that in Solomon's day, when Solomon sat on David's throne and built the Temple in Jerusalem. God promised that when David's son sinned, he would discipline him, which he did with Solomon and many other Davidic kings who followed him. But while this dynasty was one of the longest-lasting ancient empires—four hundred years—there did come a day when no son of David was sitting on the throne in Israel. It raises the question: What happened to God's promise to David that his house, his kingdom, and his throne would last forever?

Over many years the people of Israel struggled to hold on to the promise. Finally an angel came to Mary, telling her that she was going to have a son, saying, "The Lord God will give to him the throne of his father David, and he will reign over the house of Jacob forever, and of his kingdom there will be no end" (Luke 1:32-33, ESV). This was going to be the Son, the King, whom generations had longed and waited for ever since God made his covenant with David!

Even now this Son of David sits on the throne at the right hand of God. And because we know that Jesus is on the throne, we can stop our worrying and our vain attempts to control everything. The one who is seated on the throne is not only able to supply our needs and protect us; he has at his disposal everything needed to fulfill all of his promises. Because he is on the throne, our joy doesn't have to be so tied to our circumstances, and our sense of security doesn't have to be so easily shaken. The Lord rules over all.

※ ※ ※

Lord, you reign over our difficult circumstances. You reign over our ongoing conflict. You reign over our carefully crafted plans. And you can be trusted. You are a good King.

MAY 26

It Will Be Granted

Yes, I am the vine; you are the branches. Those who remain in me, and I in them, will produce much fruit. For apart from me you can do nothing. Anyone who does not remain in me is thrown away like a useless branch and withers. Such branches are gathered into a pile to be burned. But if you remain in me and my words remain in you, you may ask for anything you want, and it will be granted! JOHN 15:5-7

WE PRAY AND PRAY for our kids and wait for God to answer. And then we read these words of Jesus, and it seems both too good to be true and somehow out of our reach. What is Jesus really saying?

Jesus connects two things: his words and our prayers. He's saying that if we will listen to his words in such a way that they become a part of who we are, he will listen to our prayers. When we think God is holding out on us, it may be that we're asking for what is simply not best for us. Our prayers may be too small for his massive blessing to fit inside. Only biblical desires are big enough for God to satisfy. Jesus is promising that as the words of the Bible take root in us in such a way that they begin to shape our wants, and therefore shape our prayers, our petitions become grantable.

We live in a world in which so many voices want our attention—hundreds of channels on TV, the Internet, e-mail, and cell phones. But Christ calls us to tune ourselves to hear his voice, to "let the word of Christ dwell in you richly" (Colossians 3:16, ESV). Jesus is seeking to save us from superficiality in our prayers for our children. As the words of Scripture become a part of our thoughts and emotions, we discover that our voice becomes one with his in prayer. Our desires are purified and magnified into his will. Instead of trying so hard to get God to go along with our ideas, we discover that we are being saved from our boring pettiness and small expectations.

❊ ❊ ❊

Lord, I don't want my prayers for _____ to be limited by my own earthbound desires. I want to pray prayers for _____ that are shaped by your desires for _____ as revealed in your Word. I long for the miracle of experiencing the voice of your Word taking precedence over my own inner voice.

He Will Convict

It is best for you that I go away, because if I don't, the Advocate won't come. If I do go away, then I will send him to you. And when he comes, he will convict the world of its sin, and of God's righteousness, and of the coming judgment. . . . When the Spirit of truth comes, he will guide you into all truth. JOHN 16:7-8, 13

AS PARENTS WE HAVE LOTS OF ROLES and responsibilities in the lives of our children. We're meant to provide for and protect them, to teach and train them toward godliness. But sometimes we slip back into thinking that it is up to us to bring about the change they need. We act as if it is solely our responsibility to point out what they should and should not do. We argue as if it is up to us to convince them of what is true. Sometimes our earnest desire to help usurps the role of the Helper. Sometimes our loving inclination to guide usurps the role of the Spirit of Truth. Sometimes we act as if it is our job to be the Holy Spirit in their lives.

We were never meant to be the Holy Spirit to them. In fact, we can't be. Instead we are meant to trust that the Holy Spirit will do his work of comforting, convicting, teaching, and guiding in their lives.

We are people in need of the Holy Spirit ourselves. We need the Spirit to comfort us and convict us of our own sin. We need the Holy Spirit to guide us into truth. We need the Holy Spirit to pray for us when we don't have the will or the words. And we desperately need the Holy Spirit to empower us to stay quiet when we should not speak. Certainly we can encourage, exhort, and even admonish, but only the Holy Spirit can generate genuine spiritual life where there is deadness. Only the Holy Spirit can instill a desire for the things of God in the hearts of our children.

❊ ❊ ❊

Lord, I officially resign from seeking to be the Holy Spirit in _____'s life. I want to honor you by believing and trusting that you are at work. The same Spirit that hovered over creation and brought forth life and light and beauty is able to hover over _____'s life and bring forth life and light and beauty.

Like Father, Like Son

David's son Absalom had a beautiful sister named Tamar. And Amnon, her half brother, fell desperately in love with her. Amnon became so obsessed with Tamar that he became ill. She was a virgin, and Amnon thought he could never have her. . . . As she was feeding him, he grabbed her and demanded, "Come to bed with me, my darling sister." "No, my brother!" she cried. "Don't be foolish! Don't do this to me! Such wicked things aren't done in Israel." . . . But Amnon wouldn't listen to her, and since he was stronger than she was, he raped her. 2 SAMUEL 13:1-2, 11-12, 14

WHEN WORKING OUR WAY through 2 Samuel, we read in chapter 11 about David sending messengers to get Bathsheba, another man's wife, so that he could sleep with her. Just two chapters later we read about David's son Amnon raping his half sister, Tamar. Surely the placement of these accounts so close together is meant to show us one of the ways in which David experienced a natural consequence of his sin—having a son who committed the same sin he did.

Children tend to become like their parents in many ways. When they have our good looks, our intellectual prowess, or our athletic abilities, we take pride in the ways they are like us. But often we see that our children take after us in the ways we sin as well. And we take no pride in this. It breaks our hearts. But hopefully it does more than that. Hopefully it moves us toward genuine repentance in such a way that our children want to be like us in this way too.

If we had no power outside of ourselves to break the cycle of sin passed down from parent to child, we would be bound to perpetuate our parents' sin, and our children would be bound to commit our pet sins. But we do have a power outside of ourselves. We and our children have access to "the power of the life-giving Spirit" who frees us from "the power of sin that leads to death" (Romans 8:2).

❊ ❊ ❊

Lord, it grieves me to see some of my own sin patterns in _____. It's frustrating and humbling, and a part of me is tempted to despair that the cycle will never be broken. So I'm taking hold of the hope I find in your Word, which assures me that your Spirit provides power to forsake sin, to break the cycle. May the mercy you've shown in response to my repentance loom much larger than my sin.

Our Plans, God's Plan

We can make our plans,
but the LORD determines our steps. PROVERBS 16:9

WE MAKE PLANS FOR OUR KIDS—even if we aren't conscious of them or have never stated them aloud. We have plans for their education and where that will take them vocationally. We have plans for their spiritual development and how that will shape what is important to them. We have plans for their physical development that include the sports we hope they'll play and the bad habits we hope they'll avoid.

Our plans for our kids may be godly, but that doesn't mean our plans are God's plans. And while there's nothing wrong with making plans, God's plans often don't line up with ours. Scripture is full of examples.

Jesus told Peter that his life would not end as he planned: "I tell you the truth, when you were young, you were able to do as you liked; you dressed yourself and went wherever you wanted to go. But when you are old, you will stretch out your hands, and others will dress you and take you where you don't want to go" (John 21:18).

Paul had plans to carry the gospel to Asia. But those plans didn't go as he intended. "Paul and Silas traveled through the area of Phrygia and Galatia, because the Holy Spirit had prevented them from preaching the word in the province of Asia at that time. Then coming to the borders of Mysia, they headed north for the province of Bithynia, but again the Spirit of Jesus did not allow them to go there. So instead, they went on through Mysia to the seaport of Troas" (Acts 16:6-8).

The apostle James warns us about loving our plans too much. "Look here, you who say, 'Today or tomorrow we are going to a certain town and will stay there a year. We will do business there and make a profit.' How do you know what your life will be like tomorrow? Your life is like the morning fog—it's here a little while, then it's gone. What you ought to say is, 'If the Lord wants us to, we will live and do this or that.' Otherwise you are boasting about your own pretentious plans, and all such boasting is evil" (James 4:13-16).

❀ ❀ ❀

Lord, help me to hold on to my plans for _____ loosely. Increase my confidence that your plans for _____ are good even when they don't seem that way to me. Give me the faith I need to trust that as you determine _____'s steps, every step will take _____ closer to you.

Jesus Rescues Failures

Meanwhile, as Simon Peter was standing by the fire warming himself, they asked him again, "You're not one of his disciples, are you?" He denied it, saying, "No, I am not." But one of the household slaves of the high priest, a relative of the man whose ear Peter had cut off, asked, "Didn't I see you out there in the olive grove with Jesus?" Again Peter denied it. And immediately a rooster crowed. JOHN 18:25-27

JESUS HAD TOLD PETER that Peter would deny him. But Peter didn't believe him. After Jesus explained that he had prayed that Peter's faith would not fail, his disciple had said with great confidence, "I'm ready to die for you" (John 13:37). After all, Jesus had given him the name Peter, which means "rock," saying, "Upon this rock I will build my church, and all the powers of hell will not conquer it" (Matthew 16:18). Peter believed he would stand strong.

But after Jesus was arrested, Peter discovered that he was not above denying the one he loved. Luke tells us he wept bitterly. And we feel the crush of his failure with him when we read the story.

Though Peter deemed himself a failure and went back to what he knew best—fishing—that was not the end of his story. A short time later, he looked up and heard Jesus calling to him from the shore. He sat with Jesus, eating the fish Jesus cooked him for breakfast as Jesus called him to feed his sheep. Clearly Jesus had not given up on Peter, despite his failure.

As our children make their way through this life, Satan is always ready to shove their failures in their faces. But Jesus is relentless in his pursuit of his children who have failed him and wonder if he's had it with them for good. Jesus is the great restorer of those who fail but turn to him for forgiveness.

※ ※ ※

Lord, just as Peter's failure did not define him, by faith we believe that our failures will not define us. Instead it is your grace and mercy that will define us, your restoration that will set things right, your commission that will get us going again.

But, Lord, the shame of failure is real. When shame sends _____ running away from you, go after him. Call _____ to yourself. Let _____ know that you are not finished using him, that his failure does not define him.

Near the Cross

Standing near the cross were Jesus' mother, and his mother's sister, Mary (the wife of Clopas), and Mary Magdalene. When Jesus saw his mother standing there beside the disciple he loved, he said to her, "Dear woman, here is your son." And he said to this disciple, "Here is your mother." And from then on this disciple took her into his home.
JOHN 19:25-27

WE MAY BE TEMPTED to think that if we had the perfect child, parenting would be so much easier. But Mary did have the perfect child. And her life was filled with difficulties related to this child. They began with the humiliation of being pregnant before she and Joseph were married. Later, Simeon's words "a sword will pierce your very soul" (Luke 2:35), spoken when Jesus was an infant, must have come to her mind on many sleepless nights. No doubt she wondered what Simeon's words would mean for her.

When Jesus prophesied in their hometown synagogue, surely Mary would have been there. She must have been gripped by terror that day as the people in the synagogue took Jesus to a steep hill, intending to throw him over. Then came the day when Mary went to the house where Jesus was teaching. Instead of coming out to greet her, Jesus pointed to the people gathering around him and said, "These are my mother and brothers. Anyone who does God's will is my brother and sister and mother" (Mark 3:34-35).

What sustained Mary through these experiences? Perhaps she remembered another prophecy Simeon had spoken over her newborn son: "He is a light to reveal God to the nations" (Luke 2:32). She had seen the glory of Jesus. John describes the wedding at Cana, when Jesus turned the water into wine after his mother asked him to act, as "the first time Jesus revealed his glory" (John 2:11). This glimpse of his glory must have helped sustain her on that day when she saw his agony on the cross, that day when she felt a sword piercing her very soul. On that day, everything changed in regard to her relationship with her son. He transitioned from son to Savior. While Jesus was hers by birth, she became his by faith.

❋ ❋ ❋

Lord, on those days when it seems as if there is a sword piercing my soul, give me a fresh glimpse of your glory. Remind me of your ability to turn the emptiness of our lives into fullness of joy, just as you turned water into wine.

If Only

The man from Ethiopia arrived and said, "I have good news for my lord the king. Today the LORD has rescued you from all those who rebelled against you." "What about young Absalom?" the king demanded. "Is he all right?" And the Ethiopian replied, "May all of your enemies, my lord the king, both now and in the future, share the fate of that young man!" The king was overcome with emotion. He went up to the room over the gateway and burst into tears. And as he went, he cried, "O my son Absalom! My son, my son Absalom! If only I had died instead of you! O Absalom, my son, my son." 2 SAMUEL 18:31-33

EVERY FATHER AND MOTHER who has ever watched helplessly while a child destroyed his or her life knows the heartrending grief of David's lament, "O my son Absalom! My son, my son Absalom! If only I had died instead of you!" Even though Absalom had been deceitful and betrayed his father's trust, David wanted him back. Even though he should have been relieved that Absalom was no longer a threat to his safety, David was inconsolable.

A similar grief filled the heart of the prophet Jeremiah as he walked through Jerusalem after the Babylonian destruction. He cried out in anguish over Judah's rebellious children: "For all these things I weep; tears flow down my cheeks. No one is here to comfort me; any who might encourage me are far away. My children have no future, for the enemy has conquered us" (Lamentations 1:16).

Jesus himself has been heartbroken over rebellious children. He lamented the ongoing rebellion of those who refused the reconciliation he offered when he said, "O Jerusalem, Jerusalem, the city that kills the prophets and stones God's messengers! How often I have wanted to gather your children together as a hen protects her chicks beneath her wings, but you wouldn't let me" (Luke 13:34).

❄ ❄ ❄

Lord, it helps me to know that you understand the heartbreak of a resistant, disobedient child. Only your mercy can save sons and daughters from a rebel's death. Only you can take upon yourself the death that _____ and I both deserve. So gather us under your wings and give to us the eternal life that you deserve as the obedient Son.

What about Him?

Peter turned around and saw behind them the disciple Jesus loved—the one who had leaned over to Jesus during supper and asked, "Lord, who will betray you?" Peter asked Jesus, "What about him, Lord?" Jesus replied, "If I want him to remain alive until I return, what is that to you? As for you, follow me." JOHN 21:20-22

WE'RE ALL TEMPTED to compare ourselves to others, our family to other families, our kids to other people's kids, and our parenting to other people's parenting in an effort to feel better about ourselves. Of course, while this tendency to compare didn't start with the invention of social media, its relentless barrage of photos of everyone else's fabulous vacations, creative parties, noteworthy accomplishments, and affectionate messages certainly feeds the monster. We look at the family photos and breezy write-ups and are quite certain that others have it a little easier in the parenting department, or that their kids are seemingly turning out "better" or accomplishing more than our kids.

The problem with comparing our parenting and our kids is the pride or discontent it produces. Furthermore, when we desire the life someone else has, we're saying in our hearts that what God has entrusted to us just isn't good enough. Our jealousy and covetousness point a finger at God and imply that the story he is writing for our life is wrong and that we would have written it better.

When we're tempted to ask God why we have been entrusted with particular challenges that parents around us don't seem to have, we must hear Jesus saying to us, as he told Peter, "As for you, follow me." Jesus has work for us to do in parenting the children he entrusted to us that he has not given to anyone else. There may be a level of difficulty in our situation that parents around us don't experience. But we can be sure that he is also giving us grace to parent these particular children and deal with these particular challenges as we need it.

✻ ✻ ✻

Lord, we need your help to stop focusing on how our parenting and our kids compare to other parents and their kids so we can keep our focus on following you in the work to which you've called us.

My Help Comes from the Lord

I look up to the mountains—
    does my help come from there?
My help comes from the LORD,
    who made heaven and earth!
He will not let you stumble;
    the one who watches over you will not slumber.
Indeed, he who watches over Israel
    never slumbers or sleeps. PSALM 121:1-4

AS THE PEOPLE OF GOD made their way from the plains in Judea up the hill to Jerusalem for feasts and festivals, they sang the songs of ascent, including Psalm 121. They looked ahead to the heights they had to climb and wondered how they would have the strength for them. It's a question they all asked and answered out loud together as they made their way upward. The Lord they were on their way to meet at the Temple would be their help. He could see the unseen pitfalls ahead and wouldn't let them stumble. He would never cease his careful watching over them.

Sometimes the road of launching a child into adulthood seems like a very steep hill. We wonder if we will have the strength for the long haul. We can answer our own question the way the pilgrims did. We can remind ourselves that the one who created the world we live in and the child we love is committed to helping us all along the lengthy journey. He knows the potential pitfalls and places where we could go wrong, and he will keep us on the right path. He will never become bored with or uncaring about the concerns we pour out in prayer. He will never be asleep at the wheel when it comes to sovereignly overseeing our lives and the lives of our children.

❊ ❊ ❊

Lord, I recognize my need to cultivate confidence in your promised help as we make this long journey of raising and preparing our children for adulthood. Sometimes it seems like we just won't make it all the way. So we are in need of your help. Keep us from stumbling and falling away from you. Keep watch over us in the details of the day and the anxieties of the night. Watch over our coming and going both now and forever.

To You and to Your Children

"Let everyone in Israel know for certain that God has made this Jesus, whom you crucified, to be both Lord and Messiah!" Peter's words pierced their hearts, and they said to him and to the other apostles, "Brothers, what should we do?" Peter replied, "Each of you must repent of your sins and turn to God, and be baptized in the name of Jesus Christ for the forgiveness of your sins. Then you will receive the gift of the Holy Spirit. This promise is to you, to your children, and to those far away—all who have been called by the Lord our God." ACTS 2:36-39

PETER WAS PREACHING GOD'S WORD—Joel 2, Psalm 16, and Psalm 110—to the people gathered in Jerusalem for the Festival of Pentecost. Fifty days before, Jesus had been crucified. And just a few days before Pentecost, he had ascended into heaven. Filled with the Holy Spirit, Peter was helping people see that the Scriptures they loved had always been about the person of Jesus, whom they'd rejected and crucified.

It was only a short time before—the night Jesus was arrested—that Peter had taken out a sword to try to defend Jesus. But on this day, it was the sword of the Word of God that Peter wielded. And as Peter brandished this sword, the Spirit used it to do his piercing work. Three thousand people were cut to the heart as they heard and understood the Word of God. They recognized that this promise Peter shared of Jesus as Savior required a response, but they weren't sure what that response should be.

"What should we do?" they asked Peter and the other apostles. Peter told them they needed to receive forgiveness for their sins by repenting and by believing in the name of Jesus Christ, which they would signify through baptism. They could then expect the Holy Spirit to continue working in their lives—filling them, empowering them, securing them, and gifting them. And not only them, but their children, too.

We often sense that what we say to our children is going in one ear and out the other. And much of it probably does. But what our children need far more than to hear our words is to hear God's Word in such a way that their hearts are pierced and their lives are changed.

❊ ❊ ❊

Spirit, speak to _____ through the preaching of your Word, the reading of your Word, and through my own speaking of your Word. Break through the familiarity, the resistance, and the hardness, and pierce _____'s heart in such a way that _____ will be willing to repent and be joyful about identifying with you.

Sacrifice

David replied, "I have come to buy your threshing floor and to build an altar to the LORD there, so that he will stop the plague." "Take it, my lord the king, and use it as you wish," Araunah said to David. "Here are oxen for the burnt offering, and you can use the threshing boards and ox yokes for wood to build a fire on the altar. I will give it all to you, Your Majesty, and may the LORD your God accept your sacrifice." But the king replied to Araunah, "No, I insist on buying it, for I will not present burnt offerings to the LORD my God that have cost me nothing." 2 SAMUEL 24:21-24

A HEART THAT LOVES much is willing to sacrifice. David understood this. God had told him to build an altar on Araunah's threshing floor and to offer a sacrifice there to cover his sin. When David arrived, Araunah was willing to simply give him whatever supplies he needed—oxen, threshing sledges, ox yokes, the works. But David insisted that he pay. David understood his own need to reckon with what his sin cost. He wasn't just going through the motions of religious sacrifice; he wanted to offer the Lord something from the heart.

As we seek to grow in Christ, we long for our lives to be increasingly marked by this kind of death to self, this kind of glad giving, and this kind of sacrifice. Surely parenting is one of the key tools God uses to sanctify and grow us in this way. A mother's call to sacrifice begins as soon as she discovers she's pregnant and gives up caffeine or wine. When the child is born, a father gives up time and sleep to tend to his newborn. Sacrifice, for a parent, isn't so much big gestures but more the everyday costs of playing a board game when you'd like to watch television, getting home in time for dinner when you'd like to stay late at work, and spending less time on your own hobbies so you can help your children pursue theirs.

Our children become tools in God's hands to teach us how to embrace the crucial spiritual discipline of sacrifice and to mold us into the image of Christ—the one who offered himself as a sacrifice.

✳ ✳ ✳

Lord, when I'm tempted to resent the costly sacrifices of parenting, help me to see that every time I have to die to my own plans, you are adding to my life, not taking from it. Keep up your work of shaping me into the image of your Son, no matter what it may cost me.

Kind Words

Kind words are like honey—
  sweet to the soul and healthy for the body. PROVERBS 16:24

WE MIGHT HAVE JOINED in the chant "Sticks and stones may break my bones, but words will never hurt me" when we were kids, but we know now that this children's rhyme isn't true. Most of us have vivid memories of times when we've been injured deeply by someone's taunts. But we can also remember being uplifted and encouraged and emboldened by someone's words. Either way, we've been shaped by words spoken to us in anger or insult as well as in comfort and encouragement.

So as parents, we need to ask ourselves these questions: How are my words shaping my child? Are they like punches that my child has to duck from or deflect to escape injury? Or are my words like honey that soothe the soul and bring healing to my child from the injuries inflicted by the world around them?

Even when insults are offered in jest, usually the grain of truth in them has the power to sting. Inside every child is a subconscious mind, a storage box into which people and events are constantly putting ideas, and a place where self-image is being shaped and safety among others is being gauged. And even when our kids act as if our opinion means nothing and we think they're not listening, we can be sure that our words are being heard.

When our kids head out into the world, they will be pushed around and put down. What they need is a home free of caustic comments, a place where they can retreat from the soul-crushing barbs of those who don't care for them. What they need are parents who make it their daily aim to speak words of encouragement, words of kindness, and words of assurance to show them our unconditional acceptance—both in who they are today and in glad anticipation of all they are becoming.

※ ※ ※

Lord, so often the words that come out of my mouth are thoughtless, harsh, and cold. I need your Spirit to work in me so that my words to _____ will be filled with the fruit of the Spirit, full of love, joy, peace, patience, kindness, goodness, faithfulness, gentleness, and self-control.

Loyal to the King

Observe the requirements of the LORD your God, and follow all his ways. Keep the decrees, commands, regulations, and laws written in the Law of Moses so that you will be successful in all you do and wherever you go. If you do this, then the LORD will keep the promise he made to me. He told me, "If your descendants live as they should and follow me faithfully with all their heart and soul, one of them will always sit on the throne of Israel." 1 KINGS 2:3-4

WHEN 1 KINGS OPENS, David is on the throne, but his glory days are long gone. He's old and he's cold, negligent, and passive. A second wayward son is seeking to grab the throne. Finally Bathsheba cajoles David to name Solomon the next king. As David prepares to die, he charges Solomon to live up to what Israel's kings were commanded to be and do in the Book of the Law. David calls for Solomon to be loyal to God by keeping God's commands, regulations, and laws.

Then David turns his focus to what Solomon must do to those who have been especially loyal or disloyal to David. Joab murdered two of his commanders, so he, too, must see an early grave. Shimei, who had cursed David while he fled to Mahanaim, is to have a bloody death orchestrated by Solomon. But the sons of Barzillai of Gilead, who took care of David when he was on the run, are to become permanent guests at Solomon's table.

The king was to be loyal to God. But the rest of 1 and 2 Kings reveals that Solomon and the rulers that came after him did not live up to the law's requirements for kings. Though the reign of Solomon was a high mark in the history of Israel, Solomon allowed other loves to come before his love for God. In truth, only one descendant of David was able to fully obey David's charge to Solomon, and only one King has been perfectly loyal to God. Jesus is the King we want our children to come under. Jesus deserves and demands our absolute and exclusive loyalty.

※ ※ ※

Jesus, you are the true King who did not come to abolish the law but to fulfill it. We know that when you return as King of kings and Lord of lords, you will banish all who are not loyal to you. Until then, you offer a way back into your good graces to all who have not been faithful to you. You invite your enemies to become friends. Lord, would you work in me and would you work in _____ to instill in us a deep and abiding loyalty to you as we wait for you to come again to establish your Kingdom?

The Middle Years

Restore our fortunes, LORD,
*   as streams renew the desert.*
Those who plant in tears
*   will harvest with shouts of joy.* PSALM 126:4-5

WHEN THE PEOPLE OF GOD came back to Jerusalem after being in exile for seventy years, they were filled with laughter and sang for joy. "It was like a dream!" the psalmist writes. The whole world was talking about all the Lord had done for his people.

But once they arrived back home, the Israelites faced the overwhelming challenge of rebuilding the city of Jerusalem. What once was like a dream now felt like a desert existence. Once they were filled with laughter, but now they wept as they worked. At first, everyone was celebrating what God had done; now all they could see was what they needed him to do. They prayed that God would pour out his Spirit like water on the dry ground of their lives and generate newness and joy as they kept rebuilding. They looked forward to all that God had promised but were finding it hard to keep putting one foot in front of the other in this in-between time.

Their experience is a little like parenting, which starts out with so much joy and celebration over a new tiny life. But then the novelty wears off, and the work begins. Sometimes it's so hard that we weep as we go. So what do we do in the difficult middle years as we plod along in parenting? We pray, asking God to break through. We ask him to turn the rut we're in into a river of his grace. And as we wait in hope for this divine intervention, instead of shriveling up or checking out, we keep sowing seeds of gospel truth and godly wisdom into the lives of our children.

❋ ❋ ❋

Lord, I remember the excitement and joy of having a newborn. But some days in these middle years of parenting seem so hard. So I'm asking you to rain down your grace on our home and water the seeds I'm continuing to sow, sometimes in tears. I'm believing that what I see now is not how things will be in the end. In faith I'm trusting that the ultimate outcome of _____'s life will not be shame or ruin or destruction or tears, but that one day there will be a huge harvest for all of my sowing so that we'll celebrate with shouts of joy.

Wasted Work

Unless the LORD builds a house,
the work of the builders is wasted. PSALM 127:1

GOD IS BUILDING HIS HOUSE, a Kingdom made up of families who love and worship him, a city in which he intends to dwell with his people forever. As parents, we're called to participate with him in this great work. And how do we do that? Through faith. We are called to live by faith and, as Psalm 127 tells us, to trust in the work of God to build our family.

But trusting God to build the house doesn't come naturally for most of us. In our desire and determination to be good parents, we slip into thinking that if our children are going to become lovers of God, it will be due to our diligence. We must keep them involved in church, teach them the right values, instill in them good habits, surround them with godly people, and live before them as good examples.

Of course, all of these are worthwhile endeavors. But Psalm 127 calls us away from our *I've got to do it right; it's all up to me* approach to parenting and into an *I can trust God; he's got to do it* reliance in parenting. It reminds us that all our anxious planning "from early morning until late at night" (verse 2) is not what will create what we're hoping for in the lives of our children. The Lord is the one who must do the building. He gives rest to parents who are weary of trying and failing to generate genuine spiritual fruit in the lives of their children.

⁂ ⁂ ⁂

Lord, unless you build our house, unless you do the work of calling _____ to yourself and implanting in her a desire for you and your ways, all of our work is useless. So please, Lord, do your saving, securing, building work in our home and in our hearts. Save us from the tyranny and anxiety of thinking that it is up to us to build our home into an outpost of your Kingdom. Help us to live by faith in the finished work of Christ on the cross. Give us the rest promised to those who trust you to build your Kingdom in your way and in your timing.

1 Kings 7:1-51
Acts 7:30-50
Psalm 128:1-6
Proverbs 16:31-33

JUNE 10

Nurtured and Sent

Your wife will be like a fruitful grapevine,
flourishing within your home.
Your children will be like vigorous young olive trees
as they sit around your table.
That is the LORD's blessing
for those who fear him. PSALM 128:3-4

IN PSALMS 127 AND 128, Solomon uses images that were familiar to his original readers to describe what the blessing of a happy family looks like. In Psalm 127 he uses the imagery of building a house and watching over a city. He assures parents who are busy building and protecting that these tasks are not all up to us. We can go to sleep at night instead of staying up late to work because we know that the Lord is active in the lives of our families even while we slumber.

In Psalm 128, he uses a different kind of imagery, saying that wives in happy families are like fruitful vines. He's drawing the picture of a wife who is planted next to her loving husband, where she flourishes. He compares children in happy families to young olive trees, tender young saplings that need to be nurtured. Back in 127:4, he describes children as "arrows in a warrior's hands." So, combining these two images, the reader can see that these tender shoots are to be nurtured so they become strong and can be sent out into the world like arrows. Arrows don't remain in the quiver. They are created to be propelled out into the world to fulfill their purpose.

In the final verses of Psalm 128, we discover that this happy family is not an island. The psalmist prays, "May you see Jerusalem prosper as long as you live" (128:5). At the heart of this family's happiness is their participation in the larger family of God. Together they are engaged to see the purposes of God advance and the Kingdom of God expand in the world.

⁂

Lord, we long for this life of blessing that belongs to families who fear you—a father who fears the Lord and trusts him to build the house, a mother who flourishes, and children who are being nurtured so that one day they might be shot like arrows into a world that is in such need of you.

JUNE 11

Resistance Gives Way to Repentance

You stubborn people! You are heathen at heart and deaf to the truth. Must you forever resist the Holy Spirit? That's what your ancestors did, and so do you! ACTS 7:51

STEPHEN STOOD BEFORE the high priest surrounded by people who were well aware of the facts of their Jewish history. But Stephen started at the beginning, tracing his people's repeated rejection of God's law and his prophets, and finally their crucifixion of the Messiah. And they didn't appreciate it at all. "They put their hands over their ears and began shouting. They rushed at him and dragged him out of the city and began to stone him" (Acts 7:57-58).

Perhaps the hardest, coldest heart surrounding Stephen that day was that of a young man named Saul who "was eager to kill the Lord's followers" (Acts 9:1). He was there, resisting the Holy Spirit along with the rest of the crowd. But Saul's resistance would not get the final word in his life. The day would come when his blind eyes would be opened and he could no longer refuse the Holy Spirit. It was God's intention for Saul to become his "chosen instrument to take [his] message to the Gentiles and to kings, as well as to the people of Israel" (Acts 9:15). Saul later explained that, "God, who said, 'Let light shine out of darkness,' has shone in our hearts to give the light of the knowledge of the glory of God in the face of Jesus Christ" (2 Corinthians 4:6, ESV).

The Spirit is able to overcome blinding resistance and rebellion. That is how you were drawn to Christ, and that is how your children will be drawn to Christ. God draws us to him externally by bringing us into contact with Christ in the Word. And he does so internally by overcoming our rebellion so we can see Christ for who he really is.

As parents, our job is to make the Word known and to display Christ and his work on the cross as clearly as we can while we pray that God will do his humbling, teaching, resistance-overcoming work in our children's lives.

※ ※ ※

Lord, as I think about the people who heard your Word at Pentecost and were cut to the heart, and then think of these people who heard your Word and remained "heathen at heart and deaf to the truth," I realize that it is your Spirit who cuts through resistance and convicts of sin. So, Lord, I ask you to send your Spirit to cut through any resistance that may remain in _____. Soften any stubbornness; heal any deafness that keeps _____ from embracing and following you.

Keeping Records of Wrong

LORD, if you kept a record of our sins,
who, O Lord, could ever survive?
But you offer forgiveness,
that we might learn to fear you. PSALM 130:3-4

THE GREAT LOVE CHAPTER of the Bible—1 Corinthians 13—says that love "keeps no record of being wronged." We'd really like to love our children that way, but we sometimes have very long memories in regard to past offenses. So how will we ever love like this? Psalm 130 helps us.

The psalmist was overwhelmed with a sense of God's disapproval. He had sunk down into depths of remoteness from God. His record of repeated failure had plunged him into despair. But that's when the Holy Spirit, through the Scripture, stirred his heart to look up. "From the depths of despair, O LORD, I call for your help" (verse 1).

The psalmist was not in denial about his sin. When he asks who could survive being in God's presence if he kept a list of all our offenses, the implied answer is "nobody!" But the psalmist saw something larger, something more powerful than his own sin. He saw God's generous forgiveness: "His redemption overflows" (verse 7).

From his vantage point, the psalmist couldn't see what would make this overflowing forgiveness possible, since he knew God is perfectly just. But he put his hope in God's unfailing love anyway. What he didn't know at the time was that God would deal with our sin, not by pretending it didn't exist, but by pouring out the punishment for it on his own Son. The Bible says that God "canceled the record of the charges against us and took it away by nailing it to the cross" (Colossians 2:14). The case against us—the file folder with all the facts, names, dates, photographs, and all the incriminating evidence—was nailed there, where Jesus suffered for it all.

This means that we can live and love and forgive out of the overflow. As this grace works in us, we find that we are no longer such careful record keepers of the sins and failures of our children. Just as our Father forgave us, we are able to forgive generously.

※ ※ ※

I hear your voice, Lord, giving me the good news that you have forgiven me. And I want to become as forgiving as you are. May your mercy toward me make me merciful toward
_____.

Heart Turn

The LORD had clearly instructed the people of Israel, "You must not marry them, because they will turn your hearts to their gods." Yet Solomon insisted on loving them anyway. He had 700 wives of royal birth and 300 concubines. And in fact, they did turn his heart away from the LORD. 1 KINGS 11:2-3

THERE WAS A REASON the sons and daughters of the Israelites were not to marry the sons and daughters of the Canaanites who lived around them. It had nothing to do with racial purity but everything to do with purity of devotion to Yahweh alone. Certainly the king over Israel should have led his people by guarding his own heart from the influence of idolatry by refusing to marry women who worshiped other gods. He should have refused to join his heart and life and body with women whose beliefs were not toward Yahweh.

But as wise as Solomon was in so many ways, he was profoundly foolish in regard to the vulnerability of his own heart. Earlier we read that "Solomon loved the LORD" (1 Kings 3:3), but now we read that "Solomon loved many foreign women" and that "they turned his heart to worship other gods instead of being completely faithful to the LORD his God" (1 Kings 11:1, 4).

Oh, how we want our children to love the Lord! And if God should give them the gift of a spouse, we want that spouse to encourage our child to love Christ more and more, not less and less. We realize we don't have the power to rule over our child's heart. But we know one who does. So we pray.

※ ※ ※

Lord, I long for my child to know the joy of sharing life and love with a spouse who draws him into a greater love relationship with you. Give me wisdom to guide him well and encourage him to set appropriate boundaries.

I pray for _____ today, asking you to make him wiser than Solomon in matters of the heart. Give _____ such a deep, all-encompassing love for you that his heart cannot be turned away from you. May it never be said of _____ that he knew your clear instruction regarding marrying one who is yoked to Christ but "insisted" on loving someone who would turn his heart away from you.

Crowning Glory

Grandchildren are the crowning glory of the aged;
*   parents are the pride of their children.* PROVERBS 17:6

CERTAINLY THE FIRST PART of this proverb is easy to grasp. We know that something seems to happen to people when they become grandparents—they become thoroughly convinced that they have the cutest, smartest grandchildren ever born. But the second part of this proverb forces us to stop and think. We might expect it to say that children are the pride of their parents. But it says instead that "parents are the pride of their children."

There are plenty of times as parents when we sense that we are really the embarrassment of our children. At least it can seem that way. As we think it through, we realize that we really do have the ability to bring honor or shame to our children by the way we live, the choices we make, and the legacy we leave. As much as we can be consumed with our children living lives that will bring us great joy as we age, this proverb leads us to ask if we are rightly concerned with living lives that will bring great joy to our children as they age. Are we so anchored in Christ, so dependent upon him, that our children will have cause to take pride in our authentic faith?

※ ※ ※

Lord, forgive me for often being so concerned with how the lives and choices of my children reflect on me that I give little thought to how my life and choices reflect on them. Lord, I want my life—my love for you, my faithfulness to my family, my service to God's people—to bring joy and honor to my children and grandchildren. Keep me from sin that would bring shame on my family.

What we all need is for you to shape our thoughts, feelings, and desires so that we will glory in what pleases you. May the boast of every generation in our family be that we know you and that we are joined to you in a bond that cannot be broken, in a way that is changing each of us day by day.

Harmony

How wonderful and pleasant it is
when brothers live together in harmony!
For harmony is as precious as the anointing oil
that was poured over Aaron's head,
that ran down his beard
and onto the border of his robe.
Harmony is as refreshing as the dew from Mount Hermon
that falls on the mountains of Zion.
And there the LORD has pronounced his blessing,
even life everlasting. PSALM 133

WE WANT OUR CHILDREN to have good friends and a happy life. But we want more than that. We want them to live in deep relationship with brothers and sisters in Christ. We want them to experience the lifelong belonging, refining, and dependence upon God that comes from living life in the body of Christ.

That's what the psalmist celebrates in Psalm 133. In a sense he is reflecting on the good life. He sees that it is not what the world around him says it is. Instead it is a life lived among God's people, enjoying the forgiveness and cleansing that are made available through our great High Priest. The good life is experiencing the day-to-day refreshment of Christ in the midst of a society that is parched with thirst. To share the blessings of forgiveness and cleansing with brothers and sisters is truly wonderful and pleasant. Surely this must be at the heart of our desires for our children now and into the future.

※ ※ ※

Lord, I want so much more for _____ than simply a fulfilling career, a solid marriage, a nice house, a respected name, and a series of accomplishments. I want _____ to drink deeply of the refreshing spring found in a life bound to other believers. Would you plant _____ deeply in your church, among your people? Would you give _____ a heart to persevere in the body when things get hard? Would you help _____ to see that the good life is found among people who recognize their need for forgiveness and their need for the refreshment that comes only from you?

Favoritism

God shows no favoritism. In every nation he accepts those who fear him and do what is right. This is the message of Good News for the people of Israel—that there is peace with God through Jesus Christ, who is Lord of all. . . . Everyone who believes in him will have their sins forgiven through his name. ACTS 10:34-36, 43

BEFORE PETER WENT to the home of Cornelius, a Gentile among Gentiles, he thought that the gospel was just for his own people, the Jews. They saw themselves as insiders and everyone else as outsiders who didn't deserve God's good gift of salvation through Christ. What Peter did not yet understand is that God had given his Word to his people and poured out the Holy Spirit on his people so that they would take the good news of forgiveness of sins through Christ to people of every tribe and nation in the world. Peter's experience with Cornelius was a breakthrough for him and for the rest of the church.

Throughout the Bible, we witness "insiders" presuming upon God because of the family they were born into. They assume that God will accept them even though they have no interest in repentance and belief. The same is true today. How many children grow up in Christian families and are involved in church yet have no interest in a life of repentance and belief? How many presume that God will show them favoritism when they are called to account? We need to help our children understand that they have been given a great privilege in having grown up hearing the gospel. But it must be responded to. God must be feared. The gospel must be believed.

※ ※ ※

Lord, you have poured out your blessing on our family by giving us your Word and allowing us to hear your gospel. But we don't want to presume upon your goodness. Don't let me or my children be lulled into complacency and presumption.

I pray that you would cause _____ to fear you and do what is right. There is peace with you for _____ through Jesus Christ. Protect her from presuming upon you for favoritism. Let her experience your grace and your mercy. May _____ hear your invitation and take hold of all that you have made available to those who put their belief in you.

Hobbling between Two Opinions

Then Elijah stood in front of them and said, "How much longer will you waver, hobbling between two opinions? If the LORD is God, follow him! But if Baal is God, then follow him!" But the people were completely silent. 1 KINGS 18:21

THE CHILDREN OF ISRAEL were supposed to be the servants of God. But they still had plenty of Canaanite neighbors who did their best to make the worship of Baal attractive. In time, the Israelites decided to add a little Baal worship to their worship of Yahweh. They didn't see it as a big deal, when really it was great wickedness. They knew the first commandment: "You must not have any other god but me" (Exodus 20:3), but apparently they didn't believe it had to be that black-and-white, that all in or all out.

The time had come for a showdown. King Ahab and all the people of Israel were summoned to Mount Carmel, home turf for the prophets of Baal. There Elijah called for God's people to stop wavering between worshiping Baal and worshiping Yahweh. They needed to take a firm stand and go all out one way or the other—either in following Baal or Yahweh.

When we hear Elijah's indictment of their indecision, we recognize that we and our children struggle against the same double-mindedness. We want to serve God, but we want to make a lot of money. Our children want to please God, but they want to be popular. They want the security of heaven for later, but right now they want to have fun. But Jesus says we simply can't serve two masters.

Our children may have grown up with Bibles that have their names imprinted on them, and they've probably heard hundreds of sermons and taken the Lord's Supper. The reality, though, is that most are wavering between living for Christ and loving the world. They may not have come yet to a settled determination in their own minds about the Bible—if it is the Word of God or the invention of man. They may be wavering as to whether being a Christian will be the source of their identity or an occasional activity.

Perhaps we and our children need to take to heart Elijah's challenge to our one-foot-in-the-world, one-foot-in-the-Word way of life: *If the Lord is God, follow him!*

※ ※ ※

Lord, you deserve so much more than our part-time devotion. You demand our total worship. You have set before us life and death, blessing and cursing, eternal glory or eternal misery. Show us our wavering ways. Put an end to our hobbling between the way of the Cross and the way of the world.

Faithful Love

He remembered us in our weakness.
   His faithful love endures forever.
He saved us from our enemies.
   His faithful love endures forever.
He gives food to every living thing.
   His faithful love endures forever.
Give thanks to the God of heaven.
   His faithful love endures forever. PSALM 136:23-26

LOVE GETS US UP in the middle of the night to feed our infants and keeps us awake until they get home when they're teenagers. Love is why we fill our calendars with their sports activities and empty our pockets on their education. Love for our children makes us want to open up the beauty of the world to them as well as shield them from its brokenness.

We truly, deeply, sacrificially love our children. But our love has limits. No matter how tuned in we are to their needs, we don't always have the ability to grasp the real issues behind some of their struggles or the wisdom to address them. We don't always have the power to protect them from the things life throws at them. We can't always provide them with what they need most.

This is why we don't mind the repetitive nature of Psalm 136. We need its truth pounded into our souls. Twenty-six times we feel the drumbeat of the unwavering, unending, inexhaustible, unlimited love of God for us and for our children. Over the course of the psalm's twenty-six verses, the psalmist rehearses God's love for his people demonstrated through his faithful acts: the world he made for us, the redemption from slavery he accomplished for us, the protection from evil he provides for us, and the gracious way he cares for us.

❈ ❈ ❈

Lord, the very best news and the most blessed reality of this day is your faithful love toward us and our children. Were it not for your faithful love, we would have no hope and no song. We see in this psalm what divine love looks like. It looks like the beauty of creation, the rescue of redemption, and the rest of provision. It looks like being remembered, being rescued, being provided for. We rest today, not in our love for _____, but in yours. Your faithful love toward _____ endures forever.

Wisdom Can't Be Bought

It is senseless to pay to educate a fool,
    since he has no heart for learning. PROVERBS 17:16

AT FIRST BLUSH this proverb could appear to be about the senselessness of investing good money in educating a foolish child. But that's only because we bring our modern ideas of school tuition costs to the ancient text. The practice of paying a teacher was unknown until the Middle Ages.

What Proverbs 17:16 presents is the picture of a person who has no inclination to engage in a patient process of becoming wise and assumes instead that wisdom can be bought with money. This fool has heard the proverb writer's instruction to "get wisdom," which is "better than gold," but rather than submitting to God in holy fear, rather than experiencing slow growth through patient study of God's Word, and rather than being willing to be transformed from the inside, he digs in his pockets to pay for the quick fix. It's like a person who has no interest in investing in a marriage relationship and offers money to a prostitute, thinking that he or she can buy love. Just as love cannot be bought, neither can wisdom be purchased.

We've been told since the first chapter of Proverbs that the fear of the Lord is the beginning of wisdom. Wisdom is given freely to anyone who recognizes his or her need for it and asks God for it. James writes, "If you need wisdom, ask our generous God, and he will give it to you. He will not rebuke you for asking" (James 1:5).

✳ ✳ ✳

Generous God who gives wisdom, you save foolish people from an empty life so that we can be filled with the wisdom of Christ. Save me, Lord, and give me a heart that longs to learn your ways. And, Lord, save _____ from the foolishness of thinking there are shortcuts to becoming a wise person. Give _____ a desire for the wisdom that comes only from you.

The Power of Your Right Hand

Though I am surrounded by troubles,
*   you will protect me from the anger of my enemies.*
You reach out your hand,
*   and the power of your right hand saves me.*
The LORD will work out his plans for my life. PSALM 138:7-8

WHEN DAVID WROTE IN PSALM 138 about the hand of God that reached out to protect him, surely he was thinking about what the hand of God had done in the past. David knew the hands of God "laid the foundations of the earth, [his] right hand . . . spread out the heavens above" (Isaiah 48:13). Surely the same hands that created something out of nothing could provide what he needed. David remembered the song of praise Moses sang when the Israelites were safely across the Red Sea: "Your right hand, O LORD, smashes the enemy" (Exodus 15:6). Surely the same hands that crushed Pharaoh's armies could defeat the enemies surrounding him.

David remembered that Moses told God's people before they entered the Promised Land that "the LORD your God brought you out [of Egypt] with his strong hand" (Deuteronomy 5:15). Surely the same hands that led a whole nation out of slavery could lead him away from the fears that had gripped him and into the rest God provides. David remembered Joshua telling God's people after they walked across the dried-up Jordan River that the Lord "did this so all the nations of the earth might know that the LORD's hand is powerful, and so you might fear the LORD your God forever" (Joshua 4:24). David expected the same powerful hand to deal with whatever would try to prevent him from experiencing God's plans for his life.

What David could not yet see clearly was the greatest work of protection and salvation the Lord's hands would provide—when God incarnate would give his hands over to evil men to have nails driven into them. Jesus invites all who doubt the power of God's hands to save to "look at my hands. Put your hand into the wound in my side. Don't be faithless any longer. Believe!" (John 20:27).

※ ※ ※

Lord, how I need to remember your history of reaching out your hand to save to remind me that this is who you are and what you do. I believe that you are working out your plans for _____ 's life and that you will protect him from the enemy of his soul. Save _____ by the power of your right hand through the work of your nail-pierced hands.

171

Every Day of My Life

You made all the delicate, inner parts of my body
*   and knit me together in my mother's womb.*
Thank you for making me so wonderfully complex!
*   Your workmanship is marvelous—how well I know it.*
You watched me as I was being formed in utter seclusion,
*   as I was woven together in the dark of the womb.*
You saw me before I was born.
*   Every day of my life was recorded in your book.*
Every moment was laid out
*   before a single day had passed.* PSALM 139:13-16

THE KEY WORD IN PSALM 139 is *know*. It opens with David's declaration that the Lord has searched him and knows him. David expresses the comfort he finds in the truth that God not only knew him when he was being formed in the womb, but knew how his life would take shape. David says that the story of his life—every single day—had been written in God's book long before it even began.

This personal making, knitting, seeing, weaving, recording work of the sovereign God is, in many ways, comforting. But it can also be somewhat disconcerting. When the way our child was "woven together" in the darkness of the womb includes birth defects, we wonder how we can say sincerely, "Your work is marvelous." On the day an accident happens or a serious illness begins, we struggle to believe a good God could have recorded this in the book of our child's life before he or she was born.

The sovereignty of God—his ordaining of how our lives and the lives of our children will unfold—can be a very difficult truth to understand. If he is in control of everything, we wonder why he has allowed this universe to be ordered in such a way that brings pain. But while God's sovereignty can be hard to accept, it is also a soft place to land. Because God is sovereignly bringing history and our lives to their appointed ends, we can rest.

❊ ❊ ❊

Lord, your sovereignty is a solid rock underfoot when the winds of difficulty blow in our lives. It confronts what seems absurd in our existence. Your sovereignty is our greatest hope as we face an uncertain and unknown future. Help me to trust your sovereign plans for each day of _____'s life.

A Miracle of Life

Elisha said to her as she stood in the doorway, "Next year at this time you will be holding a son in your arms!" "No, my lord!" she cried. "O man of God, don't deceive me and get my hopes up like that." But sure enough, the woman soon became pregnant. And at that time the following year she had a son, just as Elisha had said. 2 KINGS 4:15-17

THE WEALTHY WOMAN from Shunem had not asked for a son, yet Elisha sought this blessing for her. But when the child was still young, he died suddenly. The heartbroken mother went to find Elisha. When he heard her plight, he went with her back to her home. "When Elisha arrived, the child was indeed dead, lying there on the prophet's bed. He went in alone and shut the door behind him and prayed to the LORD. Then he lay down on the child's body, placing his mouth on the child's mouth, his eyes on the child's eyes, and his hands on the child's hands. And as he stretched out on him, the child's body began to grow warm again!" (2 Kings 4:32-34). Elisha stretched himself out over the boy, uniting with him in every way, overpowering death and imparting life from God.

Just over the hill from Shunem is the village of Nain, where hundreds of years later, Jesus arrived. As he approached the village, a funeral procession was coming out, carrying the dead body of a young man, followed by his weeping mother. Luke records, "When the Lord saw her, his heart overflowed with compassion. 'Don't cry!' he said. Then he walked over to the coffin and touched it, and the bearers stopped. 'Young man,' he said, 'I tell you, get up.' Then the dead boy sat up and began to talk! And Jesus gave him back to his mother" (Luke 7:13-15).

Just as Elisha identified himself with the dead boy mouth to mouth, eyes to eyes, and hands to hands, so Jesus identified with us in every way so that he could bring us back from death to life.

✷ ✷ ✷

Lord, it is just this kind of miracle we need to be brought from death to life. As parents, we are as helpless to breathe spiritual life into the lives of our children as the woman from Shunem and the mother in Nain were to restore life to their sons. But you can. Won't you cover _____ and make her warm to the truth of the gospel? Won't you speak to _____ and call her to awaken to you?

Rebuilt Ruins

This conversion of Gentiles is exactly what the prophets predicted. As it is written:

"Afterward I will return
  and restore the fallen house of David.
I will rebuild its ruins
  and restore it,
so that the rest of humanity might seek the LORD,
  including the Gentiles—
all those I have called to be mine." ACTS 15:15-17

SOME ZEALOUS JEWISH CHRISTIANS began to tell the Gentile Christians in Antioch that if they weren't circumcised as required by the law of Moses, they couldn't be saved. But Paul and Barnabas disagreed vehemently. So the church sent the two men to Jerusalem to meet with the apostles and elders to get some clarity on the issue. As they talked, James pointed out that Gentiles coming to Christ was exactly what the Old Testament prophets said would happen.

He quoted the prophet Amos, who promised God's people that though they were about to be trampled by the Assyrians, the day would come when they would be restored. Why would God rebuild his people from the ruins? "So that the rest of humanity might seek the LORD, including the Gentiles" (verse 17).

Many years after Amos gave this prophecy, Jesus came into the world and began this restoration process by calling a believing remnant of Israel to himself and then sending them out to invite the Gentiles in. First there were twelve apostles. Then there were five thousand converts in Jerusalem. Then the gospel began to spread throughout the known world.

God is still at work reclaiming his people from the ruins. He is not looking for perfect people or families to accomplish his work in the world. He uses those who have been ruined by sin and are being restored and renewed by the power of God to call others to himself. He wants the world to see what grace accomplishes in the lives of broken people and broken homes so that others will seek out that grace for themselves.

❊ ❊ ❊

Lord, come into our ruin, and do your work of rebuilding. May your gracious renovation of our lives be a light to those around us in need of your restoration.

Foolish Children Bring Grief

Foolish children bring grief to their father
  and bitterness to the one who gave them birth. PROVERBS 17:25

MOMS AND DADS never set out on the journey of parenting expecting their children to bring them great sorrow. We want to think that the pain of child rearing ends with labor and delivery, but most parents soon discover otherwise. We feel the hurts inflicted on our child as well as the hurts inflicted by our child. Parenting over the long haul often includes the pain of relational conflict, unfulfilled expectations, and wasted opportunities. But the greatest grief for a Christian parent is the pain of having a child who rejects Christ.

Godly parents sometimes have children who are not godly. And it scares us. Because we'd like to think that if we live the right way and teach our children the right things, then we can be sure our children will live and believe like we do. But it's just not that neat and tidy. Scripture includes plenty of examples of godly parents having ungodly children as well as of wicked parents having godly children. There's simply no one-to-one correlation between the spiritual condition of parents and that of their children. But most of us don't have to go to the Bible to know this is true. We know godly parents whose hearts have been broken by children who have rejected Christ.

We can teach God's Word to our children, urge them to trust in Christ, and pray for their salvation. But no parent can make a child live a truly godly life. Only God can do that. This means that parents who grieve over their child's rejection of the Christ they love can grieve without guilt. Just as we dare not take all the credit for the grace of God in the lives of our children who have chosen to live the life of faith, neither should we assume all the blame for a child's choice to reject it.

❊ ❊ ❊

Lord, when I feel grief over my child's foolish choices, it helps to know that you have felt that same sorrow. Remind me, too, when _____ brings me grief, that I am guilty of bringing you grief. Help me to extend the same glad forgiveness to _____ that you have extended to me.

Everyone in His Household

The jailer called for lights and ran to the dungeon and fell down trembling before Paul and Silas. Then he brought them out and asked, "Sirs, what must I do to be saved?" They replied, "Believe in the Lord Jesus and you will be saved, along with everyone in your household." And they shared the word of the Lord with him and with all who lived in his household. Even at that hour of the night, the jailer cared for them and washed their wounds. Then he and everyone in his household were immediately baptized. He brought them into his house and set a meal before them, and he and his entire household rejoiced because they all believed in God. Acts 16:29-34

After a severe beating, Paul and Silas had been handed over to the jailer in Philippi. That night, the jailer and the other prisoners heard sounds coming from their cell. It wasn't groaning or cursing, but instead prayer and hymn singing. Around midnight an earthquake rocked the prison. The doors flew open, and the prisoners' chains fell off. When the jailer saw open doors, he assumed that all of the prisoners had made their escape and that he would be executed for losing them. So he drew his sword to kill himself. But then he heard a voice shouting from the darkness of the prison, assuring him that all the prisoners were still there.

Perhaps the jailer had heard the local fortune-teller's announcement that these men had come to proclaim a way of salvation. Or maybe he had been moved by their singing and wanted that kind of hope. Perhaps he assumed the earthquake and the release of their chains were a supernatural vindication of them and their message. Whatever it was, the jailer was thoroughly shaken in body and soul, convinced that the salvation these men preached was something he wanted.

But Paul and Silas were not content for this salvation to come just to the jailer. God loves to save not just individuals but entire families, which is exactly what happened that day in Philippi. Paul and Silas shared the word of Christ with everyone in the jailer's household, and all took hold of it by faith.

※ ※ ※

Lord, how we long for your salvation to come to our entire household. We want to experience this kind of rejoicing, this kind of reorientation in our home. Shake our home in whatever way is needed so that everyone in our family will want the security that is found in you.

Those Whose God Is the LORD

May our sons flourish in their youth
  like well-nurtured plants.
May our daughters be like graceful pillars,
  carved to beautify a palace. PSALM 144:12

WHEN WE READ PSALM 144, we can picture David asking God to give him victory over the enemies who threaten the safety and well-being of God's people. In the final part of the psalm, it's as if David imagines what life will be like when God answers his prayer. The victory that God gives will lead to blessing for all who live under the reign of the king. Their children, who are described in Psalm 128 as "young olive trees," will continue to grow. Their sons will become like "well-nurtured plants" instead of being cut down. Their daughters will stand tall in beauty and strength instead of cowering in fear. Rather than going hungry or languishing in need, they'll have plenty to eat and to trade. And instead of living in constant fear of being attacked, they will live a life of joy and peace.

In other words, when the Lord gives victory to his king, all who live under his rule will enjoy the benefits of that victory. And just as the blessing of the people in David's day was tied to their king, so our blessing is tied to that of our King. All who are joined to Christ are blessed "with every spiritual blessing in the heavenly realms because we are united with Christ" (Ephesians 1:3).

When we read or sing this psalm, we hear our King Jesus praying for those who live under his rule. He's praying that we will receive all the benefits of his victory accomplished on the cross. He's praying that our sons will grow and flourish and not experience being cut down by the enemy. He's praying that our daughters will be strong and beautiful, inside and out, rather than living in fear of enslavement. He's praying that our families will prosper and live in safety within the city he has secured for his people.

※ ※ ※

Joyful indeed are those whose God is the Lord. Day by day we experience the blessing that is ours because we are united to Christ. May _____ flourish like a well-nurtured plant. May _____ be like a graceful pillar, carved to beautify a palace. May our family enjoy the satisfaction and security of having Jesus as our King!

JUNE 27

Let Each Generation Tell

Let each generation tell its children of your mighty acts;
let them proclaim your power.
I will meditate on your majestic, glorious splendor
and your wonderful miracles.
Your awe-inspiring deeds will be on every tongue;
I will proclaim your greatness.
Everyone will share the story of your wonderful goodness;
they will sing with joy about your righteousness. PSALM 145:4-7

WE PASS ALONG many lessons to our children that we do not particularly intend to teach them. They pick up on and often mimic our mannerisms, attitudes, and aptitudes. In this final psalm of David, he urges us to purposefully pass along to our children a commitment to telling, proclaiming, meditating on, sharing, and singing about who God is and what he has done. David seems to have exploited all of the vocabulary he can muster to describe the outgoing, declaring nature of praise we should have. He encourages parents not to limit their praise to private devotions or even public worship. He wants us to talk to our kids about what really amazes us, encourages us, and makes us want to sing—God himself.

It is David's glad intention to praise God every day, forever. But he doesn't want this proclamation of praise to end with him. He encourages every generation to tell the next about God's mighty acts, his glorious splendor, and his righteousness. Once again, David used every expression possible to extol what makes God worthy of such praise—a list of what to talk about with our kids around the table, in the car, in good times and bad.

❋ ❋ ❋

Lord, loosen my tongue to tell _____ of your mighty acts, which I read about in your Word and experience in my own life. Let me proclaim to _____ your power demonstrated both in history and in the present as your divine power is at work in me. As I tell of your greatness, fill me with hope that your awe-inspiring deeds are not merely a thing of the past. May everyone in our home sing with joy and share the story of your goodness to us!

The Dead Man Revived

Elisha died and was buried. Groups of Moabite raiders used to invade the land each spring. Once when some Israelites were burying a man, they spied a band of these raiders. So they hastily threw the corpse into the tomb of Elisha and fled. But as soon as the body touched Elisha's bones, the dead man revived and jumped to his feet!
2 KINGS 13:20-21

ELISHA HAD A POWERFUL, life-giving prophetic ministry. He fed people in the midst of a famine, raised a boy from the dead, cleansed a leper, and played the kinsman-redeemer to the faithful within Israel. But as we discover in this strange little story of a corpse thrown into his grave, Elisha was a source of life even after his death.

This miracle of a dead person coming back to life after touching Elisha's bones provided a picture of hope for the resurrection for God's people. Even though the people in that day were about to be thrown into the grave of exile, there was still hope for resurrection. And even though the prophets were dying, Israel could be saved by clinging to the prophetic word. Death would not be the end of their story if they would take hold of the word of life spoken by the prophets.

In time, one greater than Elisha would come. And when he died, "tombs opened. The bodies of many godly men and women who had died were raised from the dead" (Matthew 27:52). But the miracle did not end there. Even now, spiritually dead people are made alive again when they are joined to Christ so that his grave becomes their grave: "For you were buried with Christ when you were baptized. And with him you were raised to new life because you trusted the mighty power of God, who raised Christ from the dead" (Colossians 2:12). All of those who are joined to Christ are already experiencing this new life. And when he comes again, the transformation from death to life will be complete: "Christ was raised as the first of the harvest; then all who belong to Christ will be raised when he comes back" (1 Corinthians 15:23).

※ ※ ※

Lord, we appreciate this picture of a dead man being revived by contact with your prophetic Word. It's what we want for _____. We long for your resurrection power to break into this dead and dying world and instill _____ with new life.

Just Like It

King Ahaz then went to Damascus to meet with King Tiglath-pileser of Assyria. While he was there, he took special note of the altar. Then he sent a model of the altar to Uriah the priest, along with its design in full detail. Uriah followed the king's instructions and built an altar just like it, and it was ready before the king returned from Damascus. 2 KINGS 16:10-11

FROM THE VERY BEGINNING, when God brought his people out of slavery in Egypt, he told them that they were to be set apart from every other nation. They were meant to live in purity, loving and enjoying the blessing of the one true God so that all the nations around them would want to worship their God. But instead of remaining distinct, they slowly became just like everyone around them.

In this scene in 2 Kings, Ahaz, the king over Judah, no longer makes any pretense of worshiping or trusting the one true God. He has turned to pagan nations to make alliances that he thinks will ensure their safety. When he visits a town to the north that has been captured by Assyria, the altar in the middle of town catches his eye.

When Ahaz returned to Jerusalem, it was out with the old altar and in with the new. He launched an all-out redesign of the Temple to make it more like the temples of other nations. But this overhaul only led to disaster as the sacrifices offered on the newly designed altars "were his downfall and the downfall of all Israel" (2 Chronicles 28:23, NIV).

Still today, we don't particularly relish standing out because of our worship of God and obedience to his ways. This can be especially hard for our children as they seek to find their place in the world. So we must lead by example as well as by teaching them God's Word, which says, "Don't copy the behavior and customs of this world, but let God transform you into a new person by changing the way you think. Then you will learn to know God's will for you, which is good and pleasing and perfect" (Romans 12:2).

※ ※ ※

Lord, we want to be yours and to live for you alone, but we feel the tug of the world that seeks to cast us into its mold. Give _____ courage today to be different from those around him. Help _____ to see that worshiping anything other than you will be his downfall.

Away from His Presence

This disaster came upon the people of Israel because they worshiped other gods. . . . They had followed the practices of the pagan nations the LORD had driven from the land ahead of them, as well as the practices the kings of Israel had introduced. . . . Because the LORD was very angry with Israel, he swept them away from his presence. 2 KINGS 17:7-8, 18

ISRAEL CAME INTO THE LAND of Canaan charged with the duty of purging the land of pagan shrines and establishing the exclusive worship of Yahweh. But when we come to 2 Kings 17, we realize that, in a tragic reversal, the land was back to its preconquest state, full of idolatrous shrines. "They even sacrificed their own sons and daughters in the fire" (verse 17). Instead of raising their children to love and obey the Lord, they put their sons and daughters into the stone arms of a false god and watched as their children burned in the fire.

A god who is not aroused to anger when children are thrown into the fire could not be good. But our good God gets angry. While he is slow to anger, his perfect anger is among his perfections. For two hundred years he repeatedly sent his prophets to Israel to warn them that if they did not abandon their worship of idols, they would be plucked out of the land. When they refused to listen, the Lord "swept them away from his presence"—just as he'd ejected Adam and Eve from the Garden because of their disobedience.

Likewise, there will come a day when every person will stand before this unchanging God. All who have refused to listen to his warnings, all who have spurned his offers of grace, will be driven away from his presence.

✳ ✳ ✳

Lord, we know a day is coming when you will pour out your anger on those who live for themselves, who refuse to obey the truth and instead lead wicked lives. But we also know that you poured out your anger on Christ so that all who find refuge in him will not be swept away from your presence but instead will be brought safely home to you. So we ask, Lord, that you would be patient in your anger. We ask that you would draw _____ into the safety of your fold and keep _____ in the safety of your presence forever.

JULY 1

What Are You Trusting In?

Then the Assyrian king's chief of staff told them to give this message to Hezekiah:
"This is what the great king of Assyria says: What are you trusting in that makes you
so confident? . . . What god of any nation has ever been able to save its people from
my power? So what makes you think that the LORD can rescue Jerusalem from me?"
2 KINGS 18:19, 35

THE LORD HAD USED the Assyrian armies to deal with the people of the northern kingdom of Israel. Now the Assyrian king was threatening the southern kingdom of Judah.
He sent his army to the walls of Jerusalem, where his warriors began to call out to King
Hezekiah's best men. After reminding them that the Lord had not rescued the northern
kingdom from Assyria, they had a message for the king in the form of a question: "What
are you trusting in that makes you so confident?"

Isn't this the question that our enemy constantly hurls at us as parents? Our enemy
mocks our confidence that God will save and secure our children. Our enemy points
out all the young people around us who have fallen victim to his deceptions and false
promises. Then he asks us why we think the Lord is going to rescue our children.

Hezekiah shows us what to do when we hear the mocking, taunting voice of our
enemy. "When King Hezekiah heard their report, he tore his clothes and put on burlap
and went into the Temple of the LORD" (19:1). Hezekiah turned to humble prayer. We,
likewise, must humbly pray for God to act. Next Hezekiah sought out a prophet who
would speak God's Word to him. So must we open God's Word to hear him speak to us.
Hezekiah's main concern was that Yahweh would vindicate his own name. He prayed,
"Now, O LORD our God, rescue us from his power; then all the kingdoms of the earth
will know that you alone, O LORD, are God" (19:19). In the same way, our hearts must
be set on God glorifying himself through the salvation of our children.

❉ ❉ ❉

Lord, I am trusting in you, the God who saves your people. You love to deliver your own.
So I ask you to rescue _____ from the power of the evil one. Show yourself strong in
the world by your saving power!

My Lifetime

Isaiah said to Hezekiah, "Listen to this message from the LORD: The time is coming when everything in your palace—all the treasures stored up by your ancestors until now—will be carried off to Babylon. Nothing will be left, says the LORD. Some of your very own sons will be taken away into exile. They will become eunuchs who will serve in the palace of Babylon's king." Then Hezekiah said to Isaiah, "This message you have given me from the LORD is good." For the king was thinking, "At least there will be peace and security during my lifetime." 2 KINGS 20:16-19

WHEN HEZEKIAH BECAME deathly ill and cried out to the Lord in tears, God graciously extended his life by fifteen years. But then Hezekiah's pride got the best of him. Wanting to show off, he took some visitors from Babylon on a tour of his royal treasuries. God then sent the prophet Isaiah to tell Hezekiah that one day his sons and daughters would experience the consequences of his prideful parade of the kingdom's riches. Babylon would come and clean them out. Not only would they take all of its monetary treasure to Babylon, they would carry away the very best of Jerusalem's sons and daughters and make them servants in Babylon.

We might expect that Hezekiah would respond with heartache, pleading with the Lord to turn back this future judgment. But he didn't. He was just glad this reckoning wasn't going to happen during his lifetime. Where Hezekiah had sought Yahweh's mercy in the matter of his *own* life, he now selfishly cared nothing about the welfare of the generations to come.

Like every other king, even this seemingly good king had a dark side. Clearly, the sons and daughters of God needed a better King. And that is what we've been given in Jesus. Instead of being concerned about his own comfort, Jesus laid down his life so that future generations could live.

❋ ❋ ❋

Lord, as much as I want to think of myself as a good parent, I know that my own selfish interests often get in the way. Sometimes I don't think about how my children and grandchildren will experience the consequences of my pride, my prayerlessness, and my pretending. I thank you for being a better parent to _____ than I will ever be. You love perfectly and purely.

JULY 3

Truly Happy

Oh, the joys of those who do not
    follow the advice of the wicked,
    or stand around with sinners,
    or join in with mockers.
But they delight in the law of the LORD,
    meditating on it day and night. PSALM 1:1-2

FINDING AN ENGLISH TRANSLATION for the Hebrew term *ashre*, expressed by the first words of this psalm, isn't easy. "Truly happy" might be the best English translation. But *happy* can often signify a fleeting emotion. So often we say that we want our kids to be happy. But really we want much more than that. We want them to experience what is expressed here in Psalm 1. *Ashre* conveys a deep sense of well-being, contentedness, and fulfillment.

The first thing we learn in Psalm 1 about those who enjoy this kind of happiness is what they do not do. They do not follow, stand, or join the wicked, sinners, or mockers. The psalmist's choice of words—*follow, stand, join*—seems to describe a progression of engagement that makes its way through thinking, behaving, and belonging. So happy people don't absorb the ideas and values or follow the advice of those who live their lives assuming that God is irrelevant. They don't conform to the behavior or lifestyle of those who sin with no conscience. They don't keep company with cynics who get a good laugh by making fun of the things of God.

It's not that truly happy people can't be influenced by anything, however. It's that the central influence in their lives is not the advice offered on social media or the opinion of the cool kids at school. It is something quite different—the Scriptures. These happy people have implanted the Word of God in their minds and souls. They don't drag out their Bible every now and then because they ought to. They read it often because they want to. This is the happiness we want for our children.

✳ ✳ ✳

Lord, I want _____ to have this kind of blessed life. I want _____ to have this kind of happiness. So I pray that _____ will recognize the wicked and refuse to follow their lead. I pray that _____ will refuse to join in with those who mock what is precious to you. I pray that the Scriptures would increasingly become the controlling influence in _____'s life.

Your Inheritance

The king proclaims the LORD's decree:
"The LORD said to me, 'You are my son.
  Today I have become your Father.
Only ask, and I will give you the nations as your inheritance,
  the whole earth as your possession.'" PSALM 2:7-8

PERHAPS YOU'VE GIVEN some thought to what you intend to pass along to your children as an inheritance. In Psalm 2, we discover that God the Father has told the Son what he intends to give to him as an inheritance—the nations.

Psalm 2 is a psalm David wrote for his own coronation, and it was likely used at the coronation of future kings in the Davidic line. When David was installed as God's representative to reign over his people, he entered into a new and unique relationship with God, one of royal sonship.

But while this psalm was originally written about David, ultimately it is about his greater son, Jesus. Though he had been eternally the Son of God in the presence of God, he, too, entered into a new relationship with God the Father on the day he was resurrected from the dead—that of royal sonship (Acts 13:33).

In Psalm 2, the Son says that God told him only to ask, and he would give him the nations for his inheritance. And in the Gospel of John, we overhear Jesus making just that request. In his prayer immediately prior to the Crucifixion, Jesus prayed, "Father, the hour has come. Glorify your Son so he can give glory back to you. For you have given him authority over everyone. He gives eternal life to each one you have given him" (John 17:1-2). We, as believers, are the inheritance Jesus asked for.

Just as David, the Lord's anointed, needed only to ask God to grant him power over his enemies and make them part of his own kingdom, so Jesus, the Lord's Anointed, needed only to ask God to grant him power over those who were his enemies. And in overcoming death, Jesus indeed overcame them.

There is something far more precious than the inheritance you may leave your children. Far more significant is that you and your children are part of the inheritance God has given to his Son.

❊ ❊ ❊

Lord, Father of King Jesus, thank you for giving such a glorious inheritance to your Son. How we long for the day when he comes back to reign and the whole earth bows to him as King!

Our Family Tree

The descendants of Adam were Seth, Enosh, Kenan, Mahalalel, Jared, Enoch, Methuselah, Lamech, and Noah. The sons of Noah were Shem, Ham, and Japheth.
1 CHRONICLES 1:1-4

THE FIRST CHAPTERS of 1 Chronicles are not just a catalog of the names of dead ancestors. They are a rich history of the people of God. This is the family through whom God was working out his plan to bless all the families of the earth. As we read through the names, we get our spiritual bearings. This first chapter reminds us of who we are by telling us about our roots. These are the saints and sinners we come from—a long line of moms and dads, sons and daughters who are connected to Christ by faith.

If we are in Christ, what we're reading is our own family tree. As Gentile believers, we have been grafted into the gnarled old olive tree of Israel. We've become a part of this family, not through birth, but by rebirth, not because of the blood that flows through our veins, but by the belief that has taken hold of our hearts.

We are not orphans. We are not on our own. We have a place, an identity that flows from being part of this family.

As much as we want our children to have a sense of identity that comes from being a part of our own immediate and extended family, what we want in a far deeper way is for our children to have a sense of identity that comes from being a part of God's family. We want them to look through this family tree and see that it has had its share of notorious sinners. This means that there is no sin our kids can commit that will disqualify them from belonging to the family of God. What distinguishes those who belong to this family is that they know how to take hold of the grace made possible by our one special brother, Jesus.

※ ※ ※

Lord, we could just as easily have been included in the line of those who are eternally separated from you. But you have drawn us to yourself by grace. You have made us your own through adoption. You are at work in us, giving us the family resemblance as you transform us into your own glorious image. So, Lord, give _____ a deep sense of belonging and a deep sense of gratitude for being brought into your family.

No Guarantees

The descendants of Solomon were Rehoboam, Abijah, Asa, Jehoshaphat, Jehoram, Ahaziah, Joash, Amaziah, Uzziah, Jotham, Ahaz, Hezekiah, Manasseh, Amon, and Josiah. 1 CHRONICLES 3:10-14

IN THIS PART of the genealogy of the royal line of David, we discover that the spiritual health of our children is not fully dependent upon us. When we read the stories of the kings who descended from Solomon, we discover that:

Rehoboam's son was Abijah. A bad father raised a bad son.
Abijah raised Asa. A bad father raised a good son.
Asa raised Jehoshaphat. A good father raised a good son.
Jehoshaphat raised Jehoram. A good father raised a bad son.

There is no formula; there are no guarantees. Sometimes genuinely and consistently godly people have children who grow up witnessing the spiritual integrity of their parents, and yet these children fail to take hold of it. Other times, completely godless parents have children who grow up and become radically converted, wholly devoted followers of Christ.

So what does this mean for us as parents? It means that while we want to live before our children in a way that demonstrates the inherent blessing of belonging to Christ and models a life that is pleasing to him, we don't take credit when they choose to live that way too. Neither do we take the blame when they choose to walk away from a godly life and toward a worldly one. It means that we put our faith not in our perfect presentation of a godly life, but in the power of the Holy Spirit to convict and convince our children, as well as to draw them in and keep them.

❊ ❊ ❊

Lord, we can see from the history of your people that good parents have had the great joy of rearing children who have walked in your ways as well as the great sorrow of seeing their children walk away from faith. How we long for _____ to love you and live for you! Keep us from despair and from pride. Keep us trusting in you.

Your Shield of Love

Let all who take refuge in you rejoice;
*   let them sing joyful praises forever.*
Spread your protection over them,
*   that all who love your name may be filled with joy.*
For you bless the godly, O LORD;
*   you surround them with your shield of love.* PSALM 5:11-12

THOUGH DAVID WAS THE KING over God's people, he understood that God was the true King. So each morning, David approached God in prayer. He didn't presume that God would hear his prayer and welcome him into his royal presence, yet clearly he expected it. But when we read the entirety of Psalm 5, we might wonder why. David wrote that the Lord detests murderers and deceivers. David was a murderer and a deceiver. How could he be so confident that God would hear his prayer and welcome him?

David did not presume to enter God's presence based on his own clean record. He didn't have one. Rather, he said it was because of God's unfailing love that he could enter God's house. This generous grace made David want to live in a way that was pleasing to God.

David was able to seek refuge in God because he was confident that the Lord's protection would be spread over him (verse 11). Of course, the Lord could spread his protection over David—and over us and our children—because there was no protection for his own Son. All the punishment we deserve was poured out on Christ so that God could pour out all the blessing Christ deserved on us.

❊ ❊ ❊

Listen to my cry for help, my King and my God,
*   for I pray to no one but you.*
Listen to my voice in the morning, Lord.
*   Each morning I bring my requests to you and wait expectantly.*
Lead _____ in the right path, O Lord.
Spread your protection over _____,
*   that _____ may be filled with joy.*
Bless _____, O Lord; surround _____ with your shield of love.
    ADAPTED FROM PSALM 5:2-3, 8, 11-12

How Long?

I am sick at heart.
How long, O LORD, until you restore me? PSALM 6:3

HOW VERY HARD it is to wait on God. Some of us have prayed earnestly (which, for some of us, means only two or three times) for him to work, and we think of ourselves as having persevered in prayer. But when we've prayed for months or years and see no visible signs of change, no tangible evidence of God at work, we can begin to lose hope. We wonder not only if heaven is closed to us, but if there really is anyone in heaven who is listening and able to act.

So David's words in Psalm 6 help us. They give us words to express our frustration with what appears to be slowness on God's part. But they also remind us to whom we're praying. That's what kept David praying for what seemed to him to be much too long. He knew that it is God's essential nature to be merciful. He was praying to a God of unfailing love. He was praying to a God who hears, who answers, who rescues.

When we are sick at heart about the direction of or the difficulty in our child's life, we can be sure that our God will restore us to a healthy confidence that he is at work. When we are worn out from sobbing over the pain in our child's life, we can be sure that the Lord has heard our weeping. He has heard our pleas and will answer. It may not be today or tomorrow. In fact, God may not accomplish all the healing and restoration we long for in this lifetime. But we can be sure that the day will come when his work in our lives and in the lives of our children will be brought to completion. And in light of eternity, it won't seem as if it took very long at all.

※ ※ ※

Lord, a part of me asks with the psalmist, "How long?" Sometimes it seems that you work so slowly. I am impatient for you to accomplish all you intend in _____'s life. But I am not hopeless. Even when I don't see you working, I will believe you are. Even when it seems as if it's taking too long, I will trust you to accomplish all you intend to accomplish and have faith that you will complete it right on time.

A Treasure

The man who finds a wife finds a treasure,
and he receives favor from the LORD. PROVERBS 18:22

SOME PARENTS, from the time their children are born, spend time in prayer, asking God to guide their sons to find wives who will be a treasure to them, or asking God to guide their daughters toward husbands who will treasure them over a lifetime. They know how critical the choice of a spouse is, so they've made it a matter of prayer.

Others of us may want a good marriage for our child, but we've spent little time praying about our child's developing desires for a spouse, the process of them finding a spouse, or their preparation to be someone's spouse. We've failed to see the gift of a loving, godly spouse as a grace from God.

God doesn't give a spouse to our child as a quid pro quo for having prayed long enough and hard enough. It is a gift, pure and simple. And yet the Lord is pleased when we do not presume upon him for this great gift or when we don't take for granted the gift he has given. So we are called to pray for the Giver of all good gifts to grant the favor of a treasured spouse to our sons and daughters.

※ ※ ※

Lord, we don't want to presume that you will grant _____ the favor of a treasured companion for life in this world through the gift of marriage. Perhaps you will call and equip _____ to be single. We want to trust you with that. But, Lord, if marriage is what you have for _____, we ask that even now you would be preparing _____ to be a faithful and loving spouse. Give _____ eyes to look for and to see in another person the qualities that wear well over a lifetime of daily life together. Work in _____ to begin now the process of dying to self so that _____ might be able to love selflessly and sacrificially. Give _____ great wisdom and insight into potential spouses, great restraint in the midst of loneliness, and great joy in accepting this favor from you.

Fulfilling Our Destiny

What are mere mortals that you should think about them,
*   human beings that you should care for them?*
Yet you made them only a little lower than God
*   and crowned them with glory and honor.*
You gave them charge of everything you made,
*   putting all things under their authority.* Psalm 8:4-6

WHEN THE PSALMIST wrote Psalm 8, we sense he was looking up and marveling at the sky and the world all around him. But more than that, he was filled with wonder as he considered that God had put humans in charge of his creation, intending that we would fill the earth and subdue it.

Unfortunately, something went wrong with this original creation. That's what the writer of Hebrews acknowledges when he quotes Psalm 8, reminding his readers that the Fall kept us from fulfilling our original destiny. "At present, we do not yet see everything in subjection to him" (Hebrews 2:8, ESV). Humanity is supposed to rule the earth, but in reality, we are subject to this cursed creation in dreadful ways. Sin ruined everything; nothing is the way it was created to be.

But that does not mean that God's original plan for humanity has been abandoned. When we look around, we see that what Psalm 8 describes about humanity being crowned with glory and honor is not true of us. But we have reason for hope: "We . . . see Jesus, who was made lower than the angels for a little while, now crowned with glory and honor because he suffered death" (Hebrews 2:9, NIV). Through our union with Christ, we fulfill the destiny originally designed for us.

The world, and even some corners of the church, tell our children they must work hard and dream big to fulfill their destinies. But in Psalm 8 we discover the destiny that matters. This destiny becomes a reality, not through hard work, but by saving faith.

❋ ❋ ❋

Lord, as we consider the destiny you have in mind for the people you created, we realize this is what we want most for _____. We don't want _____ to settle for the glory and honor that the world offers. We want _____ to be crowned with the glory and honor that come from you. As _____ is joined to Christ, _____ takes hold of the destiny you have in mind for all of your people—ruling and reigning with you in a new heaven and new earth.

JULY 11

Integrity

Better to be poor and honest
than to be dishonest and a fool. PROVERBS 19:1

THERE COMES A DAY when a child tells his first lie, when he deceives in order to get something he wants or to get out of something he doesn't want to do. When that happens, a part of our heart breaks as we realize in a more personal way that our child is a sinner and that sin and self-preservation come as naturally to him as they do to us.

But of greater concern is when our children fall into a pattern of lying and become comfortable with deception. We long for them to be people of integrity—people who can be trusted to do what they say they will do, who are the same in private as they are in public, who are incorruptible and committed to honesty in dealing with others.

Certainly we can model integrity for our children. Proverbs tell us, "The righteous man walks in his integrity; His children are blessed after him" (20:7, NKJV). Our children benefit from our ongoing integrity. More than anyone else, they are in a position to see who we are behind the scenes. They notice when we pay full price for their ticket or meal—or when we lie about their age to save a few bucks. They listen as we notify the cable company that we should be charged for service to another room—or watch as we hook up cable we haven't paid for. They see us working hard because we know we're on the clock—or hear us tell our boss we're working from home when we're actually doing other things. By modeling integrity in our own lives, we encourage our children to act with integrity.

But our children need much more than our example or our rules. They need the Holy Spirit to fill them with a love for truth and a disdain for dishonesty. They need him to help them partake of the divine nature, which is one of perfect integrity. As our children are in Christ, they will increasingly become people of integrity.

※ ※ ※

Lord, show me the little ways I compromise that leave a legacy of something less than integrity for my children to see and follow. Show me how to challenge and correct the ways _____ *acts with a lack of integrity so that by the power of the Holy Spirit,* _____ *might know the joy of a clean conscience, a good reputation, and an unhindered relationship with you.*

The Power of God at Work

I am not ashamed of this Good News about Christ. It is the power of God at work, saving everyone who believes—the Jew first and also the Gentile. This Good News tells us how God makes us right in his sight. This is accomplished from start to finish by faith. As the Scriptures say, "It is through faith that a righteous person has life."
ROMANS 1:16-17

AT SOME POINT, we may feel a bit embarrassed to be the family that is so different from other families. We believe the gospel, and we live differently because of it. It impacts every area of our lives, creating a different set of values than those held by families who have not embraced Christ. But while we might feel some embarrassment, feelings of embarrassment don't reflect reality. The gospel is the greatest truth ever known and the best news ever given. As we lean into it and depend upon it day after day, we can be sure it will prove true. It will not ultimately lead to shame but will bring us into eternal safety and joy in the presence of a holy and glorious God.

We don't want the gospel to be one aspect of our home and family that we trot out only on Sundays. Instead, we want it to be at the center of our home, a constant topic of conversation and celebration, the very fabric of the way we process life together. We want to make this gospel clear to our children from their earliest days because it can be grasped at an early age. And as our children grow, we want them to see again and again that their parents are not ashamed of the Good News about Christ. That's why we do more than talk to our neighbors about church. We unashamedly talk about Christ and the change he has brought to our lives. Out of a desire to pursue holiness, we refuse to be embarrassed by the boundaries we've put in place for our family's entertainment and activity choices. Our confidence in the gospel makes us incredibly happy and unashamed people.

❋ ❋ ❋

What good news it is that you have made a way for us to be made right with you and have peace with you! This truth, this gospel, has the power to change everything. So we ask that its power go to work in our home. May this good news of a righteousness provided to us in Christ transform our interactions and expectations. Work in us and in _____ through the good news of your grace toward sinners.

God Gave Them Up

The wrath of God is revealed from heaven against all ungodliness and unrighteousness of men, who by their unrighteousness suppress the truth. . . . And since they did not see fit to acknowledge God, God gave them up to a debased mind to do what ought not to be done. ROMANS 1:18, 28, ESV

GOD'S ANGER is not an out-of-control outburst over a petty matter. Instead, he is provoked to anger by that which destroys what he created in his image. Paul tells us in Romans 1:18 that God is even now revealing his anger against ungodliness and unrighteousness. Ungodliness is wanting to have nothing to do with God. And unrighteousness is a perverse reaction to what God commands—living a life that celebrates the opposite of his loving law.

So how does God show his anger toward those who don't want anything to do with him? Three times we read in Romans 1 that God "gave them up." God gives up those who don't want to know him or obey him so that they are free to pursue lives away from him. He gives them up to what they want. He stands back and takes his hand off those who want his hand to be removed from their lives.

The good news that Paul presents in Romans, however, is that even though God "gave up" humanity to live apart from him, he did not give us up ultimately or forever. Instead he sent his Son into our godless and unrighteous world and *gave him up* to experience all the judgment we deserve. "Since he did not spare even his own Son but gave him up for us all, won't he also give us everything else?" (Romans 8:32).

God has not ultimately given us up or given up on us but has been patient in his anger so that we might come to him in repentance. And this is the patience we want to show to our children. Just as he kept reaching out to us in love, so we refuse to give up on our children but keep on reaching out to them in love.

❊ ❊ ❊

God, if you were to give us up ultimately and forever, we would have no hope. But instead you are patient, kindly calling us to repentance. And because you have not given up on us, we will not give up on _____. Instead, we will be patient for you to work to bring about the change that you see fit. Today is a day for grace, not for giving up.

Accountability

God does not show favoritism. When the Gentiles sin, they will be destroyed, even though they never had God's written law. And the Jews, who do have God's law, will be judged by that law when they fail to obey it. . . . And this is the message I proclaim—that the day is coming when God, through Christ Jesus, will judge everyone's secret life. ROMANS 2:11-12, 16

DIFFERENT PEOPLE have different advantages when it comes to the amount of revelation they've been given. But Paul makes clear in Romans 2 that God will not show favoritism to those who had access to more truth. Rather, judgment for all will be according to the truth they had. Everyone, Paul writes, has had the truth of God's moral law written on their hearts.

Of course, many of us have had much more than that. Think of how many Bibles we have in our homes, how many sermons we've heard, how many opportunities we've had to hear the truths of God's Word. Think about all of the truth we've resisted, ignored, or simply failed to work into our lives. We'll be held accountable for how we've lived in light of all that we have heard.

But it is not just sobering for us. It is sobering as we think about our children. They're growing up in a home where their parents care enough about the things of God to be reading this book. They have heard, perhaps since their earliest days, about a God who loves them and intends for them to know him and live for him. Yet they may have learned how to go through the motions of religiosity without opening their hearts to Christ.

When we stand before God on Judgment Day, the question for us and for our children will be: In view of how little or how much revelation you possessed, how did you live? How did you respond in your heart and your actions to what you knew? The day is coming when our hearts will be exposed. So we pray that our children will not fail to embrace the truth they've been given.

❊ ❊ ❊

Lord, we pray that on that day when what is hidden beneath the surface is revealed, what will become evident in _____ will be a deep and genuine love for you, borne out over a lifetime of living for you.

Motivated by Pride

Satan rose up against Israel and caused David to take a census of the people of Israel. So David said to Joab and the commanders of the army, "Take a census of all the people of Israel—from Beersheba in the south to Dan in the north—and bring me a report so I may know how many there are." 1 CHRONICLES 21:1-2

IT'S NOT IMMEDIATELY CLEAR what the problem was with the census David instructed his officers to take. But clearly if Satan rose up and was the driving force behind David's decision, we know it couldn't be good. Even Joab, who was not exactly a bastion of godliness, begged David not to do it, saying, "Why must you cause Israel to sin?" (verse 3). But David was not deterred. In fact, over the following nine months, he never pulled back but kept pushing ahead.

We get a sense of what was in David's heart when the tally was reported: "There were 1,100,000 warriors in all Israel who could handle a sword, and 470,000 in Judah" (verse 5). Of course, God had promised to preserve David's kingdom. It was never about the size of his army but about the faithfulness of his God, so David had no need to be concerned about the number of swords he could send onto the battlefield. Evidently David wanted the census so he could exult in the size of his army. He just wanted the count to puff himself up.

Taking a census wasn't a sin in itself. There were provisions for it in God's law. The problem was the motivation. David was driven by pride, which is number one on the list of the sins that God hates (Proverbs 6:16-19). Pride is such a sneaky sin, especially when it is at the heart of our motivation for doing something that isn't necessarily a sin. How we need, and how our children need, to examine what is driving us—especially when we want to count the "likes" on our social media post, the wins or records set in athletics, or the number of As on our children's report cards. What we need is for God to do whatever it takes to humble us so that we will not be seduced by the sin of pride.

※ ※ ※

Lord, we find ourselves so easily justifying actions that are motivated by pride. And because we live in a world filled with prideful chest-thumping over what we accomplish, it seems normal, not sinful. So give us eyes to see our pride, lips willing to confess it, and hearts that are changed and made clean by the sacrifice of your Son.

No One Does Good

All have turned away; all have become useless. No one does good, not a single one.
ROMANS 3:12

MOST OF US COULD MAKE a list of the ways our children need to change. We could catalog the sins our children need to repent of. But we would be very uncomfortable naming our own sins and confessing our own need for ongoing repentance. Especially to our children. We don't want them to know what big sinners we are. We have no problem admitting that we have sinned in a general sense, but we certainly don't want to get specific. We think we preserve our credibility for disciplining them by keeping our sin under wraps, but what we're really doing is depriving our children of what they need most from us—an example of living in light of the gospel.

Our children must do more than make a single decision for Christ; they need a daily experience of grace through Christ. We all do. But if we are unwilling to admit our constant need of a Savior, how will our children grow in their understanding of their own daily need for Jesus? We simply can't share the gospel with our children if we're not living in it ourselves.

Since every single person in our house is a sinner, it will not be news to our children that we sin. But it could be a real turning point for how they understand the gospel if we are honest with them about our own struggle against sin and our own need for the grace of repentance. On those days when our sins are on display for all to see, instead of justifying or hiding them, we can simply and humbly acknowledge that we need Jesus just as much as everyone else in our home. We can lead our children to Jesus and teach them the truth of the gospel by becoming the chief repenters in our families. Our children will learn what it looks like to walk humbly with their God by observing us walking closely with our God in repentance and obedience.

❄ ❄ ❄

Lord, I would love for _____ to think that I am better than I really am and that I'm more devoted to you than I really am. Somehow I've believed that to parent well I can't let my children know about my sin. But that is not wisdom; it's pride. When I present Christianity as a system of rules rather than as a welcome for sinners, I push _____ away from you rather than toward you. So give me the courage to come clean. Give me the strength to be weak.

Counted as Righteous

For the Scriptures tell us, "Abraham believed God, and God counted him as righteous because of his faith." When people work, their wages are not a gift, but something they have earned. But people are counted as righteous, not because of their work, but because of their faith in God who forgives sinners. ROMANS 4:3-5

AT SOME POINT we begin to teach our children how a bank account works. There are deposits and withdrawals, debits and credits. Banking also provides an illustration to help our children understand what it means to be a Christian.

Paul uses an accounting analogy when he says that Abraham was counted as righteous. In other words, when Abraham believed God, a credit was made to his spiritual account. God didn't merely pretend that there was some righteousness in Abraham's account; he made an actual deposit. Long before Jesus came and lived a righteous life—but in anticipation of that righteous life—God credited the righteousness of Christ to Abraham's account. He didn't pay Abraham for something he had earned. The righteousness of Christ was placed in his account as a gift.

This is the deposit we long to see made to our child's account. We know what our child has earned—the same thing we've earned, the same thing every person has earned: "For the wages of sin is death." So we're asking for a gift—a gift that can only come from God, a transfer that can only be made by his hands. We're asking for "the free gift of God . . . eternal life through Christ Jesus our Lord" (Romans 6:23).

❄ ❄ ❄

Lord, I can never earn enough or save enough to make the kind of credit to _____'s account that must be made for _____ to be counted as righteous before you. I am bankrupt when it comes to the kind of righteousness that is needed. So I come to you asking that you would make a deposit of the perfect righteousness of Jesus to _____'s account. Make _____ rich with all the goodness of Jesus.

Endurance

We can rejoice, too, when we run into problems and trials, for we know that they help us develop endurance. And endurance develops strength of character, and character strengthens our confident hope of salvation. And this hope will not lead to disappointment. For we know how dearly God loves us, because he has given us the Holy Spirit to fill our hearts with his love. ROMANS 5:3-5

WE CAN BECOME DISCOURAGED at any stage of the parenting journey. In the earliest years, we wonder how long it will take for our children to sleep through the night. Then we wonder how long it will be until our child listens and obeys. Later we wonder how long it is going to take for our teenager to come to his senses. In every period of waiting, we're tempted to lose hope, which can make parenting a heavy burden.

Parenting well requires endurance. Love over the long haul. A willingness to wait for God to work. So one of the most important tasks for a parent is simply to refuse to give up when things are hard.

When we need strength to endure, the Spirit brings to mind the truths of Scripture to infuse us with hope. When we're tempted to think that we are the wrong parents for our children, the Spirit reminds us that God placed them with us so they could know him (Acts 17:26-27). When we're tempted to think that our children will never turn toward God, the Spirit reminds us that God works in and through families (Acts 11:14; 16:31). When we're afraid that something has happened that will ruin our children's lives, the Spirit reminds us that nothing can separate them from God's love (Romans 8:35-39). The Spirit reminds us that the hardest circumstances in our kids' lives are not outside of God's plan, but are part of his plan to bring good (Romans 8:28).

※ ※ ※

Lord, when we run into problems with _____ , help us to remember that you work in the midst of problems and trials to develop something in us that could come no other way. We would never find refuge in the hope of salvation if we never felt the need for it. So we refuse to look for the quick and easy fix. Instead, we invite you to have your way in us to develop endurance. Give us the patience, wisdom, and love we need for parenting in all the years to come.

A Father's Charge

Now, with God as our witness, and in the sight of all Israel—the LORD's assembly—I give
you this charge. Be careful to obey all the commands of the LORD your God, so that
you may continue to possess this good land and leave it to your children as a permanent
inheritance. And Solomon, my son, learn to know the God of your ancestors intimately.
Worship and serve him with your whole heart and a willing mind. 1 CHRONICLES 28:8-9

IN 1 CHRONICLES 28, we read King David's wise and careful charge to his son Solomon
as he released the reins of the kingdom to him. David told Solomon to be careful to
obey all the commands of the Lord. Shortly after, when God invited Solomon to ask
him for anything, Solomon chose to ask for wisdom.

This was a very promising beginning of Solomon's reign. But we discover problems
shortly thereafter. First was the alliance Solomon made with Egypt by marrying the
daughter of Pharaoh. He did so even though God had commanded Israel's kings never
to return to Egypt (Deuteronomy 17:16; 1 Kings 3:1). Then there was the offering of
sacrifices at the high places, even though God had commanded Israel to destroy these
sites (Deuteronomy 12:2-5; 1 Kings 3:3).

David charged Solomon to serve God with his whole heart, and he seems to be on the
right path when we read in 1 Kings 3:3 that "Solomon loved the LORD"—something not
said about any other person in the Bible. But at the end of his story, we read that Solomon
"loved many foreign women" and that "his heart was not wholly true to the LORD his God"
(1 Kings 11:1, 4, ESV). Clearly a dramatic change had taken place in Solomon's affections.
If only Solomon had followed his father's charge to give himself wholeheartedly to God.

Solomon shows us that even the wisest people sometimes foolishly disregard the
godly guidance of their parents. The problem was not that David was unclear or
inconsistent or that David called Solomon to do something unreasonable. The issue
was not with David's parenting, but with Solomon's heart.

❊ ❊ ❊

Lord, when we are tempted to heap blame on ourselves for the ways in which _____
has failed to embrace the godly guidance we have given, help us to remember that some-
times the judicious instructions of parents go unheeded. Sometimes wisdom offered is
not taken hold of. Help us to remember that it is your voice _____ must hear, your
Word _____ must heed.

Give Yourselves Completely

Do not let any part of your body become an instrument of evil to serve sin. Instead, give yourselves completely to God, for you were dead, but now you have new life. So use your whole body as an instrument to do what is right for the glory of God. ROMANS 6:13

PARENTING BEGINS with the delivery of a little body that we are tasked to care for. As our children grow, we can pray that every part of their bodies will be given over to please God.

※ ※ ※

Lord, from head to toe, inside and out, from beginning to end, may no part of _____'s body become an instrument of evil to serve sin. Instead, may _____'s whole body be an instrument to do what is right for your glory!

Don't let _____'s feet take him to places where darkness will envelop him and seduce him. Instead, let his feet take him to places where he can push back the darkness and radiate your light.

Don't let _____'s appetites for sex or food or drink make him a slave to them. Instead, sanctify his appetites for sex and food and drink so that all of them cause him to look to you for the satisfaction he craves.

Don't let _____'s heart go after passions that will take the place that should be reserved for you alone. Instead, break _____'s heart with the things that break your heart. Capture _____'s heart with a passion for your gospel and your glory.

Don't let _____'s mouth be used to speak what is false or filthy or futile. Instead, fill _____'s mouth with words of truth, words of purity, words of meaning and purpose. May _____'s mouth be full of blessing, encouragement, and peace.

Don't let _____'s hands grasp the things of this world too tightly. Instead, give him hands that are willing to work and hands that touch others in great compassion.

Don't let _____'s eyes seek out what is corrupting or contaminating. Give _____ a love for what is beautiful and pure.

Don't let _____'s ears tune in to voices that doubt or mock the things of God. Instead, give him ears that are open to your Word and your ways.

Don't let _____'s intellect be captured by the thought patterns of this world. Instead, fill his mind with the depths of your knowledge and wisdom.

Serving God in the New Way

When we were controlled by our old nature, sinful desires were at work within us, and the law aroused these evil desires that produced a harvest of sinful deeds, resulting in death. But now we have been released from the law, for we died to it and are no longer captive to its power. Now we can serve God, not in the old way of obeying the letter of the law, but in the new way of living in the Spirit. ROMANS 7:5-6

WE LOVE IT when our kids make us look good by what they do. We'd much rather see our children's names on the honor roll than on the detention list. But when we expect ongoing good behavior based solely on their knowledge of and determination to obey the rules, we set up our children for failure and despair. If they must constantly strive to live up to a set of moral expectations or social constructs, however formally or informally they are communicated, life will be drudgery. Absolute success will be an impossibility. Peace and joy will be elusive. And at some point, our children will likely give up.

So what we want is not kids who live by the rules, but kids who live in the Spirit. We want our kids to experience the "but now" of Romans 7:6. We want them to experience a miracle accomplished by a work of God. At the moment of conversion, we want God to implant in our children a desire to please him. We want our kids to experience the joy and freedom of living for Christ out of a deep inner desire put there by God himself. Our attempts at imposing rules can't accomplish this. Only God can.

This "new way of living in the Spirit" doesn't become a reality in an instant, but over a lifetime. So what we're looking for in our kids is not perfection, but growth. We don't expect them to "arrive" at any point, but we pray that they will continually be moving forward in genuine service and love for God.

⁕ ⁕ ⁕

Thank you, Lord, for not leaving _____ on her own, with no power to change. You have lifted the burden of creating change off _____'s shoulders. You keep meeting _____ with transforming grace. Free _____ from dutiful obedience imposed from the outside. Empower _____ to say no to sinful desires by the power of your indwelling Spirit. Impart to _____ a love for holiness.

No Condemnation

Now there is no condemnation for those who belong to Christ Jesus. ROMANS 8:1

NEVER HAS THERE BEEN better news. Never has there been a better reason to take a deep breath and release all your fears and regrets. If you are in Christ, joined to him by faith, there is no condemnation hanging over you, threatening you, accusing you.

It's not that you have never done anything worthy of judgment. It is not that all parents just need to give themselves a break. Parents who are outside of Christ, who have not taken hold of Christ, have plenty of reason to feel dread over their failures to live up to God's standards. But the unbelievable good news for imperfect parents who are in Christ is that all the condemnation we deserve for not being patient enough, for not being attentive enough, for simply not *being* enough has been laid upon Christ. All of the condemnation we deserve for cutting our children to pieces with our words, for being harsh with our children out of anger, for crushing their spirits with our unrealistic expectations, has been laid on Jesus. This means that God can turn to those who are in Christ and assure us: "There is no condemnation for you. You don't have to keep on carrying such a heavy weight of guilt and regret."

When our children struggle, it is easy to find reasons to be quite sure it is our fault. So what do we do with that? We will probably never be able to figure out exactly what causes difficulties in their lives. But when we are convinced that there is no condemnation for those who are in Christ Jesus, we can admit our failings freely, humble ourselves before our children, and begin to find healing together.

※ ※ ※

Lord, these words—"no condemnation"—are two of the most beautiful words in the world. And yet some days they are hard for me to believe, hard for me to take hold of. On one hand, I'm quick to blame someone or something else for the struggles my kids face. But deep down I condemn myself. Help me to live and love in the reality of the freedom that comes from your grace. And most of all, may my embrace of this gospel truth change how my children deal with the self-condemnation that threatens their peace.

We Wait

Against its will, all creation was subjected to God's curse. But with eager hope, the creation looks forward to the day when it will join God's children in glorious freedom from death and decay. For we know that all creation has been groaning as in the pains of childbirth right up to the present time. And we believers also groan, even though we have the Holy Spirit within us as a foretaste of future glory, for we long for our bodies to be released from sin and suffering. We, too, wait with eager hope for the day when God will give us our full rights as his adopted children, including the new bodies he has promised us. ROMANS 8:20-23

"GROANING as in the pains of childbirth." It's a dramatic picture, a vivid memory for many moms especially. The pain seemed unbearable. We wanted it to be over as soon as possible. The reason we were willing to endure it, however, was that we knew the pain would prove profitable. After the delivery, we would welcome a new life worth all the waiting. The painful groans of childbirth would give way to the incredible joys of holding a baby in our arms and in our hearts.

Our groaning didn't end when our children were born, however. In many ways, it was only the beginning. Paul says that we groan even as we wait with eager hope. So what does that mean for parents? It means that we aren't surprised by trouble. We don't expect the Christian life to unfold without struggle. Because we know death and decay are realities of the fallen creation we live in, we don't accuse God of wrong when our children are impacted by the effects of the curse. We're not surprised when accidents happen or natural disasters strike or deadly viruses infect. We groan, but we don't give up. In the midst of our sorrow is a radiant, confident hope that a day is coming that will make all of the pain of this life worthwhile—a day of glory so great that our sufferings will seem small by comparison.

※ ※ ※

Lord, sometimes I groan as I think about waiting for you to free the world from death and decay. The curse is so real. We feel its effects in our family. We see its effects in our community. We experience its effects in our bodies. But you also enable us to anticipate a future glory. Help us to savor every foretaste of what is to come and wait with eager hope.

Everything

We know that God causes everything to work together for the good of those who love God and are called according to his purpose for them. For God knew his people in advance, and he chose them to become like his Son, so that his Son would be the firstborn among many brothers and sisters. ROMANS 8:28-29

PERHAPS THE HARDEST WORD to swallow in Romans 8:28 is the word *everything*. That means not one thing falls outside of this promise. It is the "everything" in this verse that is both a stumbling block and a blessed solace. In his sovereignty, God is committed and able to use even the worst things we can imagine for our ultimate good and for the ultimate good of our child.

But perhaps that's where the rub comes most profoundly. As hard as it can be to believe that God can and will cause everything to work together for the good in our own lives because we belong to him, it can be much harder to believe this for our children. When we see hurts and hardship take their toll in our children's lives, it can be so terribly difficult to rest in God's promise, believing that he will use this struggle to cause them to become more like Christ. We want to be able to see a specific "good thing" come from the hard thing before we are willing to believe it is true.

Without some evidence, we are prone to stew in worry and perhaps give in to despair. But taking hold of this truth and promise keeps us focused on God's purpose in our children's lives—which is to make them more and more like Jesus. Grabbing hold of this purpose requires that we let go of our desires for a comfortable life for our children. But it enables us to embrace a life of purpose and meaning even when that includes pain.

❈ ❈ ❈

Lord, either everything works for good, or nothing makes sense. I believe, but help my unbelief. Give me a deep and undergirding confidence that you can and will cause everything to work together for the good of anyone who belongs to you. Your sovereignty over these hard things can be difficult to accept, but it is also my greatest source of comfort.

Revelation

IN PSALM 19, David delineates the perfections of Scripture and the impact of God's Word. This is the influence we pray that his Word will have in our children's lives.

The instructions of the LORD are perfect, reviving the soul.

Lord, may _____ receive rather than resist the perfect instruction in your Word. And may _____'s soul be revived rather than burdened in receiving your instruction.

The decrees of the LORD are trustworthy, making wise the simple.

Lord, may _____ put his full trust in what you decree for his life. Make _____ wise as he trusts you with the truths he does not fully understand.

The commandments of the LORD are right, bringing joy to the heart.

Lord, give _____ the outrageous joy of discovering that everything you command is for his good and for your glory.

The commands of the LORD are clear, giving insight for living.

Lord, _____ needs the insight that comes only from you to make his way through life. Give him understanding of your clear commands and a heart to obey.

Reverence for the LORD is pure, lasting forever.

Lord, you are worthy of honor and awe. Take away any casual attitude toward sin and fill _____ with a sense of reverential awe toward you.

The laws of the LORD are true; each one is fair.

Lord, while the world around _____ tells him lies, your word is eternally and perfectly true. Give him ears to listen to your truth.

They are more desirable than gold, even the finest gold.

Lord, _____ has so many cravings that threaten this supreme desire. Give him a burning desire for your Word.

They are sweeter than honey, even honey dripping from the comb.

Lord, _____ has tasted so many sweet things in the world you've created. Give him a sweet tooth for your Word.

ADAPTED FROM PSALM 19:7-10

In What Will You Put Your Trust?

Some trust in chariots and some in horses,
but we trust in the name of the LORD our God. PSALM 20:7, ESV

IT WOULD HAVE BEEN perfectly natural for the king of Israel to put his trust in the size and capabilities of his standing army. That's the way life worked in his day. But David was determined to turn to a completely different source of security. Rather than relying on human ability, he was determined to trust in God alone.

Similarly, it is perfectly natural for parents today who are concerned about their children to put their trust in many things that seem to offer security. Parents put their trust in good neighborhoods and good schools, good experiences and good examples, good health and good opportunities. On top of that, they rely on their own efforts at good parenting.

So where will you put your trust? At the heart of what it means to follow God is to make him the center and source of our security. We no longer depend on worldly defenses and safeguards. Our child's future does not depend on the protection, opportunities, or oversight we can provide. We trust in the name of the Lord our God.

Instead of trusting in savings accounts and insurance policies, we trust the God who provides for his own. Instead of trusting in health regimens and safety precautions, we trust in the God who protects his own. Instead of trusting in our own plans and dreams, we trust in the God who preordains every day of our lives. Instead of trusting in what we can achieve or what our kids can achieve, we trust in what Christ has accomplished on our behalf.

※ ※ ※

Lord, so many things falsely promise security. But the only true and lasting security in this uncertain world is Christ. So help me, Lord, when I am tempted to put my hope and confidence in what may seem promising but is ultimately unstable. Keep calling me back to trust you with everything about _____'s life.

Open Arms

Later Isaiah spoke boldly for God, saying, "I was found by people who were not looking for me. I showed myself to those who were not asking for me." But regarding Israel, God said, "All day long I opened my arms to them, but they were disobedient and rebellious." ROMANS 10:20-21

THE OPEN ARMS of a parent offer refuge, acceptance, safety, and belonging. This is the way God describes himself—arms open wide to pull a child close. God puts this picture in front of us to help us understand his posture toward us and toward our children.

We might expect a completely different posture from our heavenly Father. We might expect that his arms would be crossed in anger and frustration, or at his sides, waiting for us to make the first move. We might expect that he would want to keep us at a distance. But no. His arms are open, welcoming us to come near to be loved and cared for.

"All day long" he opens his arms to us. "All day long" is a very long time. God is patient and persistent. The day of grace has not ended, and so his arms are still open, beckoning his children to come to him.

It's such a beautiful picture that we can hardly understand why anyone would ever refuse to be embraced in this way, why anyone would choose to disobey or rebel against such a loving Father. But that was the reality for many Jewish people who had been exposed to this revelation of the Father's heart over a lifetime. They refused his glad welcome. It is also the reality of many today who grow up surrounded by the good news of God's invitation but refuse to enter his embrace. Oh, that our children might run into his open arms!

❋ ❋ ❋

Lord, I can see you there, arms open, welcoming _____ to come to you. You have extended that offer through the many sermons she has heard, prayers she has prayed, and Bible readings she's experienced over the years. Overcome any lingering resistance so that _____ will find herself at home in your presence. Enfold _____ in an embrace that nothing on earth or in heaven will ever diminish or disturb.

Impossible to Understand

Oh, how great are God's riches and wisdom and knowledge! How impossible it is for us to understand his decisions and his ways! ROMANS 11:33

INTERESTINGLY, in Paul's great letter to the Romans, after explaining so much about God's plan and purposes, Paul himself admits that it is impossible for us to understand all of God's decisions and ways. He says that God's judgments, or decrees, cannot be searched to the bottom and that his paths cannot be followed to the end. We will never completely comprehend all he is doing, nor will we ever come to full clarity about why.

It's not that we can never expect to know anything about God's ways. But we can only understand what is revealed to us. And as much as God has made known to us, he has not divulged everything, particularly the detailed explanations and answers to all of our "why" questions. While he knows the path that lies ahead for us and for our children, we don't. He calls us to live by faith in his sovereign and loving purposes. He asks us to trust him with what is beyond our ability to understand.

God has gone ahead of us, cutting a path for human history and for our lives. And his ways are beyond our tracing out—we cannot fully grasp exactly why he has ordained that the world and our lives are taking a particular course.

What path is God taking you or your child down that is inscrutable—impossible to understand or accept as the intended route for your lives? God knows what he is doing. His depths of knowledge, wisdom, and mercy are unfathomably deep, so we can trust him even when we find his ways inscrutable. We might not know what he's doing, but we can be sure that *he does.*

❋ ❋ ❋

Lord, I want to stop insisting that I must understand everything you're doing in our lives before I am willing to accept it. Forgive me for foolishly thinking that my plans would be better than yours. Forgive me for arrogantly thinking I know more than you about the solutions to my problems. I might not understand your decisions, but I want to accept them. And I might not be able to trace your ways, but I want to go, and I want _____ to go, wherever you lead.

You Will Learn to Know

Don't copy the behavior and customs of this world, but let God transform you into a new person by changing the way you think. Then you will learn to know God's will for you, which is good and pleasing and perfect. ROMANS 12:2

IF THERE'S ANYTHING we want for our kids, it is that they would know and walk in the will of God. But how are they going to know what his will is? Should they expect to hear him speak to them about big and small decisions in their subconscious thoughts? Should they "try on" particular decisions to see if they have "a peace" about them? Should they seek to interpret God's voice through their circumstances?

As much as we and our children might like to receive divine messages telling us specifically what to do and where to go, nothing in the Bible indicates that God guides us in this way. Just because God spoke in a certain way to particular believers at one point in redemption history doesn't mean that's the way he speaks to ordinary believers today.

Yet we can be sure that God will guide our children. He won't necessarily provide them with a map that tells them exactly where to go and what to do, but he has provided them with a compass. This compass is his word to us in the Bible. It will constantly and unerringly point our children toward God's will for their lives.

We don't want our children to leave decision-making behind in pursuit of divine messages. We don't want them to be in continual pursuit of a supernatural, extrabiblical word from God that will tell them where to go and what to do. We don't want them to try discerning God's will solely through feelings of peace or through interpreting the circumstances of life, which can be ambiguous. We don't want them to live in fear of missing the message. Instead, we want the minds of our children to be transformed as the work of the Spirit applies the Word of God to their hearts, awakening a response and leading them to follow him. We want them to have the mind of Christ so they will be able to discern what is good and pleasing and perfect.

✺ ✺ ✺

Lord, do your transforming work in _____ through your Word, that _____ might learn to know your heart, your mind, and your desires. Give _____ the mind of Christ so that he will be able to make wise decisions that will be pleasing to you. Guide him in your way and by your Word to embrace your will.

Authority

Everyone must submit to governing authorities. For all authority comes from God, and those in positions of authority have been placed there by God. So anyone who rebels against authority is rebelling against what God has instituted, and they will be punished. ROMANS 13:1-2

IT MIGHT BE EASIER to dismiss Paul's instructions to submit to governing authorities if we could argue that the rulers in his day were so just and good that they deserved such submission. But of course Jesus was executed on the pretext of treason, and Paul himself was accused of insurrection. A time of intense persecution for Christians in Rome was around the corner. It was into that reality that Paul instructed those who were the recipients of the saving grace of God in Christ to respond in submission to civil government. "The authorities are God's servants, sent for your good," Paul wrote in verse 4. Paul recognized that even unjust civil authorities restrain the tidal wave of evil that would break over the world without them.

Of course, there is an even larger principle in this passage that has import for the way we raise our children. It is that God puts all authority in place. To live in full recognition of God's sovereignty over the world is to recognize, and to help our children recognize, that every authority they come under has been put there by God. It's easy for us to encourage our kids to respect the authority of teachers we admire, coaches we appreciate, and bosses we look up to. But when our child tells us about an unworthy teacher, when we observe a coach treating our child unfairly, or when we recognize that a boss has done little to earn our child's respect, it is so much harder to encourage our kids to rightly submit to this authority. That's when we must remember that submission is not primarily motivated by the person to whom we submit, but is an act of obedience and submission to the Lord himself.

❊ ❊ ❊

Lord, we want _____ to learn to live under your authority. And that means submitting to human leaders—even, and perhaps especially, those who don't earn her respect. Most of all, we want _____ to gladly submit to your authority. So help _____ to make the connection. Grant _____ the grace to submit to every authority as unto you.

We Give Account

Remember, we will all stand before the judgment seat of God. For the Scriptures say, "'As surely as I live,' says the LORD, 'every knee will bend to me, and every tongue will declare allegiance to God.'" Yes, each of us will give a personal account to God.
ROMANS 14:10-12

PARENTING really matters to us. We want to get it right, and we're aware of the many ways in which we don't. So in our desperation to prop ourselves up in the parenting department, we are sometimes tempted to sit in judgment over other parents. We judge them to be too involved or completely oblivious, too lax or too harsh. From our vantage point, we're quite sure their kids' struggles are a result of their compromises and inconsistencies.

But Paul calls us down from the perch from which we look down on our brothers and sisters. He reminds us that we are all destined to stand before one Judge—one high and holy Judge before whom we will be required to give a personal account for how we've parented the children he has entrusted to us.

Jesus said that we will give an account on Judgment Day for every idle word we have spoken. Oh my. Harsh words. Unhelpful words. Hypocritical words. Jesus told the story of a steward who was entrusted with resources and called to account for how he invested them upon the master's return. We, too, will be called to give an account on the day our Master returns. Oh my. We've been given so much time and so many financial, spiritual, and educational resources to raise children who will love and serve the Lord. But we know we've wasted time, wasted opportunities, and wasted effort on things that simply don't matter while neglecting what will matter for eternity. We simply have no standing to judge others. We stand in need of mercy.

❀ ❀ ❀

Lord, we ask your forgiveness for the condescending comments and quick judgments we've made about the ways other people parent their kids. We ask your help to keep our focus on being ready to stand before you ourselves instead of on pointing out the failures of others. How could we persist in extending anything but mercy to others when you have granted so much mercy to us?

Accept Each Other

Therefore, accept each other just as Christ has accepted you so that God will be given glory. ROMANS 15:7

SOMETIMES WE SEE OURSELVES—our interests, our temperament, our beliefs, our mannerisms—reflected back in the lives of our children. But other times we see exactly the opposite. Sometimes our children grow and flourish in the direction of our dreams for them. But other times our vision for our children doesn't match up with how they are turning out.

We don't find it difficult to accept and affirm those areas in our children that are a positive reflection of ourselves. We feel respected and affirmed by our kids when they follow in our footsteps and agree with our positions. The rub comes when God gives us children who think differently than we do, value different things than we do, and process life differently than we do. When this is the case, we may feel justified in withholding our affirmation, approval, and acceptance.

But then we read the words of Paul, who instructs us to accept each other. He's telling us to go beyond mere tolerance to warm acceptance of those in the body of Christ who are different than we are—including our children.

This can sometimes seem like a tall order. And Paul seems to realize that genuine acceptance is never easy. So he provides us with both a motivation and a resource to accept others. Remembering and relishing the acceptance we've received from Christ provides what we need to accept others.

If you think about it, when we talk about acceptance in the church, we mostly talk about it in terms of us accepting Jesus. But the reality here is that Jesus accepted us even when we thought much differently than he does, valued things much differently than he does, and processed life much differently than he does. He didn't require that we clean up our lives first. Like the father of the Prodigal Son, he ran to us, embraced us, and welcomed us into his family. Oh, that we might have the grace to accept our children in this way.

❆ ❆ ❆

Lord, I need your grace to accept _____ in the same welcoming, affirming, gladhearted way in which you accepted me. I need words of affirmation and encouragement. I need a countenance of joy and openness. I need a willingness to let go of my expectations for _____ so I can accept and celebrate _____'s life as it unfolds.

Forgetfulness

While in deep distress, Manasseh sought the LORD his God and sincerely humbled himself before the God of his ancestors. And when he prayed, the LORD listened to him and was moved by his request. So the LORD brought Manasseh back to Jerusalem and to his kingdom. Then Manasseh finally realized that the LORD alone is God!
2 CHRONICLES 33:12-13

MOSES REPEATEDLY WARNED the people of Israel to remember the Lord when they settled in the Promised Land, saying, "Take care, lest you forget the covenant of the LORD your God, which he made with you, and make a carved image, the form of anything that the LORD your God has forbidden you" (Deuteronomy 4:23, ESV). But they did forget.

Their failure to remember reached its zenith in the days when Manasseh—a man whose name meant "forgetfulness"—reigned over Judah. The king over God's people was supposed to rule in righteousness, leading in loving the Lord exclusively. But Manasseh led them in worshiping idols and forsaking the Lord. The king over God's people was also supposed to listen to what God had to say to him through the prophets, but Manasseh killed the prophets who pointed out his sin.

Because Judah, along with her king, forgot God, God did something Judah would never forget—"the LORD sent the commanders of the Assyrian armies, and they took Manasseh prisoner. They put a ring through his nose, bound him in bronze chains, and led him away to Babylon" (2 Chronicles 33:11). Judah watched as her king was treated like an animal. But in that faraway land, God reminded this forgetful king of his steadfast love, and Manasseh sincerely humbled himself before God. We might wonder if it was too little too late. But while Manasseh deserved God's judgment, he experienced God's mercy.

Manasseh shows us that there is no evil we or our children can do that is so great that God will not show mercy when we call out to him in repentance. When we humble ourselves in this way, we are sure to experience his abundant mercy.

※ ※ ※

Lord, we so easily lose sight of all it means that you have bound yourself in covenant love to us. But we really don't want to forget. We ask you to protect _____ from forgetfulness of your love. We ask that _____ would cling so closely to you that it would not require deep distress to make her realize that you alone are God. May _____ never forget she can do no evil so great that you will not show mercy when she repents.

Nothing to Hide

Declare me innocent, O LORD,
for I have acted with integrity;
I have trusted in the LORD without wavering.
Put me on trial, LORD, and cross-examine me.
Test my motives and my heart.
For I am always aware of your unfailing love,
and I have lived according to your truth. PSALM 26:1-3

IN THIS PSALM, one could mistake David's confidence for pride as he boldly invited the God who sees and knows all to fully investigate his actions and motives and publicly declare him to be an authentic believer. He claimed to have always had his focus on the steadfast love of God and to have lived day in and day out in line with God's character and commands. In another claim that could come off as arrogant, David distinguished himself from liars, hypocrites, and those who do evil.

But David was not speaking with pride. If he was driven by confidence in his own record, he wouldn't have asked God to redeem him. He wouldn't have asked God to show him mercy. Instead, David closed his psalm by imploring God, "Redeem me and show me mercy. Now I stand on solid ground, and I will publicly praise the LORD" (Psalm 26:11-12). David knew he could not depend on his own record of integrity to earn favor with God. He stood instead on the solid ground of God's grace for sinners. Of course he couldn't grasp this grace as clearly as you and I can on this side of the Cross. He didn't know exactly how what happened on the altar made his dirty hands clean, but he trusted the Lord without wavering. He lived according to the truth he had been given.

This is the kind of confident faith we long to see flourish in our children. We want the grace of God to become so real to them that they can throw open the windows of their lives, confident they have no need to hide anything from God since all has been dealt with at his altar. We desire to see an increasing congruity between God's character and their character take shape, an increasing confidence in grace for sinners.

❈ ❈ ❈

Lord, we long for you to work in _____'s life so that _____ can pray this kind of confident, nothing-to-hide, everything-to-expect prayer to you.

Relentless Compassion

*All the leaders of the priests and the people became more and more unfaithful. They
followed all the pagan practices of the surrounding nations, desecrating the Temple
of the LORD that had been consecrated in Jerusalem. The LORD, the God of their
ancestors, repeatedly sent his prophets to warn them, for he had compassion on his
people and his Temple. But the people mocked these messengers of God and despised
their words. They scoffed at the prophets until the LORD's anger could no longer be
restrained and nothing could be done.* 2 CHRONICLES 36:14-16

IN THESE VERSES, we see that Yahweh is a persistent and patient Father, providing every
opportunity for his children to obey and thereby enjoy all of his blessings. He gave the
Israelites priests who took their concerns into the presence of God and offered their
sacrifices on the altar of God. But the priests were unfaithful and began to exploit
God's people and lead them astray. He came down to dwell among his people in the
Temple's Most Holy Place, but they desecrated his house by offering sacrifices to other
gods within its holy walls. He sent prophets who warned of what would happen if the
Israelites persisted in their rebellion. But instead of listening to the prophets, the people
mocked them.

These final verses in 2 Chronicles present a seemingly sad ending in light of all of the
promises God had made to them and all of the blessings he had poured out on them.
But though this is the end of the history recorded in this book, it is nowhere near the
end of the story. God would continue to extend himself to his rebellious children. The
day would come when he would send a better priest to dwell with his people, not in
the Temple but among them as one of them. Rather than sending his Word through a
prophet, the Word would become flesh.

God did not give up on his people in the face of their rejection. He continued to
pursue them and draw them to himself. And this is still God's character. This is the God
in whom we have put our hope for our children. Though they may so far have resisted
and rejected God's provision or mocked and scoffed at God's Word, don't give up. He
is relentless in his pursuit of his people.

❈ ❈ ❈

*Lord, you are a relentless Father, pursuing us in love. Help me to pursue _____ while
modeling your kind of faithfulness, your kind of persistence, your kind of compassion.*

Stirred Up

God stirred the hearts of the priests and Levites and the leaders of the tribes of Judah and Benjamin to go to Jerusalem to rebuild the Temple of the LORD. Ezra 1:5

THE PEOPLE OF GOD were far away from the land where God had promised to dwell with them, far away from the Temple where they had gone to find forgiveness, far away from being all that they were meant to be. They were five hundred miles east of Jerusalem in Babylon, living in a foreign culture that was intent on assimilating them. But then a new regime came into power. The Persians overtook the Babylonians. God "stirred the heart" of the Persian king, Cyrus, to send out a proclamation that all of the Jews who wanted to could go back to Jerusalem to rebuild the Temple.

So who would go? "Everyone whose spirit God had stirred" (verse 5, ESV).

To bring his people home to himself, God stirred up the pagan king to release them. Then he moved in the hearts of some of his people, giving them the desire to leave Babylon behind and find their home in God's land. In several waves, over several decades, a remnant of God's people went home to start over—to start over in the land, to start over on the Temple, to start over with God, and to be the people he had always intended for them to be. Going back to Jerusalem was not merely a geographical relocation. It was a personal transformation, a whole-life reorientation—away from the world that wanted to assimilate them and toward the city where God intended to sanctify them.

God still stirs up people to leave the world, with all of its familiarity and comforts, and to enter the city of God, where true security can be found. We long for this stirring in the hearts of our children so that they will be drawn to make their home in God.

❀ ❀ ❀

Lord, you stir the hearts of pagan kings, and you move in the hearts of your people. Won't you kindle a fire in _____'s heart to leave behind the Babylon of this world and come home to you? Won't you stir until _____ moves?

So We Can Know

It was to us that God revealed these things by his Spirit. For his Spirit searches out everything and shows us God's deep secrets. No one can know a person's thoughts except that person's own spirit, and no one can know God's thoughts except God's own Spirit. And we have received God's Spirit (not the world's spirit), so we can know the wonderful things God has freely given us. 1 CORINTHIANS 2:10-12

EARLIER PAUL SPOKE about "the kind of wisdom that belongs to this world or to the rulers of this world" (verse 6). Our first thought may be that he was talking about those with political or governmental power. But Paul was referring to the thought leaders of his day, the people with influence on the culture. These were people who had a huge hole in their grasp of what was ultimately true and important. These "rulers of the world" saw what happened at the cross as weak and ineffective, even ridiculous and despicable. They just didn't get it. Yet they kept talking.

Certainly, if we were looking to identify the "rulers of the world" today, those who significantly influence the way people think, we would point to afternoon television gurus, political talk-show hosts, popular bloggers and columnists, entertainers and athletes. These voices dominate the conversation in our culture, sometimes in 140 characters.

But this is not the wisdom we want our children to absorb. These are not the voices we want our children to listen to. The "wisdom that belongs to this world" simply can't help them understand "the mystery of God—his plan that was previously hidden, even though he made it for our ultimate glory before the world began" (verses 6-7). This is what they need most to know, but they need more than simply the facts about God's plan of redemption through Christ. They need another dimension of revelation that takes place in their very spirits. They need God's Spirit, not the world's spirit, to impress upon them the wisdom of God's plan and why it's essential for an abundant life. Only God's Spirit can enable our children to "know the wonderful things God has freely given us" (verse 12).

❋ ❋ ❋

Lord, the temptation to try to be the Spirit in _____'s life is strong. I find myself always listening for a voice that can speak your truth to _____ in a way that _____ will hear and receive. But there is only one way _____ will come to know all you have freely given us in Christ, and that's as you reveal these wonderful things by your Spirit.

The Voice of the Lord

The voice of the LORD echoes above the sea.
  The God of glory thunders.
  The LORD thunders over the mighty sea.
The voice of the LORD is powerful;
  the voice of the LORD is majestic.
The voice of the LORD splits the mighty cedars;
  the LORD shatters the cedars of Lebanon. PSALM 29:3-5

WHEN WE READ PSALM 29, we get the sense that David is looking up at the sky, watching the progress of a storm sweeping over all of Israel. But he's not just watching it. He is hearing what the Lord seeks to say to him through it.

The scene opens in heaven, where supernatural beings are paying homage to the Lord, worshiping him as the splendor of his holy presence surrounds them. But then the magnificent presence of the Lord moves from heaven to earth like a storm rushes across the sky. After first appearing over the unruly Mediterranean Sea, the Lord's presence bears down on land as it thunders from the north of Israel, where Lebanon's massive cedar trees are split by its force, down the whole length of Canaan to the wilderness of Kadesh, where his power leaves behind twisted oak trees and stripped forests. Anyone who has ever experienced a storm with thunder, bolts of lightning, and tree-twisting, forest-stripping winds has a sense of what David is describing.

The Lord's voice is shattering. The same voice that splits the mighty cedars of Lebanon can cut through any resistance our children have toward God. The Lord's voice is striking, piercing like a bolt of lightning. This voice can speak to our child like a gentle rain of gradual understanding or like a lightning strike of life-changing insight. The Lord's voice is shaking. It can jolt our children out of their apathy and comfort. The Lord's voice is stripping. Just as it leaves the forest bare, it can peel away negative attitudes and arguments from our children's hearts and minds.

❊ ❊ ❊

Lord, we can't help but long for _____ to sense your power and hear you speak. Won't you sweep down over our home in the way David saw you sweeping through Israel from north to south? Come reign as king in our hearts forever.

Evaluated

As for me, it matters very little how I might be evaluated by you or by any human authority. I don't even trust my own judgment on this point. My conscience is clear, but that doesn't prove I'm right. It is the Lord himself who will examine me and decide. 1 CORINTHIANS 4:3-4

THE INTERNET gives anyone and everyone a platform for broadcasting their opinions. With the click of a mouse, we can become amateur critics offering our unimpeachable perspective on pretty much anything—including our opinions about other people.

Judging others in a public way, however, is nothing new. Evidently there were those in the church in Corinth who were freely sharing their opinions about Paul. Paul wrote them a letter to challenge not only the measure by which these people were judging him but also their standing to judge him. "It matters very little how I might be evaluated by you or by any human authority," he wrote. Paul was not concerned even with his own rating of himself. "I don't even trust my own judgment on this point," he said. There was only one Evaluator who mattered to Paul and one examination that counted. Only the Lord's assessment of Paul mattered to him.

Oh, that we could impart this kind of freedom to our children when they are desperate to prove their worth to a world seemingly waiting to evaluate their every performance, post, and picture. The opinions of others can be so very uplifting on those days when they excel and perform well. But how they can crush our children when their critics point out their weaknesses and failures. The load of living by the evaluation of others is too heavy to bear. It is exhausting to live every day in front of a watching but critical world.

What our children need to counteract this pressure is the truth of the gospel. There, the way of weakness is the way of strength. The way of poverty is the way of riches. The way to glory is the way of humility. The gospel says that what matters is not what we think of ourselves or what others think of us, but what God thinks of us. And God ultimately evaluates us on the basis of what we think of Jesus.

❈ ❈ ❈

Lord, please save _____ from being ruled and ruined by the evaluations of others. Save _____ from the tyranny of self-evaluation, too. Instead, fix _____'s eyes on Jesus. Give _____ rest in the reality of the paradoxical way in which you evaluate human achievement.

The Grace of Discipline

It isn't my responsibility to judge outsiders, but it certainly is your responsibility to judge those inside the church who are sinning. 1 CORINTHIANS 5:12

HOW WILL WE RESPOND if and when we discover that our adult child is enslaved in sexual sin, involved in corrupt financial practices, abusing his or her spouse or employees, or drinking excessively and habitually?

If our children are in Christ, in addition to being our sons and daughters, they are our brothers and sisters in Christ. So we not only relate to them as parent to child, but also as believer to believer. And there is a big difference between the way we are to respond to an unbeliever who is trapped in sin and a believer who refuses to give up his or her sin.

Paul makes it clear that we should not expect those who are separated from Christ to embrace and obey his commands. And this applies to our adult children. So the big question in the face of an adult child's ongoing sin is not so much about the behavior but about whether he or she truly belongs to Christ. If our child has not been genuinely joined to Jesus by faith, it makes sense that he or she would sin. After all, unbelievers don't have the Spirit's power to overcome sin and temptation.

But if our child claims to be in Christ and resists repentance when confronted compassionately and patiently, the situation is different. Our child's sin impacts the entire church. The language Paul uses hits us as harsh and makes us uncomfortable. This person is to be removed from fellowship (verse 2), and thrown out and handed over to Satan (verse 5). Those in the church are "not to associate" (verse 9) with those who claim to be believers yet indulge in sin of any kind. We must see that this harsh response has an intended effect: restoration. Such discipline is not intended to communicate our disapproval but rather our fear for our child's soul.

✳ ✳ ✳

Lord, if I ever must endure seeing my child undergo the discipline of the church for ongoing sin, I'm going to need a lot of your grace. Help me to love the purity of your church more than the comfort of my child. Help me to trust your grace of discipline in _____'s life to bring about restoration.

Don't You Realize?

Run from sexual sin! No other sin so clearly affects the body as this one does. For sexual immorality is a sin against your own body. Don't you realize that your body is the temple of the Holy Spirit, who lives in you and was given to you by God? You do not belong to yourself, for God bought you with a high price. So you must honor God with your body. 1 CORINTHIANS 6:18-20

IN HIS FIRST LETTER to the church in Corinth, Paul wrote with the posture of a father. In a fatherly way he reasons with them, helping them think about their lives and their bodies in a way that reflects the reality that they belong to Christ. Eleven times throughout the letter, Paul comes alongside them and asks a question that begins with "Don't you realize?" "Don't you realize that all of you together are the temple of God?" (3:16). "Don't you realize that this sin is like a little yeast that spreads?" (5:6). "Don't you realize that someday we believers will judge the world?" (6:2). "Don't you realize that those who do wrong will not inherit the Kingdom of God?" (6:9). And then in quick succession he asks three questions that have to do with the way they use their bodies:

Don't you realize that your bodies are actually parts of Christ? (6:15)
Don't you realize that if a man joins himself to a prostitute, he becomes one body with her? (6:16)
Don't you realize that your body is the temple of the Holy Spirit, who lives in you and was given to you by God? (6:19)

Perhaps Paul is demonstrating for us the kinds of questions we should be asking our kids and asking ourselves about our kids. Do our kids realize that their sexual purity is about so much more than being good or avoiding disease or pregnancy or shame? Do they realize that if they are in Christ, they take him with them into every sexually compromised encounter? We can give our kids lots of good reasons to remain sexually pure. But Paul helps us center our appeal in the gospel reality of being joined both body and soul to Christ. It prompts us to consider asking our children: Don't you realize . . . ?

※ ※ ※

Lord, as we seek to instill in _____ a deep sense of the holiness and significance of sex, we find ourselves pushing against a very strong tide. Only the power of your gospel and the reality of _____'s belonging to you has pushback power against this tide. Give us the words and the will to keep up the fight to help _____ realize that his body belongs to you.

Great Trouble and Disgrace

I asked them about the Jews who had returned there from captivity and about how things were going in Jerusalem. They said to me, "Things are not going well for those who returned to the province of Judah. They are in great trouble and disgrace. The wall of Jerusalem has been torn down, and the gates have been destroyed by fire." When I heard this, I sat down and wept. In fact, for days I mourned, fasted, and prayed to the God of heaven. NEHEMIAH 1:2-4

NEHEMIAH'S HEART was broken by the things that break the heart of God, which is the mark of someone who truly knows and loves God. Nehemiah knew what to do and where to go with his broken heart. He turned to the one person who loved his people more than he did, who was more committed to the future of Jerusalem than he was, who had the power to deal with the "great trouble and disgrace" of his people. He began to pray. And he kept on praying.

Nehemiah was clear on whom he was praying to. He asked "the great and awesome God" (verse 5) to deal with the "great trouble." This was not just any god. This was the God who "keeps his covenant of unfailing love with those who love him and obey his commands" (verse 5). This was the God who rescued his people with his "great power and strong hand" (verse 10). This was the God who had a long history of protecting and providing for them. Nehemiah didn't come to him suggesting that his people *deserved* deliverance from their "great trouble and disgrace." He asked God to give them what they did not deserve and had not earned. That's grace. He asked God to be true to the promise to bring his people back to the Promised Land after exile.

Nehemiah shows *us* how to pray brokenhearted prayers for our kids when they are in great trouble and disgrace. We ask for grace, undeserved favor. We ask for God to prove true to the promises he has made. Prayer is not coming up with our list of what we think God ought to do and pressuring him to do it. Prayer is affirming God's gracious and mighty character, which never changes, and asking him to be true to his Word, which he always is.

❊ ❊ ❊

Lord, when someone I love is in great trouble and disgrace, I tend to fill my prayers with plans that I want you to put into action. Instead, Lord, I want to fill my prayers with your promises, calling on you to do what you have pledged to do in caring for your own. So Lord, please convict, please draw, please save, please renew.

Righteous Anger

About this time some of the men and their wives raised a cry of protest against their fellow Jews. They were saying, "We have such large families. We need more food to survive." Others said, "We have mortgaged our fields, vineyards, and homes to get food during the famine."... When I heard their complaints, I was very angry. NEHEMIAH 5:1-3, 6

THE JEWS WHO WERE WORKING together to help rebuild the wall were living in a region that had been through a famine, so food supplies were scarce. Evidently some of the city's privileged people took advantage of the situation, inflating the price of grain and loaning money for food at exorbitant rates. This meant that some people, desperate to survive, had to sell family members into slavery to cover their debts. While we might expect people in the wider, cutthroat, do-whatever-you-have-to-do-to-get-ahead world to take advantage of one another, this should never have happened among these brothers.

The way God's people lived together was supposed to demonstrate the goodness of God to the world around them. Their exploitation and enslavement of one another did exactly the opposite. Why would anyone in the surrounding area believe that Israel's God was kind, merciful, and compassionate when they saw those who worshiped him and called themselves by his name enslaving, overcharging, and taking advantage of each other?

When presented with the problem, Nehemiah became angry. But his was not an out-of-control anger. "After thinking it over, [he] spoke out against these nobles and officials" (verse 7). Nehemiah demonstrates that anger is not always sinful. Sometimes it is a perfectly appropriate response to injustice or to the misuse of God's name. Nehemiah was rightly angry about how his Jewish brothers were dealing with each other and how it reflected on God.

This scene in Nehemiah helps us to consider our own anger and the way we deal with the conflicts in our own home. It forces us to ask: Is my anger righteous or selfish? Do I yell and argue in frustration or think it over before I speak, aware of the impact my words have?

❅ ❅ ❅

Lord, it would be hard to call so much of my anger "righteous." I really do want _____ to see righteous, appropriate anger modeled in our home. So help me to be angry over what makes you angry so that you might have your way in the world. And help me to let go of the anger that is selfish and all about getting my own way.

Nehemiah 5:14–7:73a
1 Corinthians 8:1-13
Psalm 33:1-11
Proverbs 21:8-10

AUGUST 13

Quarrelsome

It is better to live in a corner of the housetop
than in a house shared with a quarrelsome wife. Proverbs 21:9, esv

Are there some quarrelsome people living in your home? Parents or children who are quick to accuse others and always looking to defend themselves, people whose first instinct is to criticize and last is to encourage? Such people seem to pour gasoline on every tiny spark of potential conflict.

Five times in Proverbs, Solomon uses vivid imagery to describe what it is like to live with such a person. According to Solomon, it's "as annoying as constant dripping on a rainy day" (27:15). To live with a quarrelsome person is worse than living "alone in the corner of an attic" (21:9) or "living alone in the desert" (21:19).

While some of us might be quarrelsome by nature, the point of the Christian life is that we have died to who we were by nature. Instead of doing what comes naturally, we experience something supernatural. Instead of harsh or cutting talk, our words are gentle (15:1). Instead of saying the first hurtful or unhelpful thing that comes to our mind, we exercise restraint (10:19). Rather than rushing to judgment about the motivations of others, we assume the best. Rather than grumbling, we give grace to each other (James 5:9). Because we've been so generously forgiven by God, we are "kind to each other, tenderhearted, forgiving one another" (Ephesians 4:32).

How beautiful and how pleasant would it be for our homes to be marked by kindness instead of quarrels? "The Holy Spirit produces this kind of fruit in our lives: love, joy, peace, patience, kindness, goodness, faithfulness, gentleness, and self-control" (Galatians 5:22-23).

❋ ❋ ❋

Lord, we need your divine help to make the tenor of our home one of peace, encouragement, and affection instead of rancor, criticism, and cynicism. Help us as parents to set the tone in our home in the way we speak to each other with kindness rather than with irritation.

Listen Closely

In October, when the Israelites had settled in their towns, all the people assembled with a unified purpose at the square just inside the Water Gate. They asked Ezra the scribe to bring out the Book of the Law of Moses, which the LORD had given for Israel to obey. So on October 8 Ezra the priest brought the Book of the Law before the assembly, which included the men and women and all the children old enough to understand. He faced the square just inside the Water Gate from early morning until noon and read aloud to everyone who could understand. All the people listened closely to the Book of the Law. NEHEMIAH 7:73–8:3

SOMETIMES THE BIBLE can seem to us like such an ancient book. Interestingly, it was already an ancient book to these people gathered at the Water Gate in Jerusalem. The Book of the Law of Moses—Genesis, Exodus, Leviticus, Numbers, and Deuteronomy—was one thousand years old. Yet the Israelites were hungry for it, confident it would speak to them, challenge them, and satisfy them. "All the people listened closely." They did not show up for this reading while letting their thoughts run elsewhere (which, can we admit, is often the case for us when we gather to hear the Word read and taught?). They took in God's Word, thought it through, and sought to understand and apply it.

Picture the scene: Ezra stood on a wooden platform flanked by thirteen Levites and surrounded by fifty thousand men, women, and children. From dawn until about noon, they listened to Ezra read from the scrolls, which were written in Hebrew. Since the people coming back from exile spoke Aramaic, it had to be translated. But more than that, it had to be explained. Ezra was surrounded by thirteen Levites. These men "read from the Book of the Law of God and clearly explained the meaning of what was being read, helping the people understand each passage" (verse 8).

And how did the people gathered there respond? "All the people chanted, 'Amen! Amen!' as they lifted their hands. Then they bowed down and worshiped the LORD with their faces to the ground" (verse 6). This was no token "amen." With their lips and with their whole bodies, they expressed submission to what they heard.

❊ ❊ ❊

Lord, we need you to save our family from week-by-week church attendance with no real longing for or listening to your Word. We need hearts that will take it in, minds that will think it over, hands that can't help but be lifted to you, and faces that bow before you. Only you can make us this alive to your Word.

He Will Show You a Way Out

If you think you are standing strong, be careful not to fall. The temptations in your life are no different from what others experience. And God is faithful. He will not allow the temptation to be more than you can stand. When you are tempted, he will show you a way out so that you can endure. 1 CORINTHIANS 10:12-13

To ENCOURAGE the people in the Corinthian church to turn away from idolatry, Paul told them to consider how the Israelites' worship of false gods had brought them only ruin and destruction. "These things happened to them as examples for us," Paul writes in verse 11.

When we read about the Israelites worshiping a golden calf or the Corinthians participating in pagan worship by visiting temple prostitutes, we're tempted to think that their acts are far removed from our modern life. But idolatry is very much a part of our modern life. Because it's in the air we breathe, we can't really see it.

What is idolatry? Idols are not necessarily bad things. They are often *good* things that have become *ultimate* things. They are legitimate desires that have morphed into destructive demands. We take a good thing—like providing for our family—and turn it into an ultimate thing, infused with ambition and greed. We take something important—like parenting—and make it into an ultimate endeavor as we allow our identity to be defined by our child's success or failure.

Our God meets us at the level of desire. He understands our weaknesses and our need for a way out of the grip of idolatry. And that's what he provides to us. As we look squarely at the inability of our idols to ever fully satisfy us, and as we look humbly at the willingness of Christ to take upon himself all the judgment for our idolatry, we find an opening for grace. He provides the way out of what once seemed like unendurable temptation to keep on looking for our significance, security, and satisfaction in something other than Christ.

✳ ✳ ✳

Lord, we love _____, but we don't want to make an idol out of our child. We are desperate for your help to order our loves so that our desires don't become demands. To get rid of our idols, we need your help in identifying them. Won't you use whatever means you see fit to reveal to us what we have come to love and depend on more than you?

Teach You to Fear

Come, my children, and listen to me,
and I will teach you to fear the LORD. PSALM 34:11

OF ALL THE THINGS we need and want to teach our children, surely the foundation for a truly successful life is this: the fear of the Lord. But what comes more naturally to us and to our children is to fear people more than we fear God and to love the praise of people more than we love to please God.

Our kids give in to peer pressure because they want to be like other kids more than they want to be like Christ. When they find it unbearable to disappoint someone, it's because they want to please people more than they want to please Christ.

Perhaps people's opinions have come to mean too much to our children because they haven't been exposed enough to the greatness of God and the perfection of his character. To grow in fear of God, we must become smaller while he becomes bigger. Our kids oftentimes need our help to gain perspective on how little the opinions of other people really matter in the long run. In this way our kids can begin to care more about what God thinks and less about what other people think.

In Psalm 34, David calls his children to listen so that he might teach them to fear the Lord. Perhaps we, too, need to make a point of teaching our children to fear the Lord—not only by talking about it, but by living it out in our words and actions. Our children need to be taught that pleasing God is more important and more significant than pleasing people. They need to be taught that Christ is the only one to whom they will give account at the end of the age. Living to hear his "well done" is the most freeing and satisfying life anyone can live.

❈ ❈ ❈

Lord, I realize it isn't just _____ who needs to fear you more and fear people less. I do too. Apparently I haven't outgrown my need for approval and acceptance from others. I need you to loom larger in my estimation. I need your approval and acceptance to carry a much heavier weight than it does now. So work in me, and as you do, may the change in me be evident to _____ so that _____ will also fear people less and fear you more.

Keeping Out Compromise

I was not in Jerusalem at that time, for I had returned to King Artaxerxes of Babylon in the thirty-second year of his reign, though I later asked his permission to return. When I arrived back in Jerusalem, I learned about Eliashib's evil deed in providing Tobiah with a room in the courtyards of the Temple of God. I became very upset and threw all of Tobiah's belongings out of the room. NEHEMIAH 13:6-8

THE FINAL CHAPTER of Nehemiah tells of his return to Jerusalem a few years after going back to Persia to resume his service to King Artaxerxes. When Nehemiah returned to Jerusalem, he found that a non-Israelite pagan named Tobiah had been given a place to work in the Temple. He also discovered that because the people were not giving their offerings, the Levites, who were supposed to carry out duties at the Temple, had to go out and work in the fields so they could eat. The people were treating the Sabbath like any other day of doing business.

Years before, the people had agreed to a costly separation from pagan wives. But upon his return, Nehemiah found that sadly, once again, Jews had married women of Ashdon, Ammon, and Moab. They had become so enmeshed in those godless cultures and religions that their children no longer spoke the language of Judah.

Nehemiah was a bit like a parent who comes home from a trip to discover that a wild party had been held at the house while he or she was gone. Clearly all of the rules he set in place and the provisions he made for his people to love and follow God had been forgotten. When Nehemiah came back to Jerusalem, it became clear that the wall he built couldn't keep out the compromise that had recontaminated God's people.

Likewise, we as parents can't build a wall high enough or strong enough to keep out the compromise that is always trying to make its way into our home and into our hearts. We can't provide the ongoing energy for our children to persist and grow in their pursuit of pleasing God. They need a better restorer. And they have one in Christ.

※ ※ ※

Lord, you know my heart for _____ to walk in your ways. You have heard my prayers. You have witnessed my work. But _____ is ultimately your child. And _____ needs much more than a godly parent. _____ needs you to keep her from compromise.

Examine Yourself

Anyone who eats this bread or drinks this cup of the Lord unworthily is guilty of sinning against the body and blood of the Lord. That is why you should examine yourself before eating the bread and drinking the cup. For if you eat the bread or drink the cup without honoring the body of Christ, you are eating and drinking God's judgment upon yourself. 1 CORINTHIANS 11:27-29

PARENTING OUR CHILDREN in the pew can be a challenge. We want to worship, and we want to bring up good listeners and glad worshipers. Depending on how the Lord's Supper is handled in the church we attend, it can be very challenging to help our hungry little children understand that the bread and the cup are for those who have been joined to Christ by faith and are not just a snack for all to enjoy during the church service.

As our children grow, the challenge may change, but it is still there—how to help our children grasp the meaning and enter into the blessing of the table, as well as examine themselves before the table. Frankly, it would be easier to let this go. But when we read Paul's words in 1 Corinthians 11, we realize that neglecting to teach our children what it means to eat the bread and drink the cup in an unworthy way is to neglect to protect them from eating and drinking God's judgment on themselves.

When Paul writes about eating and drinking unworthily, he's not concerned about whether the person *deserves* to approach the Lord's Table. If that were the case, none of us could eat and drink. To come to the table in an unworthy way is to come with a heart of indifference toward one's sin or a refusal to repent of sin. Paul calls on believers to examine themselves prior to approaching the table, not to find reasons for why they are unworthy, but to find evidence of a repentant heart—evidence of grace at work.

✳ ✳ ✳

Lord, I need this reminder of your expectation of self-examination before I come and feed on your broken body and shed blood. It is easy to go through the motions, and it's often uncomfortable to look squarely at the condition of my heart. So thank you for your Word that reminds me to examine myself. And, Lord, give me the opportunity and the words to talk to _____ about the importance of self-examination before your table. Help me to communicate this rich truth in a way that draws _____ toward your table and, therefore, toward you.

Identification with the People of God

Mordecai sent this reply to Esther: "Don't think for a moment that because you're in the palace you will escape when all other Jews are killed. If you keep quiet at a time like this, deliverance and relief for the Jews will arise from some other place, but you and your relatives will die. Who knows if perhaps you were made queen for just such a time as this?" ESTHER 4:13-14

WHEN ESTHER BECAME QUEEN, she kept her Jewish identity a secret. She kept the secret so well, in fact, that no one thought to inform her of the king's edict that her people were about to be slaughtered. But then Mordecai sent her word of the edict and advised her to plead with the king on behalf of her people.

Esther knew that if she went to see the king and he did not extend to her his golden scepter, she would be put to death. Approaching him could clearly cost her something—maybe even everything. Esther was in real danger. She was in danger of being so assimilated into the kingdom of the world that she would lose her identification with the people of God.

But Esther came clean with the king, telling him, "My people and I have been sold to those who would kill, slaughter, and annihilate us" (7:4). By identifying herself with God's people and their plight, she effectively added her name to the list of those to be slaughtered on the appointed day.

As with Esther, the pull of the pleasures of this world's kingdom on our children is strong. This kingdom wants to assimilate them so they will look like everyone else and think like everyone else and value what everyone else values. But the Kingdom of God calls them away from that. It calls them to identify themselves with the people of God. It may mean being hated and marginalized in this world, but we can assure them that aligning with his Kingdom holds out great reward when Christ, our King, returns.

❈ ❈ ❈

Lord, to witness Esther's courageous identification with you and your people causes me to look at my own life. I must ask myself if I have been this bold and committed to being a part of your people. Give me the courage I need to identify openly with you and your cause. And give _____ the extraordinary courage it takes to be different, even if it means being rejected because of identification with you.

Love

Love never gives up, never loses faith, is always hopeful. 1 CORINTHIANS 13:7

MY CHILD, if I talk to you for hours about what I think is important but never really listen to what matters to you, I'm just making noise. If I have the answer to every one of your questions and great faith to pray you through your struggles, but never admit my own questions and struggles, I'm not loving you well. If I lead our family in doing good deeds, but speak ill of others behind closed doors, I will have gained nothing—including your respect.

I want my love to be patient when I have to wait for you to get to the car or get going in life. I want my love to be kind when the rest of the world has been cruel. I don't want to be jealous when you agree with someone else's ideas or enjoy someone else's cooking or company more than mine. I don't want to boast about your achievements to make myself look good. I never want to treat you or your friends rudely. I don't want to demand my own way but to do things your way sometimes. I don't want to take out my frustrations on you or make you suffer under my moods. I refuse to keep a record of your wrongs to throw back in your face. I will never be happy when things are hard for you, but I will always be happy when you do what is right even though it may be hard.

Because I love you, I'm never going to give up on you. I'm never going to stop expecting the best of you. I'm never going to lose hope that God is working in your life. If there's one thing you can be sure of until the day I die, it's that my love will always be there for you to fall back on when the worst happens.

I don't always see things clearly or completely, and that includes things about you. But the day is coming when we will know each other perfectly. Nothing will come between us, or between us and God, and it will be better than we ever expected.

So as I look to the future I know what's important. Our faith in Christ is important. It's what links us to him. Our hope in Christ is important. It's what assures us of a future with him. But it is our love for each other and for Christ that is of supreme importance. Because that love is going to last forever.

Cursed God in their Hearts

Job's sons would take turns preparing feasts in their homes, and they would also invite their three sisters to celebrate with them. When these celebrations ended—sometimes after several days—Job would purify his children. He would get up early in the morning and offer a burnt offering for each of them. For Job said to himself, "Perhaps my children have sinned and have cursed God in their hearts." This was Job's regular practice. JOB 1:4-5

JOB WAS A GREAT AND GODLY MAN. He had plenty of wealth and what would appear to be the perfect family. But there was deep anxiety in Job's heart—that something sinister might be happening in the hearts of his children. When every birthday party came to an end for each of his ten children, he would call them together to offer a sacrifice. There seemed to be a sense of urgency as, "early in the morning," they would gather around the family altar, where Job would offer a burnt offering for each of them. A whole sacrificial animal was consumed by the fire, which pictured the hot anger of God burning up the animal instead of burning up Job's child. Perhaps Job burned one animal at a time, saying to each son or daughter, "This one is for you, just in case you have cursed God in your heart."

Evidently Job's children lived in such a way that he couldn't point to a particular sin. Evidently they hadn't cursed God with their mouths. But Job understood that what matters is not simply a veneer of religiosity or good behavior but rather inner lives inclined toward affection for God. Job also believed in the atoning power of sacrifice. So he cast his fears over his children's sins onto the altar, the place where such sins are dealt with.

Like Job, we can't see into the hearts of our children. But we can see the sacrifice available that deals with the sin of our children much clearer than Job ever could. Job put his hope in a Redeemer who would come in the future, in a sacrifice he couldn't fully grasp. We put our hope for the forgiveness of our children's sins in the Redeemer who came in the past, and in his sacrifice on the cross.

❀ ❀ ❀

*Lord, we long for so much more than outward conformity and good behavior for
_____. We long for _____ to be sensitive to the sins of the heart. We long for
_____ to have a deep and growing love for you rather than resentment toward you.
Each year of her life, may _____ look upon the once-for-all perfect sacrifice of your
Son and recognize that Christ died in her place so that she can live in you.*

Godly Parents

The godly offer good counsel;
*   they teach right from wrong.*
They have made God's law their own,
*   so they will never slip from his path.* PSALM 37:30-31

IF THERE IS ANYTHING we'd love for our children to say when they tell the story of their lives in the future, it would be that they had godly parents. We want more than for them to say that we took them to church or claimed to be Christians. We want their testimony to be that their parents were genuinely and pervasively devoted to Christ. So what does that look like according to Psalm 37?

"The godly offer good counsel; they teach right from wrong." This doesn't mean that godly parents always give good advice, but that the guidance they provide to their kids is rooted in the wisdom and justice of God himself. God's Word has become a part of who they are. "They have made God's law their own" by internalizing it so that it is part of their very fabric. Scripture grounds them in God so that they are not unstable.

Kids raised by such parents see their parents consistently loving the Lord, loving each other, and living according to God's Word. As much as they might want to try to change their parents in some ways, they know this connectedness to God will never change, and they are glad for it. It gives them security in an uncertain world. They can tell themselves with confidence: *Mom and Dad will always put Christ before anything and everything. The Bible will always shape their opinions, judgments, and counsel. When hard times hit, they will turn to God and seek to trust him. And when they die, I won't have to grieve as those who have no hope. I will have peace knowing that my parents are enjoying the "wonderful future [that] awaits those who love peace" (verse 37).*

⌖ ⌖ ⌖

Lord, _____ will never have perfect parents. But we want _____ to have godly parents. We want your Word to become so much a part of who we are that _____ can always be sure that our counsel is biblical, godly counsel. We want to walk so closely and consistently with you that _____ will have peace when we die, knowing we have found forever shelter in you.

Is God Punishing You?

You claim, "My beliefs are pure,"
and "I am clean in the sight of God."...
Listen! God is doubtless punishing you
far less than you deserve! JOB 11:4, 6

WE KNOW FROM THE FIRST CHAPTER of Job that Job had turned away from evil and that God himself had said Job was blameless. As readers, we are also privy to the wager with which Satan had challenged God. Of course, Job's friends did not have the advantage of all this information.

Even so, as they circled around Job in his suffering state, they were quite certain they knew the cause of Job's incredible suffering: It was his own fault. Job was being punished for some secret sin. In fact, according to Zophar's words in Job 11, Job was not simply getting what he deserved, but far less than he deserved! Job's friends assumed that such extreme suffering came only to someone who had committed a heinous sin that God had determined must be punished.

And we get this assumption, don't we? We assume in our suffering, or in our child's suffering, that God is punishing us. But is that how he works? Does God punish us or our children because of what we've done or failed to do?

My friend, if you belong to Christ, you can be confident that your suffering or your child's suffering is not punishment for your sin. Someone has already been punished for your sin so that you won't have to be. All the punishments you deserve for your sin—your outright rebellion against God or your utter apathy toward God; your refusal to love him with all of your heart, soul, mind, and strength; your ugliest, most shameful words and deeds—have been laid on Jesus. He was punished for your sin so you won't have to be.

※ ※ ※

Lord, your gospel goes against my instincts. It seems too good to be true. I need your help to deeply believe it is true when I jump to the conclusion that I am being made to pay for my sin, or that _____ is being made to pay for my sin. Thank you that I don't have to fear that you are going to take out your anger on me. Instead, I expect that you will pour out your love, your mercy, your grace, and your forgiveness on me.

Immovable

My dear brothers and sisters, be strong and immovable. Always work enthusiastically for the Lord, for you know that nothing you do for the Lord is ever useless.
1 CORINTHIANS 15:58

PAUL HAS JUST SPENT an entire chapter explaining the reality of the coming resurrection, impressing upon the people at the church in Corinth that resurrection is not merely something religious and unreal but a matter of "first importance" (verse 3, ESV). Because Jesus died and his body was resurrected from the grave, we can be sure that all who are joined to Christ will one day have that same experience. Death is not going to get the last word in the believer's life.

Paul then points to the difference this belief and confidence in resurrection should make in the lives of believers. It should make us strong and steadfast. Confidence in the coming resurrection keeps us going until our work is done. It makes us immovable, meaning that we don't easily lose our balance and get knocked down. Whenever the winds blow through our family in the form of difficulty, sickness, financial pressure, relational strife, or ungodly perspectives, we do not veer off course. We are resolute regarding what is true, what is reliable, and what is forever.

It's not that we are unwilling to listen to others or that we are belligerent or intolerant with other views. It's simply that we are so convinced that the gospel is true and that Christ has ultimate authority over everything—even death—that our confidence in him is unshakable.

As we persevere in the work of parenting, we can be sure that what we're doing matters beyond this life. We are not laboring to create the perfect family here and now. We are laboring for the souls of our children because we know that the day is coming when bodies will be raised to be joined to those souls, and we long to be surrounded by our children on that day. So we are strong and immovable in loving the Lord, talking about his Word, and living like we really do believe that resurrection day is coming.

❋ ❋ ❋

Lord, may the truth of the resurrection of Jesus and the certainty of the resurrection of all believers make us strong and steadfast in our parenting work. May it make us immovable as we look to you as our only hope.

Miserable Comforters

What miserable comforters you are!
Won't you ever stop blowing hot air?
What makes you keep on talking?
I could say the same things if you were in my place.
I could spout off criticism and shake my head at you.
But if it were me, I would encourage you.
I would try to take away your grief. Job 16:2-5

THE PROBLEM WITH JOB'S FRIENDS who came around him in the midst of his hardship and despair wasn't so much that what they said was wrong. Certainly much of what they said was right, good, and true, but much of it was wrongly applied and spoken at the wrong time. They made assumptions based on their beliefs that went beyond what they knew and squashed Job in the process. They decided they knew what God was doing, and they boiled down God's ways into simplistic formulas that didn't fit.

Certainly we hope that our children's suffering will never rise to Job-worthy levels. But we can be sure it will sometimes seem that way to them. Pain can't really be compared. It all just hurts to the person who is hurting. What we want is to be worthy comforters instead of worthless ones. We want to be quick to listen and slow to speak. We want to enter into their hurts and hear their hearts and be very slow to talk about it in ways that diminish their very real pain.

It is clear that Job's friends had good intentions and were not out to make him feel worse. They wanted to help him. But instead they added to his misery. Likewise, we have good intentions with our kids. We want to help them. So we must be careful with our words and come alongside them rather than condescend. We must seek to enter into their disappointment and frustration rather than offer easy answers.

❈ ❈ ❈

Lord, I want to be a genuine encourager to _____ in the hard places of life, not a miserable comforter. Silence me when it is time to be quiet. Humble me when I'm sure I'm right but my words are unhelpful. Give me a timely word fitly spoken.

Less Self-Reliant, More God Reliant

We think you ought to know, dear brothers and sisters, about the trouble we went through in the province of Asia. We were crushed and overwhelmed beyond our ability to endure, and we thought we would never live through it. In fact, we expected to die. But as a result, we stopped relying on ourselves and learned to rely only on God, who raises the dead. 2 CORINTHIANS 1:8-9

A QUICK INTERNET SEARCH turns up numerous articles on "7 Rules," "10 Ways," "4 Steps," and "3 Skills" to teach our kids to be self-reliant. Clearly self-reliance is a value of our age. And to a certain degree, we understand the benefit of teaching our kids to be self-reliant. We don't want to still be putting toothpaste on their toothbrush and setting out their clothes for them when they're adults. We want them to be able to make good decisions and act on them when we're not around. We want them to have a healthy sense of themselves as people made in the image of God for his glory that gives them the confidence to move out into the world and make a difference for Christ. But there is something more important than teaching them self-reliance.

Paul had to be taught this more important thing, and the lesson wasn't comfortable. In his second letter to the Corinthians, Paul said that he had recently experienced something so dire that he expected to die. Perhaps his detractors had started a riot in Ephesus or he'd faced the prospect of execution or he'd contracted a life-threatening illness. Whatever it was, and whatever caused it in human terms, Paul was clear about the divine purpose of this trial in his life. God was not interested in teaching Paul to be more self-reliant. God intended this hardship to teach Paul to rely more fully on him. He was at work erasing any lingering sense of Paul's own ability to grin and bear it or to struggle through difficulties on his own. God was leading Paul into a more profound awareness of his weakness, which would make him all the more receptive to God's assurance: "My power is made perfect in weakness" (2 Corinthians 12:9, ESV).

✻ ✻ ✻

Lord, I realize that your way of teaching us to rely on you more fully will likely mean that we will be reduced to having only you to rely on. And that sounds terribly uncomfortable for us and for _____. But we ask you to teach us and to teach _____ what it means to rely more fully on you instead of on ourselves.

The Right Path

Direct your children onto the right path,
and when they are older, they will not leave it. PROVERBS 22:6

THIS IS ONE OF THOSE PROVERBS we want to read as a promise. We would like to be able to be sure that if we steer our children onto the right path—meaning the path that leads to life in Christ—then they will never leave that course, even when they leave our home. But this isn't just a promise. Like many other proverbs, it is an adage that points us toward a general principle. It is what ordinarily happens, but it isn't what always happens. Parents who are passionately dedicated to Christ frequently raise children who are passionately dedicated to Christ. But this proverb provides no guarantee that the faithful efforts of godly parents will always produce godly children.

It's not that there is no correlation between the way we bring up our children and what becomes of them. The Bible charges us to bring up our children "with the discipline and instruction that comes from the Lord" (Ephesians 6:4). We have influence, but we don't have control. We simply don't have the power to bring about our child's repentance and faith. That is a burden we were never meant to bear, a burden only our heavenly Father is able to bear.

When we recognize that this is a proverb and not a promise, we can stop judging other parents whose kids seem to be straying from the path of Christ. And we can come out from underneath our own self-condemnation when our kids seem to be resisting our direction toward the right path. We can talk back to the voices inside our heads that tell us that if we had just tried harder, communicated more clearly, been more consistent, gotten our child to church more often, homeschooled, Christian schooled, public schooled, then certainly things would be different. We can rest in the sovereignty of God, casting all of our cares about the path our child is taking on the Lord, knowing he cares for us and our child.

※ ※ ※

Lord, if it is all up to me to make sure that _____ is heading on the right path toward you, then the burden is more than I can bear. So while I want to walk in wisdom, pointing and leading and prodding _____ in your direction, you must call, you must convince, you must capture _____'s heart.

239

I Will Put My Hope in God!

Why am I discouraged?
  Why is my heart so sad?
I will put my hope in God!
  I will praise him again—
  my Savior and my God! PSALM 42:5-6

THERE IS SO MUCH JOY IN PARENTING. But it can also be profoundly disheartening. We can become discouraged about our seeming inability to break patterns in our parenting that lack wisdom and grace. And we can become troubled by the direction the lives of our children are taking. Because we love our kids so deeply, such discouragement is not easily overcome. We need divine help. And that is what we're given in Psalm 42.

The psalmist uses vivid imagery from his surroundings that helps us understand what he feels like on the inside. The first image he uses is that of a panting deer that dips his head into what should be a flowing stream only to find a dry creek bed. He feels dried up inside, full of longing with no relief. And later the psalmist gives us another vivid image, taking us just north of the Promised Land, outside of its borders, to where the streams and waterfalls flowing down from Mount Hebron create the headwaters of the Jordan River. He writes, "your waves and surging tides sweep over me" (verse 7). So in these two images we understand that the psalmist feels dry like a deer that cannot find water, but he also feels as though he's drowning.

However, the psalmist doesn't just accept his thoughts as his reality; he announces the gospel to himself—not the gospel in general terms but applied personally to him: "*I* will put my hope in God! *I* will praise him again—*my* Savior and *my* God" (emphasis added). The psalmist pours out his complaint to God, but he also intentionally remembers and recites how good it is to be close to God. He speaks to his own soul, telling himself to put his hope in God.

❈ ❈ ❈

Lord, in this psalm you have given me words, not just to speak to you or say about you, but words to preach to myself. And so when I'm deeply discouraged, when I can't see the way forward and my emotions are telling me that nothing good is ahead, I will speak these words to my own soul, saying, "I will put my hope in God!"

A Covenant with My Eyes

I made a covenant with my eyes
not to look with lust at a young woman.
For what has God above chosen for us?
What is our inheritance from the Almighty on high?
Isn't it calamity for the wicked
and misfortune for those who do evil?
Doesn't he see everything I do
and every step I take? JOB 31:1-4

JOB WAS EVIDENTLY a realist about sexual temptation. He realized he could not take a casual approach to such a powerful desire, which could lead him into ruin and break the heart of the God he loved. So Job entered into a solemn and binding covenant with himself not to look with lust at a young woman. He determined not to indulge in an imaginative fantasy with her, which could lead to adultery or sexual immorality.

But notice that he didn't just say he was going to try really hard not to do this. The key is his use of the term *covenant*. Making a covenant often involved cutting animals in half, which was a way of saying, "If I don't live up to my covenant commitment, I should be cut in half like this animal." The kind of commitment Job made went deeper than restraint imposed from the outside or even self-imposed accountability. It was a rigorous internal commitment to purity solemnized by a verbal or written vow. The Bible does not require that we make this eye covenant. But it does command complete purity (Colossians 3:5). Job established an eye covenant as a means of fueling his own purity.

Perhaps a carefully considered covenant like Job's could be a tool to empower purity in your home and family too—not just for the kids but for the parents. In encouraging this level of commitment, we're not expecting perfection, but eliciting a promise to fight, a plan of escape, and a strategy of avoidance. And we don't expect that anyone will live up to this covenant through sheer willpower, but only by grace through faith in God's promised help.

※ ※ ※

Lord, let me lead the way in the battle for purity in our home. When I encounter a seductive person or image unexpectedly, I will look away, turn it off, or walk away. Grant me the grace to live this way day in and day out. I throw myself upon your mercy and strength.

AUGUST 30

God Has Made the Light Shine

Satan, who is the god of this world, has blinded the minds of those who don't believe. They are unable to see the glorious light of the Good News. They don't understand this message about the glory of Christ, who is the exact likeness of God. . . . For God, who said, "Let there be light in the darkness," has made this light shine in our hearts so we could know the glory of God that is seen in the face of Jesus Christ. 2 CORINTHIANS 4:4, 6

SATAN AIMS to blind our children's minds so they will be "unable to see the glorious light of the Good News." How does he intend to do this? "He is a liar and the father of lies" (John 8:44). Satan is always lying to us and to our children. The lies take different forms in each generation, but the overarching strategies have been essentially the same since the Garden of Eden. He casts doubt on God's Word and God's goodness, and he throws logs on the fire of our own desires to be somebody and to be in charge of our own lives.

Satan seeks to prevent our children from ever thinking deeply about things that matter, so he inundates them with what is entertaining and interesting but ultimately trivial and meaningless. He makes it seem normal to be completely obsessed with themselves and with what other people think and say about them. He magnifies the voice of the world that insists to our children that they are captains of their own destinies and that they must make something of themselves.

So what hope is there for our children growing up in this world with such a powerful force at work against them? It is this: "God, who said, 'Let there be light in the darkness,' has made this light shine in our hearts so we could know the glory of God that is seen in the face of Jesus Christ." As we read, talk about, and expose our children to God's Word, the light shines and "the darkness can never extinguish it" (John 1:5).

❈ ❈ ❈

Lord, I know that the only way anyone is ever converted is that you cause the darkened soul to see the beauty of Christ in your gospel. I can't generate the kind of light that is needed to convert anyone. But you can. So we ask you to shine your light brightly into our home that we might see your glory!

Why We Never Give Up

That is why we never give up. Though our bodies are dying, our spirits are being renewed every day. For our present troubles are small and won't last very long. Yet they produce for us a glory that vastly outweighs them and will last forever! So we don't look at the troubles we can see now; rather, we fix our gaze on things that cannot be seen. For the things we see now will soon be gone, but the things we cannot see will last forever. 2 CORINTHIANS 4:16-18

WHEN WE READ THIS PASSAGE, in which Paul describes his present troubles as "small," we're tempted to think that his life must have been much easier than our own, that he was downplaying the reality of his difficulties, or that he was just delusional. And when he says that these present troubles "won't last very long," we're tempted to think, once again, either that he had never faced chronic pain, repeated problems, or lifelong struggles, or that he was just putting a happy face on the realities of life to make Christianity look good.

But that was not it at all. Paul had found the secret of not giving up. He was experiencing an inner sense of renewal in the midst of his difficulties. How? We read later in this same letter to the Corinthians that fourteen years prior, Paul had been given a guided tour of heaven. Clearly seeing the glory of God had shaped Paul's perspective about life in this world. Because Paul saw the weight of the glory to come, he could describe the troubles of this life as "light." And because Paul briefly stepped out of time and into eternity, he was able to describe the afflictions of this life as "momentary" (verse 17, NIV).

Parenting is difficult. It's a lot harder and a much longer assignment than most of us knew when we signed on for it. Sometimes it gets so hard that we're tempted to give up—give up on pursuing meaningful relationships with our kids, give up on teaching them, give up on disciplining them, give up on expecting God to work in them. But Paul wants us to see the bigger picture. And the way we gain that perspective is to stop focusing on our troubles and fix our eyes on the glory that makes the heaviest burdens seem light and the eternal future that makes even lifelong struggles seem momentary.

✳ ✳ ✳

Lord, I really need your help to keep from focusing on current troubles. They loom so large and appear so relentless. Sometimes I want to give up. Please help me to fix my gaze on the realities that I can't see with my physical eyes. Renew me day by day.

Come Back to God!

God . . . brought us back to himself through Christ. And God has given us this task of reconciling people to him. For God was in Christ, reconciling the world to himself, no longer counting people's sins against them. And he gave us this wonderful message of reconciliation. So we are Christ's ambassadors; God is making his appeal through us. We speak for Christ when we plead, "Come back to God!" 2 CORINTHIANS 5:18-20

EACH TIME we discipline our kids, we can use it as an opportunity to vent our frustration and anger, force them into toeing the line, shame them into agonized regret, and manipulate them into changed behavior. Or we can see ourselves as following through on the task we've been given by God himself—this task of reconciling people, including our children—to him.

We were once God's enemies, opposed to all that he loved and doing the opposite of what he lovingly commanded. But instead of yelling at us, shaming us, or manipulating us, he welcomed us. He reconciled us to himself by pouring out his anger on his own Son. In this way he drew us close to himself. His kindness led us to repentance when we had done nothing to deserve it and, in fact, had done everything to earn his wrath. All of the obstacles that came between him and us were defeated by his great love.

So now, as parents who have been reconciled to God, we can live and love and discipline as reconcilers. We can point our children to the cross as the place where their sin has been dealt with. Rather than pushing them away with our angry words and cold demeanor, we can draw our children close as we remember that God's kindness led us to repentance. We can love as we've been loved and forgive as we've been forgiven.

❈ ❈ ❈

Lord, you never come to us with folded arms. Your arms are always open to us, even when we've done wrong. We want that kindness to mark our interactions with _____, even when _____ has done wrong. Thank you for this counterintuitive message of reconciliation instead of condemnation that is ours to pass along to our children. Help us to live as reconcilers by being willing to humble ourselves and make the first move toward those we've hurt.

Our Lives Will Matter Forever

"Everything is meaningless," says the Teacher, "completely meaningless!" ECCLESIASTES 1:2

IN THE BOOK OF ECCLESIASTES, we hear the voice of the Preacher. He has looked at life from every angle and is convinced that our lives have no lasting meaning or significance. He has seen everything "under the sun" (verse 9)—meaning everything that can be seen from a limited earthly perspective—and his estimation is that it is all meaningless. Our lives, he says, are like the visible vapors of our breath on a cold night—there for a second and then gone. And yet, he says, God has "planted eternity in the human heart" (3:11). Within human souls, God has placed a longing for our lives to matter beyond our limited lifetimes.

The Preacher sees that people work their whole lives and then die, seemingly letting go of everything they've worked for. His recommendation is to eat, drink, and enjoy the fruits of your labor if possible, recognizing that we "came from dust and . . . return to dust" (3:20). And after death, who's to say? The Preacher has no clear sense of what will happen when this life under the sun comes to an end.

Fortunately we can see something the Preacher could not see—something we want our children to see. Because we live in light of God's fuller revelation of himself in the person and work of Christ, we know that there is life beyond these few years lived under the sun. We live in confident hope of resurrection life beyond the grave. Though this life sometimes seems futile, Jesus has accomplished all that is necessary for the entire creation to be set free from its futility.

Everything we've done in Christ, for Christ, and through Christ will matter forever. Life under the sun is not futile. Because we are joined to Christ, we know that our lives will matter forever.

※ ※ ※

Jesus, even now you are filling the lives of all who are joined to you by faith with meaning and purpose. I pray that _____ would be steadfast, immovable, always working enthusiastically for you, knowing that nothing she does for you is ever useless.

Complete Holiness

Because we have these promises, dear friends, let us cleanse ourselves from everything that can defile our body or spirit. And let us work toward complete holiness because we fear God. 2 CORINTHIANS 7:1

THERE ARE PLENTY OF EXPERTS out there anxious to tell us how to parent our children. But much of the "how to" ignores the "why." Paul gives us a very clear "why" in 2 Corinthians 7:1: "because we fear God." Because we fear God, we are working toward increasing holiness in every aspect of our lives. Because we fear God, we are constantly confronting sin rather than ignoring it or justifying it. Because we fear God, we recognize that parenting is not solely about growth in our kids. Instead, we realize that God intends to use the process of parenting to bring to the surface sins that need to be dealt with.

It is easy to become focused on trying to keep our children from everything that will defile their body or spirit while being careless about the things that defile our own body or spirit. We can be rigid about what they watch on the screen while convincing ourselves that we won't be polluted by what we watch. We can tell them to share while we are unwilling to share with those in need.

God uses parenting to purify us even as he is at work purifying our children. Sins we never saw before rise to the surface and must be dealt with rather than ignored—sins of subtle rebellion against God; sins of idolatry as we discover financial security or personal safety has come to mean too much to us; sins of the heart such as pride, jealousy, or a sense of entitlement. Unless we "work toward complete holiness" we can become more demanding, more controlling, and more resentful as parents. But as we allow our children to play a part in our quest for complete holiness, we discover that God intends much more for us than simply raising our children. He intends to use them to push us forward in our own spiritual growth.

❈ ❈ ❈

Because I fear you, Lord, I want my life to be marked by increasing holiness. That means the sins that need to be dealt with are going to have to come to the surface. And it seems that parenting is constantly revealing the reality of my inner world. So, Lord, as you work in me, I want to work toward pleasing you more and more.

The Kind of Sorrow God Wants

I am not sorry that I sent that severe letter to you, though I was sorry at first, for I know it was painful to you for a little while. Now I am glad I sent it, not because it hurt you, but because the pain caused you to repent and change your ways. It was the kind of sorrow God wants his people to have, so you were not harmed by us in any way. For the kind of sorrow God wants us to experience leads us away from sin and results in salvation. There's no regret for that kind of sorrow. But worldly sorrow, which lacks repentance, results in spiritual death. 2 CORINTHIANS 7:8-10

IT DIDN'T BRING PAUL any pleasure to point out the Corinthians' sin and call them on it. He loved them, and he knew himself to be "chief" of sinners (1 Timothy 1:15, KJV). Though being so severe with them made him uncomfortable, he was willing to do it because he knew their salvation was at stake. He was God's messenger to bring them back to the path of repentance that leads to life.

When we see ongoing, unrepentant sin in the life of our child who claims to be a believer, love demands that we refuse to ignore it and instead help them to recognize it for what it is and call them to forsake it. No parent wants to bring sorrow to his or her child. But godly sorrow is a redemptive anguish that ensures our child's eternal happiness.

When Jesus says, "God blesses those who mourn, for they will be comforted" (Matthew 5:4), he's not talking about simply being sad over the losses and disappointments we experience in life. Neither is he talking about a general sense of sadness over not being who we want to be. He's talking about deep sorrow over specific sins that break God's heart. That is godly sorrow.

After we've taken care of getting the log out of our own eye, we can point out the splinters in our children's eyes that they cannot see. We can also pray that godly sorrow will cause them to repent and change their ways.

❋ ❋ ❋

Lord, help me to be willing to cause _____ pain now to save him from an eternity of being separated from you. Use my frank but loving words to help _____ overcome habitual sins.

The Need for Greater Wisdom

Here now is my final conclusion: Fear God and obey his commands, for this is everyone's duty. God will judge us for everything we do, including every secret thing, whether good or bad. ECCLESIASTES 12:13-14

AT THE BEGINNING OF ECCLESIASTES, a narrator introduces us to the Preacher, whose voice we hear throughout its twelve chapters. Then, at the end of the book, when the narrator speaks again to draw some conclusions from all that the Preacher has said, he speaks to "my son." So we could imagine a scene in which a man is sitting with his son or protégé, seeking to talk to him about what life means and what really matters. Throughout the book, he tells his son all about the Preacher's pursuits, questions, and conclusions. He has offered many wise observations and said many things that are true about the world, but his wisdom is limited. He is able to see life only from an "under the sun" perspective.

Then we can picture the narrator leaning in as he looks his son square in the eyes and states the conclusion that the entire book has been leading toward: "Fear God and obey his commands, for this is everyone's duty. God will judge us for everything we do, including every secret thing, whether good or bad." This very sound but limited conclusion is as far as Old Testament wisdom writing can take us. And it leaves us wanting. What was needed in the Preacher's day was a new revelation—wisdom that would come from heaven, not from under the sun.

Likewise, teaching "biblical principles" about how to live wisely in this world can take our kids only so far. Something greater is needed to overcome the seeming meaninglessness in the world. And that is to be joined by faith to wisdom incarnate, Jesus Christ. If it is up to us to merely do our duty and obey, we're all in trouble. If we anticipate being judged for every secret act we've committed apart from Christ, then we are hopeless. But we are not in trouble, nor are we hopeless. We have Jesus, the wisdom who came into this world under the sun and infused our lives with meaning.

※ ※ ※

Lord, we don't want to teach _____ all kinds of principles for living well in the world so that _____ is moral and successful on the world's terms but fails to see her need for you. We pray that _____ would fear you and keep your commands by believing the gospel and living in light of it.

Until the Time Is Right

Promise me, O women of Jerusalem,
*   by the gazelles and wild deer,*
*   not to awaken love until the time is right.* SONG OF SONGS 2:7

SEX CAN BE such an uncomfortable topic that we're a bit surprised to find a whole book in the Bible about it. But we learn from the outset of Song of Songs that sex is not inherently dirty or shameful. In fact, the picture of sexuality painted by the writer of the Song harkens back to the Garden of Eden, where Adam and Eve enjoyed the beautiful wonder of being naked and unashamed.

The Song presents sexuality as a good gift protected by marriage, not as an evil thing made permissible by marriage. Most of the world sees Christians as very prudish or repressive about sex. But the Bible makes it clear that sex is a God-blessed way to say to another person, "I belong completely, exclusively, and permanently to you." Sex creates deep intimacy, oneness, and communion between two people. God knows that human emotions come and go, and that we need something that binds us to each other. So God requires a public, legal covenant as the infrastructure for intimacy. This guarding of sexual love by public covenant is at the heart of the chorus that is repeated three times in this short book: "Promise me, O women of Jerusalem, by the gazelles and wild deer, not to awaken love until the time is right."

In this little chorus we discover a shocking message for our culture: Sexual desire can lie dormant. You can be a complete human being without having sex. Oh, how difficult it is for us as parents living in a culture that celebrates any and every kind of sexual expression to communicate a joyful celebration of sex exclusively within marriage and encourage our children "not to awaken love until the time is right."

❈ ❈ ❈

Lord, we really need your help to faithfully communicate to our children the good gift you intend sexual love to be, as well as the boundaries you have set for it. It seems at times that everything in the world is working against us as we try to pass along to our children a healthy and holy enjoyment of this good gift. We desperately need your grace to work in and through us to overcome the collective voice of the world around us.

Love Flashes like Fire

Place me like a seal over your heart,
like a seal on your arm.
For love is as strong as death,
its jealousy as enduring as the grave.
Love flashes like fire,
the brightest kind of flame.
Many waters cannot quench love,
nor can rivers drown it.
If a man tried to buy love
with all his wealth,
his offer would be utterly scorned. SONG OF SONGS 8:6-7

POPULAR MUSIC can make love seem so sentimental, so simple, so safe. Sitcoms make casual sex seem so inconsequential and unfettered. But the lover in Song of Songs knows that love is far more intense than mere sentimentalism, far more complex than mere words, far more dangerous than hurt feelings. Misuse or misdirect sexual desire and it has the power to inflict severe damage. The only way to safely maintain something with so much power is to experience it in a secure relationship sealed through lifelong commitment.

Everyone to whom we join ourselves, everyone with whom we sleep, takes a piece of us that we can never fully get back. The experience leaves an imprint deep in our souls. To play around with sexual intimacy outside of marriage is to play with fire. Perhaps your child has already been burned. If so, there is good news in the gospel: There is a balm that brings healing to sexual scars. By his wounds we are healed.

The religious leaders of Jesus' day were offended when they found Jesus eating with immoral and sexually broken people. But Jesus said, "Those who are well have no need of a physician, but those who are sick. I have not come to call the righteous but sinners to repentance" (Luke 5:31-32, ESV). Jesus did not come to join himself to people with perfect sexual histories, as if there were such a person. Jesus came for sick people—people who had been burned by sexual sin. He still does not turn his back on sin-scarred people, even if those wounds were self-inflicted.

❊ ❊ ❊

Lord, you know in a way I never can how _____ may have been burned by the misuse of sex. Help _____ to fall into the arms of the lover of her soul. Only you can bring healing to hidden places of the soul.

Weapons of War

We are human, but we don't wage war as humans do. We use God's mighty weapons, not worldly weapons, to knock down the strongholds of human reasoning and to destroy false arguments. We destroy every proud obstacle that keeps people from knowing God. We capture their rebellious thoughts and teach them to obey Christ.
2 Corinthians 10:3-5

WE DON'T TEND TO THINK of our homes as war zones. And yet sometimes we do sense that we are under attack. We know we have an enemy who has come into this world and shows up at our door with intentions "to steal and kill and destroy" (John 10:10). He intends to steal away the truth of God's Word implanted in our children's hearts so they are left with only human reasoning and false arguments. He intends to kill off the fruit of humility blossoming in our children's lives so they will pridefully assume no need for God. He intends to destroy any sense that obeying Christ will make them truly and eternally happy so they will be left only with rebellious thoughts of doing life their own way.

Once we realize that our home is, in fact, a war zone, where a battle is raging for the souls of all who live there, we realize that we have no power of our own to defeat the enemy. We are in need of divine power. And so we read God's Word together instead of just watching TV. We live by faith, not by our own ingenuity and hard work. We depend upon the power of the Holy Spirit, not simply our own good intentions. And we pray together instead of spending time in worry.

❊ ❊ ❊

God, we recognize that in our family there are some deeply entrenched ways of relating to each other, to you, and to the world around us, and we are powerless to change unless you provide us with divine power. There are some deeply held beliefs that are opposed to your Word, some prideful attitudes and rebellious ways of thinking that simply must be captured and destroyed. So will you show us how to take up your weapons to fight the battle? We want to use the weapons you provide to fight for _____'s very soul.

Bitter Fruit

My beloved had a vineyard
on a rich and fertile hill.
He plowed the land, cleared its stones,
and planted it with the best vines.
In the middle he built a watchtower
and carved a winepress in the nearby rocks.
Then he waited for a harvest of sweet grapes,
but the grapes that grew were bitter. ISAIAH 5:1-2

WHEN WE'RE AT OUR LOWEST moments as parents, far more aware of our failures than our successes, we need to remember that even our perfect heavenly Father raised way-ward children. Actually, *all* of his children have headed in the wrong direction. In Isaiah 1:2, the Lord says, "The children I raised and cared for have rebelled against me." So God understands the struggle and disappointment of raising children who rebel.

In Isaiah 5, he speaks of his children as a vineyard that he has prepared, protected, and tended with the expectation of fruit. But the vineyard has yielded bitter grapes. Perhaps, like the Lord himself, you have raised, protected, and tended your child with the expectation of a fruitful and godly life. You've waited in anticipation of sweet grapes. But at this point, there is only bitter fruit. We might know intellectually that our children are sinners who need a Savior, but we still struggle with frustration, fear, guilt, disappointment, and discouragement when we see our children make bad choices and act in ways that hurt themselves and others.

When we hear the Lord asking the question in Isaiah 5:4, "What more could I have done for my vineyard that I have not already done?" we know there is, in fact, something more he will do. He will send his beloved Son, who calls himself "the true grapevine" (John 15:1). The true vine will be crushed and will bear fruit. The Son says, "Those who remain in me, and I in them, will produce much fruit" (John 15:5).

❊ ❊ ❊

Lord, what _____ needs most is to abide in the vine that is Christ. A branch cannot produce fruit if it is severed from the vine. So graft _____ into your vine in a way that she can never be severed. Help me to trust you for the harvest in _____'s life.

Undone

Then I said, "It's all over! I am doomed, for I am a sinful man. I have filthy lips, and I live among a people with filthy lips. Yet I have seen the King, the LORD of Heaven's Armies." Then one of the seraphim flew to me with a burning coal he had taken from the altar with a pair of tongs. He touched my lips with it and said, "See, this coal has touched your lips. Now your guilt is removed, and your sins are forgiven." ISAIAH 6:5-7

A PROPHET IS ONE who speaks for God. So certainly, Isaiah, the prophet, took pride in his ability to speak. His lips spoke for God himself to the people of Israel. If he were around today, he would be speaking at the biggest conferences and followed by millions on Twitter. Surely Isaiah felt about his lips the way a surgeon would feel about his or her fingers or a soccer player about his or her feet.

But when Isaiah saw the holiness of God, he saw himself, and his lips, in a new light. In the blazing light of God's holiness, Isaiah could see that his lips were actually unfit for speaking for God. In the King James Version, Isaiah's response reads: "Woe is me! For I am *undone*" (emphasis added). Undone. In the presence of the perfect purity of God, Isaiah's sense of himself and his own goodness came completely unraveled.

As parents we want to encourage our children in their areas of strength. But these abilities and attributes can also puff them up. Our children's strengths can become so entwined with their identities that when they are proven inadequate, our children are "undone." It might be their special talent or appearance or position in their peer group. But the reality is that if their confidence and hope are in anything other than the grace of God, that "glue" is going to come apart.

❈ ❈ ❈

Lord we want to be first-rate encouragers to _____ about his strengths and abilities. We want _____ to have the sense that he has something worthwhile to contribute to your cause in the world. But we don't want _____'s identity to be anchored in his strong points, but we want your power put on display in his weaknesses. Give us wisdom to know how to encourage and affirm _____'s strengths while also encouraging him to find his identity in you.

So the Power of Christ Can Work through Me

To keep me from becoming proud, I was given a thorn in my flesh, a messenger from Satan to torment me and keep me from becoming proud. Three different times I begged the Lord to take it away. Each time he said, "My grace is all you need. My power works best in weakness." So now I am glad to boast about my weaknesses, so that the power of Christ can work through me. That's why I take pleasure in my weaknesses, and in the insults, hardships, persecutions, and troubles that I suffer for Christ. For when I am weak, then I am strong. 2 CORINTHIANS 12:7-10

WE DON'T KNOW WHAT PAUL'S "THORN" WAS. What we do know is that it was far more than a slight discomfort. Whatever the difficulty was, it brought unrelenting agony. Paul was able to see that the thorn was a provision from God to keep him from the sin of spiritual pride. But, like most of us, he wanted it removed. So he pleaded with God to take it away. God's response to his prayer was not to give Paul the healing he yearned for. Instead, he promised to give Paul more of himself, saying, "My grace is all you need. My power works best in weakness."

Perhaps you have pleaded in prayer for yourself or for your family, and God has so far said no. If so, the promise and provision God spoke to Paul, he also speaks to you. He will give you the grace you need to faithfully endure the pain he does not take away, the problem he does not solve, or the resolution he does not bring about. His divine power to persevere doesn't really work for people who think, *I can handle this.* Instead, his power works best in people—in parents—who recognize that they face something far beyond their ability to handle on their own.

In our day Christianity is often reduced to a method to make life go well. But spiritual strength is not about having such a special connection to God that we are able to convince him to say yes to our request to change our circumstances. Here is the supernatural experience that God *has* promised: the power of Christ coming down to rest on you when the worst thing you can imagine happens to you or to someone you love. He can make you content even when he does not take away the source of your agonizing pain.

※ ※ ※

Lord, we want to take hold of your promise of sufficient grace. We believe that you will give us the grace we need in the form, the timing, and the quantity we need it to face whatever may come. Our desire is that your glory and goodness would be put on display in our lives so those around us see that your divine power is enough to provide us peace in hardship.

Selfless Love

I am coming to you for the third time, and I will not be a burden to you. I don't want what you have—I want you. After all, children don't provide for their parents. Rather, parents provide for their children. I will gladly spend myself and all I have for you, even though it seems that the more I love you, the less you love me. 2 CORINTHIANS 12:14-15

PAUL TOLD THE CORINTHIANS that he considered himself their spiritual parent. He didn't want them spending their money to take care of him as he worked with them. More than that, Paul said he would gladly spend himself and all he had for the Corinthian Christians to grow to be all that God intended. Paul was willing to be used up to see his children in the faith grow up.

Just as Paul refused to use his "children" to make himself rich, neither do we want to use our children to make ourselves look good in the eyes of others. And though we likely don't see ourselves as wanting to use our children in this way, that self-perception is challenged by our reaction when we feel our children are making us look bad. Our anger or embarrassment reveals the truth.

Just as Paul carried a burden he chose not to place on his "children," so do we as parents carry the weight of many burdens that we choose not to place on our kids. And just as Paul was writing this letter to the disrespectful Corinthians for the very purpose of building up those who had torn him down, so we, as parents, keep on looking for ways to build up our children, even when they have rolled their eyes at our ideas and haven't treated us with the respect we deserve.

Of course, Paul could treat the Corinthians this way because this is how he had been treated by Christ. We can almost hear Christ saying to us, his children, "I will gladly spend myself and all I have for you, even though it seems that the more I love you, the less you love me."

Christ spent himself for us long before we loved him. It is his Spirit that enables us to spend ourselves in love for our children, even when they are not being loving to us in return.

❈ ❈ ❈

Lord, sometimes we just get tired of spending ourselves for our children—especially when we seem to receive little love and respect in return. We need your Spirit of serving and giving and spending ourselves.

SEPTEMBER 13

Isaiah 12:1–14:32
2 Corinthians 13:1-14
Psalm 57:1-11
Proverbs 23:9-11

Examine Yourselves

*Examine yourselves to see if your faith is genuine. Test yourselves. Surely you know
that Jesus Christ is among you; if not, you have failed the test of genuine faith.*
2 CORINTHIANS 13:5

PAUL WROTE THIS LETTER to the church in Corinth to address their doubts about the
genuineness of his apostolic authority. False teachers had questioned Paul's authority
because evidently he wasn't an impressive speaker and constantly experienced significant
suffering. Their message to the church in Corinth was that Paul was not the real deal.

So in his letter, Paul set them straight on what genuine faith looks like in the life of a
believer. It is a treasure in a jar of clay. It is the power of Christ shining through human
weakness. As he drew his letter to a close, he challenged them to examine themselves
to see if they were authentic believers. He wanted them to examine their own lives for
evidence of an increasing holiness and genuine affection for Christ. Their flirtation
with the false teachers and their immoral living put a question mark over their spiritual
condition. Interestingly, Paul was not asking the Corinthians if something happened in
their past that made them Christians; he was challenging them to examine themselves
in the present to see if there was genuine spiritual life.

Sometimes the beliefs and sins our children toy with put a question mark over their
spiritual condition too. The truth is, we can't know for certain the true nature of our
child's connectedness to Christ. But neither should we take it for granted that because
they have grown up in our home and in the church, or because they "made a decision"
or had an emotional spiritual experience, they have gone from death to life spiritually.
Surely some children raised in Christian homes respond to the gospel out of a desire to
please their parents or fit in rather than out of genuine repentance and faith.

We can't examine our kids and know if their faith is genuine. But we can encourage
them to examine themselves, not by comparing themselves to others or to cultural ideas
of what it means to be a Christian, but by putting their lives under the microscope of
God's Word to see what is really there.

※ ※ ※

*Lord, just like Paul prayed that his "children" in Corinth would pass the test and would
become mature, we pray for _____, that she will have the courage to examine
herself, the insight to see what is real, and the joy of knowing that she is genuinely and
savingly connected to you.*

One Person to Please

Let God's curse fall on anyone, including us or even an angel from heaven, who preaches a different kind of Good News than the one we preached to you. I say again what we have said before: If anyone preaches any other Good News than the one you welcomed, let that person be cursed. Obviously, I'm not trying to win the approval of people, but of God. If pleasing people were my goal, I would not be Christ's servant.
GALATIANS 1:8-10

PAUL WAS SAYING SOMETHING that would not win him many friends. Most people are not particularly drawn to someone who pronounces a curse on someone else. Did Paul just love ruffling feathers? Was he arrogant in his beliefs? Was he uncaring about those who faced an eternal future apart from Christ? No. Paul was willing to speak this way about those who preach a way into God's good graces other than faith in Christ's finished work because his desire to please God was so much higher on his list of priorities than pleasing people.

This is the kind of commitment to the truth of the gospel and freedom from pleasing people that we all want. And it's what we want for our children.

Our need for approval is deeply wired into us. It's not seeking after approval and the personal satisfaction it provides that Jesus condemns; it is seeking approval from the wrong source. If we're always looking for approval from other people, we'll never get enough, and it will never last long enough. In Christ we have already been given all the approval we really need and all the approval that really matters. Jesus was God's beloved Son in whom he was well pleased. Once we are joined to Christ, that approval splashes over onto us. Joined to Christ, we are accepted and approved.

Day by day, as our children come home, worn down by disapproval from others, we can keep pointing them to the one person whose approval really matters, assuring them that as they are in Christ, they already have this divine approval.

❈ ❈ ❈

Lord, please make _____ into a person who lives for your approval, not the praise of other people. By your great and sufficient grace, shrink and disable _____'s deep need for human approval. And by the power of the Holy Spirit, grant _____ greater assurance that, in you, he already has God's full acceptance and everlasting approval.

SEPTEMBER 15

Don't Fail to Discipline Your Children

Don't fail to discipline your children.
The rod of punishment won't kill them.
Physical discipline
may well save them from death. PROVERBS 23:13-14

THE LORD USES DISCIPLINE to reveal our sin to us and to train us to live rightly. The writer of Hebrews says, "God's discipline is always good for us, so that we might share in his holiness. No discipline is enjoyable while it is happening—it's painful! But afterward there will be a peaceful harvest of right living for those who are trained in this way" (12:10-11). God's discipline is clearly purposeful—that we might share in his holiness.

In the same way, we are to discipline our children. We want to impress on them the seriousness of sin and the importance of living rightly. Our discipline shares the same purpose as God's: that our children might share in his holiness and thereby be saved from eternal death. When our children do not feel the consequence of their sin, they will not understand that sin requires punishment. And if they have no grasp of punishment, how will they ever grasp their need for the one who was punished in their place for their disobedience toward God?

What a responsibility we have to discipline our children. And what a challenge it is to do so in a godly and grace-filled way. Too many times we act out of fear, embarrassment, anger, or frustration. We discipline in rash and out-of-control ways rather than reasoned and purposeful ways. We speak out of a desire to shame or manipulate our children rather than to point them toward repentance and restoration. What we need is for the grace of Christ to overflow in our lives so that we can discipline our children in that grace.

❊ ❊ ❊

Lord, save me from the sin of venting my anger or frustration on _____ and calling it "discipline." Show me how to discipline in a way that reveals who you are as a Father and trains _____ toward godliness.

A New Identity

My old self has been crucified with Christ. It is no longer I who live, but Christ lives in me. So I live in this earthly body by trusting in the Son of God, who loved me and gave himself for me. I do not treat the grace of God as meaningless. For if keeping the law could make us right with God, then there was no need for Christ to die. GALATIANS 2:20-21

PART OF THE PROCESS of growing up is figuring out who you are. Our kids are in the process of discovering their identity. The good news is that Christ doesn't merely provide a new persona for our children to try on for size and comfort; he offers himself to become their new identity. If they do not take hold of Christ, they will live out some inferior identity based on what they do or the way they're wired—the cool kid, the athlete, the scholar, the nerd, the pretty one, the rebel, the rule follower, the comedian, the cynic, the victim, the musician. But when they see themselves as joined to Christ, they will live lives of joy and peace.

Instead of allowing the world around them to define them on its terms, we want the truth about identity in Christ, found in the Word of God, to shape how our children see themselves. Based on Scripture, our children who are in Christ can say:

I am a friend of Jesus.
I am no longer a slave to sin.
I have been accepted by Christ.
My body is a temple of the Holy Spirit who dwells in me.
I am a new creature in Christ.
I have been blessed with every spiritual blessing in the heavenly places.
I am chosen, holy, and blameless before God.
I am God's workmanship created to produce good works.
I am a member of Christ's body and a partaker of his promise.
I am a citizen of heaven.
My life is hidden with Christ in God.

※ ※ ※

Lord, for _____ to think of herself in this way requires that she be transformed by the renewing of her mind. This can only happen as you, by your Spirit, use your Word to convince _____ of this true and lasting identity. Help me see the ways _____ is not yet convinced of this true identity in Christ and give me the right words at the right time to point her to who she is in you.

The Way of Faith or the Way of Law

Those who depend on the law to make them right with God are under his curse, for the Scriptures say, "Cursed is everyone who does not observe and obey all the commands that are written in God's Book of the Law." So it is clear that no one can be made right with God by trying to keep the law. For the Scriptures say, "It is through faith that a righteous person has life." This way of faith is very different from the way of law, which says, "It is through obeying the law that a person has life." GALATIANS 3:10-12

OUR CHILDREN have an enemy who is continuously at work tempting them to think and feel that because they are in a family that talks about God, goes to church, and reads the Bible, they are under God's blessing. But the book of Galatians concerns a group of people who did all of those things and yet were under God's curse.

The issue in question in this portion of Paul's letter was what determined whether the Galatians could expect to experience divine blessing or divine curse. And the answer didn't depend on whether they were church people or nonchurch people. It was about whether or not they had come to see their utter inability to keep the law of God and therefore had taken hold of Christ, who perfectly kept the law in their place. Unfortunately, they were still trying, through their religious activity and good morals, to earn the divine blessing they craved.

Efforts to fill up the local food pantry or build wells in Africa and commitments to save sex for marriage and refuse to buy lottery tickets can be law-keeping done in human strength to win God's favor, or they can be done in dependence upon the strength of Christ, out of love for Christ and a desire to bring glory to him. The question of curse or blessing hangs on *how* we obey and *who* gets the credit.

❋ ❋ ❋

Lord, we want _____ to obey your Word and live a holy life. We want _____ to experience and expect your divine blessing, not your divine curse. What we don't want is for _____ to be caught up in just trying to live by your law when he has no power to live that way and no sense of your forgiveness when he fails to live in that way.

God's Own Child

When the right time came, God sent his Son, born of a woman, subject to the law. God sent him to buy freedom for us who were slaves to the law, so that he could adopt us as his very own children. And because we are his children, God has sent the Spirit of his Son into our hearts, prompting us to call out, "Abba, Father." Now you are no longer a slave but God's own child. And since you are his child, God has made you his heir. GALATIANS 4:4-7

AS PARENTS, we're pretty sure that no one knows our child like we do, loves our child as much as we do, or is able to guide and care for our child like we can. No wonder it's so hard to leave our child for the first time with a babysitter or at Grandma and Grandpa's house for an overnight. We think that if we can just control the environment, avoid the dangers, and follow the right parenting strategies, we will be able to ensure that our children have a safe and happy childhood that will lead to a successful adulthood. In other words, we think we can be God for our children.

But in this, we vastly undervalue God's fatherhood as well as overvalue our own. When our children are out of our sight, they are not out of his sight. Right now, God is actively parenting our children.

This reality provides freedom for moms and dads who have blown it and can't figure out how to fix it: You don't have to be a perfect parent, and in fact, you never can be. Your children, however, do have a perfect parent. He knows them better than you do and knows what they need more than you do. He loves them more than you do and has more power to act out of that love than you do. He has sacrificed more for them than you have and will be able to care for them beyond your limited lifetime.

❋ ❋ ❋

Abba, Father, you sent your Son to buy my freedom so that you could adopt me as your own child. And because I'm your child, I stand to inherit everything you have to give to your children. What a loving, saving, caring, giving Father you are. You have entrusted _____ to me to parent during my limited lifetime, but you are _____'s true Father.

Longing for God

O God, you are my God;
I earnestly search for you.
My soul thirsts for you;
my whole body longs for you
in this parched and weary land
where there is no water. PSALM 63:1

DAVID IS THE KING OF JUDAH, but he's not sleeping in his own bed in the palace in Jerusalem. He's sleeping in a cave out in the wilderness, on the run from "those plotting to destroy" him (verse 9). And what really hurts is that those who want to kill him are led by his own son. The son he loves is not just alienated from him, but hostile toward him.

So what does David do? He prays. Psalm 63 is David's prayer addressed not just to God but to *his* God. And interestingly, it is not protection from Absalom nor victory over Absalom nor reconciliation with Absalom that he asks his God for. It is the nearness of God and satisfaction in God that David longs for. He thinks about the presence of God that came down to dwell among his people in the Most Holy Place in the Tabernacle. That is the presence he wants to know out in the wilderness.

In the midst of incredible difficulty, David's eyes are focused not on his circumstances, but on the glory of God he has seen at the Tabernacle. When his life is being threatened, he doesn't grasp for survival. Instead, he's convinced that God's "unfailing love is better than life itself" (verse 3). He's not busy orchestrating a defensive or offensive plan, but is lifting his hands up to God in prayer. He's not lying awake worrying about what might happen but is lying awake thinking about God and all of the benefits of belonging to him. He is not clinging to his title or his privilege or his plans but instead is clinging to God, confident that the Lord has taken hold of him and is holding him securely.

When we are at odds with our kids or worried about our kids, it can feel as if we are in a parched and weary land where there is no water. David shows us where to turn, what to do, and whom to long for. We turn to our God and lift up our hands to him in prayer, telling him how much we need him.

❋ ❋ ❋

Lord, because you are my helper, I sing for joy in the shadow of your wings. I cling to you; your strong right hand holds me securely.

What Kind of Fruit?

The Holy Spirit produces this kind of fruit in our lives: love, joy, peace, patience, kindness, goodness, faithfulness, gentleness, and self-control. GALATIANS 5:22-23

IT'S EASY TO READ PAUL'S LIST of the fruit the Holy Spirit produces in the life of the believer and turn it into a to-do list for ourselves or our kids. But Paul speaks of fruit, not fruits, of the Spirit. The fruit of the Spirit is not a checklist. All this fruit blossoms naturally in the lives of those in whom the Spirit dwells.

Just as apple trees don't grow oranges and orange trees don't grow apples, those who don't have the Holy Spirit at work in the interior of their lives can't expect to produce the kind of fruit the Holy Spirit produces. Instead they'll produce the kind of fruit that comes naturally to a spiritually dead person. But when the Holy Spirit has come to reside and work in someone, we can be sure that the fruit will be produced. Of course, growing fruit takes time, and the fruit of the Spirit grows particularly slowly. Sometimes the growth is imperceptible, but the Spirit's presence in our child's life guarantees that growth will occur.

As parents, it is not our job to produce children who behave in a way that lines up with this list of fruit. We are mere instruments in the Holy Spirit's ongoing work in the lives of our children. He is the producer of this fruit. And he has a long-term view.

When we realize it isn't our job to ensure that our children produce this fruit, it reshapes our parenting priorities. Instead of pushing them to produce these virtues by the force of their own will, we point them toward Christ, who comes to dwell within and produces this fruit by the power of his Spirit. This removes a heavy weight from our shoulders. It helps us to see our kids not as a reflection of who we are, or as a result of our brilliant or substandard parenting, but as unique people in whom the Spirit is at work in his way, in his timing, producing his fruit as he sees fit.

※ ※ ※

Holy Spirit, you are the Master Gardener. You know what you're doing in _____'s life. You also know what you're doing in my life. I long for a bountiful harvest of love for _____, joy in _____, patience with _____, kindness toward _____, goodness before _____, faithfulness in my promises to _____, gentleness in my demeanor to _____, and self-control in my responses to _____. Won't you generate that fruit in me?

Don't Give Up

Don't be misled—you cannot mock the justice of God. You will always harvest what you plant. Those who live only to satisfy their own sinful nature will harvest decay and death from that sinful nature. But those who live to please the Spirit will harvest everlasting life from the Spirit. So let's not get tired of doing what is good. At just the right time we will reap a harvest of blessing if we don't give up. GALATIANS 6:7-9

As PAUL BRINGS his letter to the Galatians to a close, he has a sober warning for them. They can't expect to "sow" a life of sinful indulgence or coldhearted legalism at odds with the Spirit and "reap" the kind of abundant, unending life that comes from the Spirit. The evidence that they have truly been "crucified with Christ" will be that they will keep on pursuing a life that reflects the purity of Christ in dependence upon the grace of Christ. So along with his warning of harvesting decay and death if they live to please themselves comes the promise of harvesting blessing if they live to please the Spirit.

The imagery of sowing and reaping leads us to ask: What is being sown in our children's lives? Whom are they living to please? How are we doing in both warning them about what they can expect if they live only to satisfy their sinful nature and encouraging them with what they can expect if they live to please the Spirit?

We all need encouragement to keep going and not give up. So when we see our children make a choice to please the Spirit instead of the sinful nature budding within them, we can encourage them to keep going, keep growing, keep enjoying the smile of God on their lives. We can assure them that one day the harvest of blessing will be bountiful, beautiful, and eternal.

❆ ❆ ❆

Lord, I know how often I want to give up in my own pursuit of a life lived in step with the Spirit and empowered by the Spirit. Sometimes I get tired of doing what is right and good. So help me to give _____ the same encouragement I need to keep sowing seeds of living to please the Spirit. Remind me to keep pointing _____ toward the reward you've promised—a harvest of happiness and holiness.

Every Spiritual Blessing

Christ . . . fills all things everywhere with himself. EPHESIANS 1:23

All praise to God, the Father of our Lord Jesus Christ, who has blessed _____ with every spiritual blessing in the heavenly realms because _____ is united with Christ. Even before he made the world, God loved _____ and chose _____ in Christ to be holy and without fault in his eyes. God decided in advance to adopt _____ into his own family by bringing _____ to himself through Jesus Christ. This is what he wanted to do, and it gave him great pleasure. So we praise God for the glorious grace he has poured out on _____, who belongs to his dear Son. He is so rich in kindness and grace that he purchased _____'s freedom with the blood of his Son and forgave _____'s sins. He has showered his kindness on _____, along with all wisdom and understanding.

God has now revealed to _____ his mysterious plan regarding Christ, a plan to fulfill his own good pleasure. And this is the plan: At the right time he will bring everything together under the authority of Christ—everything in heaven and on earth. Furthermore, because _____ is united with Christ, _____ has received an inheritance from God, for he chose _____ in advance, and he makes everything work out according to his plan.

God's purpose was that Jews who were the first to trust in Christ would bring praise and glory to God. And now Gentiles have also heard the truth, the Good News that God saves you. And when _____ believed in Christ, he identified _____ as his own by giving _____ the Holy Spirit, whom he promised long ago. The Spirit is God's guarantee that he will give _____ the inheritance he promised and that he has purchased _____ to be his own. He did this so we would praise and glorify him.

I pray for _____ constantly, asking God, the glorious Father of our Lord Jesus Christ, to give _____ spiritual wisdom and insight so that _____ might grow in knowledge of God. I pray that _____'s heart will be flooded with light so that _____ can understand the confident hope he has given to those he called—his holy people who are his rich and glorious inheritance.

ADAPTED FROM EPHESIANS 1:3-18

But God

Once you were dead because of your disobedience and your many sins. You used to live in sin, just like the rest of the world, obeying the devil—the commander of the powers in the unseen world. He is the spirit at work in the hearts of those who refuse to obey God. All of us used to live that way, following the passionate desires and inclinations of our sinful nature. By our very nature we were subject to God's anger, just like everyone else. But God is so rich in mercy, and he loved us so much, that even though we were dead because of our sins, he gave us life when he raised Christ from the dead. (It is only by God's grace that you have been saved!) For he raised us from the dead along with Christ and seated us with him in the heavenly realms because we are united with Christ Jesus. So God can point to us in all future ages as examples of the incredible wealth of his grace and kindness toward us, as shown in all he has done for us who are united with Christ Jesus. EPHESIANS 2:1-7

IN MODERN CHRISTIANITY, we have developed many terms for describing a Christian and what makes someone a Christian. We talk about "getting saved" or "accepting Christ" or "asking Jesus to come into your heart." But Ephesians 2 provides us with words that describe this reality: "you were dead . . . but God . . . raised [you] from the dead." This clarity helps us better understand our children. They were born physically alive but spiritually dead. Not just sickly. *Dead.* Completely unable to respond to God. Their regeneration must be accomplished by the Spirit through the Word. That's why we take our children to church where they can hear the Word of God preached and taught and why we read the Bible together in our homes. We can't make our child alive spiritually, *but God* can and does using his Word.

God is rich in mercy. In other words, he is not stingy with it. He showers his mercy on those who look to him for it. He loves to work in the lives of those who are dead because of sin to make them alive.

※ ※ ※

Lord, as we think of you in the age to come, pointing to those who were dead but were made alive by being united to Christ, how we long for _____ to be a glorious example of the incredible wealth of your grace and kindness toward sinners. We don't have the power to generate spiritual life in our children, but you do! So unite _____ to Christ. Raise _____ from the dead. Seat _____ with Christ in the heavenly realms.

Rooted and Grounded

I pray that from his glorious, unlimited resources he will empower you with inner strength through his Spirit. Then Christ will make his home in your hearts as you trust in him. Your roots will grow down into God's love and keep you strong. EPHESIANS 3:16-17

PAUL HAD THE HEART OF A PARENT—a praying parent—toward the believers in Ephesus. His letter to them keeps turning into prayers for them. What Paul wanted for his spiritual children in Ephesus, we also desire for our children.

We want our children to have Spirit-given strength in their inner being, specifically the strength to comprehend something that is incomprehensible apart from this divine strength—the expansive nature of the love of Christ. We want our children's lives to be rooted and grounded in the love of Christ. We don't want them to just sing "Jesus Loves Me." We want them to believe, deep in their souls, that they are loved by Christ. As their roots go deep into the love of Christ, we know they will be able to withstand the blows of a cruel world. As they become more and more grounded in his love, they won't be as vulnerable to false promises.

There is a power at work in our children—the same power that raised Jesus from the dead. So as we pray for them, we know that the one we pray to has the power to bring about more than we can ask or think.

❊ ❊ ❊

I fall to my knees and pray to the Father, the Creator of everything in heaven and on earth. I pray that from his glorious, unlimited resources he will empower _____ with inner strength through his Spirit. Then Christ will make his home in _____'s heart as _____ trusts in him. _____'s roots will grow down into God's love and keep _____ strong.

And may _____ have the power to understand, as all God's people should, how wide, how long, how high, and how deep his love is. May _____ experience the love of Christ, though it is too great to understand fully. Then _____ will be made complete with all the fullness of life and power that comes from God.

Now all glory to God, who is able, through his mighty power at work within _____, to accomplish infinitely more than we might ask or think. Glory to him in the church and in Christ Jesus through all generations forever and ever! Amen.

SEPTEMBER 25

Look to Me

Let all the world look to me for salvation!
  For I am God; there is no other. . . .
The people will declare,
  "The LORD is the source of all my righteousness and strength." ISAIAH 45:22, 24

GOD IS THE ONLY GOD. There is no other. And that includes us. Sometimes as parents we operate as if our children's salvation and sanctification are all up to us—that it is our rules, our diligence, and our wisdom that will shape them into all God intends for them to be. But we can't be God to our children, as much as we might like to be. We can't save them. We can't supply them with everything they will ever need. We can't promise that we will never fail them or leave them. We don't have the ability to see all that is going on inside them in the present or all that is ahead for them in the future. We can't be the source of all of their righteousness and strength.

But we can show them what it looks like to turn to God for salvation—not just at one time in our past, but in an ongoing way. We can allow our children to overhear when we call out to God to be saved from sins like lust, greed, or selfishness. We can confess before them that our righteousness is marred by apathy, deceit, and hypocrisy, which is why we need to be covered by the righteousness of another.

So while we can't be God or force our children to look to God, we can *show them* how to live in radical dependence on God rather than pretend that we have it all together.

❈ ❈ ❈

Lord, you are the source of all of our righteousness and strength. You are the God who saves. And so, Lord, we look to you, not only for our salvation but for the salvation of _____. Help us to remember that you are the only God. We simply can't be God in _____'s life. As you hold out your salvation to all who will look to you, will you cause _____ to look to you? Would you give _____ a heart that longs for the righteousness only you can provide and the strength that you supply?

Put On Your New Nature

Let the Spirit renew your thoughts and attitudes. EPHESIANS 4:23

Lord, I pray that you would not only bring _____ to life spiritually, but that your Spirit would empower _____ to live in a new way, a way that is quite different from peers who are still spiritually dead. They are hopelessly confused. Their minds are full of darkness; they wander far from the life you give because they have closed their minds and hardened their hearts against you. They have no sense of shame. They live for lustful pleasure and eagerly practice every kind of impurity.

But since _____ has heard about Jesus and has learned the truth that comes from you, we pray that _____ would throw off his old sinful nature and his former way of life, which is corrupted by lust and deception. Instead, let your Spirit renew _____'s thoughts and attitudes. May _____ put on a new nature, created to be like you—truly righteous and holy.

I pray that _____ would stop telling lies but would tell the truth even when it costs something. I pray that _____ wouldn't sin by letting anger control him, that he wouldn't let the sun go down while he is still angry, giving a foothold to the devil.

I pray that _____ would not steal, but would use his hands for good hard work and then give generously to others in need. I pray _____ would not use foul or abusive language, but that everything _____ says would be good and helpful, so that his words will be an encouragement to those who hear them.

I pray _____ would not bring sorrow to you by the way he lives.

I pray _____ would get rid of all bitterness, rage, anger, harsh words, and slander, as well as all types of evil behavior, and that instead, _____ would be kind, tenderhearted, and forgiving, just as you have forgiven him.

ADAPTED FROM EPHESIANS 4:17-32

Because You Are His Dear Children

Be imitators of God, as beloved children . . . for at one time you were darkness, but now you are light in the Lord. Walk as children of light. Ephesians 5:1, 8 esv

We want our children to do certain things in a certain way because of the way we do things in our family. It's just part of who we are and who we expect them to be. Likewise, there is a way we should live that is consistent with being a child of God. If we are truly his child, it simply doesn't make any sense to live in any other way.

In Ephesians 5, Paul called the Ephesian Christians to be who they really were—not who they used to be before they took hold of Christ by faith and his Spirit came to dwell in them. They used to be darkness, and then they were light. It's not just that they lived in darkness or liked darkness; they *were* darkness. Darkness was at the core of their identity. But now, they were light. The light of Christ had become the core of their identity. Christ was at the operating center of their lives. Paul wanted them to live out this new identity rather than live in the incongruity and misery of claiming to belong to Christ while living for themselves.

If we are still darkness, the deeds of darkness will feel perfectly natural. There will be no sense of incongruity. But if we are truly light, doing what darkness does may be exciting for a moment, but ultimately it will feel very wrong. Though it may take some time to turn, there will be a sense of *I must stop living this way.*

It is this family identity that we want our children to operate from far more than our biological family identity. A settled sense of identity in Christ will mean that instead of setting out to please themselves, our children will want to please the Lord. Instead of taking part in things people of the darkness do, they will see clearly where those things lead. Instead of living the life of a fool, they will live according to the wisdom of God. Instead of filling themselves up with too much wine, they will be filled with the Spirit.

※ ※ ※

Lord, we know that you are out to make us, and to make _____, a completely new person from the inside out. So, Lord, when _____ participates in what belongs to darkness, make _____ miserable. And make the light beautiful and inviting. Overcome _____'s bent toward finding identity anywhere else than in being your child.

The Discipline That Comes from the Lord

Fathers, do not provoke your children to anger by the way you treat them. Rather, bring them up with the discipline and instruction that comes from the Lord. EPHESIANS 6:4

THIS VERSE IN EPHESIANS mirrors one in Colossians—"Fathers, do not aggravate your children, or they will become discouraged" (Colossians 3:21). They are actually the only two commands to parents in the entire New Testament. Did Paul write this same instruction two times because dads have a natural tendency to approach things in a way that would provoke anger in their kids, demand things that aggravate their kids, or expect things that discourage their kids?

We basically know what discourages and provokes our kids to anger—things like mocking, yelling, unjust and excessive punishment, and hypocrisy—but we sometimes find it hard to break these patterns. Fortunately, this passage provides us with an alternative way to interact with our kids—"the discipline and instruction that comes from the Lord." But how does our heavenly Father discipline and instruct his own children?

He does not punish us for all our sins; he does not deal harshly with us, as we deserve. . . . The LORD is like a father to his children, tender and compassionate to those who fear him. (Psalm 103:10, 13)

Can a mother forget her nursing child? Can she feel no love for the child she has borne? But even if that were possible, I would not forget you! (Isaiah 49:15)

Since he did not spare even his own Son but gave him up for us all, won't he also give us everything else? (Romans 8:32)

To bring our children up in the discipline and instruction that comes from the Lord is something much more than raising them in church or using "biblical principles." It is disciplining and instructing them with the same clarity and compassion, the same firmness and forgiveness, the same toughness and tenderness, the same initiative and integrity with which our Father fathers us.

❊ ❊ ❊

Lord, I want to get rid of all bitterness, rage, anger, and harsh words in my parenting. Instead, I want to be kind, tenderhearted, and forgiving toward _____, just as you have been so very kind, tenderhearted, and forgiving toward me.

Progress

Every time I think of you, I give thanks to my God. Whenever I pray, I make my requests for all of you with joy, for you have been my partners in spreading the Good News about Christ from the time you first heard it until now. And I am certain that God, who began the good work within you, will continue his work until it is finally finished on the day when Christ Jesus returns. PHILIPPIANS 1:3-6

As PAUL THOUGHT about the believers in Ephesus, he was full of thankfulness and joy. His current circumstances (he was in prison and facing execution) were less than promising, and yet he was full of joy. What made him so happy as he thought about the believers in Philippi?

First, he was happy because he knew they shared with him faith in Christ and they were living out that faith in the world. Second, he was happy because he was confident that God was at work in them and that nothing—including his own death—could keep God from bringing his work in their lives to a glorious conclusion. God started the work, not Paul, and God would finish the work.

Whenever you pray for your child, do you make your requests with joy? If your child is in Christ, you have every cause for joy knowing that your child's greatest need has been met. And if your child is not in Christ, you have every cause for hope knowing that your child's greatest need can only be met in Christ.

As you pray for your child in whom God has begun to work, no matter how limited that work may have been to this point, and no matter how far there is to go, you can be certain that God will complete his work. It may be slow. It may be start and stop. It may take a direction you had not anticipated. What you can be sure of is that it will not stop short. It will not be halfway or halfhearted.

The day is coming when the work that God began by calling your child to himself will be complete. Every last vestige of sin will be gone. Your child will be perfected in body and soul. So be patient with God's way and God's timing. Be certain he will finish his work.

※ ※ ※

I pray that _____'s love will overflow more and more, and that _____ will keep on growing in knowledge and understanding. I pray _____ will understand what really matters, so that _____ may live a pure and blameless life until the day of Christ's return. May _____ always be filled with the fruit of salvation—the righteous character produced by Jesus Christ—for this will bring much glory and praise to you.

The Same Attitude

Don't be selfish; don't try to impress others. Be humble, thinking of others as better than yourselves. Don't look out only for your own interests, but take an interest in others, too. You must have the same attitude that Christ Jesus had.

Though he was God,
he did not think of equality with God
as something to cling to.
Instead, he gave up his divine privileges;
he took the humble position of a slave
and was born as a human being.
When he appeared in human form,
he humbled himself in obedience to God
and died a criminal's death on a cross. PHILIPPIANS 2:3-8

MOST PARENTS, whether they are Christians or not, want their children to be unselfish, not to be out to impress others, to interact with others in humility, and to be willing to serve the needs of others. The question is: Is it possible for any of us, regardless of our connection to Christ, to genuinely and pervasively have this attitude of deep humility and servanthood?

While having this kind of mind-set is challenging to the Christian, it is impossible for the unbeliever because it comes from being united to Christ. No one can work themselves into this mind-set. It is something received in union and communion with Christ. It is something he creates in us as he begins his work in us.

There's no point in trying to live the Christian life if you're not united to Christ. And we simply can't expect a child who has not yet been joined to Christ to live in obedience to him. To have the same attitude of Christ requires that we have Christ. More significantly, it requires that he has us.

❋ ❋ ❋

Lord, how we want _____ to have the same attitude that you had—that of a humble servant, looking out for others. To have your mind-set, _____ needs you! So take _____ to yourself and make _____ more like you day by day. Implant in _____ a desire and commitment to have the same attitude that Christ Jesus had.

Perspective

Truly God is good to Israel,
*   to those whose hearts are pure.*
But as for me, I almost lost my footing.
*   My feet were slipping, and I was almost gone.*
For I envied the proud
*   when I saw them prosper despite their wickedness.* PSALM 73:1-3

ASAPH BEGINS PSALM 73 with the conclusion he has come to—that God is good to his people—and then takes us along with him on the path that led him to it. He admits that he almost stumbled because as he looked at the world around him, it seemed as if people who gave no thought to God actually lived pretty well: "Did I keep my heart pure for nothing?" he wondered (verse 13). But then he lifted up his eyes to God in worship and was given clarity on what a life spent alienated from God leads to. "Then I went into your sanctuary, O God, and I finally understood the destiny of the wicked" (verse 17). He could see that their path led to ruin. He realized that if he looked only at appearances, he wouldn't see the complete picture of reality.

Worship puts God at the center of our vision so that we can finally begin to see things as they really are. It delivers us from distortion. That's why being in church as a family week by week is such a priority if we want our kids to have their perspectives shaped by what is true, real, and eternal. All week long, the world seeks to shape the way our children think about things, so we gather each week with the people of God and look to him to readjust our perspective to see beyond life in this world and into eternity.

※ ※ ※

Truly you are kind to us, Lord. How good it is to be near you! Sovereign Lord, you have been our shelter. We want to tell everyone about the wonderful things you do. We need you to keep us from slipping into believing that this life is all there is. We need you to save _____ from thinking that there is no real benefit to a life set apart to you. Save _____ from such foolishness; guide _____ with your counsel; give _____ a desire for you that is greater than anything on earth; lead _____ to a glorious destiny.

The End of the Race

I focus on this one thing: Forgetting the past and looking forward to what lies ahead, I press on to reach the end of the race and receive the heavenly prize for which God, through Christ Jesus, is calling us. PHILIPPIANS 3:13-14

WHEN WE SCAN THROUGH social media, taking in the reports of the activities and achievements of our friends' kids—complete with stunning photography—we may wonder if we've *done* enough or if we *are* enough as parents. At such times we need to be reminded of the ultimate goal of life, and thereby the ultimate goal of parenting: to reach the end of the race and receive the heavenly prize. We are not parenting our kids merely for a "successful" life in the here and now; we're preparing them for what lies beyond this life. Paul's call for us to focus on this one thing—what lies ahead for us in heaven—readjusts our perspective about this life. Not being invited to the party, or not making the team, or not getting into the school is robbed of its power to crush. A focus on heaven and a growing sense of anticipation of what awaits us there implants in us and in our children the perspective-shaping reality that the grandest experiences and greatest pleasures of this life will never fully satisfy us, but are foretastes of the ultimate satisfaction of our future home.

Focusing on what is to come fills our ordinary days of parenting with eternal purpose. Our goal becomes reaching the new creation together with our children. We stop trying to force all that awaits us in the new creation into the here and now and instead, "press on to possess that perfection for which Christ Jesus first possessed me" (Philippians 3:12). This perspective keeps us from requiring perfection from our children and being crushed by their imperfections. It also relieves us from the burden of expecting we can parent perfectly. Instead, we can confess our parenting failures to our children and seek forgiveness from Jesus.

❉ ❉ ❉

We hear you calling us to press on in this race, which is leading us toward a heavenly life with you. Forgive us for being so shortsighted to expect that we can experience all of heaven's joys and perfections in the here and now. Fill us with greater anticipation of what is to come so that our joyful expectation will spill out on _____.

OCTOBER 3

Don't Worry

Don't worry about anything; instead, pray about everything. Tell God what you need, and thank him for all he has done. Then you will experience God's peace, which exceeds anything we can understand. His peace will guard your hearts and minds as you live in Christ Jesus. PHILIPPIANS 4:6-7

As PARENTS, we tend to worry about many things. We worry about the safety of our children on the road, at school—really anywhere, anytime. We worry about their physical, emotional, and spiritual health. We worry about their relationships, accomplishments, and competence now and in the future. We also worry about whether we're doing a good job as parents—if we're seeing the real issues or if we're overreacting or underreacting to circumstances in our children's lives. We worry about how much time our kids will have to spend in counseling to get over the way they were parented!

We tend to justify our anxiety by seeing it as an indication of how much we love our children, when actually it is an indication of how little we trust our God.

Fortunately, God doesn't simply instruct us not to worry. We're given an alternative—prayer. Every time we wake up in the middle of the night and catch ourselves beginning to rehearse all of our "what-ifs" and imagine the worst outcomes, we can turn those worries into prayers. We can lay our fears before our heavenly Father, who has us, and our children, in his hands. As we rehearse his goodness, faithfulness, and power in our prayers, we find that anxiety takes a backseat to hope.

This chapter also gives us something else to think about—an alternative to feeding on anxiety-producing thoughts. "Fix your thoughts on what is true, and honorable, and right, and pure, and lovely, and admirable. Think about things that are excellent and worthy of praise" (verse 8). Instead of filling our thoughts with imagined fears, we can fix our thoughts on what is true rather than what might come true, what is pure rather than what might defile, what is admirable rather than what is troubling.

❈ ❈ ❈

God, I really don't want to feed my worries about _____. I want to be faithful to pray for _____. I believe that you are able to give me peace even when everything in _____'s life might not be what I want it to be. I want your peace to guard my heart from fear and my mind from worry as I live in you and turn to you in prayer.

We Have Not Stopped Praying

We have not stopped praying for you since we first heard about you. We ask God to give you complete knowledge of his will and to give you spiritual wisdom and understanding. Then the way you live will always honor and please the Lord, and your lives will produce every kind of good fruit. All the while, you will grow as you learn to know God better and better. COLOSSIANS 1:9-10

PAUL HAD RECEIVED a glowing report on the church in Colosse. He'd never even met the people personally, but he had faithfully prayed for them. The assessment was that they were faithful, they loved each other, and their confident hope was in heaven—not in the things of this earth. So what did this report compel Paul to do? It certainly didn't cause him to curtail his prayers for them. Instead, it prompted him to pray for them even more earnestly.

Oftentimes, we are committed to ongoing prayer when things are not going well for our child. A sense of desperation drives us to our knees. And that's a very good thing! There's no better place to turn, no better way to help than to pray for our children when they are in need. But just as Paul's prayers for the church in Colosse did not cease when there was no crisis, so we should not become complacent in our earnest prayers for our children when things are going well.

Paul's logic drove him to pray even more when he saw that God was at work, asking the Lord to continue and to increase his work in the lives of these believers. Likewise, we should persevere in prayer when we can clearly see God at work in our children's lives. We can ask him to increase their knowledge of what he really wants and to expand their wisdom and understanding of his ways. We can also ask him to help our children keep on living in a way that brings the Lord pleasure and generates all kinds of good fruit.

※ ※ ※

Lord, we pray now and will never stop praying for _____ because _____ will always need what only you can provide. We ask you to give _____ complete knowledge of your will and to give _____ spiritual wisdom and understanding. Give _____ everything needed to live in a way that will always honor and please you. Work in _____ so that _____ will produce every kind of good fruit. Nourish _____ with your Word so that he will grow as he learns to know you better and better.

OCTOBER 5

The Truth You Were Taught

Now, just as you accepted Christ Jesus as your Lord, you must continue to follow him. Let your roots grow down into him, and let your lives be built on him. Then your faith will grow strong in the truth you were taught, and you will overflow with thankfulness. COLOSSIANS 2:6-7

IT TAKES A LONG TIME for the roots of a tree to grow down deep into the soil. Through the years our children are in our homes, we are nourishing the soil of their hearts as we pour into them the truths of the Scripture and our own delight in God. Just as a tree's roots go down into the earth, we want our children's "roots" to go down into Christ. We want them grounded in him so they can bear the weight of the difficulties of life in this world.

We teach them the truth, praying that their faith will go deep and grow strong. We're holding on to the promise that when God's Word goes out, it always produces fruit:

The rain and snow come down from the heavens
  and stay on the ground to water the earth.
They cause the grain to grow,
  producing seed for the farmer
  and bread for the hungry.
It is the same with my word.
  I send it out, and it always produces fruit.
It will accomplish all I want it to,
  and it will prosper everywhere I send it. (Isaiah 55:10-11)

❋ ❋ ❋

Lord, we pray that _____ will not have a shallow faith, but that her roots will go down deep in you. We pray that the soil of _____'s heart will be receptive to your Word as it is preached, read, and discussed in our home. We pray that the day will come when _____ will overflow with thankfulness for the deep roots that grew and the solid foundation that was formed by the truth she was taught growing up.

Each Generation Should Set Its Hope Anew on God

He issued his laws to Jacob;
    he gave his instructions to Israel.
He commanded our ancestors
    to teach them to their children,
so the next generation might know them—
    even the children not yet born—
    and they in turn will teach their own children.
So each generation should set its hope anew on God,
    not forgetting his glorious miracles
    and obeying his commands.
Then they will not be like their ancestors—
    stubborn, rebellious, and unfaithful,
    refusing to give their hearts to God. PSALM 78:5-8

GOD HAS GIVEN HIS WORD to his people, and his intention is that every generation would teach his Word to the next. There is no new revelation for the next generation. The ancient Word from God remains what the next generation and the generation after needs to know.

Parents have a responsibility to teach their children what God has said. The Bible must be the central, all-permeating book in our homes. But it is also clear that our children have the responsibility to set their hope on God in a new and fresh way. Their faith has to become their own. Children must not forget what God has done as revealed in the Scriptures and must determine for themselves that they will pursue a life of obedience to God.

But while we can make ourselves teach, we can't make our children know. While maybe we can convince them to memorize or recite, we can't create in them a receptivity and responsiveness to the truth. There is a distance between our teaching and their knowing, between us having our hope set on God and our children setting their hope on him. What we need is for God to do what only he can do so that our children will give their hearts to him.

❈ ❈ ❈

Lord, we know that our confidence in you, our love for you, and our obedience to you is our own. As we teach your Word to _____, would you cause _____ to truly know who you are and what you've done? Would you cause _____ to believe that obedience to you brings real joy? Would you cause _____ to set his hope anew on you?

Clothe Yourselves

Since God chose you to be the holy people he loves, you must clothe yourselves with tenderhearted mercy, kindness, humility, gentleness, and patience. Make allowance for each other's faults, and forgive anyone who offends you. Remember, the Lord forgave you, so you must forgive others. Above all, clothe yourselves with love, which binds us all together in perfect harmony. And let the peace that comes from Christ rule in your hearts. For as members of one body you are called to live in peace. And always be thankful. COLOSSIANS 3:12-15

THERE'S A BIG DIFFERENCE between the things our kids do that demonstrate a lack of character or integrity, the things that are outright sin, and the things that simply get on our nerves. Over the course of growing up, our kids often annoy, frustrate, or embarrass us. Sometimes we are tempted to turn minor issues into major conflicts. But too many real battles must be fought for the souls of our kids to turn everything that irritates us into a conflict.

The battle we must fight is with our own unmerciful, unkind, impatient inner person. This is a struggle we must fight by faith, through the gospel, in prayer. As recipients of such tenderhearted mercy, kindness, gentleness, and patience from God, we want to extend tenderhearted mercy, kindness, gentleness, and patience in our words and demeanor to our children.

We want our family to be bound together with a sense of harmony and peace that comes from Christ ruling in our hearts. So as parents who have been shown such abundant grace by our heavenly Father, we extend grace to our children. We make allowance for our children's faults and forgive them when they offend us. We resist inflicting a "barrage of nitpicking criticism [or] put-downs because they are curious, anxious, excited, helpless, carefree, or absentminded."

We want our kids to feel securely loved. So as children who have been dearly loved by our heavenly Father, we clothe ourselves in his way of loving.

※ ※ ※

Lord, as we prepare for another day of doing our part as parents to create a home marked by tenderhearted mercy, forbearance, forgiveness, harmony, and peace, remind us of how generous you have been toward us in all of these ways. Help us to recognize what is worthy of confrontation and correction, and what we should lovingly let go.

Do Not Aggravate Your Children

Wives, submit to your husbands, as is fitting for those who belong to the Lord. Husbands, love your wives and never treat them harshly. Children, always obey your parents, for this pleases the Lord. Fathers, do not aggravate your children, or they will become discouraged. COLOSSIANS 3:18-21

NONE OF US set out to aggravate our children. But deep sighs, slammed doors, and disgruntled expressions sometimes reveal that's exactly what we've done. When we rage with angry rants and enforce more control than is necessary, when we belittle our kids or mock them, they might eventually do what we want them to do, but they will feel conquered, not trained; they will become discouraged, not disciplined.

Of course, the reason we sometimes parent this way is that we are sinners parenting other sinners. We have agendas we want our children to cooperate with—like getting out the door on time or getting a job done properly. We enjoy being right, and we want to be respected. But our motives are always mixed because our selfless love for our children is infected with self-centeredness. When our selfish desires meet up with our children's selfish desires, it is a recipe for harsh words and hurt feelings.

Paul says, "Let your conversation be gracious and attractive so that you will have the right response for everyone" (Colossians 4:6). He's encouraging us not only to saturate our interactions with our children with grace, but also to carefully weigh how our words will impact them. We must be slow to anger and slow to speak. We need the grace that we've received to flow through us, and we need wisdom from above to work its way through us so that rather than aggravating and alienating our children, we encourage and affirm them.

※ ※ ※

Lord, I so often point out the behaviors in _____ that don't reflect your grace and love while tolerating those same behaviors in myself. Please work in me the humility to ask for forgiveness when I've been harsh and unkind. Help me to be as concerned about my own need to grow in graciousness as I am concerned about the ways that _____ needs to grow and change.

Jeremiah 12:1–14:10
1 Thessalonians 1:1–2:8
Psalm 79:1-13
Proverbs 24:30-34

OCTOBER 9

Help Us for the Sake of Your Own Reputation

The people say, "Our wickedness has caught up with us, LORD,
but help us for the sake of your own reputation.
We have turned away from you
and sinned against you again and again. . . .
We are known as your people.
Please don't abandon us now!" JEREMIAH 14:7, 9

THEY HAD INHERITED a land flowing with milk and honey. It was a fruitful land that echoed the fertility of the Garden of Eden. But now all of that was in the past. We read in Jeremiah 14 that the wells were dry, the ground was parched, and everyone was confused and desperate from the relentless drought conditions. It seemed that the whole creation was groaning under the weight of Judah's sin and that God had become "like a stranger in the land" (verse 8, ESV).

Jeremiah was pleading with God for his people, knowing full well that they were getting what they deserved. There was nothing in Judah that Jeremiah could point to as deserving of God's mercy. But there were specific things about God that Jeremiah pointed to in his pleas for mercy—the credibility of God's name, the honor of God's throne, the stability of God's covenant. If God did not forgive and restore his people, his name would be brought into disrepute. God could not be God unless he saved his people. God's glory was made known by the exercise of his grace. So Jeremiah pressed in to the God who called these people to be his people and pleaded with him to save his people for the sake of his own reputation.

In this, Jeremiah teaches us how to pray for our children when it seems that everything in their lives has dried up and become desperate. Instead of asking God to do something for their sake, or based on what they deserve, we ask him to do something for his sake, based on who he is. We keep our prayers fixed on the glory of God.

❋ ❋ ❋

Lord, we ask for your help, but not because we have done anything to deserve it. The truth is, we've done nothing that could put you in our debt. We ask for your help because we know that you are a God who loves to save. You are a God who rains down grace on people who don't deserve it. So send the rains of your grace into our lives and into ________'s life. Soak us in your undeserved favor for the glory of your name.

This Word Continues to Work in You

We never stop thanking God that when you received his message from us, you didn't think of our words as mere human ideas. You accepted what we said as the very word of God—which, of course, it is. And this word continues to work in you who believe.
1 Thessalonians 2:13

Paul, Silas, and Timothy had come to Thessalonica and brought the Good News. "It was not only with words but also with power, for the Holy Spirit gave you full assurance that what we said was true," Paul wrote in 1 Thessalonians 1:5. Now, everywhere they went, they kept running into people who told them about the Thessalonians' faith in God. And for that, Paul, Silas, and Timothy just couldn't stop thanking God. They thanked him that when they brought the gospel to Thessalonica, the people there received it. They didn't think of it as just another human idea; instead, they heard it and received it as the very Word of the One True God. And what made Paul so very grateful was that the reports he heard confirmed that the Word of God was continuing to work in those who believed. The Word itself was living and active in them. It was producing joyful endurance even as they were persecuted by the people around them.

Clearly Paul really believed that the Word of God is powerful. When people receive the words of Scripture as the Word of God, when they come under its authority and welcome its cleansing, empowering work, they begin to change.

What does it mean to believe the Word of God is what accomplishes the work of God in the lives of our children? Certainly it means that we do our part to expose our children to the Word of God. But it also means that we trust the Word of God to do its work in them. We trust the Word to convict, convince, and challenge them. It may not happen in our preferred time frame or in our preferred way, but we trust it to work. We let up on our reminding and manipulating and cajoling and instead lean in to praying and trusting and waiting for God to work in our children's lives through his Word.

※ ※ ※

Lord, forgive me for operating in _____'s life as if my words are what he needs most and as if my words have the power to bring the deep growth and change that is needed. It's your Word that is needed most, your Word that has the power to bring real and lasting change.

OCTOBER 11

The Human Heart

The human heart is the most deceitful of all things,
and desperately wicked.
Who really knows how bad it is? JEREMIAH 17:9

OUR CHILDREN HEAR it every time they turn around. It's the well-meaning advice given in every sappy movie and on social media to someone seeking to make a decision—especially about matters of love: "You have to follow your heart." It sounds so good. It suggests that our hearts will lead us to what is best if we just have the courage to listen and act on what they tell us to do.

But this mantra ignores the reality about our hearts that the Bible makes clear: They cannot be trusted. "The human heart is the most deceitful of all things, and desperately wicked." In Matthew 15:19, Jesus tells us exactly what we will hear if we listen to and follow our hearts: "From the heart come evil thoughts, murder, adultery, all sexual immorality, theft, lying, and slander." This means that we should listen to our hearts only to identify what they're telling us about our desires. Then we will be able to examine those desires and take them to Jesus as either requests or confessions.

What we must understand, and what we must help our children understand, is that "our hearts were never meant to be followed, but to be led." So rather than following our hearts, which lead us to do as we please, we must instruct our hearts to do what pleases God.

⌘ ⌘ ⌘

Lord, we pray that _____ would trust in the Lord with all of her heart and would not depend on her own understanding or her own desires. May _____ seek your will in all she does and then follow the path you direct her to take.

Never Stop Praying

Never stop praying. 1 THESSALONIANS 5:17

As PARENTS, we love to fix things. When we see a problem in our child's life, we dig into our tool kit of parenting strategies, good advice, behind-the-scenes intervention, and new sets of rules, seeking to pull out what will do the job. And, of course, there's nothing wrong with any of these tools. It's just that often, our quick reliance on these methods takes the needs of our child into our own hands rather than placing them into God's hands.

Throughout the Scriptures we're encouraged to depend on God through prayer: "Never stop praying" (1 Thessalonians 5:17); "Keep on praying" (Romans 12:12); "Devote yourselves to prayer" (Colossians 4:2); "Pray in the Spirit at all times and on every occasion" (Ephesians 6:18). According to Jesus, we "should always pray and never give up" (Luke 18:1). In other words, our needs, as well as those of our family and the world, should keep us in a constant spirit of dependence expressed through prayer.

Of course, this charge to "never stop praying" speaks to more than simply the ongoing nature of prayer throughout the day. It also challenges us not to give up on prayer. Don't give up praying that your child will truly know God in a genuine way. Don't give up praying that your child will open up God's Word on his or her own. Don't give up praying that God will give your child friends who will be companions in the pursuit of godliness. Don't give up praying that God will give your child the grace for singleness or for marriage. Don't give up praying that God will convict your child of sin and provide power to overcome it. Don't give up praying that God will develop in your child a love for his or her church as well as a passion to reach a lost world with the gospel.

Give up fixing. But never stop praying. Give up worrying. But never stop praying. Give up despairing. But never stop praying.

❋ ❋ ❋

Lord, forgive me for acting as if parenting _____ is all up to me. It just isn't. I am fully dependent on you to give me everything I need to parent _____ wisely and well.

We Keep on Praying for You

We keep on praying for you, asking our God to enable you to live a life worthy of his call. May he give you the power to accomplish all the good things your faith prompts you to do. Then the name of our Lord Jesus will be honored because of the way you live, and you will be honored along with him. This is all made possible because of the grace of our God and Lord, Jesus Christ. 2 THESSALONIANS 1:11-12

PAUL KNEW GOD INTIMATELY, and he understood the will of God that had been revealed to him in the Scriptures. Because of this, when he prayed for the people he loved, he prayed for what he knew God wanted to do and provide. His prayers were never general or generic, never selfish or shortsighted, never for external or temporal matters. As we listen in on Paul praying for those he loved, we discover he has something to teach parents about how to pray for the children we love.

Paul asked God to enable these believers to live in such a way that they would deserve the name they bear—the name of Christ. In other words, he didn't want them to live with hypocrisy, calling themselves Christians while living in a way that was anything but Christlike. He asked God to give them the spiritual power they needed to do the things the Bible instructed them to do—such as exercise their spiritual gifts, endure under persecution, and provide for the needs of the poor among them. As they lived, gave, and loved in these ways, Paul's greatest desire, which had brought him to his knees, was accomplished—that "the name of [the] Lord Jesus will be honored." But that's not all: "And you will be honored along with him." These people he loved would share in the honor that Jesus himself had been given.

※ ※ ※

Lord, forgive us for focusing on temporal matters in our prayers for _____. While we know that you care about every area of our lives, we do not want to neglect praying for the things that are most important to you and the things that will bring _____ lasting joy and honor into eternity. So we ask you to enable _____ to live a life worthy of your call. We ask you to give _____ the power to accomplish all the good things faith prompts him to do. Then the name of the Lord Jesus will be honored because of the way _____ lives, and _____ will be honored along with him. This is all made possible because of your grace.

Take from My Hand This Cup

This is what the LORD, the God of Israel, said to me: "Take from my hand this cup filled to the brim with my anger, and make all the nations to whom I send you drink from it. When they drink from it, they will stagger, crazed by the warfare I will send against them." JEREMIAH 25:15-16

THE LORD GAVE his prophet Jeremiah a vision in which he handed Jeremiah a cup filled to the brim with his anger. Jeremiah took the cup first to Jerusalem—God's own city—and then to all of the kingdoms of the world and made them drink from it. It is a picture of terrifying judgment against every kingdom that opposes God's Kingdom and does evil. Yet it is also a picture of judgment that has been prepared for every sinner who rejects God and his Son, Jesus Christ.

When this cup, filled with God's white-hot, punishing anger against everything evil, was set before Jesus, he prayed, "My Father! If it is possible, let this cup of suffering be taken away from me. Yet I want your will to be done, not mine" (Matthew 26:39). Jesus agonized as he anticipated the anguish of drinking the cup of judgment and experiencing the resulting break in relationship with his Father. But he did drink it—every last drop.

We all deserve to drink from this bitter cup. But the good news of the gospel is that God's own Son consumed this cup of judgment so that all who put their faith in him do not have to drink it. Because he drank the cup of God's wrath, we and our children have been handed another cup—one filled not with judgment but with salvation. "I will lift up the cup of salvation and praise the LORD's name for saving me" (Psalm 116:13).

※ ※ ※

Lord, we deserve to drink from the bitter cup of your wrath, but Christ has emptied it in our stead. Now you hold out to us the cup of salvation. May _____ take this cup and drink deeply from it with great gratitude.

OCTOBER 15

Righteousness and Peace Have Kissed!

Unfailing love and truth have met together.
Righteousness and peace have kissed! PSALM 85:10

IN THE GARDEN OF EDEN, peace walked hand in hand with righteousness. But the day came when peace and righteousness were divorced. Sin created alienation between them so that peace and righteousness were separated. Peace could not come back unless righteousness had been satisfied, and righteousness could not be satisfied unless payment for sin was made. Then, on the cross of Calvary, the Righteous One was crucified. Righteousness took sin upon himself so that peace could come home. Righteousness and peace kissed.

At the Cross, God's unbending demand for truth came face-to-face with his mercy; his unchanging demand for perfect righteousness came together with peace made possible by Christ's atoning sacrifice. "We have peace with God because of what Jesus Christ our Lord has done for us" (Romans 5:1). This peace is permanent because God doesn't simply ignore our sins and faults; instead, Christ dealt with them fully and forever. The truth about our sin has met up with the abounding mercy of God in Christ.

Of all the loving kisses that our children have enjoyed so far and will enjoy in their future, surely it is this divine kiss that will bring them the most lasting joy. This is the kiss that makes it possible for them to face the truth about themselves with confidence that they will still be loved by God. This is the kiss that brings peace when the enemy continually reminds them of the many ways they have fallen so far short of God's standard of righteousness.

❇ ❇ ❇

Oh, Lord, we're so grateful for this divine kiss! We relish the freedom to be honest before you about our failures, knowing we will be met with mercy. We rest in the peace made possible by the righteousness of Christ we've received. May _____ see the beauty and enjoy the love and acceptance made possible by this divine kiss.

His Great Patience

I thank Christ Jesus our Lord, who has given me strength to do his work. He considered me trustworthy and appointed me to serve him, even though I used to blaspheme the name of Christ. In my insolence, I persecuted his people. But God had mercy on me because I did it in ignorance and unbelief. Oh, how generous and gracious our Lord was! He filled me with the faith and love that come from Christ Jesus. 1 TIMOTHY 1:12-14

PAUL GREW UP AT THE FEET OF GAMALIEL, the best teacher of the Old Testament Scriptures in his day. We read in Acts that Paul said, "As his student, I was carefully trained in our Jewish laws and customs. I became very zealous to honor God in everything I did, just like all of you today. And I persecuted the followers of the Way, hounding some to death, arresting both men and women and throwing them in prison" (Acts 22:3-4).

So here was Paul, raised in an intensely religious home with the finest education in the Scriptures possible from the finest teacher. And instead of seeing and believing in Christ, he became the most rabid persecutor of those who embraced Christ. Because he was exposed to so much light in the Scriptures and raged against it, he described himself as the worst of sinners. If we had known him in the height of his violence against all who followed Christ, we would never have believed that he would follow the Lord himself. And we certainly would not have believed that he would serve Christ and lead his people in the way he did.

Paul's story demonstrates that even someone who grows up in a Scripture-saturated home only to turn violently against Christ is not beyond the patience of God. Paul wrote, "God had mercy on me so that Christ Jesus could use me as a prime example of his great patience with even the worst sinners. Then others will realize that they, too, can believe in him and receive eternal life" (1 Timothy 1:16).

❊ ❊ ❊

Lord, I confess that I am often impatient to see change in _____'s life even though you are so very patient with me! You often seem to take your time to draw your own to yourself. You sometimes allow those who belong to you to rage against you before they finally bow before you. Help me to trust your timing as you patiently pursue _____ to become all that you intend for _____ to be.

OCTOBER 17

Your Children Will Come Back to You

This is what the LORD says:
"Do not weep any longer,
*   for I will reward you," says the LORD.*
"Your children will come back to you
*   from the distant land of the enemy.*
There is hope for your future," says the LORD.
*   "Your children will come again to their own land.*
I have heard Israel saying,
'You disciplined me severely,
*   like a calf that needs training for the yoke.*
Turn me again to you and restore me,
*   for you alone are the LORD my God.'"* JEREMIAH 31:16-18

IN JEREMIAH we get to look into a tender scene in which a father welcomes home his wayward child after years of separation. It's like an Old Testament Prodigal Son story. Through his prophet, the Lord reveals the turning that will take place in his rebellious child. We hear the son, Israel, express appreciation for his Father's discipline, sorrow over the way he turned away from his Father, shame over what he did in his younger days, and a desire for restoration (verses 18-19).

And then we hear the Father speak to the son. But it's not what we might expect from the spurned Father. No "I told you so" or "What took you so long?" Instead God speaks to Israel as his "darling child" (verse 20), expressing his longing to show mercy, his welcome home, his assurance of grace. The Father promises that he "will cause something new to happen—Israel will embrace her God" (verse 22).

How beautiful is the Father heart of God toward his rebellious children: "I often have to punish him, but I still love him. That's why I long for him and surely will have mercy on him" (verse 20).

❀ ❀ ❀

Father God, when our children disobey us, how we long for our hearts toward them to be as loving and merciful as your heart is toward your children when they disobey you. You discipline, but you still love. You long to show mercy. Fill us with the wisdom and will to discipline but also the heart to love and the words to woo.

Instructions on the Heart

"This is the new covenant I will make with the people of Israel after those days," says the LORD. "I will put my instructions deep within them, and I will write them on their hearts. I will be their God, and they will be my people." JEREMIAH 31:33

GOD HAD MADE A COVENANT with his people at Mount Sinai when he gave them the Ten Commandments and the rest of the law, which is called the old covenant. The people of Israel who were there that day pledged to obey it. Throughout the years, future generations recommitted to keeping it. But they didn't. They couldn't. Much later, in this prophecy given to Jeremiah, God promised that the day would come when he would make a new covenant with his people that would be different from the one he made at Mount Sinai with their forefathers.

Sin would be dealt with differently in the new covenant. No longer would God's people be required to trek to the Temple with their ram or goat or bird to offer a sacrifice for sin. In a single, once-for-all sacrifice, all the sins of their past, present, and future would be fully and finally dealt with. People would relate to God in a different way. Under the old covenant, priests entered into the presence of God in the Temple, but ordinary people could never come near. But under the new covenant, Jesus would invite them to draw near based on his perfect record of holiness. God would give his people a new power to understand and obey him.

As hard as we might want to change, and as much as we might want our children to change, we can't accomplish the kind of transformation that is needed on our own. God must do this work in us. When he performs this miracle in our hearts, we find that we want to know him in a way we just weren't interested in before. We find the Bible to be curiously inviting rather than boring. We feel drawn to Christ instead of trying to keep him at a safe distance. We find ourselves grateful for conviction rather than resistant to it.

✳ ✳ ✳

Lord, I find I am powerless to change the fundamental disposition of my own soul. I am in need of nothing less than a miracle. I need for you to create a new heart within me so that I will no longer walk in the same deep grooves engraved on my heart by years of habitual sin.

Training for Godliness

"Physical training is good, but training for godliness is much better, promising benefits in this life and in the life to come." This is a trustworthy saying, and everyone should accept it. This is why we work hard and continue to struggle, for our hope is in the living God, who is the Savior of all people and particularly of all believers. 1 TIMOTHY 4:8-10

FROM THEIR EARLIEST DAYS, it is impressed on our kids that if they want to be physically fit, if they want to be able to hit a ball harder, kick a ball longer, or run a race faster, then they have to work at it and train for it. Evidently that was understood even in the days when Paul wrote this letter to Timothy. But Paul was encouraging believers to train for something that had benefits far beyond a healthier body or a winner's trophy in the here and now. He wanted believers to train for something that would have benefits into eternity. While physical training has some short-term, limited benefit, training in godliness matters now and forever.

So while we encourage our kids to stay physically fit, we want much more for them. We want to encourage them in their training for godliness so that their spiritual muscles will grow rather than become flabby as they age. We encourage them to pump iron as they persist in understanding who God is and conforming their lives to his character, refusing to stop the effort when they feel the burn. As they train for godliness, an inner strength will grow so that they will not be so easily taken in by the latest spiritual fad and not so easily shaken when the winds of difficulty blow in their lives. They will become more likely to embrace God's promise and preach the truth to themselves rather than listen to themselves.

❋ ❋ ❋

Lord, I pray for _____ to be rigorous in training for godliness. As _____ works hard and continues to struggle at times, I pray that _____ would see fruit from the effort—that she is becoming more patient than she used to be, more self-sacrificial, more receptive to conviction, quicker to forsake a bad attitude, less likely to be easily offended, and less interested in passing along the story that will hurt someone else's reputation. Plant _____'s hopes firmly in the living God who will prove true on his promises of the life to come.

No Warmth for God's Word

The king sent Jehudi to get the scroll. Jehudi brought it from Elishama's room and read it to the king as all his officials stood by. It was late autumn, and the king was in a winterized part of the palace, sitting in front of a fire to keep warm. Each time Jehudi finished reading three or four columns, the king took a knife and cut off that section of the scroll. He then threw it into the fire, section by section, until the whole scroll was burned up. Neither the king nor his attendants showed any signs of fear or repentance at what they heard. JEREMIAH 36:21-24*

WHEN THE WORD of the Lord came to Jeremiah, he was told to "get a scroll, and write down all my messages against Israel, Judah, and the other nations" (verse 2). It was God's desire that "perhaps the people of Judah will repent when they hear again all the terrible things I have planned for them. Then I will be able to forgive their sins and wrongdoings" (verse 3).

A year later his scribe, Baruch, took the scrolls and read them at the Temple. While most people were too busy to listen and respond, one man, Micaiah, hung on every word of Jeremiah's prophecy and believed it. But when the scroll was read to the king, he had a very different response. He took a knife and cut off each section as it was read and threw it into the fire until the whole thing was burned. We can almost hear him and his officials laughing as they cut apart God's Word and threw it in the fire. In the coldness of the room, there was no warmth for God's Word—no sadness over sin, no reverent fear, no ears to hear, no heart to obey.

While this scene of rejection of God's Word is far removed from us in years, it is not far from us in reality. Whenever and wherever God's promise of judgment for sin and his promise of mercy for sinners who repent are rejected, this scene, in its essence, is repeated. But may it never be repeated among us. May we always warmly receive the whole of God's Word in our hearts and in our homes.

❀ ❀ ❀

Lord, we don't want to stand over your Word in judgment, picking and choosing what we will read, what we will receive, what we will obey, and what we will reject. We want our home to be a place where your Word is welcomed and received warmly.

Great Wealth

True godliness with contentment is itself great wealth. After all, we brought nothing with us when we came into the world, and we can't take anything with us when we leave it. So if we have enough food and clothing, let us be content. 1 TIMOTHY 6:6-8

PAUL COMMENDED TO TIMOTHY a very different kind of wealth than most of this world knows—a life ordered around enjoying God and what he gives instead of a life spent in pursuit of more money. He wanted Timothy, and us, to know that the godliness that overcomes the craving for material wealth produces great spiritual wealth.

Paul made his case for true godliness with contentment in light of what he had observed—"some people, craving money, have wandered from the true faith and pierced themselves with many sorrows" (verse 10). In other words, he had watched some people set their hearts on money, only to see it break their hearts in the end. They were blind to the reality that they could not keep what they collected since none of us leave this life with any possessions. Their money made them vulnerable to powerful temptations and filled them with harmful desires that ultimately led them into ruin. Most significantly, their craving for money and their justification for pursuing it led them away from the true faith.

As we parent our children in a world that pours on the pressure to succeed and glorifies getting more and better stuff, there is really only one way to impress upon them the genuine joy of being content with enough food to eat and clothing to wear. We, as parents, must be growing in godliness in such a way that we are increasingly content with enough food to eat and clothing to wear. We don't always have to have the best food available or the latest style of clothing. We can be content with "enough" and therefore enjoy our great wealth into eternity.

❆ ❆ ❆

Giver of all good things, would you create in _____ a longing to be godly and content with all that you provide? Will you cause _____ to crave all of the spiritual blessings in Christ instead of craving more and more money? Please save _____ from the sorrows that the love of money brings.

No Fear

God has not given us a spirit of fear and timidity, but of power, love, and self-discipline. 2 TIMOTHY 1:7

DURING THE YEARS spent raising a child, we can find plenty of things to be afraid of: germ-ridden shopping carts, raunchy cartoons, trampolines, sleepovers, the Internet, the public school system, alcohol and drugs, the influence of questionable friends, outdoor adventures . . . and then there's college. But our fears aren't limited to what might happen to or in our child. We fear losing the respect or control of our children along the way. We fear that the weaknesses in our parenting may impact our kids in ways that will be difficult for them to overcome.

What are we to do with all of these very real fears? The reality is that we live in a broken world where really bad things do happen. Sin has broken this world and distorted it, leaving much that is beyond our control. We can't avoid fearful feelings. But can we avoid giving in to fear, being filled with fear, and being controlled by fear?

When we find ourselves gazing into the future and beginning to fill with anxiety, we must turn our gaze to Christ. Then we must take hold of his love and mercy, his sovereignty and sufficiency. Instead of giving in to fear, we must ask God for the faith to trust him to provide the needed grace for whatever we're facing in the present and whatever may come in the future.

※ ※ ※

Lord, when we sense that fear is doing its best to squeeze out faith, help us to see that our fear is not from you. As your Spirit works in our lives and in our family, we have the spiritual power we need to put our trust in you rather than give ourselves over to fear. We can love without manipulation and control. We can discipline ourselves to parent _____ out of a confident hope in your sovereign and saving grace—for _____ and for us.

OCTOBER 23

Soldier, Athlete, Farmer

Endure suffering along with me, as a good soldier of Christ Jesus. Soldiers don't get tied up in the affairs of civilian life, for then they cannot please the officer who enlisted them. And athletes cannot win the prize unless they follow the rules. And hardworking farmers should be the first to enjoy the fruit of their labor. 2 TIMOTHY 2:3-6

MANY KIDS WHO GROW UP in the church today view Christianity as a way to add to or enhance their lives, rather than as a death to the lives they are living and a rebirth to new lives in Christ. There is no way young Timothy could have labored under that misunderstanding. In a letter written from prison, Paul did not warn Timothy about the cost of serving Christ and give him strategies for avoiding the imprisonment he was experiencing. Instead, he invited Timothy to endure suffering for the gospel along with him. He used three images that Timothy would be familiar with to help his protégé see what serving Christ should look like—images of a soldier, an athlete, and a farmer.

Soldiers don't expect a safe or easy life, but instead accept hardship, risk, and suffering as part of the job. Soldiers have to focus on their duties and be wholly at their commanding officer's disposal. So should Timothy and all who intend to serve Christ. Athletes in Greek games had to follow the rules of the sport to have any expectation of being awarded the prize. Likewise, we cannot flout God's laws and expect that we will one day be awarded a crown. A farmer's life is not filled with excitement, prestige, or recognition. But neither is it devoid of joy. Paul promises that the Christian who toils for the cause of Christ can anticipate the outrageous joy of fruitfulness in his own life, as well as being a part of planting and seeing gospel fruit grow in the lives of others.

We are swimming against the tide as we seek to implant this understanding of life in Christ in our kids. But just as Paul used the examples of the soldier, the athlete, and the farmer as teaching tools to instruct Timothy, so we can use them to teach our kids.

❋ ❋ ❋

Lord, would you develop in _____ the obedience of a good soldier, the discipline of a good athlete, and the willingness to work of a good farmer? And would you give us the joy of celebrating with _____ the victory of his battles as a soldier for Christ, the prize of his finishing the race, and the harvest of his toil in your fields?

All Scripture Is Useful

Continue in what you have learned and have firmly believed, knowing from whom you learned it and how from childhood you have been acquainted with the sacred writings, which are able to make you wise for salvation through faith in Christ Jesus. All Scripture is breathed out by God and profitable for teaching, for reproof, for correction, and for training in righteousness, that the man of God may be complete, equipped for every good work. 2 TIMOTHY 3:14-17, ESV

ALL SCRIPTURE IS breathed out by God. Consider that God breathed out, "Let there be light," and there was light. That's pretty powerful. The psalmist wrote, "By the word of the LORD the heavens were made, and by the breath of his mouth all their host" (Psalm 33:6, ESV). He spoke and it was. So the Word of God is powerful. But how does that power work? What can we expect will happen in our children as we teach them the Scriptures?

According to Paul's letter to Timothy, Scripture will make our kids wise—specifically, wise for salvation through faith in Christ Jesus. They will see the wisdom in placing all of their hopes in Christ. And isn't that our greatest desire for our kids?

Scripture will change what our kids believe. It doesn't just make suggestions; it is much stronger than that. Scripture will teach them what they ought to believe and challenge or put right their wrong beliefs.

When Scripture is read, taught, heard, and received, it will correct our kids' aberrant behavior. The Holy Spirit will use the Word of God to show them the places where they have veered astray. Then, by faith, they will be given the power and the desire to correct their course so that they please God.

Scripture will provide what our kids need. It will equip them to be content when they don't have everything they need by reminding them that they can do all things through Christ who strengthens them. It will prepare them for suffering by reminding them that they are sharing in the sufferings of Christ. The Bible will enable them to relate well to others by calling them to count others more significant than themselves.

※ ※ ※

Lord, there is something _____ needs more than all of my good advice and instruction. _____ needs your Word! Please use the Word you breathed out to make _____ wise for salvation, to shape what _____ believes, to change how _____ behaves, and to provide what _____ needs.

OCTOBER 25

Keep the Faith

As for me, my life has already been poured out as an offering to God. The time of my death is near. I have fought the good fight, I have finished the race, and I have remained faithful. And now the prize awaits me—the crown of righteousness, which the Lord, the righteous Judge, will give me on the day of his return. And the prize is not just for me but for all who eagerly look forward to his appearing. 2 TIMOTHY 4:6-8

IN THE THROES OF PARENTING, it can be hard to imagine a day when our task will be complete and we will be preparing to leave this life for the next. But certainly that day is coming. For some parents, deathbed farewells to children are filled with regrets and fears. But for others, those farewells are full of love and peace.

In the closing words of Paul's letter to his son in the faith, Timothy, we find a farewell that we might hope to emulate, an accomplishment we might hope to be able to claim as our own when our lives draw to a close. There was no fear in death for Paul. He had been pouring out his life as an offering, as a living sacrifice, for thirty years. Paul seemed to be at peace because he didn't see his death as the end. "I long to go and be with Christ, which would be far better for me," he had written long before to the Philippians (1:23). Now his longing was about to be fulfilled.

Paul had kept fighting. He didn't give up when things got hard. He kept the faith. He kept on taking Christ at his word, kept on relying on his finished work, and kept on guarding the gospel.

When your life is over, will your children be able to say that rather than giving in to the pressure of the world, you fought the good fight of faith; that rather than surrendering to some besetting sin, you finished the race of faith? Will they say that you remained faithful over the course of many years—through successes and failures, through good times and bad?

※ ※ ※

Lord, how I long for the day when I can look _____ in the face and praise you for the perseverance you worked in me over the long haul of life. Set my heart even now on the day when I will receive the prize standing side by side with _____ because we have eagerly looked forward to your appearing.

The Lord Is King!

The LORD is king!
   Let the earth rejoice!
   Let the farthest coastlands be glad. PSALM 97:1

IF WE LOOK for one central message in the vast book of Psalms, it would have to be that the Lord is King and is reigning on his throne over all things. When we come to Psalms 93–99, the psalmist seems to want to press the point repeatedly:

The LORD is king! He is robed in majesty. (Psalm 93:1)

The LORD is a great God, a great King above all gods. (Psalm 95:3)

Tell all the nations, "The LORD reigns!" (Psalm 96:10)

The LORD is king! Let the nations tremble!
   He sits on his throne between the cherubim. Let the whole earth quake! (Psalm 99:1)

What good news it is for parents that the Lord reigns! He reigns over your family squabble and your child's struggle. He reigns over your health crisis and your financial predicament. He reigns over the longing you have for what has never happened and the frustration you feel over the unwanted things that have happened. God is still King, and he reigns over the world and over your family.

While the good news is that the Lord reigns, the question for us is: Are we willing to submit to his authority, to let his Word hold sway in our lives? The Lord who reigns is a good King. We can entrust our lives to him. He did not come to be served; he came to serve others and give his life as a ransom for many. He does not want to wear us down; he wants to lift us up. He has no intention of taking advantage of us; he wants to give us all the advantages of belonging to him. His approval does not depend on the work we do; he has done all the work necessary to bring us into his Kingdom, his home.

※ ※ ※

King of kings, your rule over this world, over our lives, and over our home is cause for great gladness! It is our source of security. We find our identity in being your grateful subjects. Come and rule in our home and in our hearts.

OCTOBER 27

Putting the Beauty of the Gospel on Display

As for you, Titus, promote the kind of living that reflects wholesome teaching. Teach the older men to exercise self-control, to be worthy of respect, and to live wisely. They must have sound faith and be filled with love and patience. Similarly, teach the older women to live in a way that honors God. They must not slander others or be heavy drinkers. Instead, they should teach others what is good. TITUS 2:1-3

PAUL WAS LEAVING Titus behind on the island of Crete with a charge to bring order to the new churches that had been established. And this was no easy place for ministry. The people of Crete were known to be "liars, cruel animals, and lazy gluttons" (1:12). But now the Spirit was at work in those who had put their faith in Christ, and their lives were to display the beauty of Christ to the unbelieving world around them. This meant that men and women of every age and station in the church were to live self-controlled lives of simplicity, integrity, submission, soberness, wisdom, and faith. In this way they would stand out from the crowd and make the gospel attractive to all who observed their transformed lives.

What Paul instructed Timothy to teach to the generations of believers on the island of Crete, we must learn as well. Each instruction leads to self-examination. For dads: Do I exercise self-control or self-indulgence? Do I interact with my family and the world around me in a way that is worthy of the respect I so want from my wife and kids? Am I filled with love and patience, or do I have a very short fuse around the house? For moms: Am I careful to honor God with my life and to honor other people in my conversations? Am I sober-minded or a slave to too much wine? Am I continuing to learn so that I'm prepared to teach and train others? Am I appropriately submissive or stubbornly assertive?

※ ※ ※

Lord, we never want to bring shame on the Word of God by our lack of self-control, our foolish actions, our enslavement to alcohol, or our lack of love for each other. Help us to be open to radical change so that we might put the hope of the gospel on display to the world around us.

Always Ready to Do What Is Good

Remind the believers to submit to the government and its officers. They should be obedient, always ready to do what is good. They must not slander anyone and must avoid quarreling. Instead, they should be gentle and show true humility to everyone.
TITUS 3:1-2

THROUGHOUT PAUL'S LETTER preparing Titus to lead the churches in Crete, his aim has been that Titus would "teach them to know the truth that shows them how to live godly lives" (1:1). The grace that has come to those living on the island of Crete should produce godliness. For the Cretans and for us, that means, "We are instructed to turn from godless living and sinful pleasures. We should live in this evil world with wisdom, righteousness, and devotion to God" (2:12).

Paul tells Titus to be clear with the Cretan Christians about what God requires of his people. In the same way, we want to be clear with our children about what it means for us to live in a way that is consistent with what we say we believe. We want to boldly call our children who are in Christ to live godly lives.

Heading the list of traits of godly living is submission to governmental authority. This subjection is further defined by Paul's instructions to remind the believers on Crete to "not slander anyone" and "avoid quarreling. Instead, they should be gentle and show true humility to everyone." And lest we think this would have somehow been easier in Titus's day, before cable news and our current contentious political climate, we have to remember that "these were the times of Caesars, occupational armies, and coliseums."

As we seek to determine what godliness should look like in our own homes, we realize that the laws we obey and the language we use to discuss governmental issues and officials on social media and in our conversations—at church, at work, and around the dinner table—will be impacted if we want to obey Paul's instruction to "submit to the government and its officers." It means that we won't misrepresent any person's record or motives. We will avoid a quarreling, harsh, and arrogant demeanor, and we will show true humility to everyone.

※ ※ ※

Lord, we want and need your grace at work in our lives to make us willing to submit to authority and to create in us a commitment to integrity in what we say about other people. Help us as parents to lead the way in treating people with gentleness and humility.

A Life of Integrity

I will sing of your love and justice, LORD.
I will praise you with songs.
I will be careful to live a blameless life—
when will you come to help me?
I will lead a life of integrity
in my own home.
I will refuse to look at
anything vile and vulgar.
I hate all who deal crookedly;
I will have nothing to do with them.
I will reject perverse ideas
and stay away from every evil.
I will not tolerate people who slander their neighbors.
I will not endure conceit and pride. PSALM 101:1-5

IN THIS SONG, King David stated his resolve to rule over God's people with integrity. Of course, David—and the many kings who followed him—fell far short of this ideal . . . except for the true Son of David, Jesus. He was the only King who ever sang this psalm and lived it perfectly.

Psalm 101 sets forth the kind of life of integrity that befits not only a king but also all who live under his rule. Like David, we need the determination to allow the grace of God to work its way through every area of our lives.

❇ ❇ ❇

Lord, please give _____ a heart filled with praise for you so that he will sing of your love and justice. Be quick to help _____ as he seeks to live a blameless life—one in which no charges can stick because he is quick to confess and repent. Instill in _____ a commitment to lead a life of integrity in his own home. Make _____ the same person in private that he is in public, so that he has nothing to hide, no secret, shameful life. Give _____ a resolve to refuse to look at the vile and vulgar images that are so readily available. Surround him with friends and associates who are committed to integrity in their businesses and relationships. Give _____ an aversion to evil and perversity. Develop in _____ a love for honesty and genuine humility.

Lamentations 3:1-66
Hebrews 1:1-14
Psalm 102:1-28
Proverbs 26:21-22

OCTOBER 30

Dare to Hope

I will never forget this awful time,
as I grieve over my loss.
Yet I still dare to hope
when I remember this:
The faithful love of the LORD *never ends!*
His mercies never cease.
Great is his faithfulness;
his mercies begin afresh each morning.
I say to myself, "The LORD *is my inheritance;*
therefore, I will hope in him!" LAMENTATIONS 3:20-24

IT IS WONDERFUL that the Bible includes Lamentations—this book of divinely inspired lament over unbearable suffering and lost hope. It assures us that God does not expect a stoic response from his people, as if the hurts inflicted on us have no effect, as if somehow we are immune from feeling loss deeply and desperately. But the beauty of Lamentations is that it is not simply a venting of despair. By crying out to God, the writer of Lamentations seeks to gain perspective on his suffering. And clearly that's what happens.

It seems the mere mention of the divine name (verse 22) gets him thinking about the perfections of God—his faithful love that never ends, his mercies that never cease. So instead of continuing to listen to his despairing thoughts, he begins to talk back to himself. It's as if he says, *Self, everything you need, you have forever, so turn away from your despair and take hold of hope in God!*

It's good to know that our heavenly Father does not shush the laments of his children. Neither should we discount the laments over the very real losses our kids experience. Instead, we can encourage them to turn toward God with their sorrows rather than turn away from him.

❋ ❋ ❋

Lord, when the sorrow of this life overwhelms ________, may ________ turn to you to pour out lament and gain perspective rather than turning away from you and becoming bitter. Fill ________ with the hope that only comes from the promise of your faithful love—your abundant mercy now and the inheritance that is to come.

OCTOBER 31

He Is Able to Help Us

Therefore, it was necessary for him to be made in every respect like us, his brothers and sisters, so that he could be our merciful and faithful High Priest before God. Then he could offer a sacrifice that would take away the sins of the people. Since he himself has gone through suffering and testing, he is able to help us when we are being tested.
HEBREWS 2:17-18

WHEN OUR CHILDREN ARE BORN, they are completely dependent on us. As they grow, they learn to do some things for themselves and become less dependent. But the goal of parenting is not merely to raise children who no longer need their parents or who are completely self-reliant. The goal of parenting is to raise children who know where to turn and are willing to go to the right place for help. Here in Hebrews, we discover the resource our children need when they are facing temptation. It's not their parents they need as much as their Brother, Jesus.

"Now Jesus and the ones he makes holy have the same Father. That is why Jesus is not ashamed to call them his brothers and sisters" (verse 11). For Jesus to call us his brothers and sisters is an affirmation of intimacy, shared experience, and loyalty. He was made like us in every way—including becoming vulnerable to temptation.

We tend to think it must have been easier for Jesus to resist the temptations Satan threw at him than it is for us to resist the temptations Satan throws at us. But Jesus didn't exploit his inherent deity to overcome temptation. He faced it in his full humanity, using only the weapons we have at our disposal: the Word of God, the Holy Spirit, and trust in his heavenly Father. When our children go to their brother, Jesus, in the midst of temptation, he points them toward these same resources. Jesus helps them battle temptation in a way that only he can.

❊ ❊ ❊

Lord, when _____ feels tempted to do what is easy rather than what is right, remind her that Jesus knows how she feels. He was tempted that way too. When _____ feels overwhelmed with demands on her time and energy, remind her that Jesus knows how she feels. When _____ feels crushed by the sorrows of this broken world, remind her that Jesus knows how she feels.

Rebellious Children

"Son of man," he said, "I am sending you to the nation of Israel, a rebellious nation that has rebelled against me. They and their ancestors have been rebelling against me to this very day." EZEKIEL 2:3

"THE CHILDREN I RAISED and cared for have rebelled against me" (Isaiah 1:2). Who said that? God did. Perhaps you are looking at the way your child is living, and you think you must be a bad parent. You think you have failed. Hear this: Nobody could have been a better parent than God, and yet his children rebelled. His children did outrageously foolish, self-destructive, wicked things. If your heart is breaking over your child's rebellion, your Father knows exactly what that feels like.

God's first son, Adam, heard God's command not to eat of the tree of the knowledge of good and evil in the Garden. But he rebelled against God and ate. God's second son, the nation of Israel, heard God's Word given to Moses at Sinai. He heard that he was to have no other gods but God, that he was not to bow down to idols or misuse God's name, that he was to keep the Sabbath holy, that he was not to murder or commit adultery or lie or covet. But this son also rebelled and refused to obey God's law.

What the children of Israel needed was not a more perfect parent. They already had that. What they needed was a brother to be born into the dysfunctional human family, one who would not rebel. This brother would take all of the ugly rebellion of his brothers and sisters upon himself, so it would be nailed to the cross.

※ ※ ※

Lord, it helps me to remember that you understand the heartbreak of having a rebellious child. In this very moment, I find a deeper fellowship with you through this shared experience. I know that there is something _____ needs even more than a perfect parent. My only hope as a rebel child—and _____'s only hope as a rebel child—is to be joined by faith to the only child of yours who did not rebel. We need the perfect obedience of Jesus to be transferred to our account. And we need more than that; we need his glad obedience to you to become a growing reality in our lives. Father, do the transforming work only you can do to change us from rebellious children into obedient sons and daughters.

NOVEMBER 2

The Word of God Is Powerful

*The word of God is alive and powerful. It is sharper than the sharpest two-edged
sword, cutting between soul and spirit, between joint and marrow. It exposes
our innermost thoughts and desires. Nothing in all creation is hidden from God.
Everything is naked and exposed before his eyes, and he is the one to whom we are
accountable.* Hebrews 4:12-13

THERE IS A LIMIT to the power of our words in our children's lives. There's a limit to our
ability to see into our children and know what is really going on inside them. And there
is even a limit to their accountability to us. The Word of God has the real power in their
lives. His Word has the ability to penetrate their thoughts and motives. It prepares them
for their ultimate accountability before him.

Often the challenge for us as parents is to trust that God's Word really will accomplish his work in our children. Yet when we trust his Word to work, we can stop trying
so hard to convince or coerce them. We don't have to feel as if we've failed when we
don't see the responsiveness we prayed for. We can expect that God's Word is working
in ways and places that we can't see.

When the Word of God goes to work in our children's lives, it will expose shallow
beliefs and faulty expectations that have become a part of their thinking. It will challenge their assumptions about how this life with God works. Idols will come out from
behind the shadows where they can no longer be coddled and protected. The Word of
God will help them see the ways in which they want to use God instead of love God. It
will break through surface religiosity and even accumulated Bible knowledge to reveal
the state of their souls and the incongruity of their behavior.

It is not up to us to create change in our children; it is up to us to bring them under
God's Word and then trust him to do the convincing and changing. And we know he
will, because his Word is active.

❋ ❋ ❋

*Lord, work in _____ to place her life under the influence and authority of your
Word. Lead _____ to make herself accountable to its expectations, to submit herself
to its demands, to accept its truth. Humble _____ so that she might allow the Word
of God to judge her thoughts and motives. Use your Word to shape her perspective, set
her priorities, and show her what is truly valuable and beautiful.*

He Learned Obedience from the Things He Suffered

While Jesus was here on earth, he offered prayers and pleadings, with a loud cry and tears, to the one who could rescue him from death. And God heard his prayers because of his deep reverence for God. Even though Jesus was God's Son, he learned obedience from the things he suffered. In this way, God qualified him as a perfect High Priest, and he became the source of eternal salvation for all those who obey him. HEBREWS 5:7-9

DO YOU KNOW WHAT it is to offer up prayers and petitions with loud cries and tears? So does Jesus. Do you know what it is to ask God for the strength to submit to his plan when it brings you pain? So does Jesus. This is why he is able to deal compassionately with us when we are in the heat of the battle over obedience. Jesus is gentle with us because he has cried out to God like we have.

But what does this passage mean when it says that Jesus "learned obedience" from what he suffered? Was he in some way disobedient before? No. This means that his obedience was tested and proven. His was not automatic obedience. It was authentic obedience. His obedience was prayed for, begged for, cried out for, and wept over with tears. Jesus learned through his own experience what it feels like when following God comes with a cost.

So also God the Father experienced the pain of watching his Son suffer. No father has loved his son as perfectly as our heavenly Father loved Jesus, yet his love made room for his Son's agony. If the Father had not allowed the Son to suffer, the glorious good of becoming "the source of eternal salvation for all those who obey him" would not have been accomplished.

❊ ❊ ❊

Heavenly Father, your own Son, Jesus, learned obedience from what he suffered, so I ask that _____ would learn and live out obedience in the midst of the suffering in this life. Keep me from always sweeping in to save _____ from suffering so that you might accomplish the good that you intend in and through it.

NOVEMBER 4

Impossible

It is impossible to bring back to repentance those who were once enlightened—those who have experienced the good things of heaven and shared in the Holy Spirit, who have tasted the goodness of the word of God and the power of the age to come— and who then turn away from God. It is impossible to bring such people back to repentance; by rejecting the Son of God, they themselves are nailing him to the cross once again and holding him up to public shame. HEBREWS 6:4-6

THIS PASSAGE can be very disconcerting—especially for parents whose children seemed at one point to love the things of Christ but now appear to be walking away from faith. If we're not careful, we can read into these verses that a person with real faith can lose it and then be barred from restoration. But that is not what these verses are saying. Those who are genuinely joined to Christ can never be separated from him. Those who have been adopted by him can never be disowned by him. Those who have been made alive in Christ can never lose that life.

It is possible to "taste the heavenly gift" (6:4, ESV) and "the goodness of the word of God" and to be "enlightened" by the light of Christ that spills into one's life—and even to benefit from the work of the Holy Spirit in this world—but never consume, swallow, or commit to the gospel message. It is possible to nibble at the edges of life in Christ and decide, *I don't really like this. It is not for me. It's not worth it. I don't want it.* This is the person this passage is talking about. The Holy Spirit will give us a taste of the richness of Christ, but he will not make us eat.

This passage is not describing believers who are in danger of losing their salvation. It is about unbelievers who are in danger of losing their opportunity to receive salvation. It is talking about those who see who Jesus is and what he offers up close, those who experience personally some of the joy, hope, and blessings that he gives and decide they don't want Christ. Salvation is forever out of their reach, not because God withdraws the offer, but because they have hardened their hearts and rejected it.

❈ ❈ ❈

Lord, _____ has seen who you are and what you offer up close. You have allowed _____ to experience the joy and blessing and hope you give. Please don't let _____ taste and then refuse to fully take hold of you. Don't let _____ reject your generous offer of yourself.

A Life That Cannot Be Destroyed

Jesus became a priest, not by meeting the physical requirement of belonging to the tribe of Levi, but by the power of a life that cannot be destroyed. HEBREWS 7:16

EVERYBODY KNEW that someone couldn't be a priest unless he was from the tribe of Levi. Yet the writer of this letter was trying to convince the Hebrew people that someone (Jesus) who wasn't even a descendant of Aaron was the perfect High Priest. He built his case by reminding them that one thousand years before Aaron, there was a priest of God who was appointed by God and respected by Abraham—Melchizedek. Jesus is not a priest by ancestry, like the Aaronic priests; he is a priest by appointment, like Melchizedek. Jesus is a priest because of who he is, not because of the family he came from.

In the Old Testament priesthood, serving had nothing to do with character, ability, personality, or holiness. It was about the family you were born into. But the priesthood of Jesus is about who he is, what he has accomplished, and what he is doing, even now.

Because Jesus, our Mediator before God, has a life that cannot be destroyed, there will never be a day that he is not before the throne of God pleading our case. There will never be a day that he is not interceding with God about our needs. There will never be a day that his perfect record of righteousness will fail to cover us.

And because Jesus has a life that cannot be destroyed, all who are joined to him have lives that cannot be destroyed. What security this brings! What an antidote to fear this offers! If your child is joined to Christ, not only does he or she have everything to gain in the life to come because Jesus is pleading his or her case before the heavenly Father; your child has nothing to fear in this life. And neither do you. When your child is joined to Jesus, his or her life cannot be destroyed because Jesus' life cannot be destroyed. Like Jesus, your child may pass through physical death, but like Jesus, you can be sure that he or she will rise again.

❈ ❈ ❈

Lord, I am grateful that it is not up to me to plead _____'s case before your throne. Jesus is there, interceding, upholding, keeping, and mediating for _____. I can rest. The power of a life that cannot be destroyed is protecting and preserving _____'s life.

Live!

Give [Jerusalem] this message from the Sovereign LORD: You are nothing but a Canaanite! Your father was an Amorite and your mother a Hittite. On the day you were born, no one cared about you. Your umbilical cord was not cut, and you were never washed, rubbed with salt, and wrapped in cloth. No one had the slightest interest in you; no one pitied you or cared for you. On the day you were born, you were unwanted, dumped in a field and left to die. But I came by and saw you there, helplessly kicking about in your own blood. As you lay there, I said, "Live!" And I helped you to thrive like a plant in the field. You grew up and became a beautiful jewel. EZEKIEL 16:3-7

EZEKIEL WAS SPEAKING for God to the Jewish captives who had been dragged away from Jerusalem into exile in Babylon. Through his prophet, God had been impressing upon his people all that he had done for them and the way they had sinned against his goodness to them. In Ezekiel 16, the Lord speaks to his people, describing them as an abandoned baby dumped by the roadside, unwanted, uncared for, left to die . . . until he, the Father they had not known, walked by. He came into the field and saw this discarded child no one wanted and said, "Live!" What an act of grace. God willed his people to live; he helped them to thrive; he nurtured them as they grew.

This is true about all who are children of God. We were helpless and destined to die until God set his love on us and gave us life. We were rescued when we should have perished because we were lifeless and useless. But the Father passed by and saw us lying there and said, "Live!"

※ ※ ※

You are the God who takes discarded children and makes them your own. Make us your own. Call us to life. You bring awakening where you want, when you want, and to whom you want. Your life-giving power is not activated by our schemes and tactics, but by your Spirit. So we ask you to come by and see us, and see _____. Call us to life as only you can! Help us to thrive! Nurture us as we grow to become your beautiful jewel.

Better Covenant, Better Promises

Now Jesus, our High Priest, has been given a ministry that is far superior to the old priesthood, for he is the one who mediates for us a far better covenant with God, based on better promises. HEBREWS 8:6

GOD MADE A COVENANT with Israel in the days of Moses that was founded on grace: "I am the LORD your God, who rescued you from the land of Egypt, the place of your slavery" (Exodus 20:2). God set the terms of this covenant: "*If* you will obey me and keep my covenant, you will be my own special treasure from among all the peoples on earth; for all the earth belongs to me" (Exodus 19:5, emphasis added). Essentially he told them: "If you obey me, I'll bless you, and if you disobey me, I'll curse you."

They did not obey. But God didn't give up on his people. He made a new promise through the prophet Jeremiah: "I will put my instructions deep within them, and I will write them on their hearts" (31:33). The new covenant was inaugurated by Jesus. Jesus replaced the "If . . . then" nature of our relationship with God with "I will." The old covenant of legal threats was replaced by the new covenant of full provision in the person of Christ. And while this new covenant doesn't do away with the law, it internalizes the law in our hearts. It changes us from people who pursue holiness through behavior modification efforts into people who long for a genuine inner holiness that emerges from hearts filled with the Holy Spirit.

It's when the Spirit awakens us to the beauty of Christ that we can finally see that this is where the law was meant to lead us all along—not to better behavior, but to Christ. And this is the challenge for us as parents: to lead our children not merely toward better behavior, but to Christ.

※ ※ ※

Lord, you have given us a better covenant with better promises than you gave through the old covenant. No longer do we live in the fear of "If . . . then" but in the freedom of "It is finished!" So we ask you to save us from impressing upon our children a gospel of trying harder to live up to a standard outside of themselves. Instead, help us to communicate the Good News clearly so that they can live freely under the new covenant, which empowers us from the inside to live holy lives.

NOVEMBER 8

The Parents' Sins

The person who sins is the one who will die. The child will not be punished for the parent's sins, and the parent will not be punished for the child's sins. Righteous people will be rewarded for their own righteous behavior, and wicked people will be punished for their own wickedness. But if wicked people turn away from all their sins and begin to obey my decrees and do what is just and right, they will surely live and not die. All their past sins will be forgotten, and they will live because of the righteous things they have done. EZEKIEL 18:20-22

As THEY SUFFERED IN EXILE, the people of Israel repeated this proverb: "The parents have eaten sour grapes, but their children's mouths pucker at the taste" (Jeremiah 31:29; Ezekiel 18:2). Whenever they repeated this saying, they were complaining that they were being punished for the sins of their parents. In other words, they were accusing God of injustice.

Setting them straight, God told them that while their parents and grandparents did sin and deserved punishment, this younger generation was not, in fact, innocent. They had actually repeated the sins of their parents in even greater measure. Thus, the punishment being poured out on them was unquestionably deserved. Following their parents' example, the children had also been eating the sour grapes of sin.

It was not God's unfairness that was the problem; their sin was the problem. They were simply in denial. But while Ezekiel took away their excuse, he did not leave them crushed under the weight of the reality of getting what they deserved. He promised grace and mercy. He pleaded with them to turn and live. He promised that their past sins could be forgotten by the one they'd sinned against.

※ ※ ※

Righteous Father, as parents we know exactly what we deserve. We deserve to eat the sour grapes of judgment for all the idols we have served and the laws we have broken. But instead, you are feeding us the very best foods. You are blessing us instead of cursing us. And we ask, Lord, that you would extend this blessing to _____. Draw _____ to turn away from sin and toward you. Flood _____'s life with the good news that past sins will be forgotten and the future will be filled with life.

A Purified Conscience

Under the old system, the blood of goats and bulls and the ashes of a heifer could cleanse people's bodies from ceremonial impurity. Just think how much more the blood of Christ will purify our consciences from sinful deeds so that we can worship the living God. For by the power of the eternal Spirit, Christ offered himself to God as a perfect sacrifice for our sins. HEBREWS 9:13-14

MOST PEOPLE who are troubled by feelings of personal guilt today are told that they should see a therapist. Guilt is considered unproductive and unnecessary. But this completely ignores the reality of the gift that God has given to us in the form of a conscience. Our conscience is that internal voice that sits in judgment over our will, accusing us when we violate its standard and giving approval when we fulfill it.

When our conscience bothers us, we have only two options. One option is to seek to kill or silence the conscience through self-medication or self-justification. This is the way of the world. The other option is to test our feelings of guilt against the truth of God's Word and then apply the Word, either by correcting false feelings of guilt with the truth or by confessing what is very real guilt to our gracious God. All who belong to him can expect to be forgiven and have their consciences cleansed.

When our children experience legitimate guilt over violating what is clearly revealed in Scripture as displeasing to God, it is something to celebrate. A conscience that is sensitive to sin is a great gift, a sign of the Spirit's work of conviction. But it is also important that our children are confident in the available remedy for a conscience that needs to be cleansed—the blood of Christ. The good news of the gospel that we want to share with our children again and again—especially in the hard and dark times of facing up to sin—is that Christ has removed our very real guilt and is at work in us by his Spirit, filling us with new desires to please him.

❋ ❋ ❋

Lord, I thank you that you have given _____ a conscience. May it be shaped by your Word and not by the world. May _____ be sensitive to sin without being prone to unwholesome doubts about his standing before you. Develop in _____ a conscience that gives reliable feedback and makes him quick to confess, willing to experience sorrow over sin, and profoundly aware of the cleansing and forgiveness available in Christ.

Being Made Holy

By one sacrifice he has made perfect forever those who are being made holy.
HEBREWS 10:14, NIV

NOTICE WHEN THESE THINGS happened: He "*has made* perfect"—something that's already been done. Those who "*are being made* holy"—something that's happening right now. The perfection has been accomplished in the past, yet the process of being made holy is continual.

So in what way are we perfected? Our slates have been wiped clean. We've been completely forgiven. Our debts have been paid. Because we are in Christ, legally we stand before God with no cause for condemnation. He doesn't count our sins against us. We are covered, not in the spots and stains left behind by our failures and mistakes, but in the robes of righteousness given to us by Christ in place of our sin-spotted rags.

So if we're perfect, why do we need to continue to be made holy? Because while our sinless standing before God is made secure by the righteousness of Christ, we know that is not the reality in our lives. We still have a long way to go before holiness characterizes us from day to day.

But the good news of the gospel as we continue to stumble over some of the same old sins is that we are being made holy. The Spirit is at work in us by his Word so that we are becoming closer to what we've been declared to be in the courtroom of heaven. The gap between who we are in Christ and who we are in our flesh is closing as sins are identified, confessed, and forsaken. We are becoming in reality what we've been declared to be by joining ourselves to Jesus.

Are we celebrating the increasing holiness that we see in our children? Somehow it comes much more naturally for us to point out what needs to change. But to publicly praise God for his work in our children and to affirm our children for the change we see in them is to welcome and celebrate God's sanctifying purposes.

❀ ❀ ❀

Lord, I praise you for being a God who is relentless about holiness. You are holy, and as we submit to you, you are making us holy.

You Accepted It with Joy

Think back on those early days when you first learned about Christ. Remember how you remained faithful even though it meant terrible suffering. Sometimes you were exposed to public ridicule and were beaten, and sometimes you helped others who were suffering the same things. You suffered along with those who were thrown into jail, and when all you owned was taken from you, you accepted it with joy. You knew there were better things waiting for you that will last forever. HEBREWS 10:32-34

IT WASN'T EASY for the early Christians who were being addressed in the letter of Hebrews to follow Christ. They were ostracized in the business community, rejected by their families, unwelcome at the Temple, and some had their property confiscated. Yet when everything they owned was taken from these believers, they "accepted it with joy." This is stunning. If we consider it carefully, we wonder how it could really be true. More significantly, we wonder if it would be true of us.

The writer of Hebrews tells us how these early believers were able to respond to loss in the midst of persecution in this way. They "knew there were better things waiting for [them] that will last forever." They were able to let go of their worldly possessions because they knew what was waiting for them in heaven was better.

Our children instinctually know what truly makes us happy and what has the power to rob us of joy. So they know if Christ is our true satisfaction or merely an inherited tradition. They know if he is the passion of our lives or if we're merely going through the motions. It becomes evident when our commitment to Christ costs us something—like the investment of our time in a service project rather than a favorite sporting event, or a gift of money to gospel work that we were going to spend on a vacation. When we accept financial loss, the loss of health, the loss of advancement, and the loss of opportunity or freedom with genuine joy instead of self-pity or resentment, it becomes evident to our children that we're not depending on this world to make us happy. Our joy is anchored in the life to come.

❊ ❊ ❊

Lord, everything you are, and everything you provide now and in the life to come, is everything I need and more than I could ever ask for. Increase my confidence in what you have prepared for me so that I will respond to losses in this life with joy and contentment.

Faith

Faith shows the reality of what we hope for; it is the evidence of things we cannot see.
HEBREWS 11:1

TYPICALLY WHEN WE SAY we "hope" for something, what we're really saying is that we're not sure it is going to happen, but we want it to. This is wishful thinking, not biblical hope. There is nothing uncertain about biblical hope. What the Bible promises may not yet be realized, but it is certain.

How do we know? On what basis do we have hope? God has promised. To have faith is to risk everything on believing that everything God has promised is completely reliable. Noah believed what God said when he warned him about the flood, so he built the ark. Abraham believed what God said when he promised to bless him, so Abraham followed God's instruction and went to the place where God told him to go. Sarah believed God when he said she would have a child, so she trusted him even in her old age.

Yet Hebrews 11 says, "All these people died still believing what God had promised them. They did not receive what was promised, but they saw it all from a distance and welcomed it" (verse 13). They died waiting for the promised Messiah. They didn't receive everything in this life that was promised to them by God. But what they received in the next was far better than anything they could have imagined.

So much of modern Christianity is about harnessing the power of God to get what we want in the here and now and to become better people in the here and now. But the essence of our faith is nothing like that. We want our children to be willing to step out to follow a God they have never seen with their eyes, whose voice they have never heard with their ears, trusting a reality that the collective voice of the world says does not exist and does not matter. We want them to believe that there is something that can be found only in God that is more durable, dependable, and delightful than anything in this world—and then live in that confidence.

❋ ❋ ❋

Lord, please don't let _____ settle for a generic, domesticated kind of faith that is acceptable to the world. Instead, fill _____ with a countercultural confidence that anticipates all that you have promised—not in the here and now, but in a heavenly homeland.

Better to Suffer for the Sake of Christ

It was by faith that Moses, when he grew up, refused to be called the son of Pharaoh's daughter. He chose to share the oppression of God's people instead of enjoying the fleeting pleasures of sin. He thought it was better to suffer for the sake of Christ than to own the treasures of Egypt, for he was looking ahead to his great reward. HEBREWS 11:24-26

MOSES GREW UP "educated in all the wisdom of the Egyptians" (Acts 7:22, NIV). He likely learned linguistics, mathematics, astronomy, architecture, music, medicine, law, and the fine art of diplomacy. Ironically, the training Moses would need to lead his people out of Egypt and shepherd them in the desert was provided in the household of the pharaoh himself. While Exodus doesn't tell us about what went on in Moses' life during these years, the writer of Hebrews allows us to see what motivated Moses, what he valued, and where he chose to place his confidence. Moses "thought it was better to suffer for the sake of Christ than to own the treasures of Egypt."

Moses, who had lived for several years in the Hebrew home of his believing parents before being schooled in the halls of Pharaoh's palace, knew about the Christ, the offspring of the woman God had promised would one day be born who would put an end to the suffering and cruelty in this world. Moses held on to this promise. It was his confidence in the Christ that enabled him to walk away from worldly wealth, power, and privilege. He had his eyes and his heart set on something better than the treasures of Egypt—the reward that awaited him in heaven for investing all of his hopes in the promised Christ. Moses was willing to pass up temporary pleasure now for the lasting pleasure that would be his forever.

How did he do it? "It was by faith . . ." His parents told him about God's promise, and he took hold of it and lived in light of it.

❄ ❄ ❄

Lord, we have told _____ about you and your promises. Will you give _____ the faith to take hold of those promises and live in light of them? Will you give _____ the faith to choose to share in the oppression of God's people rather than enjoy the fleeting pleasures of sin? Will you shape _____'s perspective to see that it is better to suffer for your sake than to own the treasures of the world? Will you give _____ eyes to look ahead to the great reward to come?

A Harvest of Right Living

Our earthly fathers disciplined us for a few years, doing the best they knew how. But God's discipline is always good for us, so that we might share in his holiness. No discipline is enjoyable while it is happening—it's painful! But afterward there will be a peaceful harvest of right living for those who are trained in this way. HEBREWS 12:10-11

THE HONESTY of these verses is appealing. As "earthly" parents, we appreciate the writer's description of us—we're doing the best we know how to do in the area of disciplining our children. Clearly, however, the writer is drawing a contrast between our parenting and that of our heavenly Father. "God's discipline is always good for us." God is the perfect parent. His discipline is never too harsh or inappropriate. We do not always know how best to discipline our children. But God does. He always knows and does what is right.

His intention in disciplining us is that we might "share in his holiness." God wants his children to bear the family resemblance. He wants us to live in a way that demonstrates we share the passions and priorities of our Father.

Of course, we also appreciate the writer's honesty when he says that "no discipline is enjoyable while it is happening—it's painful!" Obviously, discipline doesn't feel good at the time. It feels like hardship and loss. As his children, we can endure it because we're confident that it's *purposeful*. God's discipline is never punitive. Never random. Never too harsh. Always done out of love. God's purpose is that "afterward there will be a peaceful harvest of right living for those who are trained in this way." When we are willing to be trained by his discipline—to be molded and shaped by it—something beautiful happens. Something blossoms in our lives—a peaceful harvest of right living.

❋ ❋ ❋

Heavenly Father, I have not grown beyond my need for your loving discipline. In fact, it is amazing to me that you can use even the challenges of parenting to mold me. Parenting has a way of exposing my idols and bringing to the surface the areas in which there is a need for a harvest of right living. So keep loving me by disciplining me in the way that only you can.

Unshakable

Be careful that you do not refuse to listen to the One who is speaking. . . . When God spoke from Mount Sinai his voice shook the earth, but now he makes another promise: "Once again I will shake not only the earth but the heavens also." This means that all of creation will be shaken and removed, so that only unshakable things will remain. Since we are receiving a Kingdom that is unshakable, let us be thankful and please God by worshiping him with holy fear and awe. HEBREWS 12:25-28

WHEN GOD SPOKE on Mount Sinai, he was literally laying down the law, and the force of it shook the earth. Exodus 19:18 says that "Mount Sinai was covered with smoke, because the LORD descended on it in fire. The smoke billowed up from it like smoke from a furnace, and the whole mountain trembled violently" (NIV).

But that was not the last time the earth shook. "When Jesus had cried out again in a loud voice, he gave up his spirit. At that moment the curtain of the temple was torn in two from top to bottom. The earth shook, [and] the rocks split" (Matthew 27:50-51, NIV). Why did the earth shake? Because the judgment of God was falling to punish sin.

Here in Hebrews 12, the writer reveals there will be yet another shaking in the future, when Christ returns to purge this world of sin for good. "Only unshakable things will remain," he writes.

Notice the writer says that we are "receiving a Kingdom that is unshakable." Evidently we cannot create for our children a life that is perfectly secure. It must be received. But we can point them toward the secret to receiving this life, which is eternally and ultimately secure. We can pass along the warning given by the writer of Hebrews: "Be careful that you do not refuse to listen to the One who is speaking." We can pray that God would make our children unshakable.

❀ ❀ ❀

Lord, you are the only one who can provide the security _____ needs. So we thank you for speaking in the past and continuing to speak through your Word, calling _____ to yourself and warning _____ about the shaking that will come in the future. May _____ worship you with holy fear and awe, and thereby be secure in the shaking.

Remember Your Leaders

Remember your leaders who taught you the word of God. Think of all the good that has come from their lives, and follow the example of their faith. HEBREWS 13:7

WE KNOW THAT it is our responsibility to bring our children up with "the discipline and instruction that comes from the Lord" (Ephesians 6:4). We also realize that our children benefit greatly from other voices who can speak the Word of God into their lives and serve as exemplary models of faith. So it makes sense to pray that God will give our children Sunday school teachers who will captivate their hearts and imaginations with the Bible; youth leaders who will come alongside to listen, to laugh, and to lead them wisely away from the world and toward the Word; and influences at college and in the workplace who will live holy lives of robust, contagious faith. We pray that our children will engage with the preached Word week by week rather than seeing that message as something for the grown-ups—or as they enter adulthood, as something that is very out of touch with the realities of their lives.

The writer of Hebrews has several instructions for us in regard to leaders who bring the Word of God. We are to *remember* them, *think* of all the good that has come from their lives, and *follow* their example of faith. We're also told to "obey your spiritual leaders, and do what they say. Their work is to watch over your souls, and they are accountable to God. Give them reason to do this with joy and not with sorrow. That would certainly not be for your benefit" (verse 17). Remember, think of them with appreciation, follow, obey, give them reason to watch over your soul with joy—these things should mark the way we talk about and interact with the pastors in our church. We know that our children are often more likely to do what we do rather than do what we say. They're listening when we complain or criticize, and when we affirm and honor those who teach us God's Word.

❊ ❊ ❊

Lord, we thank you for those you have placed in our lives and over our souls who have taught us your Word. You've blessed us with leaders who love you and live for you. We ask you to do that in _____'s life. At every age and stage, would you bless _____ with spiritual leaders who recognize they are accountable to you for the way they watch over _____'s soul? And would you cause _____ to give them reason to do this with joy and not with sorrow?

Temptation Comes from Our Own Desires

*Remember, when you are being tempted, do not say, "God is tempting me." God is
never tempted to do wrong, and he never tempts anyone else. Temptation comes from
our own desires, which entice us and drag us away. These desires give birth to sinful
actions. And when sin is allowed to grow, it gives birth to death.* JAMES 1:13-15

As PARENTS, our instinct is to protect our kids from anything that might tempt them
toward sin. If we could, we'd put up a fence between our home and the rest of the world.
But this ignores an important reality. Sin has already infected our children. They were
born with a preexisting condition. The greatest sinful influence on them is their own
depravity. It's the sin within them rather than the sin outside of them that we have to
parent them through.

This means that all of our attempts to raise our children inside a safe, spiritual
cocoon are useless because temptation operates inside the cocoon, inside our children's
hearts, at the level of their own desires.

So if building a wall around our children will not protect them from sin, is there
anything we can do that will encourage them not to act sinfully upon their desires? We
can create an atmosphere in our homes that continually exposes their emotions to what
is "true, and honorable, and right, and pure, and lovely, and admirable" (Philippians
4:8). As these good things go to work in their minds, they will shape their emotions.
They will strengthen them on the inside, impacting their desires so they won't be so
easily enticed and dragged into sin.

❈ ❈ ❈

*Lord, it is so easy to parent primarily out of fear, to be more afraid of Satan and the world
getting their hands on _____ than to be confident in your faithfulness to finish the
good work you have begun. So, Lord, keep working in _____ to sanctify _____'s
thoughts and desires, and to give _____ a fighting chance in the battle against sin.*

Slow to Anger

Understand this, my dear brothers and sisters: You must all be quick to listen, slow to speak, and slow to get angry. Human anger does not produce the righteousness God desires. JAMES 1:19-20

SURELY EVERY PARENT has responded to his or her child with ungracious, angry impatience on occasion. We're frustrated because we're late. We're annoyed with the attitude, the situation, the inaction, or the mess, so we vent our frustration on our children, justifying it as a need to teach them respect, order, and timeliness.

But James calls us back from the ledge of unloading our anger on our children. He challenges us to reconsider our sense that our anger is not only justified, but also effective. He challenges us to reconsider our assumption that the passion of our anger gets the attention of our kids and pushes them toward change.

What might happen if we took this admonition to heart in our interactions with our kids—from toddlers to teenagers to twentysomethings? What if we really believed that our anger does not, in fact, produce the righteousness God desires in us or in our children but actually does damage? What if we were willing to change the rhythm and pattern of our instinctive anger and replace it with an inclination to listen—to draw out what is really going on in the hearts of our children? What would happen if, instead of venting our accusations and complaints, we slowed down before responding, making sure our words were kind and tender? What if we were slow to speak and instead took time to listen, to see, to love, and to change our response to one of grace?

In essence, James is calling us to parent in the way that we have been parented by God. "The LORD is compassionate and merciful, slow to get angry and filled with unfailing love. . . . The LORD is like a father to his children, tender and compassionate to those who fear him. For he knows how weak we are; he remembers we are only dust" (Psalm 103:8, 13-14).

❊ ❊ ❊

Lord, you are our model for parenting our children. When we are at our worst, you are never on your last nerve. You are slow to get angry, filled with love and tenderness. Fill us with your love, your tenderness, and your patience so we can shower it on _____.

The Tongue

The tongue is a small thing that makes grand speeches. But a tiny spark can set a great forest on fire. And among all the parts of the body, the tongue is a flame of fire. It is a whole world of wickedness, corrupting your entire body. It can set your whole life on fire, for it is set on fire by hell itself. JAMES 3:5-6

"GRAND SPEECHES." Most parents have made those a time or two—lofty lectures about sharing, about telling the truth, about being kind to each other, about getting a job done. So many grand speeches. With the best of intentions, it is easy for us to use our authority as parents to drill our kids down into the ground with our lectures. We also know that our tongue has been a flame of fire in our home—ignited by a spark of frustration so that it burns harsh words and hurtful evaluations of our kids deep into their souls. Our words, and perhaps more significantly our condescending or belittling tone, have singed tender places inside our children.

Our facial expressions and body language can communicate to our kids that they are a nuisance, unimportant, difficult, disappointing, and dumb. Sometimes we use sarcasm or put-downs in ways that our children take to heart as our real estimation of them.

Jesus said, "Whatever is in your heart determines what you say" (Matthew 12:34). The way we speak to and respond to our children—both in terms of what we say as well as the tone with which we say it—exposes the condition of our hearts. In this way, God uses the task of parenting to reveal our neediness for deep heart change produced by the Holy Spirit—the kind of heart change that transforms the way we talk to and about our children.

❈ ❈ ❈

Lord, I am a parent with unclean lips, and I live among a people of unclean lips. Without Jesus to cleanse my tongue, soften my heart, and renew my mind, I would have no hope of my tongue becoming a source of blessing rather than a source of cursing to _____. Create in me a clean heart, O God, and renew a right spirit within me. And give me the privilege of speaking into _____'s life out of this clean heart and right spirit.

NOVEMBER 20

You Are Jealous of What Others Have

You want what you don't have, so you scheme and kill to get it. You are jealous of what others have, but you can't get it, so you fight and wage war to take it away from them. Yet you don't have what you want because you don't ask God for it. And even when you ask, you don't get it because your motives are all wrong—you want only what will give you pleasure. JAMES 4:2-3

As EMBARRASSING as it is to admit, most of us envy other parents and their kids at one point or another. When we're struggling to conceive, we can feel jealous toward those couples who seem to just look at each other and get pregnant. We can be envious of those who have babies who sleep through the night early on, toddlers who can already read, elementary-aged kids who seem to have more friends than our child, teenagers who get the lead in the school play or the starting position on the team when our child doesn't, or young adults who seem to be progressing toward an education or vocation more smoothly than our child.

As he is wont to do, James gets to the heart of the issue—our motives. We want our children to make us look good. But God has different intentions for our parenting. His goal is not to make us impressive but to make us holy. Rather than bringing us glory, God intends for our parenting to bring him glory. So he provides exactly what we need to overcome our jealousy and envy: "He gives grace generously. As the Scriptures say, 'God opposes the proud but gives grace to the humble'" (James 4:6).

❋ ❋ ❋

We humble ourselves before you, God, naming and confessing our sin of jealousy. Forgive us for wanting parenting success so we will look good in front of others instead of wanting our neediness for your grace to put your glory and goodness on display. We need your power to resist the devil's attempts to twist and contort our parenting and ruin our relationships by tempting us to be jealous of other parents and their kids. We need your grace to stand against the desire to be impressive. We come close to you, believing that you will come close to us.

Confess

Confess your sins to each other and pray for each other so that you may be healed. The earnest prayer of a righteous person has great power and produces wonderful results.
JAMES 5:16

IT'S NOT HARD to admit to our kids that we are sinners in a general sense or to say that we need God's forgiveness. It's not even terribly hard to confess sins we committed long ago. What's hard is practicing the regular confession of present sins in the presence of our children. What's hard is being vulnerable enough in front of them to confess as sin the gossip they overheard, the greed that shaped our recent business deal, the compromise that kept us from turning the channel, or the apathy that allows us to complain about and criticize our neighbors while never sharing the gospel with them.

We prefer to be the voice of authority and virtue to our kids, not the lead confessor or repenter. But how can we expect our kids to confess their sins and pray for each other as a means to experience healing from sin if we never confess our sins? How can we be surprised when our kids lie about or hide their sins when we live in self-denial about our own sins or seek to keep them under wraps?

As we model for our children a regular pattern of confession and glad repentance, we show them how a follower of Jesus handles sin in his own life. To hear Dad regularly confessing sin to Mom and his kids, but especially confessing sin to God; to listen as he prays for forgiveness and asks for the prayers of his family to defeat a particular sin; and then to watch him experience the joy of restored fellowship with God and a purified conscience—surely this is what convinces our kids that they don't have to be perfect and can overcome sin in community.

※ ※ ※

Lord, I confess that I've been slow to confess. When I'm courageous enough to name and admit my sin, I like for it to be between you and me. Frankly, I don't like either the embarrassment or the accountability that comes with confessing my sins to the people who will know if there is any real change in my life. But there is something I love more than my privacy—someone I love too much to disobey your Word in this way. Lord, as I confess my sin in the presence of _____, would you please use it to encourage _____ that sin can be brought out into the light and that there is grace and mercy available from me and from you?

A Priceless Inheritance

All praise to God, the Father of our Lord Jesus Christ. It is by his great mercy that we have been born again, because God raised Jesus Christ from the dead. Now we live with great expectation, and we have a priceless inheritance—an inheritance that is kept in heaven for you, pure and undefiled, beyond the reach of change and decay. And through your faith, God is protecting you by his power until you receive this salvation, which is ready to be revealed on the last day for all to see. 1 PETER 1:3-5

YOU MAY OR MAY NOT be able to leave your children a financial inheritance. But if they are joined to Christ, you can be sure that they are heirs to a far greater inheritance than you could ever provide. Any wealth that we leave to our kids is vulnerable—vulnerable to misuse, unstable markets, theft, or lost value. But the inheritance that awaits our child who is united to Christ is beyond the reach of any force that would diminish or defile it.

The new birth brings our children into a new family in which they have a share in the greatest of all inheritances. It is being kept—not in a vault but in heaven, the place of ultimate security and wealth, the place of incredible joy and satisfaction. No one in God's family will be disappointed when the inheritance is granted on the last day. We'll be full of joy to receive all that God has for us and all he will be to us.

But God does more than keep an inheritance for us and for our children. He also keeps us for the inheritance. Through faith God is "protecting you by his power until you receive this salvation." Your children's salvation does not depend on their ability to hold on to Christ, but on Christ's ability to hold on to them. Christ is keeping an inheritance for your child, and he is keeping your child for the inheritance.

❊ ❊ ❊

I see your outstretched hands, Lord, reaching out to _____. In one hand you hold an inheritance, and in the other you hold _____. Both are safe with you. And when you come, you will bring the two together, and the inheritance will be _____'s to enjoy forever.

Set Your Hope Fully on Grace

Preparing your minds for action, and being sober-minded, set your hope fully on the grace that will be brought to you at the revelation of Jesus Christ. As obedient children, do not be conformed to the passions of your former ignorance, but as he who called you is holy, you also be holy in all your conduct, since it is written, "You shall be holy, for I am holy." 1 PETER 1:13-16, ESV

THROUGHOUT CHAPTER 1 of his first epistle, Peter talks about the future that awaits those who have been born again to a living hope. He's speaking to those who can anticipate resurrected life in the presence of God through the resurrected life of Jesus. Peter isn't looking for an "Isn't that nice" response to this living hope. Instead, he wants us to think about it with soberness. More than that, he wants us to set our hope fully on "the grace that will be brought to you at the revelation of Jesus Christ." He wants our life in Christ now and into eternity to be both a driving and a steadying force.

This also gets at the heart of what we want for our children. We're not really interested in our kids growing up to become adults who go through the motions of church attendance or have a vague sense of spirituality. We don't want faith to be merely something they grew up with and take for granted. Instead, we want them to have informed, passionate optimism about what they are living for.

As our children "set their hope fully" on the grace that will deliver them from the suffering of this life and reward them with an inheritance in the life to come, it will change how they live in the here and now. This new passion will fuel holy living. Young people who have set their hope fully on the grace that will be brought to them at the revelation of Jesus Christ will be quite different from most others in this world. But they will be exactly who God has called them to be—full of unshakable hope and a passion for holiness.

❊ ❊ ❊

Holy Lord, we can set the glorious truth of hope in Christ before _____. But only you can work in _____ to cause her to set her hope fully on the grace to come when you return. Only you can reveal the worthlessness of worldly passion and replace it with a passion for holiness. So as the one who called _____ to this hope and holiness, create this confident expectation and desire deep in _____'s soul.

Unfading Beauty

Don't be concerned about the outward beauty of fancy hairstyles, expensive jewelry, or beautiful clothes. You should clothe yourselves instead with the beauty that comes from within, the unfading beauty of a gentle and quiet spirit, which is so precious to God.
1 PETER 3:3-4

WHEN WE READ Peter's words to women, telling them not to be concerned about hairstyles, jewelry, or clothing, we wonder if he was really married, or if he was ever around a woman. Being concerned with our appearance seems innate to being a woman—especially a young woman growing up in a culture obsessed with physical beauty. And because of our culture's worship of physical attractiveness, the idea of being beautiful "on the inside" is anathema to most females. It sounds like code language for "ugly." So what is Peter commending here?

The point here is not to ban flattering hairstyles or stylish clothing. It's about the vastly superior value of inward beauty over being a slave to fashion and appearance. Peter is commending modesty and restraint in dress. More than that, he's helping us to value what God values more than what the world values. He's telling us what God puts a high price tag on, what is precious to God, what catches his eye. This quality—a gentle and quiet spirit—comes from within and has the potential to become more beautiful with age rather than fading in beauty over time.

Peter is calling us to be countercultural in determining what is beautiful. His words challenge us as moms to be more concerned about clothing ourselves with a gentle and quiet spirit, a deep and abiding trust in God, than we are about keeping up with the latest fashions. As we do so, we'll be more likely to lead our daughters toward valuing this kind of beauty too.

❊ ❊ ❊

Lord, to be more concerned about being beautiful on the inside than we are about being attractive in our appearance and dress seems like a very tall order in our image-obsessed culture. It will become a reality in our lives only as we are joined to Christ, who had no beauty or majesty to attract us to him, nothing in his appearance that we should desire him. Fill us with the spirit of Christ, who was willing to bear our ugliness so that we might become beautiful to God.

Determined Not to Defile Himself

The king ordered Ashpenaz, his chief of staff, to bring to the palace some of the young men of Judah's royal family and other noble families, who had been brought to Babylon as captives. "Select only strong, healthy, and good-looking young men," he said. "Make sure they are well versed in every branch of learning, are gifted with knowledge and good judgment, and are suited to serve in the royal palace. Train these young men in the language and literature of Babylon." DANIEL 1:3-4

THE KING OF BABYLON sent his soldiers into the homes of Jerusalem to round up the best and brightest young men—young enough, he hoped, not to be so set in the ways of Jerusalem that they would resist the ways of Babylon. Once they were brought to the king's palace, the full-court press to become Babylonian was applied. Since each of their names was actually a statement of faith in the God of the Jews, those names were replaced with names that spoke of Babylonian deities. Daniel and his friends were evidently willing to accept new names, learn the language, and read the literature of Babylon. However, "Daniel was determined not to defile himself by eating the food and wine given to them by the king" (verse 8).

We don't know exactly why Daniel drew the line here, in regard to food. But perhaps he knew that once you get a taste for the high life, it is difficult to do anything that would put you at risk of losing it. Perhaps Daniel recognized the message that was being sent at every mealtime, namely: *The king's palace is the place to be; here's where the doors of opportunity are; taste the success; this is the fast track; enjoy.* Perhaps Daniel knew that if he embraced everything placed before him in Babylon, it wouldn't be long before his soul would be consumed by it and he would think he simply had to have it. Perhaps Daniel recognized that he needed a daily reminder that Babylon was not his home and that he belonged to another Kingdom and another King.

※ ※ ※

Lord, as this world opens up the doors of opportunity for _____, seeking to intoxicate _____ with the splendors of life in the kingdom of the world, don't let _____ become so consumed with the good things the world offers that he loses his sense of identity as a citizen of a holy nation set apart to God. Don't allow obedience to your law to become a relic, a cultural thing he looks back on but has grown beyond. Help _____ to place a guard on his heart so that every day when he says no to something, he will be reminded that he belongs to another Kingdom, another King.

We Will Never Serve Your Gods

Shadrach, Meshach, and Abednego replied, "O Nebuchadnezzar, we do not need to defend ourselves before you. If we are thrown into the blazing furnace, the God whom we serve is able to save us. He will rescue us from your power, Your Majesty. But even if he doesn't, we want to make it clear to you, Your Majesty, that we will never serve your gods or worship the gold statue you have set up." Daniel 3:16-18

Just picture the scene. Thousands of people from throughout the kingdom of Babylon gathered to dedicate the ninety-foot golden image that Nebuchadnezzar had set up. He intended to unify all these conquered peoples from various lands by setting before them one object of worship—his own greatness. A world-class orchestra provided a soundtrack as the people fell down to worship the golden image. Surely common sense screamed to Shadrach, Meshach, and Abednego: *Keep a low profile and live to fight another day. . . . There's nothing to be gained by dying now when you have such valuable positions of influence. . . . What matters is what's in your hearts, so bowing wouldn't be a big deal.* Yet in the sea of people with faces to the ground, three men remained standing, knowing full well a fire was being stoked for all who refused to bow.

These three had heard Daniel's interpretation of the king's dream—God's revelation that all the world's powers would turn to dust and blow away in the wind. Evidently this made them less impressed by the image they were being told to bow down to and the person telling them to do it. They knew they were part of a Kingdom to come that cannot be destroyed, even by fire, so they were less afraid of the flames. Their confidence in their true King and his ability to deliver them was far greater than their fear of the human king and his ability to destroy them.

✹ ✹ ✹

Lord, please fill _____ with a deep sense of belonging to a Kingdom that cannot be destroyed. Give _____ the courage to face the fires of persecution. In the fires of life, may _____ experience your presence like never before.

Everything

By his divine power, God has given us everything we need for living a godly life. We have received all of this by coming to know him, the one who called us to himself by means of his marvelous glory and excellence. And because of his glory and excellence, he has given us great and precious promises. These are the promises that enable you to share his divine nature and escape the world's corruption caused by human desires.
2 PETER 1:3-4

"EVERYTHING WE NEED." Really? This is an extraordinary claim.

Most people would agree that in Christ, God has given us everything we need for the faith compartment of our lives. But that is not what Peter is claiming here. He says that in Christ we have not only everything we need for faith but everything we need for centering our lives on God in every area.

As we share in the divine nature as parents, we have the wisdom we need to decide when to say yes and when to say no. We have the resources for patience and kindness when we are under pressure. We have the courage we need for facing the difficult diagnosis. We have the comfort we need in the midst of loss. We have the healing we need for the wounds of our past. We have the strength we need when we are overwhelmed.

Likewise, as our children come to know the one who has called them to share in his divine nature, God gives them everything they need for living a godly life. They have the understanding they need to take hold of the gospel and to live in light of it. They have the fruit of the Spirit beginning to blossom and grow. They have the spiritual resources they need to face ridicule, disappointment, loneliness, changing moods, failure, and rejection as well as success and popularity.

❋ ❋ ❋

Lord, it is a relief to be reminded that it is not up to me to supply everything _____ needs. I'm simply not up to the task. But you are good enough and powerful enough to give _____ everything needed for living a godly life. Give _____ the faith to take hold of your promises, share in your nature, and thereby escape the world's corruption caused by human desires.

You Have Not Measured Up

This is the message that was written: MENE, MENE, TEKEL, and PARSIN. . . . Tekel
means "weighed"—you have been weighed on the balances and have not measured up.
DANIEL 5:25, 27

THE BOOK OF DANIEL begins by telling us that Nebuchadnezzar took "the sacred objects from the Temple of God" and "placed them in the treasure-house of his god" in Babylon (1:2). In Daniel 5:2, we read that many years later, King Belshazzar was hosting a great feast and "gave orders to bring in the gold and silver cups that his predecessor, Nebuchadnezzar, had taken from the Temple in Jerusalem" so that he and his friends could drink from these exotic artifacts to toast their gods.

But then the real owner of these Temple cups brought the party to a deathly silence. A human hand appeared and began to write words on the wall that no one understood: *Mene, mene, tekel*, and *Parsin*. The king's legs gave way beneath him out of fear. After being summoned to tell the king what the writing meant, Daniel said: "You have proudly defied the Lord of heaven and have had these cups from his Temple brought before you. You and your nobles and your wives and concubines have been drinking wine from them while praising gods of silver, gold, bronze, iron, wood, and stone—gods that neither see nor hear nor know anything at all. But you have not honored the God who gives you the breath of life and controls your destiny!" (Daniel 5:23).

Daniel explained that the words on the wall meant that God had numbered the days of Belshazzar's reign, the he had been weighed on God's scales of justice and did not measure up. His kingdom would be divided.

King Belshazzar saw the handwriting on the wall: He had been "weighed in the balances and found wanting" (5:27, ESV), and the days of his kingdom were numbered. We also deserve to have "weighed and found wanting," "a failed kingdom," and "days are numbered" inscribed on the walls of our lives. Instead, all of us who are joined to Christ have written across our lives: "made worthy by the worth of Christ," "coheir of an eternal kingdom," and "numbered among those whose lives will matter forever."

※ ※ ※

Lord, we can never measure up to all we should be as parents, and _____ can never
measure up to your holy standard. We need the grace made possible by the only one who
has measured up. Write your story of grace over _____'s life.

Patient

The Lord is not slow to fulfill his promise as some count slowness, but is patient toward you, not wishing that any should perish, but that all should reach repentance.
2 PETER 3:9, ESV

HERE IS THE HEART of God toward us and toward our children: His desire is that we would not perish but instead that we would all reach repentance.

Sometimes, when we're waiting for those we love to come to repentance or grow in grace, it can seem as if God is so very slow. But hasn't God always worked to bring about his purposes rather gradually?

After Adam and Eve disobeyed in the Garden, God began working slowly, over centuries, until "the right time came," when "God sent his Son" (Galatians 4:4) to deal with the disaster of the Fall. This means that for all those years, God was preparing the world for the coming of the Savior. God was patient toward his children, sending prophet after prophet with warning after warning, giving them time to respond to his mercy. Consider the patience of Jesus. Those closest to him were so slow to understand and slow of heart to believe all that the prophets had spoken and all that he had taught them. But Jesus didn't give up. He was patiently at work, sending his Spirit to transform a group of confused men into apostles, who then boldly proclaimed the truth of the gospel.

God doesn't demand instant recognition, instant repentance, and instant maturity from his children. So neither should we demand that our children respond to his grace on our timeline. He is willing to go over the same things again and again, in situation after situation ordained by his sovereign grace. We need to give God time to work in the lives of our children. We should expect him to work as much through their failures as he does through their obedience. After all, isn't that how he works with us?

❋ ❋ ❋

I thank you, God, for your patience toward me and toward _____. Won't you fill me with your patience as I wait for your powerful grace to accomplish all that you intend in _____'s life?

NOVEMBER 30

That You May Fully Share Our Joy

We proclaim to you the one who existed from the beginning, whom we have heard and seen. We saw him with our own eyes and touched him with our own hands. He is the Word of life. This one who is life itself was revealed to us, and we have seen him. And now we testify and proclaim to you that he is the one who is eternal life. He was with the Father, and then he was revealed to us. We proclaim to you what we ourselves have actually seen and heard so that you may have fellowship with us. And our fellowship is with the Father and with his Son, Jesus Christ. We are writing these things so that you may fully share our joy. 1 JOHN 1:1-4

JOHN AND THE OTHER apostles enjoyed person-to-person fellowship with the Son of God who existed from the beginning and became flesh—Jesus Christ. By being joined to him by faith, they entered into the fellowship Jesus has with his Father. It is this communion John wanted his fellow believers to enter into.

Fellowship is the experience of sharing something significant with others. It's the pleasure of being in a group in which you see eye to eye on what matters most. It's having similar values and responding with the same kind of affections to what really counts. So to say we have fellowship with the Father and his Son means that we have come to share their values and enjoy their presence.

The relationship John and the other apostles enjoyed with the Father through the Son had brought unspeakable and unstoppable joy to their lives, even though all of them faced harsh persecution. But there was more joy to be had by John. John longed for those he was writing to, those he called "my children" throughout this epistle, to enter into this fellowship he shared with the Father and the Son. In that way, his joy would be complete.

Joy is enhanced when it is shared. And when Jesus is the joy of our lives, our joy increases when we share it with those we love. This is why we long for our children to fully share the joy of our fellowship with the Father through the Son.

※ ※ ※

Lord, this is the joy we long for—to share the joy of fellowship with the Father and the Son with _____. Reveal yourself in fresh, new ways to _____. Draw _____ into closer and closer fellowship with you.

Do Not Love This World

Do not love this world nor the things it offers you, for when you love the world, you do not have the love of the Father in you. For the world offers only a craving for physical pleasure, a craving for everything we see, and pride in our achievements and possessions. These are not from the Father, but are from this world. And this world is fading away, along with everything that people crave. But anyone who does what pleases God will live forever. 1 JOHN 2:15-17

WHAT IS "THE WORLD" that John says we are not to love? This is the same disciple who wrote that "this is how God loved the world: He gave his one and only Son, so that everyone who believes in him will not perish but have eternal life" (John 3:16). Clearly, in John's writings, the word *world* has a wide range of meaning.

When John writes here that we are not to love the world, he's talking about the world that has abandoned its Creator and lives apart from his rule. To love this world is to love the values and pursuits of the world that stand opposed to God.

John says we are not to love this world "nor the things it offers you." Does this mean we shouldn't buy fashionable clothing or go to Disney World? Actually, John seems to be more concerned about what's inside of us than the world outside of us. He warns us about our internal cravings for physical pleasure, material possessions, and personal glory. Loving the things of the world, according to John, is about the lustful look, the greedy gaze, and the wardrobe designed to impress or seduce. John wants us to understand that we simply cannot love all that God is and has to offer, and still love this world and all it has to offer.

The world has great appeal to us and to our kids. It is constantly wooing us into a love relationship, offering us pleasure in many forms. But it also lies to us. It refuses to tell us that it won't last. The truth is that the world is fading away, while "anyone who does what pleases God will live forever."

※ ※ ※

Lord, we need wisdom in this battle against the world in our home. Help us to recognize the internal battle going on in _____ as the world seeks to shape and satisfy _____'s cravings that only you can truly satisfy. This lifelong battle with worldliness cannot be won by sheer willpower or personal resolve, but only as our love for the world is replaced with a love that will never disappoint.

DECEMBER 2

God's Children

Since we know that Christ is righteous, we also know that all who do what is right are God's children. See how very much our Father loves us, for he calls us his children, and that is what we are! 1 JOHN 2:29–3:1

"FOR HE CALLS US HIS CHILDREN." What a beautiful picture. God points to us and says, "They're mine. Those are my kids." This is astonishing love and grace, since we are well aware of the disparity of conduct between Christ, who is perfectly righteous, and us, who are not.

But those who are truly God's children are not altogether unrighteous. Sin is the exception, not the rule, in their lives. "Those who have been born into God's family do not make a practice of sinning, because God's life is in them" (1 John 3:9). In other words, our orientation and aim have changed. While we still have sinful patterns—some that will plague us for life and others that we will finally conquer or control—new habits of holiness are our prevailing lifestyle. Real and radical change has happened and continues to happen inwardly and outwardly.

Our Father is not up in heaven amused or frustrated by our efforts to live in a way that pleases him. Like the father who cherishes the pencil holder made by his child at school, or the mom who enjoys the burned toast prepared by her child on Mother's Day, God is pleased at our attempts at obedience, even when we miss the mark. We are his children, and he loves us unconditionally.

We have the opportunity to mirror the way we are loved by our heavenly Father as we love, affirm, and encourage our children's efforts toward holy living. Our smile on their lives serves as a dim, yet still meaningful, reflection of his smile.

❊ ❊ ❊

Lord, _____ is your child. Help _____ make a decisive break with the big sins that have no place in the life of a member of your family. And help _____ root out the small sins—the bits of worldliness, compromise, inconsistency, and indiscretion that take away from your reflection.

Real Love

We know what real love is because Jesus gave up his life for us. 1 JOHN 3:16

WHEN OUR CHILDREN ARE SMALL—so innocent and so dependent—"I love yous" come easily. Whether they are terrific or terrible, we tell our toddlers over and over that we love them. But as they grow older, "I love yous" can too easily be replaced with "Your room is a mess!" and "What's up with these grades?"

And it works in the other direction too. The crayon-colored pages that said "I luv you, Mommy and Daddy" are often replaced by rolled eyes, big sighs, and slammed doors. And in those moments, instead of saying, "I love you," we vent our frustration. When our children come home embracing those things we worked so hard to train them to reject, our words and expressions often communicate more scorn and condemnation than affection. It's not that we don't love them anymore. It's that our love generates more volatile emotions such as hurt, rejection, disappointment, and anger. When our children's messes invade our orderly world, it can be challenging to say "I love you" in a way our kids can hear and receive.

But that's precisely the time when they need to hear it the most. That's when it has the power to penetrate the hardest of hearts. Our "I love you" plants a seed that over time can grow roots and bear fruit. In the darkest of moments with our kids, expressing genuine, tenderhearted love has the power to soften their hearts.

Because this is the way we have been loved, we can communicate love to our kids even when they are too hardened to engage with us. Jesus loved us when we were in the dark, when our lives were a mess, when we were full of rebellion—not when we were sweet and innocent. His "I love you" expressed at the Cross penetrated and softened our hearts. His love toward us enables us to respond to our children in the mess and alienation and say, "I love you. No matter how hard you push, no matter what you do or don't do, I will always love you."

❈ ❈ ❈

Lord, when it costs me something to love _____, remind me of what it cost you to love me when I was at my worst. May your never-ending, never-failing love flow through me to _____.

DECEMBER 4

Test Them

Dear friends, do not believe everyone who claims to speak by the Spirit. You must test them to see if the spirit they have comes from God. For there are many false prophets in the world. This is how we know if they have the Spirit of God: If a person claiming to be a prophet acknowledges that Jesus Christ came in a real body, that person has the Spirit of God. 1 JOHN 4:1-2

THE APOSTLE JOHN was committed to confronting heretical beliefs that were being taught in his day, namely that Jesus only appeared to have a body. So he defined the truth about who Jesus is—that Jesus existed in eternity past as the Son of God, and that when he came as the Christ, he took on a bodily existence common to humanity.

John was not content for his spiritual children to have a vague or squishy understanding of the person and work of Jesus. What they believed about Jesus mattered. John wanted them to be careful to whom they listened, because not "everyone who claims to speak by the Spirit" can be trusted. He warned about following voices that were in vogue, telling them to stick with what had been taught and written about Jesus by the apostles.

Even in our day, some people who talk about Jesus sound very spiritual, but they diminish or distort who he is and what he came to accomplish. There is the Jesus who gets prayed to before a singing competition and thanked at award shows and athletic championships. Along with this pop-culture Jesus, there is the social-activist Jesus, the great-teacher Jesus, the pacifist Jesus, the rebel Jesus, and many more.

Part of parenting our kids toward knowing and loving Jesus is keeping a close watch on the orthodoxy of those who are speaking into their lives about the person and work of Christ. John writes about people who "belong to this world, so they speak from the world's viewpoint, and the world listens to them." He continues, "But we belong to God, and those who know God listen to us" (1 John 4:5-6). Who is "us"? The apostles. In other words, the way we know someone is speaking the truth about Jesus is that their teaching conforms to what the apostles wrote and taught about him in Scripture.

❋ ❋ ❋

Lord, I need greater clarity on who you are so that I'll be equipped to recognize error when it is being taught. Help me to know when I should be concerned about the voices _____ is listening to, and give me wisdom about how to challenge those voices and point _____ to the truth in the Scriptures.

Kept Safe

We know that God's children do not make a practice of sinning, for God's Son holds them securely, and the evil one cannot touch them. 1 JOHN 5:18

WE ALL WANT TO KEEP OUR KIDS SAFE. And in a world that can seem so very threatening, we want to assure them that they are safe. But what safety can we truly promise our kids in this world? Christians get all the same cancers and experience all the same catastrophes as everyone else. More than that, many Christians are targeted and mistreated around the world specifically because they are believers. Jesus told his disciples that "there will be great earthquakes, and there will be famines and plagues in many lands, and there will be terrifying things. . . . There will be a time of great persecution. You will be dragged into synagogues and prisons, and you will stand trial before kings and governors because you are my followers. . . . Your parents, brothers, relatives, and friends . . . will betray you. They will even kill some of you" (Luke 21:11-12, 16). Then, having told them that some of them would be killed, he added something that might seem strange: "But not a hair of your head will perish!" (Luke 21:18).

How do we put these two things together in our minds, and just as importantly, how do we communicate them to our children so they can rest in the perfect safety provided to all who are in Christ? John says about all of those who are joined to him, "God's Son holds them securely, and the evil one cannot touch them." While Satan wants to harm us and our children, and to have us for eternity, Christ has taken us from the clutches of the evil one. Once Christ has laid hold of us, once his life flows into ours, nothing and no one can take that life. Once our children are in his hands, they are beyond Satan's grasp.

We simply can't promise perfect physical safety to our children in this world. And yet we can assure them that if they are in Christ, they are perfectly and eternally safe. The fallenness of this world might impact them, and the enemy might tempt them, but the evil one can never have them. Christ died to save them, and he lives to keep them. He intercedes for them at the right hand of the Father. He has purchased them with his own blood, and he will never let them go.

❋ ❋ ❋

Lord, you are Lord over even the evil one. All who belong to you are perfectly and eternally safe. And all who are opposed to you are completely and eternally condemned. Take _____ to yourself. Hold _____ securely.

Those Who Trust in the Lord

Those who trust in the LORD are as secure as Mount Zion;
*   they will not be defeated but will endure forever.*
Just as the mountains surround Jerusalem,
*   so the LORD surrounds his people, both now and forever.* PSALM 125:1-2

"THOSE WHO TRUST IN THE LORD." Is that you? Really? Trusting the Lord is the foundation of faith and relationship with Christ, but it can be so very difficult to live consistently in this way—especially when it comes to our children.

Psalm 125 speaks some sense to us as parents when we are tempted to put our trust in anything other than God. It tells us that our lives are as secure as Mount Zion. In other words, our lives are as likely to crumble, as likely to be destroyed, as Mount Zion is likely to come down. Not only do our lives have the stability of Mount Zion; they have the protection of the one who made the mountains. Our protection is his personal project. It is not assigned to lesser beings. Jehovah himself encircles his people. His protection is not occasional or temporary. It is now and for all time.

Of course, the reason Mount Zion—the place where God's people dwell—cannot be shaken is because of what happened on the hill of Golgotha. On the afternoon when Christ died, "The earth shook, rocks split apart" (Matthew 27:51). Three days later, the earth shook again when the stone was rolled away from his tomb. The only reason the Lord "surrounds his people, both now and forever" is because of that Friday when the Father did not surround his Son.

Trusting God means connecting ourselves and entrusting our children to the one person who will endure forever. We simply can't provide this kind of security for our children. As much as we love them, we can't surround them with this kind of impenetrable protection. So we trust in the Lord to be their security and protection.

❊ ❊ ❊

Lord, I want to do more than just give lip service to trusting you. I want to deeply, consistently, pervasively entrust my life and _____'s life to you.

Strong in Spirit

This letter is from John, the elder. I am writing to Gaius, my dear friend, whom I love in the truth. Dear friend, I hope all is well with you and that you are as healthy in body as you are strong in spirit. Some of the traveling teachers recently returned and made me very happy by telling me about your faithfulness and that you are living according to the truth. I could have no greater joy than to hear that my children are following the truth. 3 JOHN 1:1-4

IN THE BRIEF LETTER of 3 John, we get to read a personal letter between the apostle John and a man named Gaius. Gaius was one of John's beloved spiritual children who kept the faith and supported the spread of the gospel. John calls this friend "beloved" and reveals the content of his prayers for him. "Beloved, I pray that all may go well with you and that you may be in good health, as it goes well with your soul" (verse 2, ESV). His prayer for Gaius is that he would have good physical health as well as good spiritual health.

In the typical church we do a lot of asking for prayer about health concerns. We check in with each other in regard to health issues. But we don't do as well when it comes to sickness of the soul. We are hesitant to ask for prayer when our souls are ailing. And it can easily be the same in our families. We can be very tuned in to the physical health of our children while rarely, if ever, checking in with them on the state of their souls.

What makes a soul sick is knowing the truth about Christ and resisting or rejecting that truth. The incongruity of claiming to belong to Christ while living as one who belongs to the world robs a soul of vitality. John found great joy in hearing that his spiritual child, Gaius, was living out the truth of the gospel. Likewise, our greatest joy comes from hearing and seeing that our children are not struggling with a sickness of soul caused by inconsistency in living out what they claim to believe, but are following the truth.

※ ※ ※

Lord, grant me this privilege! Give me the joy of hearing that _____ is following the truth. Save _____ from the soul sickness caused by hypocrisy and hiding. Let _____ experience the strength of spirit that comes from living according to your Word.

Able to Keep You

Now all glory to God, who is able to keep you from falling away and will bring you with great joy into his glorious presence without a single fault. All glory to him who alone is God, our Savior through Jesus Christ our Lord. All glory, majesty, power, and authority are his before all time, and in the present, and beyond all time! Amen. JUDE 24-25

JUDE'S LETTER BEGINS by telling us as believers that we are *called* and *loved* by our heavenly Father and that we are *kept* "safe in the care of Jesus Christ"(verse 2). Then he ends his brief letter with the assurance that God is able to keep us from falling away and will bring us into his glorious presence where no accusation of sin against us will stick.

In between these two assurances that believers are kept safe by God is the reminder Jude gives of the Israelites who were rescued from Egypt but were not kept due to their unfaithfulness and were destroyed (verse 5); angels who rebelled and are being kept, not for salvation, but for judgment (verse 6); and people in Jude's day who claimed to be in Christ but who lived immoral, rebellious lives (verse 10). They would not be kept either, but were bringing about their own destruction.

It will take a work of God to keep your child spiritually alive and following Christ over the course of a lifetime, and to bring your child into the presence of God full of joy and without fear of condemnation. He is the giver of this life, the moment-by-moment sustainer of this life. Yet your child has a part to play also, as made clear by Jude: "But you, dear friends, must build each other up in your most holy faith, pray in the power of the Holy Spirit, and await the mercy of our Lord Jesus Christ, who will bring you eternal life. In this way, you will *keep yourselves* safe in God's love" (verses 20-21, emphasis added). Even as your child is being kept by God, he must keep himself in the love of God by putting himself among the people of God. As believers, we build one another up in faith by praying in the power of the Holy Spirit and by waiting expectantly for the day when God will bring us into his glorious presence.

❋ ❋ ❋

Now all glory to you, God, who is able to keep _____ from falling away and will bring _____ with great joy into his glorious presence without a single fault. All glory to you who alone are God, our Savior through Jesus Christ our Lord. All glory, majesty, power, and authority are yours before all time, and in the present, and beyond all time! Amen.

Lost Years

The threshing floors shall be full of grain;
  the vats shall overflow with wine and oil.
I will restore to you the years
  that the swarming locust has eaten. JOEL 2:24-25, ESV

GOD'S PEOPLE had suffered the loss of their entire harvest as swarms of locusts marched like an insect army through their fields. For four consecutive years, the locusts laid waste to every vine and tree and field. But it wasn't merely a natural disaster; it was divine judgment. In the midst of the famine, the Lord called out to his people through his prophet Joel, wooing them back to himself with an incredible promise: "I will restore to you the years that the swarming locust has eaten."

In the midst of the devastation came the promise of an incredible reversal if God's people would turn to the Lord, who is merciful and compassionate. "He is eager to relent and not punish," Joel says of the Lord (verse 13).

This same merciful and compassionate Lord restores what the consequences of sin have taken from us—all the years of glad service to Christ lost to apathy and busyness, all the loveless years lost to bitterness and anger, all the indulgent years spent trying to fill up the emptiness with alcohol, and all of the Christless years resisting the Savior's drawing love. The Lord restores the distracted years when you didn't give your children the attention they needed. He restores the angry years when you were more likely to yell or hit instead of listen and love. He restores the demanding years when your rigid standards drove your child away.

Take heart. There is hope. God can restore to you the years eaten up by sinful patterns and misguided priorities. He can deepen his fellowship with you so that your love for him can be greater than you've known before. He can multiply your fruitfulness so that your impact for Christ can be greater than it's ever been. He can break down the barriers between you and your child so that your mutual affection can become stronger than you ever imagined.

※ ※ ※

Lord, I don't deserve the kind of restoration that you promise. But I know that you are a God of grace, giving your people what we don't deserve and could never earn. As I turn to you, restore the years that sinful patterns have stolen from me.

You Don't Love Me as You Did at First

I know all the things you do. I have seen your hard work and your patient endurance. I know you don't tolerate evil people. You have examined the claims of those who say they are apostles but are not. You have discovered they are liars. You have patiently suffered for me without quitting. But I have this complaint against you. You don't love me or each other as you did at first! Look how far you have fallen! Turn back to me and do the works you did at first. REVELATION 2:2-5

EACH OF THE LETTERS John wrote down for the seven churches in Asia addressed their faithfulness to Christ in the midst of a threatening pagan culture. Two of the seven churches received only commendations, no criticisms, from Jesus. One of the churches received only criticism and no commendation. But four of the churches got mixed reviews. Jesus told four of them that he had something against them—including the church in Ephesus.

The church in Ephesus was commended for their hard work and patient endurance. But there was a significant problem: They simply didn't love Jesus in the way they once did. So Jesus called them to turn back to him and live for him. He called them to declare his gospel boldly like they did when they first came to him.

Sometimes we as parents can get this same kind of wake-up call from our own kids. We long and pray for them to take hold of Christ and become passionate about him. And then they do! They get excited about reading their Bibles and being with other believers to worship. Their enthusiasm can challenge us to evaluate our own passion for Christ. They want us to be as excited as they are about serving Jesus, even if it takes us out of our comfort zone.

Perhaps this is one of many ways the Lord uses our children to sanctify us as parents. Sometimes their fresh and passionate love for Jesus reminds us of the fresh and passionate love for Jesus we once had that over the years may have waned.

❄ ❄ ❄

Lord, I want to love you in the way I did when our love was new. How can I pray for _____ to love Christ if my love for you has grown cold? Stir in me fresh passion for you as I do the things I did when I first began this life in you.

The Day of the Lord

What sorrow awaits you who say,
  "If only the day of the LORD were here!"
You have no idea what you are wishing for.
  That day will bring darkness, not light. Amos 5:18

SOMETIMES IT SEEMS like we spend a lot of our lives focused on a day in the future. As we were growing up, we looked forward to that last day of school that would launch us into a season of fun and freedom. Now as parents we often count down to the day when school will start again! But there are also days to come that we dread.

There is a day spoken of throughout Scripture—a day of divine intervention in human history called "the Day of the Lord," or sometimes simply "the day" or "that day." It is described as a day when burdens will be lifted, honor bestowed, salvation accomplished, redemption completed, abundance enjoyed, satisfaction made full, and healing made plentiful. It sounds like a day to long for. And it is. But this is not all that the Bible tells us about that day.

We also discover in the Scriptures that the Day of the Lord will be a day of humiliation, destruction, cruelty, doom, darkness, retribution, distress, anguish, and ruin. When we read these descriptions, this day seems like one to dread. So which is it? Will the Day of the Lord—the day that Christ returns—be a day of mourning or a day of joy? Will it be a day of incredible loss or a day of indescribable gain?

The reality is that it will be both. Those who have feared the Lord by believing his gospel and who are joined to Christ by faith can wake up every morning wondering, with an eager heart, if this will be the day God will intervene in human history. But those who have rejected God's offer of mercy and ignored his gracious invitation into the safety of his fold should wake up every day thinking about his coming with a sense of sickening fear.

✳ ✳ ✳

Lord, as we anticipate the day—your day, when you come to punish and put away evil and set all things right in your world—we long for it to be filled with joy and victory for everyone in our family. We long to experience the glory of your coming side by side with _____. Fill us all with glad anticipation for your day.

DECEMBER 12

A Plumb Line

Then he showed me another vision. I saw the Lord standing beside a wall that had been built using a plumb line. He was using a plumb line to see if it was still straight. And the LORD said to me, "Amos, what do you see?" I answered, "A plumb line." And the Lord replied, "I will test my people with this plumb line. I will no longer ignore all their sins." AMOS 7:7-8

"ANY JOB WORTH DOING is worth doing well." This is the kind of standard we often set for our kids. We want them to learn to finish a task while striving for excellence at every step. Doing so will serve them well throughout life. But we also know that our strict standards can become a source of great discouragement to our kids, giving them the sense that they can never please us. As much as our children need an ideal to shoot for, they also need grace for when they come up short.

That is what we've all received as God's children. "We all fall short of God's glorious standard" (Romans 3:23). The prophet Amos was given a vision of the way the children of Israel had not lived up to God's rigorous standard. Amos saw a plumb line. A plumb line is a string with a weight fastened to the end that helps a builder keep the walls of a structure straight (or "plumb"). It works like a level, revealing if the walls are becoming crooked and thus vulnerable to collapse. Compared to the "plumb line" of God's perfect law delivered at Sinai—the standard God expected of his people—the nation of Israel was completely crooked and destined for collapse.

A plumb line is an unrelenting measure, as is God's law. And the reality is that we are hopelessly crooked. But the good news of the gospel is that Jesus comes to us and says, "So you don't measure up? I do. I lived up to God's standard perfectly. And by grace through faith, I will give you my own perfect record so that when God tests you with his plumb line, instead of condemning you for your crookedness, he'll bless you for my holiness." May such magnanimous love inspire us to extend grace to our own kids when they fall short!

✳ ✳ ✳

Lord, help me to deal with the ways _____ does not live up to my standards with the same grace you extend to me. Your cross has become the plumb line by which my life is judged. You took the condemnation for my crookedness and give the grace that conforms me to your holiness.

A Throne in Heaven

As I looked, I saw a door standing open in heaven, and the same voice I had heard before spoke to me like a trumpet blast. The voice said, "Come up here, and I will show you what must happen after this." And instantly I was in the Spirit, and I saw a throne in heaven and someone sitting on it. REVELATION 4:1-2

As JOHN SUFFERED on the island of Patmos for his bold testimony for Jesus, he was enabled to look into heaven and write down what he saw. As we read his words in Revelation, we get to witness what the suffering Christians of the first century and struggling believers of every age have needed to see. We get a glimpse of the ultimate reality that we, along with our children, need to see—God on the throne.

The centerpiece of heaven, the focal point of this universe, is God ruling and reigning, surrounded by a sea of glass that perfectly mirrors his glory back to him.

Our modern Western culture suggests that to love a child is to tell her that she is special and unique, and that everything she does is wonderful. We're not supposed to throw away her artwork. She gets a ribbon for participating. This could easily give our child the impression that the world revolves around her. But that simply isn't true. Our children are cherished members of our family, but they're not the center.

It is the prosperity gospel that teaches that we are the focus of the universe and that God is here for our happiness. The biblical gospel is that while God's love overflows for his people, we were made for him. God is at the center of the universe—not us, and not our children.

❅ ❅ ❅

Lord, you demonstrated your love for us, not by making us the center of your universe, but by going to the cross so that we can enjoy making you the focal point of our lives and the source of our joy forever. We want to put you in your rightful place—at the center of our family, on the throne of our lives.

Salvation's Source

My salvation comes from the LORD alone. JONAH 2:9

THE BOOK OF JONAH ends without telling us what happened to the prophet as he sat outside Nineveh, filled with resentment that God had saved the wicked city. But the fact that we have this book detailing Jonah's frank confession of his running, his resurrection, and his resentment is evidence that God was not done working in his life. In fact, because he wanted it to take center stage in his story, we find the settled conclusion of Jonah in the very center of the book: "My salvation comes from the LORD alone." This truth, which reverberated throughout Jonah's life and experiences, makes all the difference to us and to our children when it is at the center of our lives too.

Salvation begins and ends with the Lord. It is his work from start to finish. He is the one who initiates and accomplishes it. He *has saved* us by putting our sin upon Christ and crediting Christ's righteousness to us. He *is saving* us by sanctifying us by his Word and Spirit. And he *will save* us by glorifying us at the Resurrection.

Our salvation and that of our children is not in our own hands or in theirs. It is not determined by our own ability to find, understand, or trust in the Lord; nor does it depend on our own ability to change. Our salvation comes through the sacrifice of another, the obedience of another. Praise God that salvation comes from the Lord alone!

❀ ❀ ❀

Lord, we have no greater need, no more desperate a prayer, than that you would save us and our children. We have no ability to save ourselves or our children. Only you can deliver us! And we refuse to presume upon you for this salvation. Instead, we call upon you and ask you to save us. As we read the story of Jonah, it fills us with hope because in it you repeatedly rescue those who have done nothing to earn your salvation but cry out to you for it anyway.

The Wrath of the Lamb

Then everyone—the kings of the earth, the rulers, the generals, the wealthy, the powerful, and every slave and free person—all hid themselves in the caves and among the rocks of the mountains. And they cried to the mountains and the rocks, "Fall on us and hide us from the face of the one who sits on the throne and from the wrath of the Lamb. For the great day of their wrath has come, and who is able to survive?"
REVELATION 6:15-17

IT WOULD NOT BE a stretch to say that the Bible is the story of a lamb from beginning to end. Throughout the Old Testament, God makes it clear that anyone who wants to be made right with God can do so only on the basis of the Lamb that he has provided.

The Lamb of God will still be at the center of God's purposes when he brings human history in this world as it is now to a conclusion. When John, on the island of Patmos, was enabled to see into ultimate reality, he saw the Lamb on the throne, "a Lamb that looked as if it had been slaughtered" (5:6), as the center of everything. Before this Lamb are those who have been washed in his blood so that their robes are white. These people have nothing to fear. Then there are those who saw no need to be washed and covered in the blood of the Lamb, and they have everything to fear. There are those who have hidden themselves in the Lamb, and those who try to hide from the Lamb.

Those who persisted in their sin, who saw no need for confession or cleansing, will have no ability to stand before the throne of God and will fall down in terror, hoping the rocks and mountains will fall on top of them. But those who fell on their faces before the Lamb and submitted to his cleansing work will fall down not in terror, hiding from the Lamb, but in adoration, praising the Lamb.

※ ※ ※

Lord, we long for the day when we will stand before your throne. On that day we will have no need for protection from the Lamb, but will be protected forever by him. The cleansing that began when we first believed will be complete, and we will stand in a purified environment as purified people. But, Lord, we don't want to stand there alone. We long for _____ to be there with us. Please call _____ to yourself; cover and cleanse _____ with the blood of the Lamb.

What Does God Want?

What can we bring to the LORD?
  Should we bring him burnt offerings?
Should we bow before God Most High
  with offerings of yearling calves?
Should we offer him thousands of rams
  and ten thousand rivers of olive oil?
Should we sacrifice our firstborn children
  to pay for our sins? MICAH 6:6-7

IN MICAH 6, it is as if the people of Judah said to God, "What do you want from us?" When they learned that God was not satisfied with the sacrifices they brought to the Temple, they began working through a series of proposals to come up with one sufficient to satisfy the God they suggested was impossible to please. They began with a year-old calf, escalated to thousands of rams, then jumped to the ridiculous ten thousand rivers of oil before suggesting the outrageous offering of a firstborn child. But Micah interrupted, stating simply and clearly what the Lord required. And it wasn't outrageous sacrifice; it was simple obedience from the heart. "No, O people, the LORD has told you what is good, and this is what he requires of you: to do what is right, to love mercy, and to walk humbly with your God" (6:8).

This is what God really wants from his people. He wants us to act justly—to do what is right even when it is costly—and to love mercy. God wants us to walk humbly with him. To live in this way is to have the praise of God on our lips and a settled determination to be obedient to God in our hearts. Of course, our children have front-row seats to know whether or not this describes us. When your spouse, a friend, or a family member hurts or disappoints you, do your children see you simmer in resentment? Do they hear you rant about the offense to your friends over the phone? Or do they see that you love to show mercy? Do they see in you that love covers a multitude of sins?

❊ ❊ ❊

Lord, we will never do justice, love mercy, and walk humbly with you perfectly. But we know that Jesus has lived this way in our place and transfers his record of perfect righteousness to all who are joined to him by faith. As he indwells us by his Spirit, we are finding the power we need to do justice, love kindness, and thereby walk humbly in your ways before you, and before _____.

Just Enough

O God, I beg two favors from you;
  let me have them before I die.
First, help me never to tell a lie.
  Second, give me neither poverty nor riches!
  Give me just enough to satisfy my needs.
For if I grow rich, I may deny you and say, "Who is the LORD?"
  And if I am too poor, I may steal and thus insult God's holy name.

        PROVERBS 30:7-9

CHAPTER 30 contains the only prayer in the entire book of Proverbs and comes under the heading, "The sayings of Agur son of Jakeh." Agur's prayer demonstrates a wise way to pray for our child's future, though it certainly cuts against the grain of the American dream.

Agur's goal in life was to never go broke and never get rich. Why? Because both would make him vulnerable to temptation—the temptation to become blind to his need for God and the temptation to dishonor God by stealing from others out of fear that the Lord would not take care of him. Agur wanted to live month to month in constant dependence on God, doing as much good with his money as he could.

Our materialistic culture—with its offers of easy credit, its commercials designed to create dissatisfaction with what we have, and its barrage of newer, better, bigger— does not set our children up for success when it comes to making wise financial decisions. Our kids, therefore, need their financial lives shaped by Scripture's perspective on money. They need to see Mom and Dad living in glad dependence upon God rather than in constant pursuit of saving or spending more. There's a reason that Paul says that "people who long to be rich fall into temptation and are trapped by many foolish and harmful desires that plunge them into ruin and destruction" (1 Timothy 6:9). Wealth is a gift of God, but it also can prove dangerous to the soul.

        ❋ ❋ ❋

O God, I beg two favors from you;
  let _____ have them before he dies.
First, help _____ never to tell a lie.
  Second, give _____ neither poverty nor riches!
  Give _____ just enough to satisfy his needs.
Don't let _____ deny you and say, "Who is the LORD?"
  Instead, let _____ glorify your holy name.

No Matter What

I trembled inside when I heard this;
  my lips quivered with fear.
My legs gave way beneath me,
  and I shook in terror.
I will wait quietly for the coming day
  when disaster will strike the people who invade us.
Even though the fig trees have no blossoms,
  and there are no grapes on the vines;
even though the olive crop fails,
  and the fields lie empty and barren;
even though the flocks die in the fields,
  and the cattle barns are empty,
yet I will rejoice in the LORD!
  I will be joyful in the God of my salvation! HABAKKUK 3:16-18

THE LORD REVEALED to the prophet Habakkuk that he was about to do a purifying work among his people by raising up the Babylonians to take them into captivity. Habakkuk lived among God's people, so this word from God meant he and his family were about to come under attack. Habakkuk was clearly afraid about what would happen when the Babylonian invaders showed up on his doorstep. But he refused to let that fear control him.

Instead of trying to pray away what was coming, Habakkuk entrusted his life and perhaps his death to God. He entrusted his family's future to God. He chose to live by faith—not the kind of faith that believed God would miraculously show up and shield them from harm, but faith that God would preserve them through harm. Habakkuk shows us that living by faith means banking our hope on God no matter what happens in this life. He discovered the door to a joy that is not dependent upon circumstances, trusting that God was in control of both the process and the outcome.

❈ ❈ ❈

Lord, sometimes the possibility of coming catastrophe can make our family terribly afraid. We're tempted to ask you only to protect us from difficulty, but what we really want is to be a family who lives by faith in the midst of the worst of circumstances. We want to be a family who faces the uncertainty of the future with calm confidence in you. You are strong enough to preserve us through the worst things that happen in this world.

He Is a Mighty Savior

On that day the announcement to Jerusalem will be,
  "Cheer up, Zion! Don't be afraid!
For the LORD your God is living among you.
  He is a mighty savior.
He will take delight in you with gladness.
  With his love, he will calm all your fears.
  He will rejoice over you with joyful songs." ZEPHANIAH 3:16-17

WHEN JOSIAH became king at age eight, he inherited a country that had long rebelled against God. When he discovered the scroll of the Law in the Temple at age sixteen, he initiated a massive countrywide reform to return his people to faithfulness to God's law. The prophet Zephaniah appears to have been part of Josiah's reform efforts among his people. He explained the judgment they deserved for their religious pluralism, neglect of prayer, and spiritual stagnation. He called them to "seek the LORD, all who are humble, and follow his commands. Seek to do what is right and to live humbly" (2:3). Zephaniah portrayed Yahweh as a mighty warrior who would bring judgment but save the remnant who would seek him as their King.

For those who searched for him, there was hope. Zephaniah's book of prophecy ends with a song of hope and victory sung by the Lord himself over his people. The Lord's song anticipates the celebration to come when the people he has chosen for himself are restored to him, when their shame will be removed. He will live in their midst, their oppressors will be dealt with, and salvation will come to the outcast.

And he calls us to sing along with him: "Sing, O daughter of Zion; shout aloud, O Israel! Be glad and rejoice with all your heart, O daughter of Jerusalem! For the LORD will remove his hand of judgment and will disperse the armies of your enemy. And the LORD himself, the King of Israel, will live among you! At last your troubles will be over, and you will never again fear disaster" (3:14-16).

✳ ✳ ✳

Lord, because you sing this song of salvation over us, we can sing it over our children too. You removed your hand of judgment from us and laid it on your own Son. You are a mighty Savior who takes delight in _____. Your love calms our fears about the future and takes away the shame of the past.

DECEMBER 20

Haggai 1:1–2:23
Revelation 11:1-19
Psalm 139:1-24
Proverbs 30:15-16

Priorities

"This is what the LORD of Heaven's Armies says: The people are saying, 'The time has not yet come to rebuild the house of the LORD.'" Then the LORD sent this message through the prophet Haggai: "Why are you living in luxurious houses while my house lies in ruins?" HAGGAI 1:2-4

HEADING BACK TO JERUSALEM after seventy long years of exile in Babylon, the people of God were full of anticipation to live in a restored Jerusalem, worship at a rebuilt Temple, and recapture Israel's former glory as a nation. But when they arrived in Jerusalem, now a pile of charred rubble, they quickly became discouraged, and after a short time suspended their efforts to rebuild the Temple. For sixteen years, they made no progress on rebuilding the house of God.

It was into this setting that God sent his prophet Haggai, who challenged the people to resume their efforts to rebuild God's house. "It just isn't the right time," they protested, suggesting that the Lord's providence somehow prevented them from the work. But in reality they were too preoccupied with improving their own standard of living to invest themselves in the work of building God's house. So Haggai called them to examine their priorities.

Certainly it is no stretch to see ourselves in these spiritual ancestors. The demands of modern life with its traffic snarls, late nights of work, sports schedules, and homework provide us with plenty of excuses to say that "it just isn't the right time" to allow ourselves to be used by God to build his Kingdom in the world. So Haggai also speaks to us, calling on us to examine our priorities and give ourselves to gospel work in the world.

❁ ❁ ❁

Lord, forgive us for pouring so much of our energy into building our own house and taking care of our own property while giving little to your work in the world. As a family, we want to be used by you. Show us where we are too consumed building our own kingdom to be given over to building yours.

The Accuser

Then I heard a loud voice shouting across the heavens,

"It has come at last—
salvation and power
and the Kingdom of our God,
and the authority of his Christ.
For the accuser of our brothers and sisters
has been thrown down to earth—
the one who accuses them
before our God day and night.
And they have defeated him by the blood of the Lamb
and by their testimony." REVELATION 12:10-11

A VERY REAL ENEMY lurks in the hallways of our homes seeking to speak into the hearts of everyone living there. Peter tells us, "Stay alert! Watch out for your great enemy, the devil. He prowls around like a roaring lion, looking for someone to devour" (1 Peter 5:8). How does he devour?

His strategy with those outside of Christ is to keep them in the dark about their sin and to keep them thinking about anything other than their sin. But his strategy is very different for those who are in Christ. He works against believers by reminding them of their sins and failures in an attempt to make them lose heart. He wants them to think more of their sin than of their Savior and his saving, cleansing, forgiving power.

When Satan comes to accuse us, we need to recognize we're in a spiritual battle and fight back with the truth: "There is no condemnation for those who belong to Christ Jesus" (Romans 8:1). We fight back by asking, "Who dares accuse us whom God has chosen for his own? No one—for God himself has given us right standing with himself. Who then will condemn us? No one . . . not even the powers of hell can separate us from God's love" (Romans 8:33-34, 38).

✻ ✻ ✻

Lord, help me to recognize and refuse the accuser's voice when he wants to remind me of and bind me to all my past failures as a parent and as a person. And help me to recognize when the accuser seeks to devour _____ and eat _____ up with false guilt so I can encourage _____ with the truth.

In a Single Day

Hear now, O Joshua the high priest, you and your friends who sit before you, for they are men who are a sign: behold, I will bring my servant the Branch. For behold, on the stone that I have set before Joshua, on a single stone with seven eyes, I will engrave its inscription, declares the LORD of hosts, and I will remove the iniquity of this land in a single day. ZECHARIAH 3:8-9, ESV

IN ZECHARIAH'S TIME, the people of God were beginning a new day. They were back in their homeland, and they were free. But their future was unclear. Among many other concerns, they wondered if they would fall into the old sins that had plagued their forefathers and resulted in their exile, or if their future would be marked by fidelity to God. The Lord gave his prophet Zechariah a series of visions to assure his people that he was working out all aspects of their redemption.

In one of Zechariah's visions, he saw the reinstatement of a high priest named Joshua. Of course, the Hebrew name Joshua is "Jesus" in Greek. So right away, we sense that Zechariah is being shown something about the Great High Priest who will come. In fact, in the vision, Joshua is told that he and all of the other Old Testament priests are "symbols of things to come" (verse 8, NLT). So Joshua, the priest in Zechariah's vision, points to the greater Priest to come. But there are key differences.

Joshua's clothing was filthy because of sin, so God gave him fine new clothes; Jesus was stripped of his clothing as he took our sins upon himself. While a clean "Holy to the LORD" turban was placed on Joshua's head, a crown of thorns was placed on Jesus' head. While the Lord rejected the accusations Satan made against Joshua, the Lord willingly laid the guilt of humanity on Jesus. In this way, God "remove[d] the sins of this land in a single day" (verse 9, NLT).

❈ ❈ ❈

Lord, even as our family prepares to celebrate the day of your Son's birth, we are mindful of why he was born. He came to earth for this day—the day when you removed the sins of your people by putting them upon him. We praise you and thank you for removing our sin, for removing _____'s sin, and for removing the sin of all your people in a single day through this singular sacrifice.

His Name on Their Foreheads

I saw the Lamb standing on Mount Zion, and with him were 144,000 who had his name and his Father's name written on their foreheads. REVELATION 14:1

As WE PREPARE to celebrate the birth of Jesus, we see him as Mary's little Lamb, weak and needy, lying in a manger. But we know that while he came in weakness the first time, when he comes again, he will arrive in power. He will be the Lamb on the throne, surrounded by all of those who have put their hope in him, all who have been marked by his saving blood, all who have been completely transformed into his likeness.

In the Old Testament priesthood, the priest wore a turban of fine linen with a gold plate affixed to the front that was engraved with the words "Holy to the LORD." This signified that he and the people he represented were set apart by God and to God to be a holy nation. When we get to the book of Revelation, we see that what God intended all along was for the people of God to be a kingdom of priests, representing and displaying his glory throughout all of his creation. In John's vision of the future, we see that people "from every tribe and language and people and nation" have been made into "a Kingdom of priests for our God" (Revelation 5:9-10).

Throughout Revelation, all of the people of God, not just a select few, are clothed as priests in white and linen. Their purity is not put on as a garment over an otherwise-sinful self but is a true, inner perfection that is theirs because they have been washed by the blood of the Lamb. These priests do not enter the Most Holy Place only once a year. Instead, the whole earth has become God's throne room where all "will see his face, and his name will be written on their foreheads" (Revelation 22:4).

When we enter into the presence of the Lamb, "Holy to the LORD" will not merely be an ornament on a turban that we will put on and take off. Our belonging to him will be written into our very being.

❋ ❋ ❋

Lord, as we gather around the manger in our thoughts this Christmas, our hearts are stirred with a longing to gather around your throne and to be there with all of those we love. Please write _____'s belonging to you into her very being. Protect _____ from being claimed and marked by the beast that rules this world, and preserve _____ to be a part of the great choir singing a new song before your throne.

DECEMBER 24

Zechariah 6:1–7:14
Revelation 15:1-8
Psalm 143:1-12
Proverbs 30:24-28

Show Me Where to Walk

Let me hear of your unfailing love each morning,
for I am trusting you.
Show me where to walk,
for I give myself to you. PSALM 143:8

DAVID WAS IN A DARK and difficult situation. "My enemy has chased me. He has knocked me to the ground and forces me to live in darkness like those in the grave" (verse 3). He was waiting in the dark and didn't know what would happen next. So what did he do? "I lift my hands to you in prayer," he told God (verse 6).

Advent is a time of anticipation, a time of waiting for the Light to come into the darkness. And we, as parents, know a lot about waiting. Our task rarely produces immediate results. We often wonder if all our efforts to parent well are having any lasting effect on our kids. Our investment is future oriented, a deposit made toward the yet-unseen years of their adulthood. Like David, we wait in the dark and wonder what is going to happen. But we don't wait alone or with no resources. We have a Lord who listens. We call out to the Lord who has promised to show us where to walk when we can't see the way forward.

✻ ✻ ✻

Lord, let me hear of your unfailing love each morning, including this morning as we prepare to celebrate the birth of your Son,
for I am trusting you.
Show me where to walk on this pathway of parenting _____,
for I give myself to you.
Rescue me from my enemies of discouragement and fear over _____'s future, LORD;
I run to you to hide me.
Teach me to do your will,
for you are my God.
May your gracious Spirit lead me forward
on a firm footing.
I'm raising _____ for the glory of your name, O LORD, not mine.
Because of your faithfulness, bring me out of this distress.
I am your servant.
ADAPTED FROM PSALM 143:8-12

We Have Heard That God Is with You

Among the other nations, Judah and Israel became symbols of a cursed nation. But no longer! Now I will rescue you and make you both a symbol and a source of blessing. So don't be afraid. Be strong, and get on with rebuilding the Temple! ZECHARIAH 8:13

THE BIRTH OF JESUS is the fulfillment of a promise first given in the Garden when God promised that one day a child would be born, a descendant of Eve, who would crush the head of the serpent. The promise is then traced to Abraham. God promised to bless him and told him, "All the families on earth will be blessed through you" (Genesis 12:3).

Here in Zechariah, the promise of a blessing and of being a blessing is made once again to the descendants of Abraham who have returned to the land God gave their forefather many centuries before. It must have been hard for them to believe, because everything about their circumstances made it appear that they were under God's curse rather than recipients or conduits of his blessing. Zechariah was saying that not only would they shed any sense of being cursed, but that God would make them both a symbol and a source of blessing.

How would this happen? God would come to them. He would work in them in such a way that "the people of one city will say to the people of another, 'Come with us to Jerusalem to ask the LORD to bless us. Let's worship the LORD of Heaven's Armies. I'm determined to go.' . . . Men from different nations and languages of the world will clutch at the sleeve of one Jew. And they will say, 'Please let us walk with you, for we have heard that God is with you'" (Zechariah 8:21, 23).

Today, as we celebrate the coming of the one promised in the Garden, the one promised to Abraham through whom all the families of the earth would be blessed, the one who is Immanuel, God with us, we long for God to fulfill the promise he made through Zechariah. We long to live with such peace and joy that people—neighbors, coworkers, and family members who are outside of Christ—will take hold of us and say, "Please let us walk with you, for we have heard that God is with you."

※ ※ ※

Lord, please work in our family today to make us both a symbol and a source of the blessing that comes only through Christ. Make us strong so we can get on with being used by you to build your spiritual temple—your church—in our day.

Your King

Rejoice, O people of Zion!
  Shout in triumph, O people of Jerusalem!
Look, your king is coming to you.
  He is righteous and victorious,
yet he is humble, riding on a donkey—
  riding on a donkey's colt. Zechariah 9:9

It was clear from the angel's announcement to Mary that the child she carried would be a king. "The Lord God will give him the throne of his ancestor David," he told her (Luke 1:32). But of course Jesus wasn't born in a palace, but rather in a place where animals were kept. He slept in the trough animals ate from. Clearly he would not be a king like other kings. And yet, the wise men came looking for "the newborn king of the Jews" (Matthew 2:2).

When Jesus began his ministry, people wondered if he was truly the King God had promised would come. At one point we read, "When Jesus saw that they were ready to force him to be their king, he slipped away into the hills by himself" (John 6:15). Finally the day came when Jesus was prepared to present himself as King to his people. But he did it unlike any other king in the ancient world. In order to present themselves in all their power and splendor, ancient kings would ride into the cities they ruled over astride a stout white stallion. But when Jesus entered the royal city of Jerusalem, he did not arrive on a warrior steed. He came humbly, riding on a donkey.

Even though his fellow Jews had the prophecy from Zechariah, they didn't recognize—or perhaps did not want to recognize—what Jesus was saying about himself when he entered Jerusalem this way. By arriving on a donkey instead of a warhorse, Jesus was saying, "I am not coming to slay you but to serve you. I'm coming not with a sword, but with salvation." This is the kind of King who has come to us, the kind of King who invites us and our children to come under his loving rule. He is righteous, always doing what is right. He is victorious over the power of death and hell. Yet he is humble.

❈ ❈ ❈

Lord, you came so gently and humbly to us, your people. And the world crucified you instead of bowing to you. Forgive us. Give _____ eyes to see that you are a good King. Overcome all resistance and rebellion. Bring _____ under your loving rule.

They Will Come Running

I will strengthen Judah and save Israel;
  I will restore them because of my compassion.
It will be as though I had never rejected them,
  for I am the LORD their God, who will hear their cries.
The people of Israel will become like mighty warriors,
  and their hearts will be made happy as if by wine.
Their children, too, will see it and be glad;
  their hearts will rejoice in the LORD.
When I whistle to them, they will come running,
  for I have redeemed them. ZECHARIAH 10:6-8

SHEPHERDS in biblical times herded their flocks by whistling or piping to them. That is the imagery Zechariah used to describe the way God was going to come and guide his people. The shepherds among God's people had failed to lead them in his ways, but he promised to send a true Shepherd.

Some parents have trained their young kids to come running home when Mom or Dad open the door and whistle. Oh, if only it was that easy to get our kids to come home to God when they're wandering away from him! While we don't have the ability to create gladness and responsiveness toward God in our children simply by whistling, he does. In fact, that's what he has promised to do in the lives of his people and their children. "When I whistle to them, they will come running, for I have redeemed them," he says.

Here is hope for lost sheep. Our confidence is not based on their ability to find their way to God. Left on our own, none of us can or will come running in his direction. Our hope is that the Shepherd will come to find his lost sheep, pluck them out of danger, and carry them on his shoulders into the safety of his fold. When he whistles, they will come running.

✳ ✳ ✳

Great Shepherd, we are waiting for you to do your work of restoration, listening for you to whistle, and watching for _____ to come running in your direction.

DECEMBER 28

A Fountain Will Be Opened

On that day a fountain will be opened for the dynasty of David and for the people of Jerusalem, a fountain to cleanse them from all their sins and impurity. ZECHARIAH 13:1

THROUGHOUT THE PROPHECIES of Zechariah, God said over and over in a variety of ways that he was going to do something good for the recently returned exiles living in and around Jerusalem. These were people who had committed blatant social and moral sins; they were passively rebellious and spiritually apathetic. Zechariah wooed them with incredible visions of the future in which God would bring peace and restoration. This would be accomplished by the Messiah, who would "pour out a spirit of grace and prayer on the family of David and on the people of Jerusalem" (12:10). However, when the Messiah came proclaiming grace, his people would pierce him. But his piercing would become the means by which a cleansing fountain would be opened for him to wash away their sin.

During Zechariah's ministry, the people were at work to rebuild the Temple, where they would resume the offering of animals as a sacrifice for sin. But Zechariah was promising something far better than the fountain of the blood of animals that would flow at the rebuilt Temple. This fountain would not flow from the neck of an animal but from the pierced side of the Son of God. The blood from this fountain would not only cover their sin; it would cleanse them from sin, and it would empower them to say no to sin.

❊ ❊ ❊

Lord, you have opened up a fountain of cleansing and invited us in to be purged of sin. Don't let _____ resist or refuse your invitation to be washed in your fountain. Cleanse away the sin that has left shameful stains on the interior of _____'s life. Make _____ pure as only you can.

The Book of Life

I saw the dead, both great and small, standing before God's throne. And the books were opened, including the Book of Life. And the dead were judged according to what they had done, as recorded in the books. . . . And anyone whose name was not found recorded in the Book of Life was thrown into the lake of fire. REVELATION 20:12, 15

WHEN THE APOSTLE JOHN was given a vision of what is to come at the end of human history as we know it, he "saw a great white throne and the one sitting on it" (verse 11). All of humanity was standing before the throne, and the books were opened. John actually saw two kinds of books. The first, the Book of Life, is a record of the names of those God calls his own. It is a list of all whom God chose "in Christ to be holy and without fault in his eyes" and whom he "decided in advance to adopt . . . into his own family by bringing [them] to himself through Jesus Christ" (Ephesians 1:4-5).

This Book of Life appears throughout Scripture. The first place we read about it is in Exodus when Moses was willing for his name to be blotted out of the Lord's book in exchange for forgiveness for his people (Exodus 32:32, ESV). The psalmist wrote about the Lord's book in which the names of those "enrolled among the righteous" (Psalm 69:28, ESV) are found. The prophet Daniel wrote that God's people will be delivered. And who will those people be? "Everyone whose name shall be found written in the book" (Daniel 12:1, ESV).

But "the books" mentioned in Revelation 20:12 are quite different from the Book of Life. These books are a record of all that everyone has done and failed to do. No one wants to be judged solely on the basis of what is recorded in "the books." No record of our actions could ever list enough good deeds to save us. What we want is to be judged on the basis of what is in the Book of Life—our names, written by the hand of God in such a way that they can never be erased. As grateful as we are that our children are a part of our family, this family—the one listed in the Book of Life—is the one we long for them to be a part of forever.

❈ ❈ ❈

Lord, in faith I pray that when you open the books, what you find will not bring condemnation but will be confirmation that _____ is yours. I pray that it will not be a record of _____'s feeble, fleshly works but of the righteousness of Christ, both imputed by grace and imparted through the grace of the Spirit's sanctifying power.

The Holy City

He took me in the Spirit to a great, high mountain, and he showed me the holy city, Jerusalem, descending out of heaven from God. . . . The city wall was broad and high, with twelve gates guarded by twelve angels. And the names of the twelve tribes of Israel were written on the gates. There were three gates on each side—east, north, south, and west. The wall of the city had twelve foundation stones, and on them were written the names of the twelve apostles of the Lamb. REVELATION 21:10, 12-14

THE APOSTLE JOHN described how the new Jerusalem will descend out of heaven from God. For the meaning of that to sink in, we need to think for a minute about the old Jerusalem. David captured Jerusalem from the pagan Jebusites before dishonoring it with adultery and murder. This was the city that later became infamous for its child sacrifice and unlawful sorceries. This was the city that mocked the integrity of Jeremiah and turned a deaf ear to the preaching of Isaiah. Jerusalem is the city that rejected and crucified Jesus. Isn't this the most unlikely of places to serve as a model for our eternal home? What insight does this give us into the nature of heaven?

This tells us that God is making a holy city out of our idol-loving, God-defying, Christ-rejecting city of man. God is taking moms and dads who worship idols of pleasure and pride, sons and daughters who love to hate God, families who continually reject the riches of Christ for the trinkets of the world, and he is remaking us into a city he intends to live in.

The foundations of this city are built on the twelve sons of Israel and the twelve apostles. In other words, this Holy City of God is being built on the foundation of the grace of God at work in the lives of ordinary, fearful, unfaithful, inconsistent human beings. This means that there is nothing so evil or unredeemable, nothing so obscure and unworthy in our lives that it cannot, even now, be fashioned into the foundation stones of the new city of heaven.

❊ ❊ ❊

Lord, you really are making all things new! Your Holy City will be filled with flagrant but forgiven sinners. And that gives us hope.

Turned Hearts

Look, I am sending you the prophet Elijah before the great and dreadful day of the LORD arrives. His preaching will turn the hearts of fathers to their children, and the hearts of children to their fathers. Otherwise I will come and strike the land with a curse. MALACHI 4:5-6

THE STORY THAT BEGAN in Genesis 1 with God's repeated blessing of all that he had made ends here in Malachi 4 with God threatening to "come and strike the land with a curse." Yet couched in the threat is a promise. In the very last verse of the very last book of the Old Testament, we find an enormous dose of gospel hope specifically for parents.

God promised his people that he was going to send someone who would preach his Word before the Messiah came. As a result of this prophet's ministry, many parents and children would turn toward God. With their faith renewed, they would turn toward one another as well. Reconciliation with God would result in reconciliation between generations. Repentance would lead to healing for whole families.

Four hundred years later an angel appeared to a priest named Zechariah in the Temple in Jerusalem and told him that his wife was going to have a son whom they should name John. "He will be a man with the spirit and power of Elijah. He will prepare the people for the coming of the Lord. He will turn the hearts of the fathers to their children, and he will cause those who are rebellious to accept the wisdom of the godly" (Luke 1:17).

Just as the Spirit worked through his prophet John the Baptist to do a work in the hearts of parents and children in his day, the Spirit is still at work in the lives of hard-hearted parents and hard-hearted kids to soften and turn their hearts toward one another. The power of God's grace is the hope of every parent and child longing for reconciliation and relationship.

❋ ❋ ❋

Father, you have turned your heart toward me in Jesus Christ. Your grace at work in me is turning my heart toward my parents so that my desire to honor them as you've commanded is growing. And your grace is turning my heart toward _____, confident that your grace is at work in _____'s heart too.

Notes

January 4:   Portions adapted from Nancy Guthrie, *The Wisdom of God: Seeing Jesus in the Psalms and Wisdom Books* (Wheaton, IL: Crossway, 2012), 195.

January 9:   Portions adapted from Nancy Guthrie, "Is Anything Too Hard for the Lord?" in the *ESV Women's Devotional Bible* (Wheaton, IL: Crossway, 2014), 19.

January 10:   Portions adapted from Nancy Guthrie, *Hearing Jesus Speak into Your Sorrow* (Carol Stream, IL: Tyndale House, 2009), 24–25.

January 16:   Portions adapted from Nancy Guthrie, *The Promised One: Seeing Jesus in Genesis* (Wheaton, IL: Crossway, 2011), 221–222.

January 17:   Portions adapted from Nancy Guthrie, *The Promised One: Seeing Jesus in Genesis* (Wheaton, IL: Crossway, 2011), 264.

January 31:   Portions adapted from Nancy Guthrie, *The Lamb of God: Seeing Jesus in Exodus, Leviticus, Numbers, and Deuteronomy* (Wheaton, IL: Crossway, 2012), 80–81.

February 2:   Portions adapted from Nancy Guthrie, "Grumbling and Grace in the Wilderness," in the *ESV Women's Devotional Bible* (Wheaton, IL: Crossway, 2014), 86.

February 6:   Portions adapted from Nancy Guthrie, *The Lamb of God: Seeing Jesus in Exodus, Leviticus, Numbers, and Deuteronomy* (Wheaton, IL: Crossway, 2012), 126–127.

February 9:   Portions adapted from Nancy Guthrie, *Hearing Jesus Speak into Your Sorrow* (Carol Stream, IL: Tyndale House, 2009), 17.

February 12: I was helped in understanding today's verses by John Piper, "The Lord, a God Merciful and Gracious" (sermon, Bethlehem Baptist Church, Minneapolis, October 7, 1984).

February 15: Portions adapted from Nancy Guthrie, *The Lamb of God: Seeing Jesus in Exodus, Leviticus, Numbers, and Deuteronomy* (Wheaton, IL: Crossway, 2012), 175.

February 17: Portions adapted from Nancy Guthrie, *The Lamb of God: Seeing Jesus in Exodus, Leviticus, Numbers, and Deuteronomy* (Wheaton, IL: Crossway, 2012), 202.

February 18: Portions adapted from Nancy Guthrie, *One Year of Dinner Table Devotions and Discussion Starters* (Carol Stream, IL: Tyndale House, 2008), January 8.

February 21: Portions adapted from Nancy Guthrie, *The Lamb of God: Seeing Jesus in Exodus, Leviticus, Numbers, and Deuteronomy* (Wheaton, IL: Crossway, 2012), 204–205, 208.

March 5:   I was helped in understanding the command in today's passage by John Piper, "Love Your Neighbor as Yourself, Part 2" (sermon, Bethlehem Baptist Church, Minneapolis, May 7, 1995).

March 8:   Portions adapted from Nancy Guthrie, *The Lamb of God: Seeing Jesus in Exodus, Leviticus, Numbers, and Deuteronomy* (Wheaton, IL: Crossway, 2012), 223–224.

March 11:   Portions adapted from Nancy Guthrie, *The Wisdom of God: Seeing Jesus in the Psalms and Wisdom Books* (Wheaton, IL: Crossway, 2012), 173–174.

March 13:   I was helped in understanding today's verses by John Piper, "He Will Turn the Hearts of the Fathers to the Children" (sermon, Bethlehem Baptist Church, Minneapolis, December 27, 1987).

March 14:   Portions adapted from Nancy Guthrie, *The Lamb of God: Seeing Jesus in Exodus, Leviticus, Numbers, and Deuteronomy* (Wheaton, IL: Crossway, 2012), 230–231.

March 23:   Quotes taken from Paul David Tripp, *New Morning Mercies: A Gospel Devotional* (Wheaton, IL: Crossway, 2014), February 23.

March 30:   Portions adapted from Nancy Guthrie, *The One Year Book of Hope* (Carol Stream, IL: Tyndale House, 2005), 378.

April 2:   I was helped on today's passage by Christopher Wright, *Deuteronomy*. New International Biblical Commentary (Peabody, MA: Hendrickson Publishers, 1996), 235–236.

April 13:   I was helped in understanding today's story by Chad Bird, "When Valleys of Trouble Become Doorways of Hope," *Flying Scroll* (blog), September 30, 2015.

April 14:   Portions adapted from Nancy Guthrie, *Hearing Jesus Speak into Your Sorrow* (Carol Stream, IL: Tyndale House, 2009), 103.

April 15:   I was helped in understanding today's psalm by Derek Kidner, *Psalms 73–150*. Kidner Classic Commentaries (Downers Grove, IL: InterVarsity, 2008), 302–303.

April 21:   I was helped on today's topic by Kathy Keller, "Don't Take It from Me: Reasons You Should Not Marry an Unbeliever," *The Gospel Coalition* (blog), January 22, 2012.

April 22:   I was helped on today's passage by Kim Riddlebarger, "We Will Serve the Lord" (sermon, Christ Reformed Church, Anaheim, CA, November 11, 2007).

April 24:   Portions adapted from Nancy Guthrie, *The Son of David: Seeing Jesus in the Historical Books* (Wheaton, IL: Crossway, 2013), 71–72.

May 5:   Portions adapted from Nancy Guthrie, *The Son of David: Seeing Jesus in the Historical Books* (Wheaton, IL: Crossway, 2013), 97.

May 11:   Portions adapted from Nancy Guthrie, *The Lamb of God: Seeing Jesus in Exodus, Leviticus, Numbers, and Deuteronomy* (Wheaton, IL: Crossway, 2012), 105.

May 14:   Portions adapted from Nancy Guthrie, *The Son of David: Seeing Jesus in the Historical Books* (Wheaton, IL: Crossway, 2013), page 127.

May 15:   Portions adapted from Nancy Guthrie, *The Son of David: Seeing Jesus in the Historical Books* (Wheaton, IL: Crossway, 2013), 129–134.

May 17:   Portions adapted from Nancy Guthrie, *Hearing Jesus Speak into Your Sorrow* (Carol Stream, IL: Tyndale House, 2009), 73–74.

May 20:   Portions adapted from Nancy Guthrie, *Hearing Jesus Speak into Your Sorrow* (Carol Stream, IL: Tyndale House, 2009), 126.

May 25:   Portions adapted from Nancy Guthrie, *The Son of David: Seeing Jesus in the Historical Books* (Wheaton, IL: Crossway Books, 2013), 157.

June 9:   I was helped on today's passage and in more general ways throughout the entire book by Rose Marie Miller, Deborah Harrell, and Jack Klumpenhower, *The Gospel-Centered Parent* (Greensboro, NC: New Growth Press, 2015), 10–12.

June 24:   I was helped on this passage by Bob Deffinbaugh, "Wisdom and Child-Rearing (Part 1)," Bible.org.

June 28:   I was helped on today's passage by Peter J. Leithart, *1 and 2 Kings*. Brazos Theological Commentary on the Bible (Grand Rapids, MI: Brazos Press, 2006), 233–234.

June 29:   I was helped on today's passage by Peter J. Leithart, *1 and 2 Kings*. Brazos Theological Commentary on the Bible (Grand Rapids, MI: Brazos Press, 2006), 246–247.

July 3:	Portions adapted from Nancy Guthrie, *The Wisdom of God: Seeing Jesus in the Psalms and Wisdom Books* (Wheaton, IL: Crossway Books, 2012), 89, 97–98.
July 13:	I was helped on today's passage by Colin Smith, "Wrath" (sermon, The Orchard Evangelical Free Church, Arlington Heights, IL, July 15, 2001).
July 14:	I was helped on today's passage by John Murray, *The Epistle to the Romans*. The New International Commentary on the New Testament (Grand Rapids, MI: Eerdmans, 1968), 77.
July 29:	I was helped in understanding this illustration of the Bible as a compass by Phillip D. Jensen and Tony Payne, *Guidance and the Voice of God* (Sydney, Australia: Matthias Media, 1997), 97.
August 2:	Portions adapted from Nancy Guthrie, "Forgetting the God Who Does Not Forget His People" in the *ESV Women's Devotional Bible* (Wheaton, IL: Crossway, 2014), 452.
August 5:	Portions adapted from Nancy Guthrie, *The Son of David: Seeing Jesus in the Historical Books* (Wheaton, IL: Crossway, 2013), 230–231.
August 9:	I was helped on today's difficult passage by Stephen T. Um, *1 Corinthians: The Word of the Cross*. Preaching the Word (Wheaton, IL: Crossway, 2015), 91–101.
August 14:	Portions adapted from my chapter, "Coming Together around God's Word," in *God's Word, Our Story: Learning from the Book of Nehemiah* (Wheaton, IL: Crossway, 2016), 97–98.
August 19:	Portions adapted from Nancy Guthrie, *The Son of David: Seeing Jesus in the Historical Books* (Wheaton, IL: Crossway, 2013), 263–264.
August 21:	I was helped on today's passage by Christopher Ash, *Job: The Wisdom of the Cross*. Preaching the Word (Wheaton, IL: Crossway, 2014), 34–35.
August 23:	Portions adapted from Nancy Guthrie, *The Wisdom of God: Seeing Jesus in the Psalms and Wisdom Books* (Wheaton, IL: Crossway Books, 2012), 50.
August 28:	Portions adapted from Nancy Guthrie, *The Wisdom of God: Seeing Jesus in the Psalms and Wisdom Books* (Wheaton, IL: Crossway Books, 2012), 75–77.
August 29:	I was helped on today's passage by Bob Sorge, "Why You Should Make a Covenant with Your Eyes," *Charisma* magazine, August 8, 2013.
September 2:	Portions adapted from Nancy Guthrie, *The Wisdom of God: Seeing Jesus in the Psalms and Wisdom Books* (Wheaton, IL: Crossway, 2012), 218–230.
September 3:	I was helped on today's passage by Gary Thomas, *Sacred Parenting* (Grand Rapids, MI: Zondervan, 2004), 20–21.
September 5:	Portions adapted from Nancy Guthrie, *The Wisdom of God: Seeing Jesus in the Psalms and Wisdom Books* (Wheaton, IL: Crossway, 2012), 228–229.
September 6:	Portions adapted from Nancy Guthrie, *The Wisdom of God: Seeing Jesus in the Psalms and Wisdom Books* (Wheaton, IL: Crossway, 2012), 246, 250–251.
September 7:	Portions adapted from Nancy Guthrie, *The Wisdom of God: Seeing Jesus in the Psalms and Wisdom Books* (Wheaton, IL: Crossway, 2012), 252.
September 10:	I was helped on today's passage by J. D. Greear, "3 Reasons God's Holiness Terrifies Us," J.D.Greear.com (blog), September 7, 2015.
September 28:	I was helped on today's passage by John Piper, "Marriage Is Meant for Making Children . . . Disciples of Jesus, Part 2" (sermon, Bethlehem Baptist Church, Minneapolis, MN, June 17, 2007).
October 2:	I was helped on today's passage by Stephen Witmer, "Parents, You Can't Build Heaven Here," *Desiring God* (blog), October 28, 2015.

October 6:   I was helped on today's passage by John Piper, "Raising Children Who Are Confident in God" (sermon, Bethlehem Baptist Church, Minneapolis, February 25, 1996).

October 7:   Quote from Tim Kimmel, *Grace-Based Parenting* (Nashville: Thomas Nelson, 2004), 61.

October 8:   I was helped on today's passage by Tim Kimmel, *Grace-Based Parenting* (Nashville: Thomas Nelson, 2004), 39.

October 11:   Quote from Jon Bloom, "Don't Follow Your Heart," *Desiring God* (blog), March 9, 2015.

October 18:   Portions adapted from Nancy Guthrie, *The Word of the Lord: Seeing Jesus in the Prophets* (Wheaton, IL: Crossway, 2014), 178–179.

October 20:   Portions adapted from Nancy Guthrie, *The Word of the Lord: Seeing Jesus in the Prophets* (Wheaton, IL: Crossway, 2014), 174.

October 23:   I was helped by John R. W. Stott, *Guard the Gospel: The Message of 2 Timothy* (Downers Grove, IL: InterVarsity, 1973), 52–58.

October 28:   Quote from Bryan Chapell, *1–2 Timothy and Titus: To Guard the Deposit*. Preaching the Word (Wheaton, IL: Crossway, 2012), 389.

November 3:   Portions adapted from Nancy Guthrie, *Hoping for Something Better* (Carol Stream, IL: Tyndale House, 2007), 64.

November 4:   Portions adapted from Nancy Guthrie, *Hoping for Something Better* (Carol Stream, IL: Tyndale House, 2007), 83.

November 5:   Portions adapted from Nancy Guthrie, *Hoping for Something Better* (Carol Stream, IL: Tyndale House, 2007), 68.

November 7:   Portions adapted from Nancy Guthrie, *The One Year Book of Discovering Jesus in the Old Testament* (Carol Stream, IL: Tyndale House, 2010), October 31.

November 8:   I was helped on today's passage by Iain M. Duguid, *Ezekiel*. The NIV Application Commentary (Grand Rapids, MI: Zondervan, 1999), 234–244.

November 10:   Portions adapted from Nancy Guthrie, *Hoping for Something Better* (Carol Stream, IL: Tyndale House, 2007), 104–105.

November 12:   Portions adapted from Nancy Guthrie, *Hoping for Something Better* (Carol Stream, IL: Tyndale House, 2007), 124–125.

November 13:   Portions adapted from Nancy Guthrie, *The Lamb of God: Seeing Jesus in Exodus, Leviticus, Numbers, and Deuteronomy* (Wheaton, IL: Crossway, 2012), 49–50.

November 14:   Portions adapted from Nancy Guthrie, *Hearing Jesus Speak into Your Sorrow* (Carol Stream, IL: Tyndale House, 2009), 77.

November 15:   Portions adapted from Nancy Guthrie, *The Lamb of God: Seeing Jesus in Exodus, Leviticus, Numbers, and Deuteronomy* (Wheaton, IL: Crossway, 2012), 133.

November 17:   I was helped on today's passage by Tim Kimmel, *Grace-Based Parenting* (Nashville: Thomas Nelson, 2004), 24, 215–216.

November 25:   Portions adapted from Nancy Guthrie, *The Word of the Lord: Seeing Jesus in the Prophets* (Wheaton, IL: Crossway, 2014), 196–198.

November 26:   Portions adapted from Nancy Guthrie, *The Word of the Lord: Seeing Jesus in the Prophets* (Wheaton, IL: Crossway, 2014), 200–201.

November 30:   I was helped on today's passage by John Piper, "Eternal Life Has Appeared in Christ" (sermon, Bethlehem Baptist Church, Minneapolis, January 27, 1985).

December 11:   Portions adapted from my chapter "Ultimate Goals: Heading for That Day," in *Word-Filled Women's Ministry: Loving and Serving the Church* (Wheaton, IL: Crossway, 2015), 227–228.

December 12: Adapted from Nancy Guthrie, *The One Year Book of Discovering Jesus in the Old Testament* (Carol Stream, IL: Tyndale House, 2010), December 3.

December 16: Portions adapted from Nancy Guthrie, *The Word of the Lord: Seeing Jesus in the Prophets* (Wheaton, IL: Crossway, 2014), 102.

December 18: Portions adapted from Nancy Guthrie, *The Word of the Lord: Seeing Jesus in the Prophets* (Wheaton, IL: Crossway, 2014), 153–154.

December 28: Portions adapted from Nancy Guthrie, *The One Year Book of Discovering Jesus in the Old Testament* (Carol Stream, IL: Tyndale House, 2010), December 19.

December 29: Portions adapted from Nancy Guthrie, *The One Year Book of Discovering Jesus in the Old Testament* (Carol Stream, IL: Tyndale House, 2010), November 17.

December 30: Portions adapted from Nancy Guthrie, *The One Year Book of Discovering Jesus in the Old Testament* (Carol Stream, IL: Tyndale House, 2007), June 30.

December 31: I was helped on today's passage by John Piper, "He Will Turn the Hearts of the Fathers to the Children" (sermon, Bethlehem Baptist Church, Minneapolis, December 27, 1987).

About the Author

NANCY GUTHRIE lives in Nashville, Tennessee. She speaks at conferences around the country and internationally, and is currently pursuing graduate studies at Reformed Theological Seminary Global. She and her husband, David, are the cohosts of the GriefShare video series used in more than 10,000 churches around the world, and they host Respite Retreats for couples who have faced the death of a child. She is the author of numerous books, including *Holding On to Hope, Abundant Life in Jesus,* and *The One Year Book of Discovering Jesus in the Old Testament.* She also hosts the *Help Me Teach the Bible* podcast at The Gospel Coalition. You can find more information about Nancy's family and ministry at www.nancyguthrie.com.

BY NANCY GUTHRIE

BOOKS	BIBLE STUDIES
Holding On to Hope	*Hoping for Something Better*
The One Year® Book of Hope	*The Promised One*
Hearing Jesus Speak into Your Sorrow	*The Lamb of God*
	The Son of David
When Your Family's Lost a Loved One (with David Guthrie)	*The Wisdom of God*
	The Word of the Lord
What Grieving People Wish You Knew about What Really Helps (and What Really Hurts)	
One Year® of Dinner Table Devotions and Discussion Starters	
The One Year® Book of Discovering Jesus in the Old Testament	
Abundant Life in Jesus	
The One Year® Praying through the Bible for Your Kids	
Seeing Jesus	

CP1149